C000144224

Chelsea

Player by Player

Chelsea

Player by Player

Peter Lovering

Hamlyn

ACKNOWLEDGEMENTS

The author would like to thank the following for their encouragement and assistance:
Frank Blunstone, Barry Bridges, Joe Fascione, Ron Harris, Colin Lee, John Mortimore,
Ken Shellito, the late Peter Sillett, Nigel Spackman, David Webb, Ray Wilkins, Steve
Small, Ivan Ponting, Deirdre Fenney, Jocelyne Bia, Trevor Davies, Charles Richards,
Ron Hockings and all at Colorsport.

The author is also grateful for permission to reproduce photographs. The vast majority are
from Colorsport, with additional contributions from Allsport and Ron Hockings.

Efforts have been made to trace copyright holders of all photographs used in this book.
We apologise for any omissions, which are unintentional, and would be pleased to include
appropriate acknowledgement in any subsequent edition.

First published in Great Britain by Guinness Publishing in 1993

This revised and updated edition published in 1998 by Hamlyn an imprint of Reed
Consumer Books Limited, Michelin House, 81 Fulham Road, London SW3 6RB and
Auckland, Melbourne, Singapore and Toronto.

ISBN 0 600 59497 1

Copyright © Peter Lovering

Oringal design: Steve Small. Updated: Bob Bickerton

Printed and bound in Spain by Graphycem

A catalogue record for this book is available from the British Library

All rights reserved. No part of this publication may be reproduced, stored in a retrieval
system, or transmitted in any form or by any means, mechanical, photocopying, recording
or otherwise, without the permission of the copyright holders.

INTRODUCTION

It was inevitable that I would come to think of Chelsea as 'my team'. My father had been a lifelong Blues supporter and it never occurred to me to question the faith I had been born into. Growing up in the 1960s, I took it for granted that they were one of England's top clubs, even though the 1955 League Championship was the only major honour they had won. During Tommy Docherty's reign the Blues always seemed to be in the thick of the fight for silverware and under Dave Sexton, of course, they would lift the FA Cup and European Cup-Winners' Cup in successive seasons. I cheerfully assumed that they would continue to challenge for the game's glittering prizes in the years ahead but I was soon to learn that success has to be earned and that Chelsea's sojourn among football's élite had been strictly temporary.

The Blues' decline was to be swift and inglorious. They were relegated in 1975 and although they were firmly re-established in the top flight by the mid-Eighties (with the exception of a single season in Division Two in 1988/89) there were plenty of occasions when it seemed that the gap separating them from the handful of clubs that dominate English football had become unbridgeable. Since the first edition of this book was published in 1993, however, a spectacular transformation has taken place at Stamford Bridge. The ground has been redeveloped, a compact, modern stadium with an intimidating atmosphere emerging in place of the wide-open spaces and crumbling terraces of old, but the changes on the playing side have been even more dramatic. In the last two seasons Chelsea have won the FA Cup, Coca-Cola Cup and European Cup-Winners' Cup, and it says much that a fourth-place finish in the Premiership in 1997/98 was considered something of a disappointment. However, it is not just the Blues' results that have delighted the Stamford Bridge faithful; some of their football has been simply breathtaking. The arrival of world-class players such as Ruud Gullit, Roberto Di Matteo, Frank Leboeuf, Gianluca Vialli and Gianfranco Zola has made Chelsea London's most exciting team and given new life to the old boast that they are 'the Manchester United of the South'.

All those players are featured in this book, of course, along with the stars of the Sixties and Seventies and the enthusiastic youngsters who carried the hopes of the Blues' dwindling band of supporters in the dark days when the club's very survival was in doubt. It includes every player who has appeared in a first-team match for Chelsea since 1960/61, the season that saw the departure from Stamford Bridge of Jimmy Greaves, the arrival of Tommy Docherty and the start of the club's modern era. My aim has been to provide a considered assessment of each player, but where he has made so few appearances that this seemed impossible I have confined myself to the facts and figures of his career.

A number of excellent works of reference on Chelsea have been published over the last ten years, so I have provided only the essential statistical information: games played (with appearances as a substitute shown in brackets), goals scored, other clubs and so on. The figures quoted for each player's Chelsea career refer to matches played in League football (including the play-off games in 1987/88), the FA Cup, the League Cup in its various guises, the Full Members' Cup and European competitions but not the FA Charity Shield. A full breakdown is given at the back of the book. The records quoted for other clubs refer to League matches only (excluding play-offs). The dates in large type indicate the seasons during which each player appeared in the Blues' first team, not when he joined or left the club. Honours listed are those won as a Chelsea player with the exception of international caps. The years mentioned after the number of caps won indicate the dates of the player's first and last international appearances. Statistics are complete to 15 May 1998. Transfer fees quoted are those given in the press at the time.

Although *Chelsea – Player by Player* focuses on the period since 1960/61, I have prefaced this cavalcade of heroes with a glance at some stalwarts from the 1950s – in particular the redoubtable side that captured the League Championship in 1955. Could it be that the day is not too far distant when the Blues finally manage to emulate their achievement?

Peter Lovering
London
May 1998

CONTENTS

8 FIFTIES FAITHFULS	JIM BARRON	98 DUNCAN McKENZIE
10 PETER SILLETT	BARRY LLOYD	JOHN SPARROW
12 PETER BRABROOK	CHICO HAMILTON	99 EAMONN BANNON
13 REG MATTHEWS	GEORGE LUKE	MICKY NUTTON
14 JOHN SILLETT	55 ALEX STEPNEY	100 COLIN VILJOEN
15 MEL SCOTT	KINGSLEY WHIFFEN	TREVOR AYLOTT
16 RON TINDALL	ROGER WOSAHLO	101 PETAR BOROTA
17 JOHN MORTIMORE	COLIN WALDRON	102 CLIVE WALKER
18 TONY NICHOLAS	GEOFF BUTLER	104 GARY CHIVERS
DEREK GIBBS	STEWART HOUSTON	105 PHIL DRIVER
19 SYLVAN ANDERTON	PAUL McMILLAN	ALAN MAYES
STAN CROWTHER	56 ALAN BIRCHENALL	106 STEVE FRANCIS
20 JIMMY GREAVES	57 JOHN DEMPSEY	DENNIS ROFE
22 CHARLIE LIVESEY	58 DAVID WEBB	107 TOMMY LANGLEY
JOHNNY BROOKS	60 PETER OSGOOD	108 PETER RHOADES-BROWN
23 MIKE HARRISON	62 KEITH WELLER	109 CHRIS HUTCHINGS
MICKY BLOCK	63 MARVIN HINTON	KEVIN HALES
24 DAVID CLISS	64 CHARLIE COOKE	110 BRYAN ROBSON
TERRY BRADBURY	66 TOMMY BALDWIN	PAUL CANOVILLE
25 ANDY MALCOLM	67 STEVE KEMBER	111 MIKE FILLERY
BOBBY EVANS	68 ALAN HUDSON	112 TONY McANDREW
26 TOMMY DOCHERTY	70 IAN HUTCHINSON	GORDON DAVIES
DENNIS BUTLER	72 CHRIS GARLAND	113 JOEY JONES
GORDON BOLLAND	73 PETER HOUSEMAN	114 COLIN PATES
COLIN SHAW	74 RON HARRIS	116 DOUG ROUGVIE
DENNIS SORRELL	76 PETER FEELY	117 COLIN LEE
ERROL McNALLY	TONY POTRAC	118 JOHN BUMSTEAD
27 MICHAEL PINNER	MIKE BROLLY	120 MICKY THOMAS
JOHN DUNN	TOMMY ORD	121 EDDIE NIEDZWIECKI
JIM MULHOLLAND	LEE FROST	122 DAVID SPEEDIE
DENNIS BROWN	BOB ILES	124 KERRY DIXON
IAN WATSON	77 JOHN SITTON	126 NIGEL SPACKMAN
JOHN O'ROURKE	GARY JOHNSON	128 PAT NEVIN
28 FRANK UPTON	JIM DOCHERTY	130 KEITH DUBLIN
29 ALLAN HARRIS	TIM ELMES	KEITH JONES
30 DEREK KEVAN	JIMMY CLARE	131 DALE JASPER
TOMMY HARMER	MARK FALCO	TONY GODDEN
31 KEN SHELLITO	PAUL WILLIAMS	132 GORDON DURIE
32 FRANK BLUNSTONE	78 PADDY MULLIGAN	134 DEREK JOHNSTONE
34 BERT MURRAY	79 TOMMY HUGHES	TERRY HOWARD
35 GRAHAM MOORE	DEREK SMETHURST	ROBERT ISAAC
36 BARRY BRIDGES	80 MICKY DROY	JOHN MILLAR
38 EDDIE McCREADIE	82 TEDDY MAYBANK	DUNCAN SHEARER
40 JOHN BOYLE	JOHN SISSONS	LES FRIDGE
41 GEORGE GRAHAM	83 DAVID HAY	135 JOHN McNAUGHT
42 ALAN YOUNG	84 STEVE SHERWOOD	COLIN WEST
TOMMY KNOX	RAY LEWINGTON	JOHN COADY
43 JIM McCALLIOG	85 JOHN PHILLIPS	BILLY DODDS
JOE FASCIONE	86 GRAHAM WILKINS	MICKY BODLEY
44 JOHN HOLLINS	87 STEVE FINNIESTON	PERRY DIGWEED
46 TERRY VENABLES	88 KEN SWAIN	136 DARREN WOOD
48 PETER BONETTI	89 BILL GARNER	137 JERRY MURPHY
50 TONY HATELEY	90 GARY LOCKE	ROY WEGERLE
51 JOE KIRKUP	92 BRIAN BASON	138 MICK HAZARD
JIM THOMSON	DAVID STRIDE	139 CLIVE WISON
52 BOBBY TAMBLING	93 IAN BRITTON	140 JOE McLAUGHLIN
54 JIM SMART	94 RAY WILKINS	141 GRAHAM ROBERTS
BILLY SINCLAIR	96 GARRY STANLEY	142 TONY DORIGO
TOMMY ROBSON	97 STEVE WICKS	144 KEN MONKOU

145 KEVIN McALLISTER
146 ROGER FREESTONE
    JASON CUNDY
147 PETER NICHOLAS
148 ALAN DICKENS
    DAMIAN MATTHEW
149 DAVE BEASANT
150 VINNIE JONES
151 PAUL ELLIOTT
152 GARETH HALL
153 KEVIN WILSON
154 ANDY TOWNSEND
156 TOM BOYD
    CLIVE ALLEN
157 TONY CASCARINO
    MICK HARFORD
158 DAVID LEE
159 GRAHAM STUART
160 ROBERT FLECK
161 GAVIN PEACOCK
162 JOHN SPENCER
163 ANDY DOW
    MAL DONAGHY
164 ANTHONY BARNESS
    DARREN BARNARD
165 MARK STEIN
166 DAVID HOPKIN
    NEIL SHIPPERLEY
167 GLEN HODDLE
168 DIMITRI KHARINE
169 KEVIN HITCHCOCK
170 SCOTT MINTO
    JAKOB KJELDBJERG
171 PAUL FURLONG
172 DAVE MITCHELL
    JOE ALLON
    MICHAEL GILKES
    STEVE LIVINGSTONE
    IAN PEARCE
    GRAHAM RIX
    NICK COLGAN
173 GERRY PEYTON
    JOE SHEERIN
    NEIL CLEMENT
    PAUL PARKER
    CRAIG FORREST
    STEVE HAMPSHIRE
    NICK CRITTENDEN
    JON HARLEY
174 FRANK SINCLAIR
175 EDDIE NEWTON
176 TERRY PHELAN
    DAVID ROCASTLE
177 ERLAND JOHNSEN
178 STEVE CLARKE
180 DENNIS WISE
182 RUUD GULLIT
183 ANDY MYERS
184 MARK HUGHES

186 DAN PETRESCU
187 CRAIG BURLEY
188 ROBERTO DI MATTEO
189 GIANLUCA VIALLI
190 DANNY GRANVILLE
    PAUL HUGHES
191 MARK NICHOLLS
    JODY MORRIS
192 MICHAEL DUBERRY
193 FRANK LEBOEUF
194 GIANFRANCO ZOLA
196 FRODE GRODAS
    ED DE GOEY
197 BERNARD LAMBOURDE
    CELESTINE BABAYARO
    LAURENT CHARVET
198 TORE ANDRE FLO
    GUSTAVO POYET

199 GRAEME LE SAUX
200 TED DRAKE
    TOMMY DOCHERTY
201 DAVE SEXTON
    RON SUART
    EDDIE McCREADIE
202 KEN SHELLITO
    DANNY BLANCHFLOWER
    GEOFF HURST
    JOHN NEAL
203 JOHN HOLLINS
    BOBBY CAMPBELL
    IAN PORTERFIELD
    DAVID WEBB
204 GLEN HODDLE
    RUUD GULLIT
    GIANLUCA VIALLI
205 PLAYERS' STATISTICS

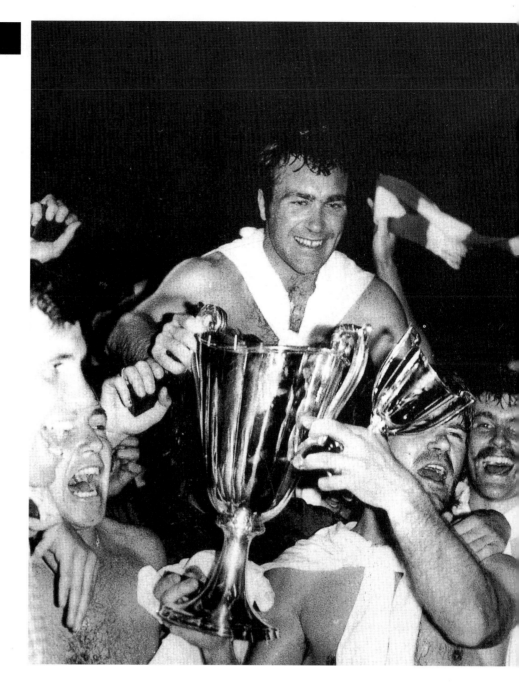

FIFTIES FAITHFULS

The high-water mark of Ted Drake's nine-year reign as Chelsea manager was undoubtedly the League Championship triumph in 1954/55. Combining several dependable stalwarts he had inherited with an array of imaginative signings, Drake had welded together a resolute, purposeful team that managed to carry off the title with an impressive surge in the second half of the season. As that side broke up, seemingly unable to sustain the mighty effort that had brought them glory, he placed his faith in youthful exuberance, and many of Drake's Ducklings are featured in the main part of this book.

However, a number of players who provided sterling service during the second half of the fifties did not survive into the new decade. Some were talented youngsters who failed to command a regular first-team place and soon moved on, others were solid journeymen who lacked the qualities required for a long career at the top; a few of them are featured here, together with the men who brought the Championship to Stamford Bridge, to set the scene for what follows.

Back row *(left to right)*:

KEN ARMSTRONG (47/8-56/7, wing-half, 401 games, 30 goals).

RON GREENWOOD (52/3-54/5, centre-half, 66 games, 0 goals).

DEREK SAUNDERS (53/4-58/9, wing-half, 222 games, 9 goals).

BILL ROBERTSON (50/1-59/60, goalkeeper, 214 games, 0 goals).

STAN WILLEMSE (49/50-55/6, full-back, 220 games, 2 goals).

PETER SILLETT (53/4-61/2, full-back, 287 games, 34 goals).

Front row:

ERIC PARSONS (50/1-56/7, winger, 176 games, 42 goals).

JOHN McNICHOL (52/3-57/8, inside-forward, 202 games, 66 goals).

ROY BENTLEY (47/8-56/7, forward, 366 games, 149 goals).

LES STUBBS (52/3-58/9, inside-forward, 122 games, 35 goals).

JIM LEWIS (52/3-57/8, winger, 95 games, 40 goals).

LEAGUE CHAMPIONS 1954/55

STAN WICKS

SEAMUS O'CONNELL

CHICK THOMSON

DICK WHITTAKER

LEN CASEY

IAN MacFARLANE

ALAN DICKS

LES ALLEN

STAN WICKS (54/5-56/7, centre-half, 80 games, 1 goal).

SEAMUS O'CONNELL (54/5-55/6, inside-forward, 17 games, 12 goals).

CHICK THOMSON (52/3-55/6, goalkeeper, 59 games, 0 goals).

JOHN HARRIS (45/6-55/6, centre-half/full-back, 364 games, 14 goals).

JOHN HARRIS

DICK WHITTAKER (55/6-59/60, full-back, 51 games, 0 goals).

LEN CASEY (55/6-58/9, wing-half, 37 games, 0 goals).

IAN MacFARLANE (56/7-57/8, full-back, 43 games, 0 goals).

ALAN DICKS (52/3-57/8, centre-half, 38 games, 1 goal).

LES ALLEN (56/7-59/60, forward, 49 games, 11 goals).

PETER SILLETT

Rather like a Rolls-Royce, there was nothing showy or flamboyant about Peter Sillett but his quality was readily apparent to the discerning observer. Placid and undemonstrative, he remained resolute and imperturbable in the heat of battle, calmly intervening to avert disaster when there was panic and confusion all around, but it could be argued that his sane, civilised attitude to the game prevented the powerfully built full-back from doing complete justice to his exceptional natural talent.

Peter joined Chelsea in May 1953 for £12,000, renewing a family link with Ted Drake, who had played alongside his father at the Dell in the early thirties. In his first season at Stamford Bridge he made only a dozen League appearances, but he broke into the team midway through the next campaign and made a significant contribution to the Blues' mould-breaking Championship triumph.

A hard, uncompromising defender who feared no one, Peter was not particularly quick nor was he an exceptional tackler but his complete mastery of the subtle arts of full-back play meant that wily opponents like Stanley Matthews and Tom Finney rarely escaped his shackles. He kicked the ball beautifully, picking out his man with precision, and his ferociously struck free-kicks yielded a number of highly spectacular goals, none better than an astounding effort from 40 yards against Manchester United in September 1959 that flew past the startled goalkeeper into the top left-hand corner of the net. However, he is probably best remembered as a deadly penalty-taker. He took on the potentially embarrassing role after five successive misses by John Harris and Roy Bentley had threatened to undermine the Blues' growing Championship challenge and performed it with characteristic aplomb. Never was his nerve subjected to a more rigorous examination than when he was given the chance to settle an enthralling and potentially decisive encounter with Wolves on Easter Saturday from the spot with 15 minutes remaining, but his trusty right foot did not fail him. The ball rocketed past Bert Williams, the 75,000 crowd erupted and the title was within Chelsea's grasp.

Peter was an automatic choice for the next six seasons, his only significant absence coming at the start of 1956/57 following a knee operation. Although he preferred to play on the right, Chelsea's failure to find a long-term replacement for Stan Willemse meant that he was often obliged to switch to the other flank, where he performed with equal distinction. His versatility ensured that he was a regular member of the party selected for international matches – he travelled to the 1958 World Cup in Sweden, for instance, without getting a game – but the lack of a steady partner at club level may well have hampered his efforts to add to the three full England caps he won on the summer tour in 1955.

The rapid break-up of the Championship-winning team meant that within a few seasons of joining the Blues as a 20-year-old Peter was one of the few seasoned professionals on the Stamford Bridge staff and his encouragement made an invaluable contribution to the development of many of the club's young players, including his eventual successor Ken Shellito. Sillett succeeded Derek Saunders as captain in 1959, but a broken leg sustained in the third game of 1961/62 effectively ended his Chelsea career. He had recovered by the end of the season but there was no place for him under the Docherty regime and he joined Guildford City that summer, a lack of confidence in the leg prompting him to decline offers from a number of League clubs. He was only 29 and it was a decision he subsequently regretted, but it was characteristic of the man that he should have accepted the cards he had been dealt without complaint.

BORN: Southampton, 1.2.33.
GAMES: 287. GOALS: 34.
HONOURS: League Championship 54/5.
3 England caps (55).
OTHER CLUBS: Southampton 51/2-52/3 (59, 4).

1953/54-1961/62

PETER BRABROOK

It is easy to forget that Peter Brabrook was still a month short of his 25th birthday when he left Stamford Bridge in October 1962. He had been unchallenged as the Blues' first-choice right-winger for five seasons and the torrent of goals that, for most of that period, had successfully compensated for the side's defensive shortcomings owed much to the enterprising East Ender's skill and consistency.

Peter was 17 when he was given his first taste of League football, making three appearances at inside-left as the 1954/55 Championship battle neared its climax, and the following season he shared the number eight shirt with Johnny McNichol. However, in November 1956 he was switched to outside-right in place of Eric Parsons and it was soon apparent that he had found his true position. Few of Drake's Ducklings were to make the transition to senior football with such assurance and within two seasons he had become the first product of the Chelsea Juniors to play for England, making his full international debut in the play-off against the Soviet Union in the 1958 World Cup in Sweden.

Pace and good ball control with either foot made Brabrook a formidable opponent. He was a direct, attacking winger who ran at defences and frequently left them trailing bemused in his wake, never more impressively than when he beat three men before pushing the ball past the 'keeper at Upton Park in February 1960. He crossed the ball well, his centres helping Ron Tindall to many of his goals, and if he didn't have Frank Blunstone's tenacity – well, there were very few who did. He was also a reliable goalscorer, regularly meeting crosses from the left with a well-placed header.

However, the departure of Ted Drake and the appointment of Tommy Docherty prompted wholesale changes at Stamford Bridge. When Brabrook was left out of the team at the start of 1962/63 it became clear that his departure would not be long delayed and within weeks he had been transferred to West Ham United for £35,000.

BORN: Greenwich, 8.11.37.
GAMES: 270. GOALS: 57.
HONOURS: 3 England caps (58-60).
OTHER CLUBS: West Ham United 62/3-67/8 (167, 33);
Leyton Orient 68/9-70/1 (72, 6).

1954/55-1961/62

REG MATTHEWS

Moving to Stamford Bridge was probably the biggest mistake Reg Matthews ever made. A magnificent natural goalkeeper with quite astonishing reflexes, he had begun his career with his home-town club, Third Division Coventry City, and performed so impressively that he earned five England caps without the benefit of the publicity surrounding more fashionable teams. When he joined Chelsea in November 1956 he became the most expensive 'keeper in the country, but he was unable to settle in London and continued to live in Coventry. As a result he could not train with his team-mates regularly and, not surprisingly in the circumstances, he produced his best form only intermittently during his time with the Blues, although in mitigation it should be said that the protection he received from his defence was often rudimentary.

Reg was a little round-shouldered with an ambling gait that scarcely betrayed the fact that he was a professional athlete, but once he donned the green jersey he was transformed. Agile and acrobatic, he was at his best on his line but came out for crosses with authority and was utterly fearless when diving at the feet of onrushing forwards. He smoked heavily to calm his jangling nerves and his excitability caused more than a few anxious moments for his defenders, but he generally emerged from the frequent goalmouth mêlées clutching the ball.

Significantly, Reg's best performances for the Blues came on visits to the Midlands, with a superlative display in a rousing 2-1 win against Wolves in January 1959 outstanding, and by the closing weeks of 1959/60 his position as Chelsea's first-choice 'keeper was in doubt. A bruised ankle allowed Peter Bonetti to prove his class and Matthews was able to reclaim the position only briefly before moving on to Derby County in October 1961.

BORN: Coventry, 20.12.33.
GAMES: 148. GOALS: 0.
HONOURS: 5 England caps (56).
OTHER CLUBS: Coventry City 52/3-56/7 (111, 0);
Derby County 61/2-67/8 (225, 0).

1956/57-1960/61

JOHN SILLETT

Few wingers enjoyed playing against John Sillett. He possessed only a fraction of his elder brother Peter's abundant natural talent but made far greater use of the ability he had been granted, his determination and unquenchable aggression ensuring that his technical limitations were rarely exploited.

John started his career with Southampton and joined Chelsea as a 16-year-old when Peter moved to Stamford Bridge from the south coast club. At that stage he was a bustling centre-forward but by the time he made his League debut at Old Trafford on New Year's Day 1957 he had been converted to full-back. A dislocated kneecap that September delayed his progress and he was 22 by the time he was given his first extended run in the side at the beginning of the 1958/59 season. He started on the left with Peter at right-back, but John was happier on the other flank (and less adaptable than his brother) and therefore made the majority of his appearances over the next three years in the number two shirt.

Ferocious in the tackle and utterly fearless, John invariably performed with passion and unwavering commitment, rapidly coming to be recognised as one of football's hard men. He lacked his brother's composure but had the pace to sprint back and close the door when a rash lunge appeared to have left it wide open. He lost his place after a 6-0 defeat at Bolton in March 1959 but fought his way back into the side the following season and for the next 18 months the pairing of Sillett (P) and Sillett (J) was broken only when the junior partner was held to be responsible for some particularly painful thrashing and consigned to the reserves for a few weeks.

John's technique may have been unsophisticated but he was a solid professional who worked hard at his game. However, when Tommy Docherty succeeded Ted Drake he quickly decided that Ken Shellito was the better long-term prospect and in April 1962 Sillett was transferred to Third Division Coventry City.

BORN: Southampton, 20.7.36.
GAMES: 102. GOALS: 1.
OTHER CLUBS: Coventry City 61/2-65/6 (109, 1);
Plymouth Argyle 66/7-67/8 (38, 1).
MANAGER: Hereford United (74-78 and 91-92);
Coventry City (87-90).

1956/57-1961/62

MEL SCOTT

Mel Scott was given his chance to claim a first-team place against Wolves in March 1958 and seized the opportunity so impressively that by the following September he had graduated to the England under-23 side. Quick and agile, the 18-year-old centre-half was remarkably assured and appeared to possess all the qualities required for success. He had a good touch and read the game well, favouring the timely interception rather than the crunching tackle, and if his distribution was only fair no doubt that would improve with experience.

However, there was a fundamental weakness that would prove to be Mel's undoing: he was not quite tall enough to dominate in the air and lacked the physical presence to handle big, aggressive centre-forwards. He was the first-choice number five for most of the following season but the Blues' unswerving commitment to attack meant that the defence was often hopelessly exposed and, with the goals-against tally steadily mounting, his confidence was gradually eroded. For all his undoubted ability, the youngster was making too many mistakes, although his pace often allowed him to retrieve the situation. He gave the impression of being content to rely on the natural gifts he had been granted, rather than working to make the fullest possible use of his talent – or perhaps it was simply that too much had been demanded of him so early in his career. Following the arrival of Sylvan Anderton in March, Ted Drake decided to switch John Mortimore back into the middle and for the next two years Scott was consigned to the reserves.

Mel reclaimed his place towards the end of 1960/61 and played regularly the following season but was unable to recapture the form that had marked his arrival in the First Division. He was once again displaced by Mortimore and it became increasingly apparent that he had no future at Stamford Bridge. In March 1963 he joined Brentford, a move which did little to revive his fading career.

BORN: Claygate, 26.9.39.
GAMES: 104. GOALS: 0.
OTHER CLUBS: Brentford 62/3-66/7 (156, 2);
Chicago Sting; Oakland Clippers.

1957/58-1961/62

RON TINDALL

Chelsea have had many centre-forwards more gifted than Ron Tindall, but none who has tried harder. Popular in the dressing room and utterly selfless on the pitch, he was a true 'team man', who could be relied upon to play his part to the full.

Ron scored on his debut, at home to West Bromwich Albion in November 1955, but even after Roy Bentley's departure to Fulham the following September he had to fight to retain his grip on the number nine shirt, as first Les Allen and then Charlie Livesey attempted to snatch it from him. It was as if Ted Drake felt he ought to be able to find someone more stylish to fill the position, but soon discovered that the replacements, no matter how stylish, were less effective than the original incumbent.

Tindall was the ideal target man, with the strength to hold the ball before bringing team-mates into the game, and harassed colleagues knew that he would be easy to find with a long pass. Brave and athletic, he was majestic in the air and most of his goals were scored with his head, including a hat-trick against Newcastle in November 1960. Less adept when the ball was on the ground, he was not the quickest or most elegant of movers, but formed a formidable attacking partnership with Jimmy Greaves, his flicks presenting Jimmy with many of his openings.

It was entirely characteristic that Ron, a natural all-round sportsman who played cricket for Surrey during the summer, should take on the role of emergency goalkeeper and perform it with distinction, and he gave further evidence of his boundless versatility by moving to left-back for a while in the autumn of 1959 following the arrival of Livesey from Southampton.

Tindall was one of a number of players to leave Stamford Bridge following Drake's replacement by Tommy Docherty, moving to West Ham United in November 1961 in part-exchange for Andy Malcolm.

BORN: Streatham, 23.9.35.
GAMES: 174. GOALS: 70.
OTHER CLUBS: West Ham United 61/2 (13, 3);
Reading 62/3-63/4 (36, 12);
Portsmouth 64/5-69/70 (161, 7).
MANAGER: Portsmouth (70-73).

1955/56-1961/62

JOHN MORTIMORE

John Mortimore's Chelsea career divides neatly into two halves – separated by a frustrating two-year sojourn in the wilderness when he was probably at his peak.

After a distinguished spell as an amateur with Woking, during the course of which he made three League appearances for the Blues, John joined the professional staff at Stamford Bridge in August 1957, although he continued to pursue his career as a teacher for several years. He had been signed as a replacement for Ken Armstrong at right-half, but proved to be most effective when playing in the centre of the defence. Dominant in the air, he was a tight marker with a firm tackle who used the ball constructively but lacked the pace to be a top-class wing-half.

Solid and dependable, Mortimore was a first-team regular for three seasons but then found himself out of favour as first Bobby Evans and then Mel Scott – neither of whom excelled 'upstairs' – occupied the number five shirt. John came close to joining Chester as player-manager but resumed his duties at centre-half in the last three matches of 1961/62 and lent some much-needed experience and composure to Docherty's exuberant young side over the next three seasons. A League Cup winner's medal in 1965 was a richly deserved reward for the tall defender's loyalty, and only an over-zealous referee's whistle prevented him from giving the Blues the lead in that season's FA Cup semi-final against Liverpool.

John had been appointed coach in succession to Dave Sexton earlier that year but was reluctant to accept Docherty's suggestion that he should give up playing to concentrate on his new role, and when he was left out in favour of Marvin Hinton at the start of the following season he decided to move on to Queens Park Rangers, subsequently embarking on a highly successful coaching career, much of which has been spent as assistant manager of Southampton.

BORN: Farnborough, 23.9.34.
GAMES: 279. GOALS: 10.
OTHER CLUBS: Queens Park Rangers 65/6 (10, 0); Sunderland (0, 0).
MANAGER: Ethnikos, Greece (twice); Portsmouth (73-74);
Benfica (twice); Real Betis, Spain; Belenenses, Portugal.

1955/56-1964/65

TONY NICHOLAS	DEREK GIBBS

While physical prowess alone can bring considerable success at junior level, something more is needed if a youngster is to make a similar impact in League football and it was the absence of this extra dimension from his game that prevented Tony Nicholas from fulfilling his undoubted potential. A strong, powerfully built inside-forward with two good feet, he had pace and covered a lot of ground in 90 minutes, but his athleticism could not conceal the fact that he was essentially an instinctive player who lacked the speed of thought and tactical awareness needed to trouble First Division defences and he failed to maintain his early progress.

Nicholas was given his senior baptism in August 1956 as Ted Drake set about the wholesale reconstruction of his Championship-winning side, and he had several extended runs in the first team over the next four seasons but never succeeded in making his place secure. His most productive spell was in the autumn of 1957 when he scored six goals in nine appearances including a splendid individual effort in a 6-1 win against Burnley, but the pressing need was for someone to supply the ammunition for Jimmy Greaves. The arrival of Johnny Brooks in December 1959 effectively spelled the end of Tony's chances at Stamford Bridge and the following November he was transferred to Brighton.

BORN: West Ham, 16.4.38.
GAMES: 63. GOALS: 20.
OTHER CLUBS: Brighton and Hove Albion 60/1-61/2 (65, 22); Leyton Orient 65/6 (9, 2).

Every club needs men like Derek Gibbs, dependable reserves who will give everything they have on the rare occasions they are called up to fill a gap in the first team. A hard-working, dogged inside-forward, he was a big, strong player who could run all day, shuttling up and down the pitch, but possessed only a fraction of the talent of contemporaries such as Jimmy Greaves and David Cliss. Although he occasionally looked clumsy, he passed the ball neatly enough, but his yeoman qualities were never sufficient to win him a recognised place in the side and he was restricted to a total of 25 senior appearances spread over five seasons, scoring six times.

Derek's best season was probably 1958/59, with the high spot being a third round FA Cup tie against Newcastle at St James's Park when the Blues defied a passionate Geordie crowd to record a famous 4-1 win, Gibbs scoring the third goal when he ran onto a pass from Stan Crowther and beat the advancing 'keeper, not long after he had hit the bar with a venomous drive. Defeat at the hands of Aston Villa in the next round ended dreams of Wembley for another year and shortly afterwards Gibbs returned to the reserves.

The arrival of Johnny Brooks only added to the competition for inside-forward places and in November 1960 Derek moved to Leyton Orient, but he failed to make the impression in the lower divisions that one might have anticipated.

BORN: Fulham, 22.12.34. GAMES: 25. GOALS: 6.
OTHER CLUBS: Leyton Orient 60/1-62/3 (33, 4); Queens Park Rangers 63/4-64/5 (27, 0).

1956/57-1960/61	1956/57-1960/61

SYLVAN ANDERTON

Sylvan Anderton was one of football's drudges, an honest toiler who went about his work with the unobtrusive efficiency of a diligent clerk perched high upon a stool in some sepulchral Victorian office, his quill moving ceaselessly across the pages of a weighty ledger.

Signed by Ted Drake from the club he had managed before taking over at Stamford Bridge, Reading, shortly before the transfer deadline in March 1959 to reinforce a team that had lost its way after a bright and breezy start to the season, Sylvan proved to be a sound, dependable right-half who used the ball well and covered conscientiously. Although he was a little short of drive and aggression, he contributed to a worthwhile upturn in the Blues' fortunes in the closing weeks of 1958/59 and missed only two League games the following season, forming a solid if somewhat pedestrian half-back partnership with Stan Crowther.

Powerless to resist the challenge of 17-year-old Terry Venables, a player of infinitely greater gifts, Anderton began the next campaign in the reserves but fought back with characteristic tenacity to claim a place at left-half after Christmas. Tommy Docherty's elevation to the position of chief coach presented a chance to reassert his claims but the arrival of Andy Malcolm dashed Sylvan's hopes and in January 1962 he joined Queens Park Rangers.

BORN: Reading, 23.11.34.
GAMES: 82. GOALS: 2.
OTHER CLUBS: Reading 52/3-58/9 (155, 18);
Queens Park Rangers 61/2 (4, 0).

1958/59-1961/62

STAN CROWTHER

A powerful, aggressive wing-half with a reputation as a hard man, Stan Crowther was signed from Manchester United shortly before Christmas 1958 in an effort to reinforce a defence that had been conceding too many soft goals, particularly away from home. Although he was only 23, he had already had an eventful career: having helped Aston Villa win the FA Cup in 1957, he had moved to Old Trafford in the aftermath of the Munich disaster and reached Wembley once again, becoming the first man to play in the competition for two different clubs in the same season.

Apart from a spell at the beginning of 1959/60 when he was sidelined by injury, Stan was the Blues' regular left-half for the next 18 months but he lacked the natural ability of the man he had replaced, Derek Saunders, and could not summon the self-discipline to make the fullest use of the talent he possessed. For all the Midlander's fierce tackling and unwavering commitment, the torrent of goals conceded continued unabated and at the start of 1960/61 Ted Drake looked to Terry Bradbury.

Crowther made only one more first-team appearance for Chelsea, in a League Cup tie against Workington that October, and in March 1961 he was transferred to Second Division Brighton, subsequently dropping out of League football.

BORN: Bilston, 3.9.35.
GAMES: 58. GOALS: 0.
OTHER CLUBS: Aston Villa 56/7-57/8 (50, 4);
Manchester United 57/8-58/9 (13, 0);
Brighton and Hove Albion 60/1 (4, 0).

1958/59-1960/61

JIMMY GREAVES

Jimmy Greaves is widely acknowledged as the greatest goalscorer that English football has ever produced but, in the eyes of the Stamford Bridge faithful at least, he never quite recaptured the precocious brilliance he showed during his four seasons in the Chelsea first team prior to his departure for Italy in the summer of 1961. He was rarely to be seen dropping back to help his defenders and could scarcely be described as a model professional off the field, but none of that mattered; he was a match-winner whose pace and deft control made him almost impossible to contain.

Jimmy made his League debut at White Hart Lane in the first game of 1957/58, having scored more than a century of goals as a junior the previous season, and crowned a sparkling performance by tucking home the equaliser with the precision that was to become so familiar with five minutes remaining. However, the Greaves legend really began to take shape when he returned to the side on Christmas morning after a brief spell on the sidelines, the audacious 17-year-old scoring four times in a festive romp against Portsmouth.

Greaves scored 132 goals in 169 games for Chelsea, an astonishing rate of return that kept the Blues afloat despite the manifest inadequacies of their defence. He hit five in a match on three occasions, including a remarkable 5-4 win at Deepdale in December 1959 when he appeared to score at will every time Preston drew level. A hat-trick against Manchester City in November 1960 made him the first man to score a hundred League goals before the age of 21 and it seems highly unlikely that his club record of 41 League goals in 1960/61 will ever be beaten.

The statistics of Jimmy's career are enough to reduce every striker currently plying his trade in the Premier League to abject despair, but figures alone cannot do justice to the imperious style in which his goals were taken. Not for him the ego-boosting blast into the roof of the net; he had the confidence to select his spot and roll the ball home, often having wrong-footed the hapless 'keeper. Blessed with remarkable anticipation, he was a clinical, razor-sharp finisher who pounced eagerly on the half-chance at close quarters, ruthlessly punishing the slightest lapse. He relished every opportunity to run at defences, heading for goal with characteristic singleness of purpose, and had the skill to go past his man, as he demonstrated against Birmingham in September 1959 when he picked the ball up in his own half and weaved his way past five defenders before leaving the 'keeper helpless with a stinging shot. But, above all, he made it look absurdly, joyously easy . . .

Greaves won his first full international cap against Peru in May 1959 and was a regular member of Walter Winterbottom's side thereafter, but Chelsea's failure to build a winning team around their extraordinary young marksman made it inevitable that they would lose him. In Italian football he could command vastly more than the modest sum the Blues were permitted to offer him and it was eventually agreed that he would join AC Milan for £80,000 at the end of the 1960/61 season. His last game for the club was against Nottingham Forest at Stamford Bridge and he marked the occasion in characteristically dramatic fashion by scoring all four goals in a 4-3 win. It was an emotional occasion, for the little genius had been enormously popular with fans and team-mates alike and the future looked bleak without him. However, while the Stamford Bridge crowd mourned the loss of their saviour, few could pretend that in his place their decision would have been any different.

Like many football expatriates since, Jimmy did not enjoy his stay in Italy but by the following December the maximum wage had been lifted and he was back in London – but with Tottenham, not Chelsea.

BORN: East Ham, 20.2.40.
GAMES: 169. GOALS: 132.
HONOURS: 57 England caps (59-67).
OTHER CLUBS: AC Milan;
Tottenham Hotspur 61/2-69/70 (321, 220);
West Ham United 69/70-70/71 (38, 13).

1957/58-1960/61

CHARLIE LIVESEY

The two seasons Charlie Livesey spent at Stamford Bridge represented a wasted opportunity for a player of considerable natural ability. A speedy, powerfully built centre-forward, he had failed to make the grade with the Blues as a schoolboy but was signed from Southampton in May 1959 in a part-exchange deal involving Cliff Huxford after an impressive first season in League football which had also attracted the interest of Arsenal and Birmingham City.

Charlie began his Chelsea career with something of a flourish, contributing to a bright start to the new campaign with eight goals in his first 14 appearances, including a coolly taken individual effort against West Bromwich Albion in October, but his stay with the club was to be blighted by inconsistency. All too often a good performance would be followed by a match in which he remained largely anonymous, as if he felt he had nothing left to prove, and it seemed that only when he was dropped was he prepared to assert himself.

Although he was not the most ruthless of goalscorers, Livesey possessed a cultured left foot and, like any worthwhile number nine of the period, posed a threat when the ball was in the air, but these qualities were not enough to guarantee his place and after a lively start to the following season he was once again omitted in favour of Ron Tindall, eventually joining Gillingham in August 1961.

BORN: West Ham, 6.2.38. GAMES: 42. GOALS: 18.
OTHER CLUBS: Southampton 58/9 (25, 14);
Gillingham 61/2-62/3 (47, 17); Watford 62/3-63/4 (64, 26);
Northampton Town 64/5-65/6 (28, 4);
Brighton and Hove Albion 65/6-68/9 (125, 30).

1959/60-1960/61

JOHNNY BROOKS

One of a number of players brought to Stamford Bridge by Ted Drake who had started their careers under his tutelage during his five-year spell in charge at Reading, Johnny Brooks was a stylish inside-forward whose delicate ball skills and imperious distribution had earned him three England caps at the high point of a largely successful stay with Tottenham. However, by the time he joined Chelsea in December 1959 in an exchange deal which took Les Allen to White Hart Lane – where he would earn a place in the history books as a member of Spurs' double-winning team – his career was in what would prove to be an irreversible decline.

There was no doubt of Johnny's talent. His ability to prise open even the stubbornest defence with a majestic swerve or to switch the point of attack with a crisply struck 40-yard pass should have ensured that Jimmy Greaves was kept supplied with a steady stream of goalscoring opportunities, but in a struggling team the newcomer's fragile confidence crumbled away, prompting his detractors to mutter about a lack of heart and courage.

Drake kept faith with Brooks for a year or so but his belief that he could help the 28-year-old rediscover his lost form proved unfounded. In the spring of 1961 Johnny was ousted from the first team by young Bobby Tambling and shortly after the start of the following season he moved on to Brentford.

BORN: Reading, 23.12.31.
GAMES: 52. GOALS: 7.
HONOURS: 3 England caps (56).
OTHER CLUBS: Reading 49/50-52/3 (46, 5);
Tottenham Hotspur 52/3-59/60 (166, 46);
Brentford 61/2-63/4 (83, 36); Crystal Palace 63/4 (7, 0).

1959/60-1960/61

MIKE HARRISON

Mike Harrison was a strong, athletic left-winger whose pace and powerful running troubled all but the most accomplished defenders, but he lacked the delicate skills and indomitable spirit of Frank Blunstone and was never able to establish himself as Chelsea's first-choice number 11. He made his debut at Blackpool in April 1957 when he was still five days short of his 17th birthday but had to wait until the closing weeks of the 1958/59 season before he was given an extended run in the side. He did well enough to prompt Ted Drake to accommodate Blunstone at inside-left, but the following season Harrison made only five appearances and thereafter he was firmly cast in the role of understudy.

His direct style created a steady stream of goalscoring opportunities for his team-mates but Mike is best remembered for his ability to test goalkeepers from prodigious distances with his mighty left foot, a remarkable swerving effort against Arsenal in March 1962, for example, leaving the unfortunate Jack Kelsey utterly bewildered.

Blunstone's frequent absences allowed Harrison a fairly regular taste of League football, but the arrival of Tommy Knox in the summer of 1962 marked the end of his hopes at Stamford Bridge and he soon moved on to Blackburn, giving the Lancashire club excellent service over the next five years.

BORN: Ilford, 18.4.40.
GAMES: 64. GOALS: 9.
OTHER CLUBS: Blackburn Rovers 62/3-67/8 (160, 40);
Plymouth Argyle 67/8 (15, 3);
Luton Town 68/9-69/70 (32, 6).

1956/57-1962/63

MICKY BLOCK

It seems cruel that the door to the Chelsea first team should have been opened to Micky Block so early in his career, only to be slammed in his face before he had reached his 19th birthday. His tantalising taste of First Division football was an indirect result of the injury which was to sideline Frank Blunstone for the best part of two years, the powerfully built youngster making his debut on the left wing in September 1957 and going on to record a total of 20 League appearances that season. Direct and persistent, Block possessed few of Frank's intricate skills, his preferred strategy being to run at his full-back, then knock the ball past him and use his pace to get clear, but he had a left foot of great power and precision and was not afraid to try his luck from distance.

Micky continued his public apprenticeship the following autumn, although he now faced competition for the number 11 shirt from Mike Harrison, a player of similar style who was three months younger. However, it was the return of Blunstone to fitness at the end of November that really marked the turning-point in Block's fortunes, the likeable teenager quickly finding himself relegated to the position of third choice. He remained at Stamford Bridge for another three years, making just five more League appearances, but the appointment of Tommy Docherty prompted widespread changes to the Blues' playing staff and in January 1962 he was transferred to Brentford.

BORN: Ipswich, 28.1.40.
GAMES: 40. GOALS: 6.
OTHER CLUBS: Brentford 61/2-65/6 (146, 30);
Watford 66/7 (13, 2).

1957/58-1961/62

DAVID CLISS

There have been any number of Chelsea players who have failed to do justice to their talent down the years, but rarely has the gulf between potential and achievement been wider than in the case of David Cliss. A diminutive inside-forward with the sort of audacious, delicate skills the Stamford Bridge crowd have always relished, he made his first-team debut against Preston in February 1958 and his stylish display in a 3-1 win at Villa Park two weeks later suggested that a star was in the making.

However, despite the 18-year-old's plentiful exuberance, Ted Drake appeared to feel that his lack of weight and power was an insuperable handicap and Cliss soon gave way to more robust performers. He made only seven appearances during the next two seasons and a broken leg in the first reserve match of 1960/61 dashed hopes that the experience he had gained playing in America during the summer would enable him finally to make the breakthrough.

Fully recovered, David started the following campaign in the side but the departure of Drake ended his chances of establishing himself, and in the summer he slipped into non-League football. With more application, and better luck, it could have been different . . .

BORN: Enfield, 15.11.39.
GAMES: 24. GOALS: 1.

1957/58-1961/62

TERRY BRADBURY

Brimming with youthful enthusiasm, Terry Bradbury was a tall, aggressive wing-half who was destined to discover that an abundance of effort alone could not compensate for the absence from his game of the kind of refinement generally considered essential to a First Division career.

Having waited rather longer than many of his contemporaries for his chance in the first team, he started the 1960/61 season in a completely remodelled half-back line that was completed by the Scottish veteran Bobby Evans and, on the right, 17-year-old Terry Venables. An eager, determined ball-winner who was blessed with considerable self-confidence, Bradbury tackled with great spirit and had the maturity to play within his limitations, sensibly opting for the simple pass to a colleague rather than attempting – in vain – something more ambitious, but after nine games which saw 24 goals conceded, he gave way to Sylvan Anderton. Six further appearances followed later in the campaign but consistency remained elusive.

Terry was given another run in the side during the Blues' dismal relegation battle the following winter but when he failed to win a place in Tommy Docherty's revamped team at the beginning of 1962/63 it became apparent that it was time to move on and in September he joined Southend United.

BORN: Paddington, 15.11.39. GAMES: 29. GOALS: 1.
OTHER CLUBS: Southend United 62/3-65/6 (161, 19);
Leyton Orient 66/7 (27, 0); Wrexham 67/8-68/9 (78, 4);
Chester 69/70-70/1 (90, 2).

1960/61-1961/62

ANDY MALCOLM

When Tommy Docherty succeeded Ted Drake in September 1961 it was already apparent that the team would have to be strengthened if the Blues were to avoid relegation. That verdict can only have been reinforced by a sequence of four defeats and a draw in his first five matches in charge, and in an effort to halt the slide he signed Andy Malcolm from West Ham in a deal which took Ron Tindall to Upton Park in part-exchange.

A strong, aggressive right-half with a reputation as a tight marker, Malcolm was a seasoned campaigner and there seemed to be every hope that the experience and resolve he brought to a tactically naive team might make a decisive difference when his debut at Highbury yielded a 3-0 win, Chelsea's first away victory of the season. Comfortable in possession and always wanting the ball, Malcolm soon made the number four shirt his own, assuming the captaincy in the absence of Peter Sillett, but the revival could not be sustained and relegation soon became virtually inevitable.

A fine solo goal in a 4-3 win at Fulham was probably the best moment of Andy's short stay at Stamford Bridge, but there was no place for him in the remodelled team unveiled by Docherty at the start of the following season and that October he moved on to Queens Park Rangers.

BORN: West Ham, 4.5.33.
GAMES: 28. GOALS: 1.
OTHER CLUBS: West Ham United 53/4-61/2 (283, 4);
Queens Park Rangers 62/3-64/5 (84, 4);
Port Elizabeth, South Africa.

1961/62

BOBBY EVANS

When Chelsea signed Bobby Evans in May 1960 they were buying a player of proven class. A Scottish international for more than a decade, he had served Glasgow Celtic with distinction for 16 seasons, helping the Parkhead club to a league and cup double in 1954 with a series of imposing displays at right-half before switching successfully to the number five shirt, but the Stamford Bridge crowd were to see little of the doughty tackling and measured passing that had won him such respect north of the border.

Bobby was already past his 33rd birthday when he trotted out for the first game of the new season and it soon became apparent that he was a spent force, the veteran finding it impossible to adapt to the greater pace of English football at this stage in his career. No doubt Ted Drake had hoped that his enormous experience would advance the football education of the youngsters in the team but, with Evans struggling to keep his head above water as a flood of goals were conceded, he was able to offer little assistance to others.

Bobby retained his place at centre-half until March but he was painfully aware that he had not lived up to his reputation, and in the closing weeks of the season he made way for Mel Scott before joining Newport County as player-manager in the summer.

BORN: Glasgow, 16.7.27. GAMES: 37. GOALS: 1.
HONOURS: 48 Scotland caps (48-60).
OTHER CLUBS: Glasgow Celtic;
Newport County 61/2 (31, 0);
Morton; Third Lanark; Raith Rovers.
MANAGER: Newport County (61-62); Third Lanark.

1960/61

TOMMY DOCHERTY

GORDON BOLLAND

DENNIS SORRELL

TOMMY DOCHERTY 1961/62

Wing-half. BORN: Glasgow, 24.8.28.
GAMES: 4. GOALS: 0.
HONOURS: 25 Scotland caps (51-59).
OTHER CLUBS: Glasgow Celtic; Preston North End 49/50-57/8 (324, 5);
Arsenal 58/9-60/1 (83, 1).
MANAGER: Chelsea (62-67); Rotherham United (67-68);
Queens Park Rangers (68 and 79-80); Aston Villa (68-70);
Oporto, Portugal; Scotland (71-72); Manchester United (72-77);
Derby County (77-79); Sydney Olympic, Australia;
Preston North End (81); Wolverhampton Wanderers (84-85).

DENNIS BUTLER 1961/62-1962/63

Full-back. BORN: Fulham, 7.3.43.
GAMES: 18. GOALS: 0.
OTHER CLUBS: Hull City 63/4-69/70 (217, 0);
Reading 69/70-73/4 (170, 0).

GORDON BOLLAND 1961/62

Inside-forward. BORN: Boston, 12.8.43.
GAMES: 2. GOALS: 0.
OTHER CLUBS: Leyton Orient 61/2-63/4 (63, 19);
Norwich City 63/4-67/8 (105, 29);
Charlton Athletic 67/8-68/9 (11, 2);
Millwall 68/9-74/5 (244, 62).

COLIN SHAW 1961/62

Centre-forward. BORN: St Albans, 19.6.43.
GAMES: 1. GOALS: 0.
OTHER CLUBS: Norwich City 63/4-64/5 (3, 0);
Leyton Orient 65/6 (7, 0); Natal, South Africa.

DENNIS SORRELL 1961/62-1963/64

Wing-half. BORN: Lambeth, 7.10.40.
GAMES: 4. GOALS: 1.
OTHER CLUBS: Leyton Orient 58/9-60/1 (37, 1) and
64/5-66/7 (74, 3).

ERROL McNALLY 1961/62-1963/64

Goalkeeper. BORN: Lurgan, 27.8.43.
GAMES: 9. GOALS: 0.
OTHER CLUBS: Portadown; Glenavon.

DENNIS BUTLER

COLIN SHAW

ERROL McNALLY

JOHN DUNN

DENNIS BROWN

IAN WATSON

MICHAEL PINNER

JIM MULHOLLAND

JOHN O'ROURKE

MICHAEL PINNER 1961/62

Goalkeeper. BORN: Boston, 16.2.34.
GAMES: 1. GOALS: 0.
OTHER CLUBS: Aston Villa 54/5-56/7 (4, 0);
Sheffield Wednesday 57/8-58/9 (7, 0);
Queens Park Rangers 59/60 (19, 0);
Manchester United 60/1 (4, 0); Swansea City 61/2 (1, 0);
Leyton Orient 62/3-64/5 (77, 0).

JOHN DUNN 1962/63-1965/66

Goalkeeper. BORN: Barking, 21.6.44.
GAMES: 16. GOALS: 0.
OTHER CLUBS: Torquay United 66/7-67/8 (44, 0);
Aston Villa 67/8-70/1 (101, 0); Charlton Athletic 71/2-74/5 (104, 0).

JIM MULHOLLAND 1962/63-1963/64

Forward. BORN: Knightswood, 10.4.38.
GAMES: 12. GOALS: 3.
OTHER CLUBS: East Stirling; Morton;
Barrow 65/6-68/9 (134, 47); Stockport County 68/9-69/70 (33, 5);
Crewe Alexandra 70/1 (10, 0).

DENNIS BROWN 1963/64-1964/65

Inside-forward. BORN: Reading, 8.2.44.
GAMES: 13. GOALS: 2.
OTHER CLUBS: Swindon Town 64/5-66/7 (92, 38);
Northampton Town 66/7-68/9 (46, 10);
Aldershot 69/70-74/5 (245, 56).

IAN WATSON 1962/63-1964/65

Full-back. BORN: Hammersmith, 7.1.44.
GAMES: 9. GOALS: 1.
OTHER CLUBS: Queens Park Rangers 65/6-73/4 (203, 1).

JOHN O'ROURKE 1963/64

Centre-forward. BORN: Northampton, 11.2.45.
GAMES: 1. GOALS: 0.
OTHER CLUBS: Luton Town 63/4-65/6 (84, 64);
Middlesbrough 66/7-67/8 (64, 38);
Ipswich Town 67/8-69/70 (69, 30);
Coventry City 69/70-71/2 (54, 17);
Queens Park Rangers 71/2-72/3 (34, 12);
AFC Bournemouth 73/4-74/5 (22, 4).

FRANK UPTON

A burly, tough left-half who delighted in his reputation as a hard man, Frank Upton was possibly the least gifted member of the Chelsea team that gained promotion from the Second Division in 1962/63 but his contribution was vital. Signed from Derby County shortly before the start of the previous season, he had been dropped after just three matches and remained out of favour until the following March, when he was recalled at centre-forward in a desperate bid to drag the Blues away from the foot of the table. The move was not a success, but when Tommy Docherty paired Frank with John Mortimore at the centre of the defence in the closing fixtures he had at last discovered a foundation on which he could build a winning team.

There were no frills to Upton's game, but he was a fearsome competitor who could be depended upon to give everything he had. Good in the air and a doughty tackler, he played to his strengths, winning the ball and giving it to a colleague better equipped to do something constructive with it. His influence on his young team-mates was invaluable, and anyone he suspected of not matching his own total commitment could expect to have it drawn to his attention in no uncertain terms.

Frank scored three goals that season from carefully planned free-kick moves, but his most celebrated contribution came in the epic battle at Roker Park in May which opened the door to the First Division. Handed the number nine shirt and instructed to unsettle Charlie Hurley, the creative Sunderland centre-half, he carried out his task with undisguised relish, characteristically shaking off a knee injury to finish the game on one leg.

Having lost his place in defence to Ron Harris, Frank returned to the side the following November after a tactical reshuffle and helped the Blues establish themselves as a force to be reckoned with, but with Docherty trying to build a team that would challenge for honours, there was no long-term future for him at the Bridge and he rejoined Derby in September 1965. He later had a spell on the Chelsea coaching staff and was caretaker manager – for a day – after the departure of Ken Shellito.

BORN: Nuneaton, 18.10.34.
GAMES: 86. GOALS: 3.
OTHER CLUBS: Northampton Town 52/3-53/4 (17, 1);
Derby County 54/5-60/1 (224, 12) and 65/6-66/7 (35, 5);
Notts County 66/7 (34, 3); Workington 67/8 (7, 0).
MANAGER: Workington (68).

1961/62-1964/65

ALLAN HARRIS

During his two spells at Stamford Bridge Allan Harris was a valued member of the first-team squad but never quite succeeded in making his place in the side secure. A cool, thoughtful full-back, he was loyal and uncomplaining and could bedepended upon to give his all whenever he was called upon, but perhaps lacked the aggression needed to succeed at the highest level.

A member of the Chelsea side that won the FA Youth Cup in 1960 and 1961, Allan made his senior debut as a 17-year-old in a League Cup tie against Workington in October 1960 and went on to make a total of 21 appearances that season, all of them on the left – his preferred position, even though he was naturally right-footed. When Peter Sillett broke his leg the following August the youngster was presented with an opportunity to make the position his own and impressed many observers with his composure and maturity. Although he was occasionally betrayed by over-confidence when in possession, his reading of the game, sound positional play and measured passing suggested a bright future, but the arrival of Eddie McCreadie from East Stirling that April effectively blocked his progress.

Harris found himself in the thankless role of understudy over the next two seasons and eventually moved to Second Division Coventry City in November 1964 in search of first-team football. Eighteen months later he was back at the Bridge, deputising for McCreadie in the second leg of the Fairs Cup semi-final against Barcelona and the subsequent play-off in Spain, but for much of the following season he was on the side-lines once more. He returned to the first team at right-backin time to help the Blues to the FA Cup Final, but the frustrating 2-1 defeat at the hands of Tottenham was to be his last game for the club as he was transferred to Queens Park Rangers that summer.

BORN: Northampton, 28.12.42.
GAMES: 98 (4). GOALS: 1.
OTHER CLUBS: Coventry City 64/5-65/6 (60, 0);
Queens Park Rangers 67/8-70/1 (93, 0);
Plymouth Argyle 70/1-72/3 (64, 0);
Cambridge United 73/4 (6, 0).
MANAGER: Español, Spain.

1960/61-1964/65 & 1965/66-1966/67

DEREK KEVAN

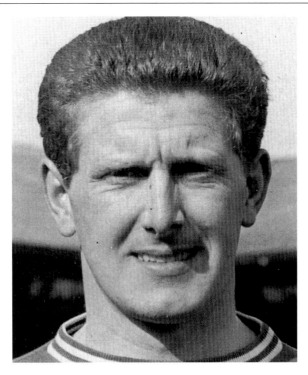

When it became apparent that the sparkling form that had taken Chelsea six points clear of their nearest rivals at the top of the Second Division table at Christmas had disappeared during the Big Freeze that brought English football to a virtual standstill in the first two months of 1963, Tommy Docherty's characteristically bold response was to pay West Bromwich Albion £45,000 for the services of Derek Kevan, their powerfully built centre-forward. The 28-year-old England international had a highly impressive scoring record but he was none too mobile and thus had great difficulty in adapting to his new team's close-passing style, which depended on seemingly non-stop running. For all his physical strength and ability to win the ball in the air, Derek was largely dependent on others to create chances for him and in a side that had lost its confidence and rhythm the service he received was predictably scanty.

Kevan experienced similar difficulty in accustoming himself to the strict discipline and demanding training Docherty had introduced to Stamford Bridge, and his Chelsea career was to be brief and unrewarding. The single goal he scored for the club could scarcely have been more important, his header after 90 seconds paving the way for the 7-0 win over Portsmouth that clinched the Blues' return to the First Division, but on the eve of the following season he was transferred to Manchester City.

BORN: Ripon, 6.3.35. GAMES: 7. GOALS: 1.
HONOURS: 14 England caps (57-61).
OTHER CLUBS: Bradford Park Avenue 52/3 (15, 8);
West Bromwich Albion 55/6-62/3 (262, 157);
Manchester City 63/4-64/5 (67, 48); Crystal Palace 65/6 (21, 5);
Peterborough United 65/6-66/7 (17, 2); Luton Town 66/7 (11, 4);
Stockport County 66/7-67/8 (40, 10).

1962/63

TOMMY HARMER

An old-fashioned ball playing inside-forward who had graced White Hart Lane in the late fifties with his close control and superb passing, Tommy Harmer was 34 when he joined Chelsea from Watford in September 1962, expecting to play in the reserves and further the education of the Stamford Bridge youngsters. Slight and frail-looking, with a deeply lined face that suggested profound knowledge acquired over many years, 'Tiny Tom' seemed ideally cast as a dressing-room sage but in the event he made five League appearances that season and finished on the winning side every time.

Although he needed a cigarette before a game to calm his jangling nerves, Tommy was a steadying influence out on the pitch, slowing things down if the pace became too frantic. He was no athlete, but his ability to hold the ball despite the earnest attentions of opponents seemingly twice his size and find a colleague with a telling pass proved invaluable as the tension mounted, especially in the epic struggle at Roker Park, where his goal – deflected into the net from a Tambling corner – earned the Blues the victory they needed to keep their promotion hopes alive.

'Charmer' Harmer played three times in the First Division the following season, having a hand in both goals in a 2-1 win at Tottenham, and remained on the Chelsea coaching staff until 1967.

BORN: Hackney, 2.2.28.
GAMES: 9. GOALS: 1.
OTHER CLUBS: Tottenham Hotspur 51/2-59/60 (205, 47);
Watford 60/1-61/2 (63, 6).

1962/63-1963/64

KEN SHELLITO

The injury which wrecked Ken Shellito's career robbed Chelsea of a richly talented right-back and left a gap in Tommy Docherty's emerging team which was never adequately filled. Having been introduced to first-team football in April 1959, Ken spent most of the next two seasons in the reserves, honing his technique, but when the chance he had been waiting for finally arrived in the wake of Ted Drake's departure he was ready to make the most of it, the 21-year-old securing his place with a series of polished displays.

However, it was during the Blues' whirlwind tour of the Second Division that Shellito's reputation began to blossom, his partnership with Eddie McCreadie quickly becoming one of the most respected in the country. An accomplished defender, he was not outstandingly quick but his positional play and reading of the game reflected a solid grounding in the traditional full-back skills and he relished a struggle for supremacy with a tricky winger. In a team committed to playing constructive football with a measured build-up from the back, his role in launching attacks was crucial, and he rarely wasted possession, picking out his man with a precise pass. Encouraged by Docherty and his coach, Dave Sexton, to support the attack at every opportunity, Ken helped pioneer the overlap, surging down the right flank, linking with his forwards and delivering a telling centre.

Shellito won what promised to be the first of many England caps on the 1963 summer tour and took over the Chelsea captaincy early the following season, but then in October he damaged his left knee against Sheffield Wednesday. He underwent four cartilage operations in the next three years as he battled with extraordinary courage and tenacity to save his career, but the knee was never right and the home leg of the Fairs Cup tie against Wiener of Austria in December 1965 proved to be his last competitive first-team match for the Blues. Finally forced to abandon his dogged fight for fitness in January 1969, he joined the Stamford Bridge coaching staff, succeeding his old full-back partner as manager in 1977.

BORN: East Ham, 18.4.40.
GAMES: 123. GOALS: 2.
HONOURS: 1 England cap (63).
MANAGER: Chelsea (77-78);
Cambridge United (85).

1958/59-1965/66

FRANK BLUNSTONE

Few ball-playing wingers have possessed the indomitable courage of Frank Blunstone. Faced by fearsome full-backs who had no hesitation in carrying out their blood-curdling threats when words alone proved insufficient to intimidate their tormentors, he remained defiant, revelling in the challenge and quite prepared to hand out as many knocks as he took. The frequent injuries that were an inevitable consequence of this aggressive approach he generally shook off without recourse to so much as the trainer's magic sponge, never mind the two weeks' rest that many of his peers might have considered unavoidable, and when a broken leg put him out of the game for nearly two years he fought his way back to fitness with characteristic grit to play the most effective football of his career.

Frank arrived at Stamford Bridge as an 18-year-old in February 1953, having learned his trade in the Third Division North with his home-town club, Crewe Alexandra, and quickly became an automatic choice at outside-left, helped on his way by a goal on his senior debut for the Blues against Tottenham. His return to the side after a lengthy injury lay-off in November was an important factor in the surge that brought the League Championship to SW6 in 1954/55, and his sparkling form that season earned him international honours against Wales, Scotland, France and Portugal. However, he played in around a hundred games in not much more than six months, many of them for the Army during the course of his National Service, and that was probably an underlying cause of the fracture to his left leg sustained in a fourth round FA Cup tie at White Hart Lane in January 1957. Back in action in a pre-season friendly against Ajax the following August, Frank suffered a recurrence of the injury and this time he was ruled out for more than a year, making his comeback at Everton in November 1958.

It says much for his character that he soon recaptured his best form, ensuring a steady supply of chances that helped Jimmy Greaves make his name and Chelsea stay in the First Division despite the shortcomings of their defence. A bubbly, lively character, full of energy and life, Frank was a direct, attacking winger, famed for a head-down dribbling style that prompted some wits to suggest that he would have ended up out in the Fulham Road if he hadn't counted the white lines as he went. Despite this, he was a good crosser of the ball and had the confidence to keep running at a defence even when things weren't going his way.

Once the baby of the side, Frank was one of the old heads of the team which won promotion in 1962/63, and he confirmed his supreme professionalism by adapting to the new tactics introduced by Tommy Docherty and Dave Sexton which called for him to drop back into midfield and make runs to create space for Eddie McCreadie's overlaps. It was a role that involved a lot of work and little glory but Frank's ability to change the character of a match with a single coruscating flash of skill remained invaluable. His two superb individual goals in a vital 3-1 win against Derby in March were typical, but possibly the best game of his long and distinguished career was the third round FA Cup tie against Spurs at White Hart Lane the following season when his perfect centre gave Bert Murray a magnificent equaliser.

Cruelly, injury was to strike Frank down once again, just as he was poised to share in the Blues' exciting pursuit of honours, a ruptured Achilles tendon suffered during a tour of the Caribbean in the summer of 1964 ending his career when he still had a huge amount to offer. After his retirement he helped with the coaching of Chelsea's young players, subsequently managing Brentford and working with Tommy Docherty at Manchester United and Derby, but he prudently declined the offer of the manager's chair at Stamford Bridge in the wake of Dave Sexton's departure.

BORN: Crewe, 17.10.34.
GAMES: 346. GOALS: 53.
HONOURS: League Championship 54/5.
5 England caps (54-56).
OTHER CLUBS: Crewe Alexandra 51/2-52/3 (48, 12).
MANAGER: Brentford (69-73).

1952/53-1963/64

BERT MURRAY

The Stamford Bridge crowd never really warmed to Bert Murray, failing to appreciate the contribution made by his unstinting efforts on the right flank to the overall effectiveness of a side justly admired for its team-work. He was regarded as an orthodox winger when he made his League debut in October 1961 but it was his ability to adapt to the more demanding role envisaged by Tommy Docherty and Dave Sexton the following season that enabled him to establish himself in the team at the expense of Peter Brabrook.

Shuttling up and down the pitch, Bert formed a formidable partnership with Ken Shellito, making runs to create space for the full-back when he broke forward, and tackling back when possession was lost. Quick and direct, with two good feet, he provided a steady service to his forwards, playing the ball in early with no unnecessary frills, and scored more than his fair share of goals, many with his head, including the equaliser in a hard-fought third round FA Cup tie at White Hart Lane in January 1964 and the winner in the replay.

When Tommy Docherty adopted a 4-3-3 formation in the wake of the injury which ended Frank Blunstone's career, 'Ruby' was called upon to show his versatility once more and abandon the flanks for a new role in midfield, to the bewilderment of some of the club's less knowledgeable followers who, seemingly oblivious to the tactical revolution that had swept English football in recent years, demanded to know why their number seven was 'never on his bloody wing'. Bert was a regular member of the side which pursued a magnificent treble that season, contributing 17 goals in 40 League appearances, a total many a striker would envy, but his involvement in the celebrated Blackpool Incident inevitably soured relations with his uncompromising manager. The emergence of Peter Osgood in 1965/66 ultimately cost Bert his place and at the end of the season, with the side that had brought the Blues so close to success breaking up as the simmering Stamford Bridge saucepan boiled over, he followed Barry Bridges to Second Division Birmingham City.

BORN: Hoxton, 22.9.42.
GAMES: 179 (4). GOALS: 44.
HONOURS: League Cup 64/5.
OTHER CLUBS: Birmingham City 66/7-70/1 (132, 22);
Brighton and Hove Albion 70/1-73/4 (102, 25);
Peterborough United 73/4-75/6 (123, 10).

1961/62-1965/66

GRAHAM MOORE

Graham Moore arrived at Stamford Bridge with a big reputation to live up to, and it would be fair to say he didn't quite manage it. He did a respectable job during his two-year stay in London, but possessed the natural talent to have achieved rather more.

A powerfully built Welsh international forward, Graham was signed from Cardiff City in December 1961 for £35,000, a club record fee at the time. The 20-year-old went straight into the first team at centre-forward and two thunderously struck goals in his third game, a 5-2 defeat at White Hart Lane, suggested that he would make a valuable contribution to the grim fight against relegation which faced the Blues in the second half of the season. However, he failed to add to them and the lack of a goalscoring touch was to prove one of his greatest weaknesses.

'Archie' had exceptional skill for a player of his size and was highly effective as a target man, receiving the ball with his back to goal, shielding it and laying it off to colleagues with aplomb. A little ponderous, he didn't have too much pace and struggled the following season as Tommy Docherty and Dave Sexton pioneered their new style of football based on constant movement. Nevertheless he played in all but six League matches, usually in the number ten shirt, and formed an effective partnership with Barry Bridges and Bobby Tambling.

Always popular in the dressing room, Graham retained his place as the Blues attempted to establish themselves in the First Division the following autumn but still the goals wouldn't come and when Docherty made a tactical switch, restoring Frank Upton to the team at the expense of a forward, he was the one to go, despite scoring twice in what was to be his last match for Chelsea, a 3-2 home defeat at the hands of Birmingham in November. Shortly afterwards he was on his way to Manchester United, where further disappointment awaited him.

BORN: Hengoed, 7.3.41. GAMES: 72. GOALS: 14.
HONOURS: 21 Wales caps (59-70).
OTHER CLUBS: Cardiff City 58/9-61/2 (85, 23);
Manchester United 63/4 (18, 4);
Northampton Town 65/6-66/7 (53, 10);
Charlton Athletic 67/8-70/1 (110, 8);
Doncaster Rovers 71/2-73/4 (69, 3).

1961/62-1963/64

BARRY BRIDGES

A potent cocktail of electrifying pace and the predatory instincts of a natural goalscorer made Barry Bridges a key member of the Chelsea team for much of the turbulent Docherty era. He was by no means a complete striker – a tendency to spurn simple chances in favour of those that looked impossible comes to mind – but he certainly made the fullest possible use of the gifts he possessed, his determination and sheer effort compensating for any deficiencies in his technique.

Although Barry made his senior debut when he was 17, scoring in a 3-2 win against West Ham in February 1959, more than two years would pass before he was given a real chance to prove himself during the Blues' miserable slide towards relegation in 1961/62. His tally of 19 goals in 32 League appearances represented an impressive achievement in a poor side, but he was unable to maintain that striking rate in the Second Division and was dropped for the decisive matches against Sunderland and Portsmouth in May to accommodate Frank Upton. When Jimmy Mulholland was preferred at the start of the following season, Bridges understandably concluded that there was no future for him at Stamford Bridge but he quickly regained his place and resumed his prolific partnership with Bobby Tambling.

Many of Barry's goals were scored at close range, his speed and outstanding awareness enabling him to pounce on a ball played into the goalmouth before anyone else had moved, as he demonstrated with the Blues' fourth goal in the FA Cup quarter-final against Peterborough in March 1965. However, he was probably at his most dangerous when running onto a through-pass down the middle and thrived on the superb service supplied by Terry Venables, although he was sometimes guilty of over-eagerness, mistiming his move and being caught offside as a result.

Barry's consistency won him full international honours against Scotland, Hungary and Yugoslavia in 1964/65 but at the end of that season he was one of eight players sent home from Blackpool after they had broken a curfew imposed by Tommy Docherty and his relations with the autocratic Scotsman were never the same again. The following October he was recalled to the England team to face Austria but three days later he was dropped from the Chelsea starting line-up against Leicester to make room for Peter Osgood, who was promised a run of a dozen games in the side. Bridges, upset that his World Cup chances were being jeopardised, asked for a transfer but, following a petition by fans outraged at the thought that their hero might be allowed to leave the club, it was decided that he should stay and he switched to a wandering role at the expense of Bert Murray, enjoying considerable success.

Two goals, the second a swerving right-foot drive, in the fifth round of the FA Cup against Shrewsbury confirmed Barry's continuing usefulness, but he was left out once more after the semi-final defeat at the hands of Sheffield Wednesday and when he was sent home from the airport prior to the first leg of the Fairs Cup tie with Barcelona there was little doubt that he would soon be moving on. Somewhat surprisingly, he went to Second Division Birmingham City and, although he had the satisfaction of playing on the winning side when Chelsea visited St Andrews in the sixth round of the FA Cup in 1968, he never really recaptured the form he had shown during his years at Stamford Bridge.

BORN: Horsford, 29.4.41.
GAMES: 203 (2). GOALS: 93.
HONOURS: League Cup 64/5.
4 England caps (65).
OTHER CLUBS: Birmingham City 66/7-68/9 (83, 37);
Queens Park Rangers 68/9-70/1 (72, 32);
Millwall 70/1-71/2 (77, 27);
Brighton and Hove Albion 72/3-73/4 (66, 14);
Highlands Park, South Africa.

1958/59-1965/66

EDDIE McCREADIE

Tommy Docherty was in the habit of describing Eddie McCreadie as the best left-back in Europe and, while that may be regarded as an example of the Doc's fondness for hyperbole, there is no doubt that the £6,000 fee he paid East Stirling for the 22-year-old Scot's services in April 1962 was one of the more successful bits of transfer business he did during his years at Stamford Bridge.

A rugged defender whose trademark was a ferocious sliding tackle, Eddie was not the most astute reader of the game in the early stages of his career but he made the transition from part-time football in Scotland to the heat of the Second Division promotion battle with characteristic assurance, immediately striking up a formidable partnership with Ken Shellito. He was inclined to be impetuous, diving in when he would have done better to have held off and settled for containing his winger, and this weakness was to prove his undoing when Stoke visited Stamford Bridge at the end of the season for a match that was crucial to the Blues' fading hopes. Stanley Matthews, by then a veteran of 48, teased and taunted Eddie like a wily bullfighter, the supremacy he gained helping the leaders to a vital 1-0 win. However, McCreadie was blessed with tremendous pace and his exceptional powers of recovery generally allowed him to repair the damage done by his impulsiveness.

Although he possessed a good left foot, Eddie's distribution was indifferent, but he took delight in every opportunity to get forward, surging down the flank with great panache. Unfortunately, he tended to lose composure when he got into the last third of the field, sometimes opting for a wildly optimistic shot from 40 yards when the situation called for a measured pass to a better-placed team-mate, but in the first leg of the League Cup final against Leicester in 1965 all his dreams of glory were realised when, playing at centre-forward in the absence of Barry Bridges, he scored the winning goal after an epic solo run that carried him the length of the pitch.

Eddie was an emotional man with a fiery temper and he was inevitably involved in regular clashes with Tommy Docherty, another Scot with a combustible temperament. His role in the ill-starred Blackpool Affair in April 1965 did nothing to improve matters and during the next year McCreadie fired off no fewer than five transfer requests, but they were all turned down and eventually an uneasy peace was restored.

Good-humoured and popular with the Stamford Bridge crowd, Eddie won his first international cap against England two weeks before the dramatic events at Blackpool and regularly represented his country for the next four years, while his flair, aggression and dauntless spirit were central to the Blues' challenge for honours during the mid-sixties. However, the later stages of McCreadie's career were to be plagued by a cruel series of injuries. He was able to play in the 1970 FA Cup final only after he had courageously decided to postpone abdominal surgery and he missed much of the following season as a result of a persistent ankle problem, but his contribution behind the scenes was invaluable and in March 1972 he was appointed club captain in succession to Ron Harris. He was able to lead the side out onto the field for much of the next campaign but his playing days were nearing their end, and his appointment as reserve team coach in the summer of 1974 marked the start of a new challenge which would see this passionate, highly intelligent man assume the arduous task of keeping the Blues in the First Division before the season was out.

BORN: Glasgow, 15.4.40.
GAMES: 405 (5). GOALS: 5.
HONOURS: FA Cup 69/70; League Cup 64/5.
23 Scotland caps (65-69).
OTHER CLUBS: East Stirling.
MANAGER: Chelsea (75-77); Memphis Rogues.

1962/63-1973/74

JOHN BOYLE

Although his unspectacular contribution went largely unnoticed by the press and the majority of the Stamford Bridge crowd, John Boyle was a key member of Tommy Docherty's squad in the mid-sixties. Tigerish tackling and unrelenting effort were the solid foundations upon which his game was built, but he possessed more ability than he was generally given credit for and his versatility ensured that he was rarely out of the team.

John arrived in senior football in style, scoring the winning goal in the first leg of the League Cup semi-final against Aston Villa in January 1965 from 25 yards, and quickly established himself as Ron Harris's deputy in the middle of the defence. With Harris spending much of the following campaign at full-back, the Scottish teenager had every opportunity to impress and his sterling performance against AC Milan at Stamford Bridge provided ample evidence of his rapid progress. However, John was most effective when employed as a ball-winner in midfield and that was where he made most of his appearances over the next three seasons, his non-stop running and neat distribution helping the Blues to the FA Cup final in 1967. Head injuries sustained in a road accident the following March interrupted his progress when he appeared to have wrested the number four shirt from John Hollins and, with Dave Sexton introducing a slightly more adventurous, cavalier style, his place came under increasing pressure.

A cartilage operation in the summer of 1969 seemed to rob Boyle's career of much of its momentum and, after a year in the shadows, he came close to joining Sheffield Wednesday in August 1970. He was recalled to the first team at right-back a couple of months later in place of the injured Paddy Mulligan and acquitted himself with distinction despite his lack of pace, but his adaptability continued to hamper his efforts to win a secure place in the starting line-up and he gradually slipped out of contention. In 1972/73 he made only a handful of appearances and, following a spell on loan at Brighton, he was transferred to Orient for a nominal fee in December 1973.

BORN: Motherwell, 25.12.46.
GAMES: 253 (13). GOALS: 12.
HONOURS: European Cup-Winners' Cup 70/1;
League Cup 64/5.
OTHER CLUBS: Brighton and Hove Albion *on loan* 73/4 (10, 0);
Leyton Orient 73/4-74/5 (18, 0); Tampa Bay Rowdies.

1964/65-1973/74

GEORGE GRAHAM

The casting of Tommy Docherty, the martinet of Stamford Bridge, in the role of the fairy godmother may appear unpromising, but there is nevertheless something in the dramatic elevation of George Graham, from the drudgery of Aston Villa reserves to a key role in a side chasing an unprecedented treble, that prompts thoughts of Cinderella. Signed for a modest £5,000 in June 1964, the 19-year-old striker made a promising start to his Chelsea career, scoring on his debut, and became established in the first team when his demanding manager decided that neither of the replacements available was going to be able to fill the boots of the injured Frank Blunstone on the left wing and switched to a 4-3-3 formation to accommodate the young Scotsman.

Poised and stylish, George always seemed to have time to spare, his air of aristocratic languor earning him the richly evocative sobriquet 'Stroller'. Although he was no great runner and lacked pace, he proved to be a prolific marksman, finding the net 17 times in 30 League appearances in 1964/65, but just as important was his role as a provider. Blessed with immaculate ball control, he was a highly effective target man and acted as the pivot of the Blues' well-balanced attack, supplying the ammunition for Barry Bridges and Bobby Tambling, whose speed was the ideal complement to Graham's guile.

The strongly built youngster was majestic in the air, his unstoppable header in the first leg of the Fairs Cup tie against AC Milan in the San Siro stadium in February 1966 – and an equally spectacular effort in the second match a week later – demonstrating the value of perfect timing. His total of 23 goals in all competitions that season was not bettered, but the team that had brought the Blues within touching distance of glory was breaking up amid mounting dressing-room disharmony. Graham's transfer request was initially refused but, with the new campaign six weeks old, he was allowed to join Arsenal, Tommy Baldwin moving to Stamford Bridge in part-exchange.

BORN: Bargeddie, 30.11.44. GAMES: 102. GOALS: 46.
HONOURS: League Cup 64/5.
12 Scotland caps (71-73).
OTHER CLUBS: Aston Villa 62/3-63/4 (8, 2); Arsenal 66/7-72/3 (227, 59); Manchester United 72/3-74/5 (43, 2); Portsmouth 74/5-76/7 (61, 5); Crystal Palace 76/7-77/8 (44, 2).
MANAGER: Millwall (82-86); Arsenal (86-95); Leeds United (96-).

1964/65-1966/67

ALAN YOUNG

During his seven years with Chelsea Alan Young made just 26 first-team appearances but that bare statement conceals a fair amount of drama as well as much invaluable work assisting the development of the club's young players in the reserves. A strapping, six-foot centre-half who was effective in the air but rather less assured when the ball was on the floor, he was brought to Stamford Bridge as a 20-year-old by his former Arsenal team-mate Tommy Docherty shortly after the abrasive Scot had replaced Ted Drake, but failed to win a place in a struggling side and soon slipped into obscurity.

A brief taste of the limelight came when Alan was recalled for the first leg of the League Cup final against Leicester three years later but he was injured after 13 minutes and had little reason to remember the Blues' courageous win with pleasure. The departure of Frank Upton and John Mortimore early the following season opened the door for him, however, and he enjoyed a run of nine League games in the autumn and also played in the Fairs Cup ties against Roma and Wiener, later emerging with credit from the 2-0 defeat at the hands of Barcelona in the first leg of the semi-final. During Chelsea's run to the FA Cup final in 1966/67 Young played – and scored – in a fourth round replay against Brighton but that was to be his last senior appearance, and after another two years of loyal and dependable service behind the scenes he moved on to Torquay United in search of new challenges.

BORN: Hornsey, 20.1.41.
GAMES: 26. GOALS: 1.
OTHER CLUBS: Arsenal 60/1 (4, 0);
Torquay United 68/9-71/2 (59, 1).

1961/62-1966/67

TOMMY KNOX

Tommy Knox had to wait two seasons for a real chance to prove himself in the Blues' first team, and when the opportunity he had waited for for so long finally arrived he was found wanting. A traditional left-winger with good close control, he had followed his former East Stirling club-mate Eddie McCreadie to Stamford Bridge in the summer of 1962 and made six Second Division appearances the following season without suggesting that he would earn a regular place in the side. Tommy was called upon only once in 1963/64 and it seemed that his Chelsea career would bring nothing but frustration, but the injury to Frank Blunstone during the summer tour of the Caribbean meant that the Scotsman started the new campaign in the number 11 shirt with every prospect of an extended run in the side.

When Tommy was able to jink his way past his full-back he could be a considerable asset, as he demonstrated when making a goal for George Graham in a 3-2 win at Hillsborough, but if that ploy failed he had little else to offer. Had he been able to reproduce the form he showed in training things might have turned out differently, but his overall contribution was disappointing and when Tommy Docherty changed his tactics to accommodate three strikers there was no longer a place for an orthodox winger in the side. The following February Knox moved to Newcastle United to seek greater success in the lower divisions.

BORN: Glasgow, 5.9.39. GAMES: 21. GOALS: 0.
OTHER CLUBS: East Stirling;
Newcastle United 64/5-66/7 (25, 1);
Mansfield Town 66/7-67/8 (34, 5);
Northampton Town 67/8-68/9 (29, 0).

1962/63-1964/65

JIM McCALLIOG

Jim McCalliog was a potentially outstanding player who might well have enjoyed great success at Stamford Bridge had he been prepared to wait a little longer for the regular first-team place he felt he deserved. A midfielder of style and authority, he became Terry Venables's acknowledged understudy in 1964/65, making his League debut against Birmingham City in November and scoring twice in a 6-1 win. Having played regularly in the early rounds of the League Cup, the young Scot did not figure in the two-legged final against Leicester City, but his ability to spot an opening and exploit it with a measured pass pointed to a bright future.

McCalliog was given the attacking role usually filled by George Graham on the opening day of the following season but it was apparent that he was most effective when employed as a midfield general, dictating the shape of the game with his cool and assured distribution. However, there seemed little prospect of a vacancy arising in that department, and the 19-year-old's mounting frustration prompted him to fire off a volley of transfer requests. Tommy Docherty was reluctant to lose a player of such ability and there was much dark muttering about the teenager having been 'tapped', but in October 1965 Jim moved to Sheffield Wednesday in a £37,500 deal and proved a point by scoring the Owls' second goal when they beat Chelsea in the FA Cup semi-final at Villa Park in April.

BORN: Glasgow, 23.9.46. GAMES: 12. GOALS: 3.
HONOURS: 5 Scotland caps (67-71).
OTHER CLUBS: Sheffield Wednesday 65/6-68/9 (150, 19);
Wolverhampton Wanderers 69/70-73/4 (163, 34);
Manchester United 73/4-74/5 (31, 7); Southampton 74/5-76/7
(72, 8); Chicago Sting; Lincoln City 78/9 (9, 0).
MANAGER: Halifax Town (90-91).

1964/65-1965/66

JOE FASCIONE

Joe Fascione can count himself a little unfortunate that his years at Stamford Bridge did not bring him greater reward. A small, skilful winger who could play on either flank, he was signed from Scottish club Kirkintilloch Rob Roy as a 17-year-old and, like his fellow countryman Jim McCalliog, had his first taste of top-flight football in the early rounds of the League Cup in 1964/65. His League baptism at Highbury the following September could scarcely have been more encouraging, the energetic youngster scoring the Blues' second goal with a glancing header from Bert Murray's corner, then helping create the third for Barry Bridges. A series of impressive displays followed, but Joe's enterprising forays down the flanks and tireless covering in midfield were not enough to secure his place in the reshuffle that followed the advent of Peter Osgood. Understandably miffed, he retired to the shadows.

Fascione was given a second chance when Dave Sexton succeeded Tommy Docherty almost two years later, but he was unable to reproduce the sure touch in front of goal that had served him so well in the reserves and after a run of six games he was displaced once again, Sexton bringing Alan Birchenall down from Sheffield United in an effort to boost the team's firepower. That was effectively the end of the road for the talented Scot and in the summer of 1969 he decided to try his luck with Durban City in South Africa.

BORN: Coatbridge, 5.2.45.
GAMES: 27 (7). GOALS: 1.
OTHER CLUBS: Durban City.

1964/65-1968/69

JOHN HOLLINS

The phrase 'model professional' is used somewhat glibly, but there is no doubt that in the case of John Hollins it is fully justified. His boundless energy and unfailing enthusiasm made him a cornerstone of the Chelsea midfield for eleven seasons, but his most remarkable achievement is to have accomplished so much in a fiercely competitive environment yet remained universally liked and respected.

Strangely enough, the three senior appearances he made as a 17-year-old in 1963/64 all ended in defeat, but he was handed the number four shirt at the start of the following season and quickly became a key component in Tommy Docherty's high-revving machine. In the early stages of his career John played his football at such a frantic pace that mistakes were inevitable, but his fizzing vitality more than compensated for his tactical naivety and over the years he would develop a more considered, focused style. His dynamic displays earned him a place in the England side that faced Spain at Wembley in May 1967, four days after he had played there for the Blues in the FA Cup final, but that was to be his only appearance in a full international – to the bewilderment of his legions of admirers at Stamford Bridge.

John had a spell at right-back in 1967/68 and found himself there again the following season when he was unable to reclaim his usual place from Peter Osgood after he had been sidelined by injury for a month, but it was not a role he enjoyed. He appeared to have lost much of his old zest but bounced back to produce the best football of his career, showing a new maturity and consistency, and was voted the fans' Player of the Year for two seasons in succession. In five seasons 'Holly' missed only four matches – the result of an ankle ligament injury in April 1971. Typically, he fought hard to get fit to take his place against Real Madrid in Athens and it was cruel that a recurrence prevented him from playing in the replay.

Sharp and alert, John was quick to pounce on any stray passes but his own distribution was not always as accurate as it might have been, largely because of over-eagerness. However, he was constantly involved, covering defenders when they went forward, tackling relentlessly in the middle of the field and making surging runs that helped create space for the forwards, and his selfless efforts were of immeasurable value to the side. He also scored many memorable goals for the Blues, none better than a spectacular solo effort against Arsenal in August 1970 that was a reward for remarkable persistence, and possessed a stunning shot, his venomously struck penalties helping him to a total of 18 goals in all competitions in 1971/72.

John's cheerful personality had always had a beneficial effect on morale in the dressing room and he was handed the captaincy at the start of 1974/75, having led the side during Eddie McCreadie's frequent absences, but his long love-affair with the Blues was destined to end unhappily. With the team struggling, his form suffered and he was rested for a spell to help him get over a niggling knee problem. The final blow came when McCreadie, the newly appointed manager, left him out for the three matches at the end of the season that would determine whether the club stayed in the First Division and that summer he followed Dave Sexton to Queens Park Rangers.

After distinguished service at Loftus Road and then at Highbury, Hollins returned to Stamford Bridge as player-coach in the summer of 1983 and, playing at right-back, was enormously influential in welding together the side which won the Second Division Championship. After Christmas he gave way to Colin Lee to concentrate on a coaching career which seemed certain to prove no less successful.

BORN: Guildford, 16.7.46.
GAMES: 591. GOALS: 64.
HONOURS: FA Cup 69/70; League Cup 64/5;
Second Division Championship 83/4.
1 England cap (67).
OTHER CLUBS: Queens Park Rangers 75/6-78/9 (151, 5);
Arsenal 79/80-82/3 (127, 9).
MANAGER: Chelsea (85-88).

1963/64-1974/75 & 1983/84

TERRY VENABLES

It is customary to describe outstanding midfield players as 'influential' but the word is more than merely a conventional acknowledgement of exceptional ability when applied to Terry Venables. During four breathlessly exciting seasons which saw Chelsea throw off their old inertia and emerge, newly minted, as serious contenders for football's glittering prizes, he exercised a dominion at Stamford Bridge that helped forge a vibrant new identity for the club and presented a challenge to the authority of Tommy Docherty that the strong-willed Scotsman ultimately found intolerable.

When the Blues were playing well, Venables was the hub around which their football revolved. He craved constant involvement, dropping deep to collect the ball from his defenders, and his ability to pierce a defence with a superbly weighted pass ensured that Barry Bridges and Bobby Tambling received a steady flow of openings. A keen student of the game, Terry took a lively interest in the tactical innovations introduced by Tommy Docherty and Dave Sexton and delighted in helping to devise free-kick routines of the kind that gave him two of his three goals in the first leg of a bad-tempered Fairs Cup tie against Roma in September 1965. The skill with which he marshalled his depleted forces that night, after Eddie McCreadie had been sent off with less than thirty minutes played, provided a perfect example of the tactical awareness that made him such an effective midfield general, but there were occasions when it seemed that the Blues had become over-reliant upon their master-strategist. When he had a poor game, as he did against Liverpool in the FA Cup semi-final the previous season, Chelsea appeared to be lost, the well-oiled machine rendered impotent by the malfunctioning of the single component that brought all the rest to life.

Venables first appeared regularly in senior football as a brilliantly precocious 17-year-old in 1960/61, his assured displays at right-half belying his inexperience, but when Tommy Docherty succeeded Ted Drake he plausibly judged that the immediate crisis called for maturity and resilience rather than the rich potential of golden youth and he lost no time in acquiring the services of Andy Malcolm from West Ham. Relegation confirmed the folly of such caution and the following season the right-flank triangle of Venables, Shellito and Murray performed with exemplary consistency as the Blues surged back into the First Division. However, it was when he was handed the number ten shirt at the expense of Graham Moore in November 1963 that Terry really began to dictate the shape of the game, his commanding displays in the middle of the pitch earning him England caps against Belgium and Holland a year later.

A born leader, Venables had become a dominant figure in the dressing room and he took over as captain when Ken Shellito was sidelined by injury, but his outstanding football brain, sharp wit and forceful personality meant that conflict with Docherty was virtually inevitable. In the wake of the semi-final defeat at the hands of Liverpool in 1964/65 he was dropped for a game that was crucial to Chelsea's hopes of winning the Championship and his involvement in the notorious Blackpool Incident shortly afterwards added to the mounting tension. With his form suffering, Terry was stripped of the captaincy in the new year and shortly before the third game against AC Milan two months later it was announced that he had been put up for sale.

Although it was subsequently decided that there would be no departures while the Blues were still pursuing honours, there seemed little hope that Terry's differences with Docherty could be resolved and before the season was over he had been transferred to Tottenham for a fee of £80,000.

BORN: Bethnal Green, 6.1.43.
GAMES: 237. GOALS: 31.
HONOURS: League Cup 64/5.
2 England caps (64).
OTHER CLUBS: Tottenham Hotspur 65/6-68/9 (115, 5);
Queens Park Rangers 69/70-74/5 (179, 19); Crystal Palace 74/5 (14, 0).
MANAGER: Crystal Palace (76-80); Queens Park Rangers (80-84); Barcelona;
Tottenham Hotspur (87-91); England (94-96); Australia (96-).

1959/60-1965/66

PETER BONETTI

A vital save can determine the outcome of a game just as decisively as the highly publicised efforts of the men commanding massive transfer fees at the other end of the pitch, and there is no doubt that in Peter Bonetti Chelsea were blessed with a real match-winner. In a first-team career that spanned 20 seasons and comprised more than 700 appearances, his professionalism and dependability provided the unshakeable foundations of a succession of famous triumphs and helped to avert at least as many humiliating disasters.

Peter was first thrust into the limelight as an 18-year-old against Manchester City in April 1960 when both Reg Matthews and his deputy Bill Robertson were injured, and performed with such verve and assurance that he quickly made the position his own. Playing behind a notoriously leaky defence, he lost no time in establishing a reputation as one of the best shot-stoppers in English football, although it is true that in the early stages of his career the astonishing agility that had earned him the nickname 'Catty' was sometimes required to compensate for positioning that betrayed his inexperience.

Peter's strength of character was never seen more clearly than during the Blues' exhilarating promotion campaign in 1962/63 when he shrugged off a couple of costly mistakes that had prompted Tommy Docherty to leave him out of the side and produced a performance in the decisive match at Roker Park in May that was nothing less than heroic, a flying leap in injury time to deny Sunderland winger George Mulhall crowning an outstanding second-half display that had seen him resist relentless pressure seemingly single-handed. The gale howling down the pitch that day exposed the weakness of his kicking, but his ability to catch the ball and hurl it out to his full-backs with pinpoint accuracy in a single flowing movement was the springboard of many attacks down the years.

Over the next three seasons, Bonetti played a key role in Chelsea's quest for honours, but amid the turmoil that engulfed Stamford Bridge in the wake of the semi-final defeat at the hands of Sheffield Wednesday in 1966 he was one of many players to seek a transfer, and when Alex Stepney was signed from Millwall it seemed certain that he would be allowed to leave. However, Peter began the following campaign in the scintillating form that had earned him the first of his seven full England caps during the summer and it was Stepney who moved on, having made just one first-team appearance.

Slim and lithe, Peter was almost boyish in appearance and there was something uncanny about the way he would repeatedly emerge with the ball clutched securely to his chest after a high centre had been swung into the Blues' penalty area, his immaculate timing and adhesive handling frustrating burly forwards who seemed certain to overwhelm him with their height and aggression. His spectacular performance in the FA Cup final in 1970 was instrumental in earning the Blues a replay and his extraordinary courage was no less crucial to the emotional triumph at Old Trafford 18 days later, Peter making a number of vital saves despite a first-half injury which impaired his mobility.

As a result of his unfailing daring, Bonetti picked up more than his fair share of injuries over the years and, with signs of fallibility beginning to appear, he came under increasing pressure from John Phillips in the early seventies. When it was announced in March 1975 that he was to be awarded a free transfer at the end of the season it appeared that his long association with the club was at an end, but after a summer in American football Peter returned to Stamford Bridge, initially on a monthly contract, and his brilliant goalkeeping helped Eddie McCreadie's young team gain promotion in 1976/77. He continued to battle for a first-team place over the next two seasons before moving to the Isle of Mull in 1979, combining life as a guest-house proprietor with appearances for Dundee United. He has since acted as a goalkeeping coach to a number of clubs, including Chelsea, and has also been involved with the England set-up.

BORN: Putney, 27.9.41.
GAMES: 728. GOALS: 0.
HONOURS: European Cup-Winners' Cup 70/1; FA Cup 69/70; League Cup 64/5.
7 England caps (66-70).
OTHER CLUBS: St Louis Stars; Dundee United.

1959/60-1978/79

TONY HATELEY

In his proper element, Tony Hateley was highly effective, if not exactly decorative. When the ball was flighted to the far post he was magnificent, all menace and power, but his lack of mobility and failure to master even the basics of ball control meant that on the floor he posed as much threat as a shark in a desert. It will be apparent, therefore, that he was a strange choice to replace Peter Osgood when the sublimely gifted youngster broke his leg in October 1966, but of course Tommy Docherty was nothing if not unpredictable.

Signed from Aston Villa for £100,000, the highest fee the club had ever paid, Tony never looked likely to prosper at Stamford Bridge, for the Blues' recent success had been based upon fluid passing movements and the speedy interchange of forwards, a style totally alien to the ungainly six-footer. He scored twice against Fulham three days after his arrival, his second goal the product of a soaring leap and a header of brutal force, but much of the time he was a spectator as his colleagues weaved their familiar patterns. Docherty encouraged his team to exploit the newcomer's strengths, sometimes to the exclusion of any other strategy, but this reaped only limited rewards as Hateley rarely received the sort of inviting crosses he needed if he was to thrive. Too often the ball was knocked forward from deep positions, denying him the opportunity to build up momentum and handing the initiative to the defence.

Tony made a valuable contribution to Chelsea's progress to the FA Cup final that season, his superb header from Bobby Tambling's centre in the fifth round against Sheffield United demonstrating how dangerous he could be, and his goal against Leeds in the semi-final – despatched past Sprake with an imperious thrust of the forehead – earned him an enduring place in the hearts of the faithful. However, nine goals in 33 appearances was not an encouraging return and at the end of the season, with Osgood approaching fitness, he was transferred to Liverpool, where he enjoyed scarcely more success.

BORN: Derby, 13.6.41.
GAMES: 32 (1). GOALS: 9.
OTHER CLUBS: Notts County 58/9–62/3 (131, 77) and 70/1–71/2 (57, 32);
Aston Villa 63/4–66/7 (127, 68); Liverpool 67/8–68/9 (42, 17);
Coventry City 68/9 (17, 4); Birmingham City 69/70–70/1 (28, 6);
Oldham Athletic 73/4 (5, 1).

1966/67

JOE KIRKUP

Signed from West Ham United in March 1966 to reinforce a squad depleted by a recurrence of Ken Shellito's knee trouble, Joe Kirkup was a polished, cultured right-back who epitomised the artistic approach to the game for which the Upton Park side were once renowned. A member of the Hammers team which had lifted the European Cup-Winners' Cup the previous spring, he settled into the Chelsea defence with a characteristic absence of fuss, making an assured debut in front of a 60,000 crowd against Manchester United, and played in all the Blues' remaining fixtures that season.

Joe was at his most impressive when he was coming forward, using the ball well and linking effectively with the attack, as when he fired home from ten yards against Blackburn after a sweeping move involving Ron Harris and Bert Murray. He sometimes appeared a little vulnerable in defence, his lack of aggression presenting a distinct contrast with the style of his full-back partner Eddie McCreadie, but he was nevertheless unfortunate to lose his place to Jim Thomson the following November. He remained out of favour for nearly a year, returning to the team on a regular basis only when Dave Sexton replaced Tommy Docherty, but the reprieve was to be short-lived and in February 1968 he was transferred to Southampton in part-exchange for David Webb, subsequently enjoying considerable success at the Dell.

BORN: Hexham, 17.12.39.
GAMES: 62 (7). GOALS: 2.
OTHER CLUBS: West Ham United 58/9-65/6 (165, 6);
Southampton 67/8-73/4 (169, 3).

1965/66-1967/68

JIM THOMSON

One of the many young Scots brought to Stamford Bridge by Tommy Docherty, Jim Thomson was perhaps the victim of his own versatility, for in the course of the 40 first-team games he started for the Blues he wore seven different shirts without ever looking likely to establish a lasting grip on any of them. A solid defender with few pretensions to creativity, his best position was probably in the middle of the back four, but the majority of his senior appearances during his time at Stamford Bridge were at right-back, while on occasion he was pressed into service in midfield, where he inevitably looked ill at ease.

After a couple of outings towards the end of 1965/66, Jim's real break came early the following season when John Hollins was dropped after asking for a transfer, Docherty insisting that when the rebel was recalled it would not be at the expense of the new boy, as if to stress that loyalty would be rewarded. Thomson played fairly regularly thereafter, his enthusiasm and unflagging effort going some way to compensate for a lack of finesse, and he was unfortunate to miss out on the Blues' appearance at Wembley in May, but he remained prone to silly mistakes. After Dave Sexton took over as manager in October 1967 Thomson's opportunities became rarer and the following September he was transferred to Burnley, where he performed valiantly for more than a decade.

BORN: Glasgow, 1.10.46.
GAMES: 40 (7). GOALS: 1.
OTHER CLUBS: Burnley 68/9-80/1 (297, 3).

1965/66-1967/68

BOBBY TAMBLING

When Jimmy Greaves packed his bags and headed for Italy in 1961 he left a gap in the Chelsea forward line that no mere mortal could reasonably be expected to fill, and it is a measure of Bobby Tambling's remarkable goalscoring prowess that within a year the Stamford Bridge crowd had ceased to mourn the loss of their old favourite and were instead hailing the emergence of a new hero. He may have been blessed with only a fraction of his illustrious predecessor's magical gifts, but Bobby's courage, spirit and cool finishing were essential ingredients in the most successful decade in the Blues' history and his total of 202 goals remains a club record.

Tambling had his first taste of senior football as a 17-year-old against West Ham in February 1959 and, like his fellow debutant Barry Bridges, scored in a 3-2 win, but it was in 1960/61 that he began to appear regularly in the first team, initially on the left wing (he remained a good crosser of the ball throughout his career) then at inside-forward. Greaves's defection that summer thrust Bobby into the limelight but he coped magnificently with the burden placed on his young shoulders, emerging from the Blues' grim battle against relegation as top scorer with 20 goals in 34 appearances, and the following season he became, at 21, the youngest player to have captained a promotion-winning side, having been appointed to succeed Peter Sillett. Needless to say, he led from the front, scoring 35 League goals, 25 of them in the 22 matches he played before the Big Freeze interrupted the team's rhythm, and his sparkling form earned him full England honours against Wales and France.

A modest, popular man, Bobby did not really enjoy the pressures of captaincy and was happy to accept Tommy Docherty's suggestion that he should pass the job on to Ken Shellito when he found goals hard to come by in the opening weeks of 1963/64. Dry spells of this kind tended to worry him, but they were to be rare occurrences over the next six seasons. Like Greaves, Tambling had days when he could do no wrong and the goals kept flying in. He scored four in a match on four occasions, most dramatically in the final game of 1962/63 when victory against Portsmouth was essential to clinch promotion, and against Aston Villa in 1966 he plundered five goals – all straightforward chances, perhaps, but all of them ruthlessly taken.

Tambling had a splendid left foot and some of his goals were highly spectacular, like the stunning free-kick he swerved round the defensive wall against Sheffield Wednesday in the fifth round of the FA Cup in 1968, but more typical was the winner against Leeds in the fourth round two years before, knocked in from close range with the minimum of fuss after George Graham had struck a post. He could usually be relied upon to hit the target when presented with an opening, and was quite prepared to accept a knock for the satisfaction of seeing the ball nestling in the back of the net, but he was at his most effective when employed as a front-runner on the left of the attack, using his pace to get clear of the defenders as he pursued a through-ball from George Graham or Terry Venables.

As his career progressed, Bobby did not enjoy the best of luck with injuries, a hamstring strain affecting him in 1965/66, abdominal problems requiring surgery on two occasions two seasons later, and a cartilage operation costing him his first-team place in August 1969. By the time he had recovered, Ian Hutchinson and Peter Osgood had formed their formidable partnership, and Bobby, having lost a little pace perhaps, was unable to force his way back in. He went to Crystal Palace on a month's loan, and then, having decided to remain in football despite his involvement with the Jehovah's Witnesses movement, made a permanent switch to Selhurst Park in June 1970.

BORN: Storrington, 18.9.41.
GAMES: 366 (4). GOALS: 202.
HONOURS: League Cup 64/5.
3 England caps (62-66).
OTHER CLUBS: Crystal Palace 69/70-73/4 (68, 12);
Cork Celtic; Waterford; Shamrock Rovers.
MANAGER: Cork Celtic.

1958/59-1969/70

JIM SMART 1964/65

Forward. BORN: Dundee, 9.1.47.
GAMES: 1. GOALS: 0.
OTHER CLUBS: Morton; Highlands Park, South Africa.

BILLY SINCLAIR 1964/65

Midfielder. BORN: Glasgow, 21.3.47.
GAMES: 1. GOALS: 0.
OTHER CLUBS: Morton; Glentoran.

TOMMY ROBSON 1965/66

Winger. BORN: Gateshead, 31.7.44.
GAMES: 6 (1). GOALS: 0.
OTHER CLUBS: Northampton Town 61/2-65/6 (74, 20);
Newcastle United 66/7-68/9 (48, 11);
Peterborough United 68/9-80/1 (482, 113).

JIM BARRON 1965/66

Goalkeeper. BORN: Tantobie, 19.10.43.
GAMES: 1. GOALS: 0.
OTHER CLUBS: Wolverhampton Wanderers 63/4-64/5 (8, 0);
Oxford United 65/6-69/70 (152, 0);
Nottingham Forest 70/1-73/4 (155, 0);
Swindon Town 74/5-76/7 (79, 0);
Peterborough United 77/8-80/1 (21, 0).

BARRY LLOYD 1966/67-1968/69

Midfielder. BORN: Hillingdon, 19.2.49.
GAMES: 8 (2). GOALS: 0.
OTHER CLUBS: Fulham 68/9-75/6 (257, 29);
Hereford United 76/7 (14, 0); Brentford 77/8 (31, 4).
MANAGER: Brighton and Hove Albion (87-93).

CHICO HAMILTON 1966/67

Midfielder. BORN: Streatham, 31.10.50.
GAMES: 3 (2). GOALS: 2.
OTHER CLUBS: Southend United 68/9 (37, 11);
Aston Villa 69/70-75/6 (208, 40);
Sheffield United 76/7-77/8 (60, 13); Minnesota Kicks;
San José Earthquakes.

GEORGE LUKE 1966/67

Wing-half. BORN: Hetton-le-Hole, 9.11.48.
GAMES: 1. GOALS: 0.
OTHER CLUBS: Newcastle United (0, 0);
Durban City.

JIM SMART

TOMMY ROBSON

BARRY LLOYD

BILLY SINCLAIR

JIM BARRON

CHICO HAMILTON

GEORGE LUKE

ALEX STEPNEY

ROGER WOSAHLO

GEOFF BUTLER

PAUL McMILLAN

ALEX STEPNEY 1966/67

Goalkeeper. BORN: Mitcham, 18.9.42.
GAMES: 1. GOALS: 0. HONOURS: 1 England cap (68).
OTHER CLUBS: Millwall 63/4-65/6 (137, 0);
Manchester United 66/7-77/8 (433, 2); Dallas Tornadoes.

KINGSLEY WHIFFEN 1966/67

Goalkeeper. BORN: Welshpool, 3.12.50.
GAMES: 1. GOALS: 0.
OTHER CLUBS: Plymouth Argyle (0, 0).

ROGER WOSAHLO 1966/67

Winger. BORN: Cambridge, 11.9.47.
GAMES: 0 (1). GOALS: 0.
OTHER CLUBS: Ipswich Town 67/8 (1, 0) and 69/70 (1, 0);
Peterborough United 68/9 (15, 1).

COLIN WALDRON 1967/68

Centre-half. BORN: Bristol, 22.6.48.
GAMES: 10. GOALS: 0.
OTHER CLUBS: Bury 66/7 (20, 1); Burnley 67/8-75/6 (308, 16);
Manchester United 76/7 (3, 0); Sunderland 76/7-77/8 (20, 1);
Tulsa Roughnecks; Atlanta Chiefs (twice); Rochdale 79/80 (19, 1);
Philadelphia Furies.

GEOFF BUTLER 1967/68

Full-back. BORN: Middlesbrough, 29.9.46.
GAMES: 8 (1). GOALS: 0.
OTHER CLUBS: Middlesbrough 65/6-67/8 (55, 1);
Sunderland 67/8-68/9 (3, 0); Norwich City 68/9-75/6 (153, 1);
Baltimore Rockets; AFC Bournemouth 75/6-80/1 (119, 1);
Peterborough United 81/2 (39, 0).

STEWART HOUSTON 1967/68-1970/71

Defender. BORN: Dunoon, 20.8.49.
GAMES: 10 (4). GOALS: 0.
HONOURS: 1 Scotland cap (75).
OTHER CLUBS: Brentford 71/2-73/4 (77, 9);
Manchester United 73/4-79/80 (205, 13);
Sheffield United 80/1-82/3 (94, 1);
Colchester United 83/4-85/6 (107, 5).
MANAGER: Queens Park Rangers (96-98).

PAUL McMILLAN 1967/68

Centre-half. BORN: Lennoxtown, 13.7.50.
GAMES: 1. GOALS: 0.
OTHER CLUBS: Clydebank.

KINGSLEY WHIFFEN

COLIN WALDRON

STEWART HOUSTON

ALAN BIRCHENALL

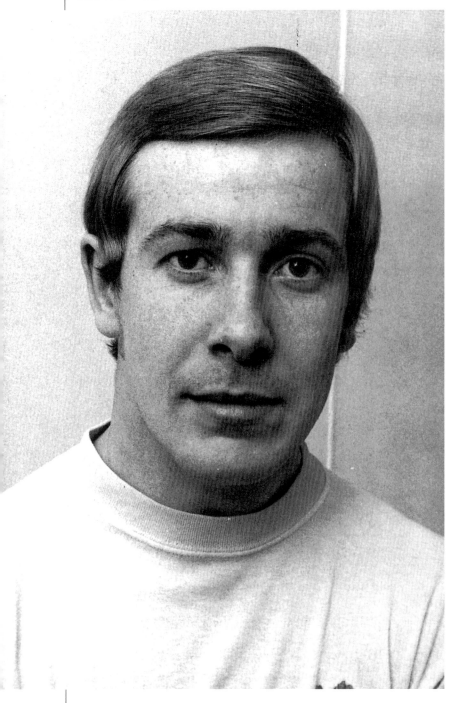

Alan Birchenall felt that he was playing the best football of his career in the autumn of 1969. He had scored with a well-struck shot in the third round of the League Cup against Leeds at Elland Road and followed that up by clinching the Blues' victory in the replay with a thumping left-foot volley. In between, the big striker had come up with two goals in a 3-0 home win against Arsenal, the first being a powerful header at the far post that had Stamford Bridge roaring its approval. All seemed to be well with the powerfully built 24-year-old's world.

Then, cruelly, it all went wrong. 'Birch' hurt his knee against WBA at the Bridge in October and was out of action for three months. While he was sidelined, Ian Hutchinson and Peter Osgood struck up their spectacular double act, but when they had to miss the home game against Newcastle in February, Alan was recalled and hoped to make enough of an impression to reclaim his place.

Instead, having looked sharp, he was carried from the field after 51 minutes with a badly gashed knee following a clash with goalkeeper Iam McFaul. The blond Midlander recovered in time to play twice more before the end of the season, but the arrival of Keith Weller confirmed that he had no future with Chelsea and in June 1970 he was transferred to Crystal Palace.

A stylist who delighted in receiving the ball with his back to goal and spreading it wide with his cultured left foot, Birchenall had been Dave Sexton's first signing for the Blues when he moved from Sheffield United in a £100,000 deal in November 1967, but his instinctive tendency to drop back into midfield meant that he was not the ideal partner for Osgood, who in this respect was a similar player. Alan's effectiveness in the air and persistent running made him popular with the fans despite his indifferent goalscoring record, and it is unfortunate that his progress should have been interrupted at a crucial stage of his career.

BORN: East Ham, 22.8.45.
GAMES: 95 (1). GOALS: 28.
OTHER CLUBS: Sheffield United 64/5-67/8 (107, 31);
Crystal Palace 70/1-71/2 (41, 11); Leicester City 71/2-76/7 (163, 12);
Notts County 75/6 *on loan* (5, 0); San José Earthquakes; Notts County 77/8 (28, 0);
Memphis Rogues; Blackburn Rovers 78/9 (18, 0); Luton Town 78/9-79/80 (10, 0);
Hereford United 79/80 (11, 0).

1967/68-1969/70

JOHN DEMPSEY

During his three and a half seasons as Chelsea's regular centre-half John Dempsey played in three major cup finals, but he was somewhat overshadowed by his more flamboyant team-mates and never received the credit he deserved for his part in the club's success. A £70,000 signing from Fulham in January 1969, the Irish international was a dependable defender who felt no embarrassment about putting the ball into touch whenever danger threatened and favoured an uncomplicated approach to the job in hand which led one journalist to describe his resolute display in the 1970 FA Cup final at Wembley as 'splendidly functional'.

Quick on the turn and able to hold his own with most forwards over short distances, John was a good close marker, with a firm tackle and plenty of strength. He was not particularly dominant in the air but when David Webb switched from full-back to join him in the middle of the back four the pair presented a formidable barrier, as well as posing a considerable threat at the other end of the field.

John is probably best remembered for the superb volley which gave the Blues the lead in the 1971 European Cup-Winners' Cup final replay in Athens, a goal which must have come as something of a relief to the undemonstrative Londoner since it was his unlucky slip deep into stoppage time at end of the first game which had allowed Zoco to equalise for Real Madrid. However, in August 1972 he suffered the first of the catalogue of serious injuries which were to blight the remainder of his career. He made just 31 first-team appearances in three seasons but appeared to have re-established himself in 1975/76, forming a solid partnership with Micky Droy as Chelsea regrouped in the Second Division. Sadly, a twisted knee cost Dempsey his place and he was unable to force his way back into the side, although he remained at Stamford Bridge for another two years, eventually taking the well-trodden path to America in March 1978.

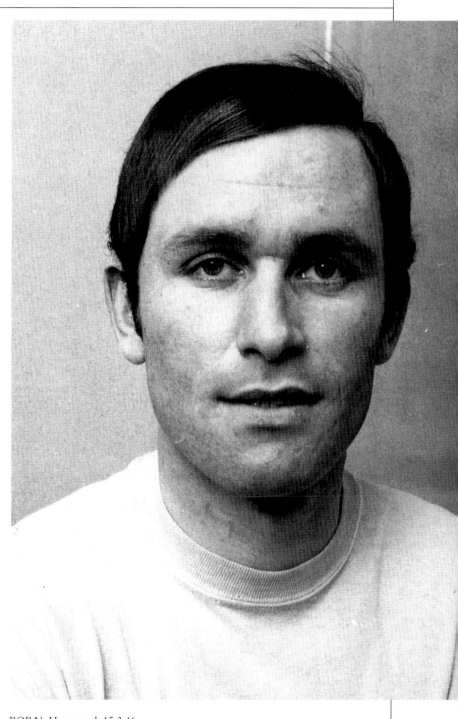

BORN: Hampstead, 15.3.46.
GAMES: 200 (7). GOALS: 7.
HONOURS: European Cup-Winners' Cup 70/1; FA Cup 69/70.
19 Ireland caps.
OTHER CLUBS: Fulham 64/5-68/9 (149, 4);
Philadelphia Furies.

1968/69-1975/76

DAVID WEBB

There was little polish or refinement about David Webb's game, but few players have been more popular with the Stamford Bridge crowd. A rugged defender with the wit, resilience and appetite for life for which East Enders are famed, he had the gift of communicating his warm, roguish personality to the fans, who shared in all his triumphs and disasters. But despite his air of jaunty defiance, Dave was a solid, dependable professional whose infectious enthusiasm made him a cornerstone of Dave Sexton's exciting team.

A hefty six-footer with rough-hewn features that helped earn him the highly apt nickname 'Desperate Dan', Webb was signed from Southampton in February 1968 in a deal which took Joe Kirkup to the Dell in part-exchange. He had played at right-back for the south coast club but Sexton, who had been his manager at Leyton Orient for a few months in 1965, initially employed him at centre-half, which had become something of a problem position. Dave distinguished himself with a swashbuckling hat-trick at Ipswich on Boxing Day, but when John Dempsey arrived shortly afterwards he was handed the number two shirt that had been vacated by Kirkup.

Webb continued to perform with characteristic gusto but he lacked the pace and agility to make a complete success of the role and his limitations were brutally exposed in the 1970 FA Cup final at Wembley when Leeds United's wily left-winger, Eddie Gray, teased and tormented him with a display of traditional wizardry. Dave bore his ordeal with the courage Chelsea fans had come to expect, making a crucial clearance in extra time, and in the replay at Old Trafford he had his revenge. While Ron Harris switched to full-back and subdued Gray in his own inimitable fashion, Webb moved into the middle alongside Dempsey to shackle Clarke, crowning an authoritative performance with the winning goal, bundled in at the far post from Ian Hutchinson's long throw.

Webb was reluctant to return to his old position and after a lame performance there against Everton in the Charity Shield – attributed by some experienced observers to the lush beard he had acquired during the summer – he was dropped, but he soon established himself as Dempsey's regular partner in the centre of the defence and it became clear that he had found his best position. A doughty competitor with unquenchable spirit, he was strong in the air and tackled like an earth-mover, and outstanding displays in both matches against Real Madrid in Athens provided ample confirmation of his growing stature.

Dave continued to score a healthy ration of goals and even made occasional appearances as an emergency striker – to considerable effect – but his willingness to do whatever was asked of him in the Chelsea cause was never seen more clearly than when he played in goal against Ipswich on Boxing Day 1971, taking over the green jersey in the absence of all three senior 'keepers and – needless to say – emerging with a clean sheet. He performed heroics of a rather more familiar kind against Spurs in the League Cup semi-final at White Hart Lane a few days later but in 1972/73 he suffered a brief loss of form and, having regained his place, missed the closing weeks of the campaign through injury.

The following season was not a happy one for the Blues and in the wake of the disharmony that led to Alan Hudson and Peter Osgood leaving Stamford Bridge, Webb became unsettled. He felt that the atmosphere at the club had turned sour, and that summer he was transferred to Queens Park Rangers for £100,000. His departure was a further indication that a golden age was drawing to a close, but he would return to Chelsea nearly twenty years later in the hope of launching another . . .

BORN: Stratford, 9.4.46.
GAMES: 298. GOALS: 33.
HONOURS: European Cup-Winners' Cup 70/1; FA Cup 69/70.
OTHER CLUBS: Leyton Orient 64/5-65/6 (62, 3);
Southampton 65/6-67/8 (75, 2); Queens Park Rangers 74/5-77/8 (116, 7);
Leicester City 77/8-78/9 (33, 0); Derby County 78/9-79/80 (26, 1);
AFC Bournemouth 80/1-82/3 (11, 0); Torquay United 84/5 (2, 1).
MANAGER: AFC Bournemouth (80-82); Torquay United (84-85);
Southend United (86-87 and 88-92); Chelsea (93); Brentford (93-97).

1967/68-1973/74

PETER OSGOOD

The efforts of the terrace choristers are rarely notable for their insight, but the song that hailed Peter Osgood as the King of Stamford Bridge succeeded in capturing the essence of the man. Regal in his bearing, imperious in his manner, he scored unforgettable goals with a swagger that bordered on arrogance, took his revenge with the cruelty of Genghis Khan when his displeasure had been aroused and had a taste for the good things in life that befitted an emperor.

It took Ossie a little time to secure the loyalty of his subjects. He scored twice on his senior debut in a League Cup tie against Workington in December 1964 but had to wait until the following September for another chance to impress, Tommy Docherty promising him a run of a dozen games in the first team. Since this was at the expense of Barry Bridges, the current England centre-forward, the reaction from the terraces was initially hostile but it soon became clear that the 18-year-old was something very special indeed.

A willowy 6ft 3in, Peter had the ability to slice his way through defences with a deceptive swerve, as he demonstrated at Turf Moor the following January when, running from his own half, he beat four Burnley defenders before rounding the keeper and stroking the ball home. He was good in the air and possessed magical ball control, but most remarkable was his gift for spotting openings apparent to no one else.

Osgood's world came crashing down when he broke his right leg in a clash with Blackpool's Emlyn Hughes in October 1966. He missed the rest of the season and during his absence he put on two stone in weight that he never managed to lose, with the result that he was no longer able to run with the ball as he once had. It took him a long time to regain his confidence and it was only after a spell in midfield in 1968/69 that the golden touch began to return. He was most effective when he dropped back a little to collect the ball and he enjoyed the most productive period of his career when he was joined in attack by Ian Hutchinson in November 1969. Ossie scored in every round of the FA Cup that season, plundering a hat-trick at QPR, and crowned it all with a superb diving header in the replay against Leeds at Old Trafford that left David Harvey bewildered.

Osgood travelled to Mexico for the World Cup that summer but he was never the type of player to find favour with Sir Alf Ramsey. Responding to the challenge of a vital match played in front of a big crowd in characteristic style, he returned from a savage eight-week suspension to score twice in the second leg of the Cup-Winners' Cup quarter-final against Bruges the following season and found the net in both matches against Real Madrid in Athens to help another trophy on its way to Stamford Bridge.

However, Peter's relationship with Dave Sexton was never easy and at the start of the next campaign he was transfer-listed for 'lack of effort'. Things were smoothed over on that occasion but the manager finally lost patience with his star player's inconsistency and dropped him, together with three others, for a game at Sheffield United on New Year's Day 1974. Following a training-ground flare-up Ossie was put on the transfer list and, after a long-drawn-out saga which saw his team-mates attempt to engineer a reconciliation, Sexton walk out in a huff and Osgood ask for his cards, he was eventually sold to Southampton for £275,000.

In December 1978 Peter returned to Stamford Bridge but he was unable to recapture the old magic and after ten rather sad months he retired from a game that had been immensely richer for his virtuosity, style and sense of drama.

BORN: Windsor, 20.2.47.
GAMES: 375 (4). GOALS: 150.
HONOURS: European Cup-Winners' Cup 70/1; FA Cup 69/70.
4 England caps (70-73).
OTHER CLUBS: Southampton 73/4-77/8 (126, 28);
Norwich City *on loan* 76/7 (3, 0); Philadelphia Furies.

1964/65-1973/74 & 1978/79-1979/80

KEITH WELLER

When Dave Sexton added Millwall's Keith Weller to his Cup-winning squad in a £100,000 deal in May 1970, he explained that he intended to employ his latest signing as a goalscoring right-winger, a declaration which occasioned some surprise since the chirpy Cockney had made a name for himself at the Den as an enterprising midfield player. However, having been a victim of the star system at White Hart Lane, Weller was desperate to prove himself in the First Division and approached the challenge presented by an unfamiliar role in a positive frame of mind.

At first things went splendidly. He scored twice from Peter Osgood knock-downs to rescue a point at Upton Park in only his third game, and his pace, control and directness made him a consistent threat to opposing defences. His determination won him the respect of his new colleagues and by Christmas the stocky Londoner's decisive finishing had brought him 12 goals, including a spectacular volley at home to Newcastle.

However, in the second half of the season Weller's form wilted. The service he received became fitful, partly as a result of the injuries to key players which continued to disrupt the side, and the goals dried up. Although he emerged as the leading scorer in a team which won the European Cup-Winners' Cup and finished sixth in the League, his confidence had suffered and he was no longer an automatic selection. When discussing his new recruit, Sexton had stressed his versatility, yet he was never given a chance to show what he could do at the heart of the side, which was a pity.

Illness and injury restricted Keith to only two matches in the opening weeks of the following campaign, and when Steve Kember and Chris Garland were signed it became clear that he no longer figured in the manager's plans. Sixteen months after his arrival at Stamford Bridge, he was transferred to Leicester City, where he gave sterling service for eight seasons and became an England player – in midfield.

BORN: Islington, 11.6.46.
GAMES: 48 (5). GOALS: 15.
HONOURS: European Cup-Winners' Cup 70/1.
4 England caps (74).
OTHER CLUBS: Tottenham Hotspur 64/5-66/7 (21, 1); Millwall 67/8-69/70 (121, 40);
Leicester City 71/2-78/9 (262, 37); New England Tea Men; Fort Lauderdale Strikers.

1970/71-1971/72

MARVIN HINTON

As a sweeper, covering behind a well-organised defence, Marvin Hinton had few peers, as he demonstrated when he was used in that role by Tommy Docherty in a number of Fairs Cup ties in 1965/66. Sadly, he was rarely given the chance to exploit his ability in the position in which he excelled.

Marvin had started his career with Charlton Athletic as a centre-half but made most of his appearances during his first two seasons at Stamford Bridge following his £30,000 transfer in August 1963 at right-back, deputising for the injured Ken Shellito. He was then switched to the centre of the back four in place of John Mortimore but was never a truly dominating defender and lacked the height to be commanding in the air.

Although Hinton was short of pace, he possessed an outstanding football brain and read the game so well that he was rarely embarrassed. Steady and totally unflappable, he looked good in possession and used the ball intelligently, and his immaculate displays that season – with an assured, polished performance in the first game against AC Milan in the San Siro stadium outstanding – earned him a place in the squad of 40 players named for the 1966 World Cup.

However, after the arrival of David Webb in February 1968 Marvin was rarely sure of a place in the first team and the following season he started only six League games. A more assertive man would probably have moved to another club in search of the recognition his talent deserved, but 'Lou' was content to remain at the Bridge in the role of understudy and his continuing value to Chelsea was underlined when he came on as a substitute for the last five minutes of extra time in the FA Cup final replay at Old Trafford in 1970 to calm rapidly fraying nerves, both on the pitch and on the terraces.

Hinton made his final senior appearance for the Blues in the last game of 1974/75. He finally left Stamford Bridge twelve months later, aged 36, but continued to play in non-League football for many years.

BORN: Norwood, 2.2.40.
GAMES: 327 (16). GOALS: 4.
HONOURS: FA Cup 69/70; League Cup 64/5.
OTHER CLUBS: Charlton Athletic 57/8-63/4 (131, 2).

1963/64-1974/75

CHARLIE COOKE

If professional football were simply a matter of gifted artists entertaining the paying public with their delightful skills, Charlie Cooke would be revered as one of the finest players ever to have laced on a pair of boots. Instead, results take precedence over every other consideration, and for much of his Stamford Bridge career the mercurial Scotsman was regarded with suspicion by managers frustrated that his exceptional talent was largely ornamental.

A superb dribbler with a gloriously deceptive body swerve, Charlie was signed from Dundee in April 1966 for a club record fee as a direct replacement for Terry Venables, but found it impossible to adapt to the team's established style, which depended on the ball being played early to speedy front-runners. All too often he would weave his way down cul-de-sacs when a simple pass would have opened up a clear path to goal, and when it became apparent that Tony Hateley was helpless without a steady supply of high crosses Charlie was moved to the wing to provide it. A typical wriggle and a pinpoint centre created the winning goal in the FA Cup semi-final against Leeds, but Cooke never produced his best form on the flanks, tending to drift out of matches if he was not at the heart of the action.

Charlie's ball-juggling skills inevitably made him a darling of the Stamford Bridge crowd and he was voted the Blues' Player of the Year the following season, but Dave Sexton was less convinced, feeling that for all his delightful artistry the maestro made insufficient practical contribution to the team. Charlie seemed to accept that he would need to harness his individualism to the collective effort, for in 1969/70 he emerged as a more rounded, complete performer, but he was still at his most effective on those rare occasions when he was given a chance to bring his skills to bear in the middle of the pitch, most memorably in the FA Cup final replay at Old Trafford when he mastered Billy Bremner and created Peter Osgood's equaliser with an exquisite chip.

Always a player to produce his best on the big occasion, Charlie was again outstanding in the matches against Real Madrid in Athens, but he was unable to summon the consistency required to earn a regular place in the Blues' midfield and in September 1972 he followed Paddy Mulligan to Crystal Palace. A deeply intelligent, thoughtful man who was often tortured by self-doubt, Cooke was to have a miserable time at Selhurst Park, but after 15 months he was recalled to the Bridge to provide some much-needed sparkle in the wake of Alan Hudson's departure. The fee of £17,000 was around a fifth of what Chelsea had received and it was soon clear that Sexton had secured a bargain. Charlie had taken a long, hard look at himself and was clearly determined to make the most of his gifts in the years left to him. By the start of the following season he was fitter than he had ever been and his inspired displays on the wing provided a rare glimmer of hope during the Blues' wretched drift towards relegation.

Having rediscovered his old passion for the game, Cooke suffered a series of unfortunate injuries over the next couple of years but he returned to the side during the closing weeks of the tense promotion campaign in 1977 and, at 34, helped steady the nerves of Eddie McCreadie's young team, holding the ball and spraying it around with much of the old assurance. The veteran was destined to enjoy one more day of glory, a delightful 35-minute cameo in the third round of the Cup against Liverpool in January 1978 paving the way for a famous victory, before making a permanent switch to the United States that summer.

BORN: St Monance, Fife, 14.10.42.
GAMES: 360 (13). GOALS: 30.
HONOURS: European Cup-Winners' Cup 70/1; FA Cup 69/70.
16 Scotland caps (65-75).
OTHER CLUBS: Aberdeen; Dundee;
Crystal Palace 72/3-73/4 (44, 0);
Los Angeles Aztecs; Memphis Rogues; California Surf.

1965/66-1972/73 & 1973/74-1977/78

TOMMY BALDWIN

When Tommy Baldwin arrived at Stamford Bridge in September 1966 as part of the deal that took George Graham to Highbury, he had started fewer than 20 League games and was regarded as no more than a makeweight, but his form over the next three seasons left no doubt that once again Tommy Docherty had recognised gold where others had seen only base metal. However, the busy striker failed to maintain his early impetus and was to be no more than a squad player – albeit an important one – for the remainder of his long career with the Blues.

Baldwin scored on his Chelsea debut at Manchester City the day after making the move across London and would prove to be a dependable marksman, his last-minute winner against Sheffield Wednesday in the sixth round of the Cup that season confirming the value of his sharpness at short range. More important, however, was the huge amount of work he got through in 90 minutes, his good close control and determination enabling him to hold the ball under pressure and create openings for others.

The turning-point in Tommy's career came when he was sidelined for four months after damaging his knee against Ipswich on Boxing Day 1968. In his absence Ian Hutchinson emerged as a formidable rival and thereafter 'Sponge' could never be sure of a place in the first team. He was undeniably unlucky with illness and injuries but his inconsistency did nothing to help his chances. When he was recalled to the side he usually performed with much of his old zest at first, but then he seemed to lose interest and, not surprisingly, he was the one to be left out again when things went wrong.

Although he played in all the Blues' cup finals in the early seventies, Baldwin understandably grew increasingly dissatisfied with his role as a reserve and when he was made available in November 1972 it seemed that his departure was unlikely to be long delayed. In the event a series of proposed deals fell through and, after an abortive spell on loan at Manchester United, he was given a free transfer in September 1975.

BORN: Gateshead, 10.6.45.
GAMES: 228 (11). GOALS: 92.
HONOURS: European Cup-Winners' Cup 70/1; FA Cup 69/70.
OTHER CLUBS: Arsenal 64/5-66/7 (17, 7);
Millwall *on loan* 74/5 (6, 1);
Manchester United *on loan* 74/5 (2, 0);
Brentford 77/8 (4, 1).

1966/67-1974/75

STEVE KEMBER

The Crystal Palace fans took Steve Kember to their hearts for his tigerish aggression and when Dave Sexton broke the Chelsea transfer record in September 1971 to take him to Stamford Bridge, the Londoner admitted he was sorry to be leaving the club he had supported from the age of five. Although he was a first-team regular throughout his four seasons with the Blues, the midfielder never looked entirely comfortable in his new surroundings and rarely produced his best form.

At Selhurst Park Steve had been a major influence on a struggling side, and he seemed to be somewhat intimidated by some of the big names and extrovert personalities with whom he now shared a dressing room. It was unfortunate that an appearance for Palace in the early stages of the League Cup prevented him from taking part in Chelsea's run to the final during his first season with the club and no doubt that added to his sense of isolation.

He was marginalised in a rather more literal sense by Sexton, who asked him to play wide on the right rather than in his preferred position at the heart of the action. There was much learned talk about the value of Kember's stamina on the flanks, but he was unable to make much impression and soon became a frustrated and bewildered figure.

Once Sexton had departed, Steve was given his chance to demonstrate his worth in the thick of the midfield battle. His confidence quickly returned and his spirited displays were an inspiration as commitment replaced panache as the Chelsea rallying cry, but it was too late for the sorrowful slide towards relegation to be reversed. Kember's personal renaissance was short-lived, and when the season had reached its melancholy conclusion he was grateful to be given the opportunity to continue his career in the First Division with Leicester City.

BORN: Croydon, 8.12.48.
GAMES: 144 (6). GOALS: 15.
OTHER CLUBS: Crystal Palace 65/6-71/2 (218, 35) and 78/9-79/80 (42, 1);
Leicester City 75/6-78/9 (117, 6);
Vancouver Whitecaps.
MANAGER: Crystal Palace (81-82).

1971/72-1974/75

ALAN HUDSON

The ascent of Alan Hudson from the obscurity of the Football Combination to the fringe of the England World Cup squad could scarcely have been more spectacular. Having made his first-team debut in February 1969, the richly talented midfielder seized the opportunity presented by a wave of injuries that afflicted Stamford Bridge at the start of the following season to establish himself as an influential member of what was rapidly developing into a thrilling Chelsea side. No less an authority than Sir Alf Ramsey, not a man renowned for his oratorical excesses, declared that there was 'no end to what this boy can achieve', and a quite breathtaking individual goal against Sheffield Wednesday in March reinforced the gifted 18-year-old's blossoming reputation. Alan was among the 40 players short-listed for service in Mexico and it seemed that the Blues had unearthed a player of genuine world class.

With his long hair flapping and his socks around his ankles, Hudson covered a huge amount of ground during the course of a match, helping out in defence one moment then surging up the field to create an opening at the other end the next. He read the game with an astuteness that belied his inexperience, and his willingness to take responsibility, running at defences before splitting them wide open with an inch-perfect through-ball, was remarkable in one so young. It is rare indeed for athleticism and artistry to be combined in such rich measure; it really did seem as though Alan had it all . . .

However, the teenager's apparently irresistible rise was brought to an abrupt halt by a nasty ankle injury picked up at the Hawthorns on Easter Monday and, despite a courageous fight, he missed both the epic confrontation with Leeds at Wembley and, to his intense disappointment, the Old Trafford rematch. Like many young footballers of exceptional ability since, Hudson, who had been brought up close to London's fashionable King's Road, just a few minutes' walk from the Blues' ground, did not find it easy to come to terms with the adulation suddenly thrust upon him, and the rest of his Chelsea career was to be marred by an exasperating inconsistency. In the end that golden promise remained largely unfulfilled.

A stress fracture of the shin hampered Alan's recovery from this setback and the form that had won him such acclaim was rarely seen the following season, but by the second half of 1971/72 he was generally considered to be back at his best. His appetite restored, his passing more perceptive than ever, Hudson was quite outstanding against Liverpool in March, dominating the game in majestic style, but that summer he suffered a severe blow when he was banned from international football for two years after declining to join an under-23 tour.

Alan's fortunes dipped once again the following winter and, frustrated at being asked to play out of position on the right flank, he demanded a transfer, marking the start of a battle of wills with Dave Sexton that could have only one outcome. The FA ban was lifted in July 1973 and, for a few weeks in the autumn, he looked sharp and eager, his desire rekindled. Chelsea suddenly recaptured much of their old swagger, but the revival was to be short-lived and Hudson was dropped, together with three others, for the game at Sheffield United on New Year's Day. He asked for a move once again and within a fortnight he had been transferred to Stoke City for £240,000, his sparkling performances for the Potteries club earning him two England caps.

Alan returned to Stamford Bridge in the summer of 1983, but illness and injury sadly denied him the chance to show whether he could reproduce the magic that had enthralled the fans a decade earlier.

BORN: Chelsea, 21.6.51.
GAMES: 187 (1). GOALS: 14.
HONOURS: European Cup-Winners' Cup 70/1.
2 England caps (75).
OTHER CLUBS: Stoke City 73/4-76/7 (105, 9) and 83/4-85/6 (39, 0);
Arsenal 76/7-77/8 (36, 0); Hercules, Spain; Seattle Sounders.

1968/69-1973/74

IAN HUTCHINSON

Any centre-half who had spent ninety minutes marking Ian Hutchinson knew he had earned his money. Brave and aggressive, the big striker allowed defenders no respite, constantly harrying them and challenging for every ball played in his direction with a ferocity that made onlookers wince. Accepting injuries as the price that had to be paid if he was to do his job, he rarely emerged from a game unscathed and his uncompromising style made it almost inevitable that his career would be cut short, but during his one full season in the Chelsea first team 'Hutch' produced a series of stirring performances that will not be easily forgotten by those who witnessed them.

Ian gained his football education in a tough school, playing as a part-timer in non-League football with Burton Albion and Cambridge United before moving to Stamford Bridge in a £5,000 deal in July 1968. He was given an extended run in the side in the closing weeks of the following season and made a dramatic impact, scoring six times in 11 appearances and impressing with his strength and enthusiasm, but the real turning-point came when he was paired with Peter Osgood against Sheffield Wednesday at Hillsborough on a cold, wet Saturday in November 1969. It was immediately apparent that their partnership had enormous potential, the lion-hearted 21-year-old drawing the enemy's fire while his stealthy partner crept in unobserved, and the Blues won 3-1, Ian rounding off a splendid display with two well-taken goals.

A superb header of the ball, the powerfully built youngster may have looked a little ungainly on the floor but his control was getting better all the time, as he demonstrated in the FA Cup semi-final against Watford four months later, turning past a bewildered defender before thumping home the Blues' fourth goal and setting up the fifth for Peter Houseman with a delicate lay-off. Then at Wembley he conjured up a last-ditch equaliser with a brave diving header, and his immensely promising season was crowned in the replay at Old Trafford when one of the prodigious long throws which had become his trademark was bundled in at the far post by David Webb for the winner.

Hutchinson looked set to maintain his progress the following winter but in December he received the first of the heartbreaking catalogue of injuries that were to wreck his career. Ironically, in view of the punishment he received every week, it was self-inflicted, a clash with a Nottingham Forest defender who had left him minus a tooth resulting in a broken bone in his arm. Two months later the combative striker damaged his right knee against Southampton and he would not return to first-team action for nearly two years, having broken his leg in a reserve game and subsequently suffered a repeat of the fracture.

Two goals on his comeback against Norwich in December 1972 were quickly forgotten when more trouble with his knee forced Ian back into hospital and he managed only a handful of appearances in 1973/74, but the following season he was able to play more regularly and showed signs of recapturing the drive and commitment that had made him so formidable. Utterly determined to overcome every setback, 'Hutch' seemed to have re-established himself in the side in the autumn of 1975 but his right knee was still causing him a lot of pain and the following February came the final announcement that the joint could take no more abuse.

His long fight for fitness had been characteristically dogged and unflinching, but Eddie McCreadie spoke for many of the fans who had followed Ian's injury-blighted career with boundless admiration when he said that it was a relief that the popular Midlander's ordeal was at an end.

BORN: Derby, 4.8.48.
GAMES: 136 (7). GOALS: 57.
HONOURS: FA Cup 69/70.

1968/69-1975/76

CHRIS GARLAND

Prior to the first leg of the 1971/72 League Cup semi-final against Tottenham at Stamford Bridge on 22 December, Chris Garland had started only four first-team games since his £100,000 transfer from Bristol City at the beginning of September and had yet to score. He had been signed to add depth to the squad, and would probably not have played if Steve Kember had been available, but he seized his chance splendidly by heading home at the near post from Peter Houseman's right-wing corner as Chelsea triumphed 3-2, and finally won over the fans with an unstoppable 20-yard drive at White Hart Lane two weeks later which helped clinch the Blues' place at Wembley.

In the final against Stoke the enthusiastic striker produced another energetic, determined performance and it took a heroic save from Gordon Banks in the closing minutes to deny him a deserved equaliser. However, those three matches were very much the highlights of the athletic blond forward's four-year stay at Stamford Bridge, during which he was rarely certain of a first-team place.

He started the following season with a flurry of goals but then picked up a persistent groin injury which hampered him for the next two years, preventing him from training for much of the time. Chris found it frustrating that Dave Sexton generally asked him to play wide on the left or the right to capitalise on his powerful running, since he felt that his most effective position was in the middle alongside a dominant centre-forward, but in truth he probably did not have the sharpness to be a regular marksman at the top level.

Something of an open-hearted country boy, Garland never really adapted to the cynicism of life in the metropolis and, with Chelsea doomed to relegation, was relieved to be given a chance to revive his career in the provinces by Leicester manager Jimmy Bloomfield in March 1975, subsequently returning to his native Bristol.

BORN: Bristol, 24.4.49.
GAMES: 111 (3). GOALS: 31.
OTHER CLUBS: Bristol City 66/7-71/2 (143, 31) and 76/7-82/3 (64, 11);
Leicester City 74/5-76/7 (55, 15).

1971/72-1974/75

PETER HOUSEMAN

It was Peter Houseman's misfortune to be victimised by a section of the Stamford Bridge crowd who were seemingly alienated by his meticulous, diffident manner – and, more to the point, didn't know a footballer when they saw one – but that should not be allowed to overshadow the outstanding service this talented player gave the Blues in a first-team career that spanned more than a decade.

Peter was still three days short of his 18th birthday when he made his senior debut against Sheffield United in December 1963, but he proved to be something of a late developer and five years would pass before Dave Sexton gave him a permanent place in the side. A cultured performer with a fine left foot, 'Nobby' blossomed as his confidence grew and he didn't miss a match in 1969/70, starting the season in midfield then settling down on the left wing when Alan Hudson broke into the team.

Houseman was a diligent worker who dropped back conscientiously to cover his full-back and his ability to hold the ball was much appreciated by hard-pressed colleagues. When he was in the mood to make the most of his skill he could be a match-winner and he crossed the ball beautifully, although he was sometimes guilty of over-elaboration. He is best remembered for his performances in the FA Cup that year, with a magisterial display on a heavy pitch in the semi-final at White Hart Lane the highlight.

Peter was a fixture in the side for the next two seasons, but as Chelsea started to struggle his own star began to wane and his first-team place came under mounting pressure. Sexton switched him to left-back at the start of 1974/75 but he lacked the aggression for the role and, with a wind of change sweeping through Stamford Bridge, he was transferred to Oxford at the end of the season.

All football's triumphs and disasters were shown for what they are, however, when this quiet, unassuming man was killed together with his wife Sally in a tragic road accident two years later.

BORN: Battersea, 24.12.45.
GAMES: 324 (18). GOALS: 39.
HONOURS: European Cup-Winners' Cup 70/1;
FA Cup 69/70.
OTHER CLUBS: Oxford United 75/6-76/7 (65, 2).

1963/64-1974/75

RON HARRIS

Judgements of Ron Harris during his playing days tended to reflect the loyalties of the person handing down the verdict. To supporters of other teams he was 'Chopper' Harris, the ruthless destroyer who would use any means, within the laws of the game or otherwise, to subdue his opponent; to the Stamford Bridge crowd he was an indomitable lionheart and probably the best tackler in English football. However, all could agree that he was a consummate professional, seemingly fashioned from toughened steel, who never flinched from a challenge and routinely played when carrying injuries that would have confined lesser men to the comfort of their armchair.

Ron had already made five League appearances for the Blues when he captained the England Youth team that won the Little World Cup at Wembley in April 1963. Tommy Docherty, impressed by the 18-year-old's fierce will to win, decided that he was the man to add resolve to Chelsea's faltering promotion challenge and recalled him to the first team against Preston four days later. He stayed there for 17 years, carrying out his allotted task with uncompromising thoroughness and invariably giving his managers – all seven of them – everything he had to offer.

Ron was at his best playing alongside the centre-half, close-marking the opposition's most dangerous forward. Men like Geoff Hurst and George Best rarely prospered with Harris sticking to them closer than their shadows, and his mastery of Jimmy Greaves was such that the little genius scored just once in more than twenty matches against the Blues and was even heard to ask why Tottenham bothered to pick him against Chelsea. It is true that Ron occasionally did things that made his team-mates cringe and was not above examining the bravery of the players he faced, some of whom were quite content to let him pass his afternoon largely undisturbed. However, he relished the opportunity to test his mettle against an opponent with an equally fearsome reputation, and one bone-splintering challenge for a 50-50 ball with Liverpool's Tommy Smith is not likely to be forgotten by those who witnessed it.

Adaptable and uncomplaining, Ron was regularly switched to full-back to plug gaps caused by injuries or loss of form, but his lack of pace was occasionally exposed in that role and there is no doubt that his willingness to play out of position for the good of the team did little to advance his own career. He replaced Terry Venables as captain in January 1966 and led the Blues to four major cup finals, inspiring his troops by his peerless example rather than the melodramatic fist-waving employed by more flamboyant characters. The much trumpeted 'clean-up' of the early seventies was widely supposed to have blunted Chopper's edge and he was briefly dropped after the crushing disappointment of defeat in the fifth round of the FA Cup and the League Cup final on successive Saturdays in the spring of 1972, the captaincy passing to Eddie McCreadie. However, Ron remained a model of solid pragmatism, content to win the ball with quiet efficiency and play a simple pass to a more gifted colleague.

Harris was named as substitute on no fewer than 30 occasions by McCreadie in 1976/77 but did his usual dependable job when he stood in for David Hay in the tense closing stages of the promotion battle. Three years later he was handed the number 11 shirt by Geoff Hurst and asked to play as a midfield destroyer. At 35, he proved so effective that one wondered what he might have achieved if he had been used in that role a decade earlier, but his relations with his former adversary were not entirely comfortable and at the end of the season he joined Brentford as a player-coach, having made 794 appearances for the Blues, establishing a record that is very unlikely ever to be broken.

BORN: Hackney, 13.11.44.
GAMES: 783 (11). GOALS: 14.
HONOURS: European Cup-Winners' Cup 70/1; FA Cup 69/70; League Cup 64/5.
OTHER CLUBS: Brentford 80/1-83/4 (61, 0).
MANAGER: Aldershot (84-85).

1961/62-1979/80

PETER FEELY 1970/71-1972/73

Forward. BORN: Camden, 3.1.50.
GAMES: 4 (1). GOALS: 2.
OTHER CLUBS: AFC Bournemouth 72/3-73/4 (9, 2);
Fulham (0, 0); Gillingham 74/5-75/6 (41, 22);
Sheffield Wednesday 75/6-76/7 (19, 2);
Stockport County *on loan* 76/7 (2, 0).

TONY POTRAC 1971/72

Forward. BORN: Victoria, 21.1.53.
GAMES: 1. GOALS: 0.
OTHER CLUBS: Durban City.

MIKE BROLLY 1972/73-1973/74

Winger. BORN: Galston, 6.10.54.
GAMES: 8 (1). GOALS: 1.
OTHER CLUBS: Bristol City 74/5-75/6 (30, 2);
Grimsby Town 76/7-81/2 (254, 27);
Derby County 82/3 (42, 4);
Scunthorpe United 83/4-85/6 (95, 15).

TOMMY ORD 1972/73

Forward. BORN: Woolwich, 15.10.52.
GAMES: 3. GOALS: 1.
OTHER CLUBS: Bristol City *on loan* (0, 0);
Montreal Olympic; Rochester Lancers;
New York Cosmos;
Vancouver Whitecaps; Seattle Sounders;
Tulsa Roughnecks;
Atlanta Chiefs.

LEE FROST 1977/78-1979/80

Winger. BORN: Woking, 4.12.57.
GAMES: 12 (3). GOALS: 5.
OTHER CLUBS: Brentford *on loan* 78/9 (6, 0);
Brentford 80/1 (15, 3).

BOB ILES 1978/79-1982/83

Goalkeeper. BORN: Leicester, 2.9.55.
GAMES: 14. GOALS: 0.
OTHER CLUBS: AFC Bournemouth (0, 0).

PETER FEELY

TOMMY ORD

LEE FROST

TONY POTRAC

MIKE BROLLY

BOB ILES

JOHN SITTON

JIM DOCHERTY

JIMMY CLARE

MARK FALCO

JOHN SITTON 1978/79-1979/80

Central defender. BORN: Hackney, 21.10.59.
GAMES: 12 (2). GOALS: 0.
OTHER CLUBS: Millwall 79/80-80/1 (45, 1);
Gillingham 81/2-84/5 (107, 5);
Leyton Orient 85/6-90/1 (170, 7).
MANAGER: Leyton Orient (94-95).

GARY JOHNSON 1978/79-1980/81

Forward. BORN: Peckham, 14.9.59.
GAMES: 18 (4). GOALS: 9.
OTHER CLUBS: Crystal Palace *on loan* (0, 0);
Brentford 80/1-82/3 (60, 13); PG Rangers, South Africa;
Aldershot 85/6-87/8 (75, 20).

JIM DOCHERTY 1978/79

Forward. BORN: Broxburn, 8.11.56.
GAMES: 2 (1). GOALS: 0.
OTHER CLUBS: East Stirling; Dundee United.

TIM ELMES 1980/81

Midfielder. BORN: Thornton Heath, 28.9.62.
GAMES: 2 (2). GOALS: 0.
OTHER CLUBS: Leyton Orient (0, 0).

JIMMY CLARE 1980/81

Midfielder. BORN: Islington, 6.11.59.
GAMES: 0 (1). GOALS: 0.
OTHER CLUBS: Charlton Athletic (0, 0).

MARK FALCO 1982/83

Forward. BORN: Hackney, 22.10.60.
GAMES: 3 (*on loan* from Tottenham Hotspur). GOALS: 0.
OTHER CLUBS: Tottenham Hotspur 78/9-86/7 (174, 68);
Watford 86/7 (33, 14); Glasgow Rangers;
Queens Park Rangers 87/8-90/1 (87, 27);
Millwall 91/2 (21, 4).

PAUL WILLIAMS 1982/83

Central defender. BORN: Lambeth, 16.11.62.
GAMES: 1. GOALS: 0.

GARY JOHNSON

TIM ELMES

PAUL WILLIAMS

PADDY MULLIGAN

Before joining Chelsea from Shamrock Rovers in a £17,500 deal in October 1969, Paddy Mulligan had combined football with a job as an office furniture salesman and it took him some time to adapt to the level of fitness expected at Stamford Bridge. The enthusiastic Irishman made only a handful of appearances during his first season but, in the wake of Eddie McCreadie's long-term injury problems, he appeared to have established a regular place in the Blues' first team at right-back the following autumn, his whole-hearted style and adventurous overlapping down the wing making him popular with the fans. He had generally played in the centre of the defence for the Republic of Ireland, but a fine match-winning goal in the home game against Arsenal when he ran onto Peter Osgood's pass, beat McNab and sent a well-struck right-foot shot past Bob Wilson demonstrated his considerable attacking ability.

A torn hamstring sustained in the second leg of the Cup-Winners' Cup tie against CSKA Sofia put him out for two months and on his return he was unable to regain the position, but the following season he started 36 games – all but two of them at right-back – and seemed to be developing into a fine player, adding poise to his natural energy and determination. The injury which kept him off the field for the second half of the League Cup final that year undoubtedly contributed to Chelsea's defeat, yet at the start of the next campaign the amiable Dubliner was in the reserves, and when the chance of a regular first-team place at Crystal Palace was offered to him, he was happy to accept.

While Paddy may not have been the most naturally gifted defender in the Football League, his attitude helped compensate for any shortcomings and his performances at Selhurst Park and, subsequently, West Bromwich Albion confirmed that he had been right to try to prove himself on this side of the Irish Sea.

BORN: Dublin, 17.3.45.
GAMES: 73 (5). GOALS: 2.
HONOURS: 51 Ireland caps.
OTHER CLUBS: Shamrock Rovers (twice); Boston Beacons;
Crystal Palace 72/3-74/5 (57, 2);
West Bromwich Albion 75/6-77/8 (109, 1).

1969/70-1972/73

TOMMY HUGHES

When Chelsea lost 5-2 at home to Leeds United in January 1970, ending all thoughts of a challenge for the Championship, Tommy Hughes was savaged by the Sunday newspapers. The Scottish under-23 international had taken the place of Peter Bonetti, who had flu, and his uncertainty was said to have been responsible for the defeat. However, the young 'keeper, playing only his sixth first-team match, had been the victim of his own courage and sense of duty, as he was also unwell and should really have been tucked up in bed with a hot-water bottle rather than facing Don Revie's men at the height of their powers. He later acknowledged that it had been a mistake to play but, however unfair it might have been, the 'accident prone' label had been firmly attached, and his reputation took a further battering when his fourth game of the season ended in another five-goal drubbing, at the hands of the Champions, Everton.

Dave Sexton still had faith in his ability, but a broken leg sustained when jumping for a high ball in a pre-season friendly against Breda at the end of July effectively ended Tommy's chances of proving his worth at Stamford Bridge. However, the big Scot subsequently established himself at Hereford, where he played for nine seasons before becoming manager.

BORN: Dalmuir, 11.7.47.
GAMES: 11. GOALS: 0.
OTHER CLUBS: Clydebank; Aston Villa 71/2 (16, 0);
Brighton and Hove Albion *on loan* 72/3 (3, 0);
Hereford United 73/4-81/2 (240, 0).
MANAGER: Hereford United (82-83).

1966/67-1969/70

DEREK SMETHURST

As he collected the medal he had earned when he came on as a substitute in the European Cup-Winners' Cup final replay in Athens in May 1971, Derek Smethurst must have felt that he could look forward to a bright future with the Blues. The 23-year-old South African striker had played in both legs of the semi-final against Manchester City, scoring the only goal of the game at Stamford Bridge when he slid the ball neatly past Joe Corrigan from a pass by stand-in centre-forward David Webb, and had also appeared in the last five League games of the season, collecting two more goals. The new campaign would surely bring many more opportunities to prove his worth . . .

Derek had made his first-team debut at Burnley the previous September, having been signed from Durban City in December 1968, and appeared to have established himself as a valued member of Dave Sexton's squad, signing a professional contract when he had fulfilled a two-year residential requirement. Tall and stylish, he was a little short of pace and lacked the drive and aggression so highly prized in English football, but he certainly had ability and appeared to be a bright prospect.

It was therefore something of a surprise when, having played in the first two games of the new season in place of Keith Weller, Smethurst was transferred to Millwall for £35,000 in September, remaining at the Den for four years before trying his luck in America.

BORN: Durban, South Africa, 24.10.47.
GAMES: 18 (1). GOALS: 5.
HONOURS: European Cup-Winners' Cup 70/71.
OTHER CLUBS: Durban City; Millwall 71/2-74/5 (71, 9);
Tampa Bay Rowdies; San Diego Sockers; Seattle Sounders.

1970/71-1971/72

MICKY DROY

Micky Droy's Chelsea career spanned no fewer than 15 seasons, during which he provided just about the only continuity (apart from the long-suffering supporters) amid seemingly unending changes in the dressing room, the manager's office and the boardroom. These years saw several periods of deep gloom in SW6, but without the courage and resilience of the huge centre-half the despair would have been even greater.

In his last full season in the first team, 1982/83, the Blues only narrowly avoided relegation to Division Three, and it was hard to remember that he had started his Chelsea career in a very different atmosphere, his third senior game being the home leg of the European Cup-Winners' Cup semi-final against Manchester City in April 1971. When Micky ran out onto the pitch for away games in those early days, his sheer size invariably drew murmurs of astonishment from the apprehensive home fans, and at 6ft 4in and 15½ stone he certainly presented an imposing sight.

Droy had learned his football in the non-League game, moving to Stamford Bridge from Slough Town at the age of 19 in October 1970, and in his first few seasons the rough edges were very apparent. He became established in the side only in the second half of 1973/74 when Dave Sexton decided that the club would have to battle its way out of trouble, and the presence of the unpolished stopper at the heart of the Blues' defence embodied the new mood of austerity at the Bridge. However, as Chelsea slipped towards the relegation trap-door the following winter, his courageous and aggressive displays were often inspirational, with a defiant performance at Upton Park outstanding. Although not entirely fit, having just recovered from injury, he headed away the stream of high balls sent in by West Ham and scored the decisive goal when he hurled himself at Peter Houseman's centre.

When Micky was ruled out by injuries for much of the second half of 1975/76, Steve Wicks was able to establish a firm grip on the number five shirt which he relinquished only briefly as Eddie McCreadie's team surged towards promotion, but Ken Shellito decided to use the two towering defenders together during the Blues' spirited fight for First Division survival the following season and the partnership proved surprisingly effective. Micky emerged as the fans' Player of the Year and his lengthy absences due to illness and then an ankle problem were undoubtedly a major factor in the side's lamentable efforts in 1978/79.

As his experience increased, 'Lurch' became more authoritative and, as his reading of the game improved, his lack of speed was rarely punished. He was now much more composed, his strength and reach making him irresistible in the tackle. He also showed increased poise on the ball, sometimes demonstrating quite remarkable finesse with his favoured left foot to dribble out of tight situations before making a searching forward pass. Although he was often sent upfield to remedy desperate situations, Droy didn't score too often, but his efforts certainly created chances for others.

Micky succeeded Ray Wilkins as club captain and his influence on a young side over the next four seasons was invaluable. He always played with total commitment, launching his mighty frame into challenges with utter fearlessness, and as a consequence he picked up a seemingly endless catalogue of niggling injuries which caused him to miss more than a quarter of the Blues' matches and affected his consistency. However, at his best – in other words, when he was fully fit – he was utterly dominant, particularly when the ball was in the air.

In the summer of 1983 John Neal recruited Joe McLaughlin and Droy started only one more first-team game for Chelsea, but he did a fine job for Crystal Palace following his move to Selhurst Park in March 1985.

BORN: Highbury, 7.5.51.
GAMES: 302 (11). GOALS: 19.
OTHER CLUBS: Luton Town *on loan* 84/5 (2, 0);
Crystal Palace 84/5-86/7 (49, 7);
Brentford 86/7 (19, 3).

1970/71-1984/85

TEDDY MAYBANK

Eddie McCreadie's decision to give 18-year-old Teddy Maybank his first-team debut in the crucial relegation battle with Tottenham at White Hart Lane in April 1975 was so daring that it deserved to succeed. However, the blond striker was unable to make much impression on a match more tense than any cup-tie, and hopes of a miraculous deliverance were dashed.

Strongly built and energetic, Maybank was at his most effective when running at defences with the ball, but in the 26 matches he played the following season he rarely produced his best form as the Blues struggled to adapt to the Second Division. Two fine headed goals at home to Carlisle in August confirmed that, despite his relative lack of inches, he was useful in the air, but for all his pace and skill he was unable to hit the target often enough and, following the fifth round Cup defeat at home to Crystal Palace, McCreadie turned to Steve Finnieston.

After joining Fulham on a one-month loan, Teddy became increasingly restless and, in spite of Chelsea's reluctance to lose a player of considerable potential, he was allowed to move to Craven Cottage permanently in a £65,000 deal in March 1977. Unhappily, injury problems meant that that early promise went unfulfilled.

BORN: Lambeth, 11.10.56.
GAMES: 32. GOALS: 6.
OTHER CLUBS: Fulham 76/7-77/8 (27, 14)
and 79/80 (19, 3);
Brighton and Hove Albion 77/8-79/80 (64, 16).

1974/75-1976/77

JOHN SISSONS

What would prove to be Dave Sexton's last major signing for Chelsea was uncharacteristically quixotic. In August 1974 he paid Norwich City £50,000 for John Sissons, the traditional left-winger who, as a slim, speedy 18-year-old, had played in West Ham's FA Cup-winning side ten years earlier. At Upton Park he became a victim of the tactical revolution which had forced his species to the brink of extinction, often finding himself held responsible for the shortcomings of the Hammers' defence, and he eventually moved on to Second Division Sheffield Wednesday. After four largely frustrating years with the sleeping giants of Hillsborough and a season in Norwich colours which had ended with the prospect of a return to the hurly-burly of Division Two, Sissons had not hesitated to accept the lifeline extended by Sexton.

In the first few games of the season the boyish-looking winger, no longer so slim or so speedy but still capable of advancing puposefully down the flank and putting over an accurate centre, looked sharp and eager but, with the team's confidence ebbing away, his form faded and after ten matches he was dropped. Sexton then departed and although Sissons played two further games, it soon became clear that he did not feature in the new regime's plans. He eventually departed for South Africa in March 1976, no doubt pondering what might have been.

BORN: Hayes, 30.9.45.
GAMES: 12 (1). GOALS: 0.
OTHER CLUBS: West Ham United 62/3-69/70 (213, 37);
Sheffield Wednesday 70/1-73/4 (115, 14);
Norwich City 73/4 (17, 2); Cape Town City.

1974/75

DAVID HAY

The signing of David Hay from Celtic in July 1974 was intended to signal the beginning of a new era at Chelsea. Chairman Brian Mears could not be accused of a lack of ambition, for the Scottish international had been outstanding in the recent World Cup, driving forward powerfully from midfield, and the fee of £225,000 made him London's most expensive footballer; but a cruel sequence of misfortunes meant that hopes of a Hay-inspired reversal of the club's decline were made to look foolish.

It took him some time to settle in his new surroundings and, as he searched in vain for his best form in a side lacking confidence, his own self-belief started to ebb away, the trickle turning into a flood when, following his return from a leg injury, the vision in his right eye became blurred. The widely admired Scotsman kept going until season's end with characteristic professionalism, but surgery was required for the removal of a cataract that summer.

David was still not sure of a place in the team the following season as the Blues failed to impress in the Second Division, but things began to improve when he was paired with Steve Wicks in the centre of the defence in February. He shackled Mick Channon ruthlessly when Southampton visited the Bridge, using his strength and intelligent positional play to great effect, and this partnership was to be the cornerstone of Chelsea's ultimately successful challenge for promotion in 1976/77.

Further problems with the same eye curtailed his season and threatened his career but, after no fewer than three operations to repair a detached retina, the steely Glaswegian made a courageous comeback 12 months later. However, the unkind fates had not yet finished with Hay and, as he fought to re-establish himself in the side in the autumn of 1978, he suffered a knee injury which would force his premature retirement a year later.

It was less than this fine player deserved.

BORN: Paisley, 29.1.48.
GAMES: 118 (2). GOALS: 3.
HONOURS: 27 Scotland caps (70-74).
OTHER CLUBS: Glasgow Celtic.
MANAGER: Motherwell; Glasgow Celtic; St Mirren.

1974/75-1978/79

STEVE SHERWOOD

When it was realised early on the morning of the home game against Ipswich on 27 December 1971 that injuries would rule out both Peter Bonetti and John Phillips, Steve Sherwood was asked to return urgently to Stamford Bridge to make his League debut, but the 18-year-old arrived just five minutes before kick-off and was not allowed to play, which was perhaps a foretaste of future disappointments. David Webb relinquished the 'keeper's jersey at Derby five days later and the 6ft 3in Yorkshireman performed valiantly, only to be beaten with seven minutes remaining when a shot from Archie Gemmill was deflected beyond his reach.

Sherwood's next opportunity came in November when he played three more League games, conceding seven goals, but he had to wait until the start of the 1975/76 season for his only extended run in the first team. A dropped corner which led to a 'Pop' Robson equaliser at Sunderland on the opening day was an unhappy beginning, and the blond giant's positioning sometimes looked suspect, so it was no surprise when, after a 4-1 defeat at Southampton in October, Eddie McCreadie turned to Peter Bonetti to steady the ship. Steve, the younger brother of Olympic athlete John Sherwood, moved on to Watford the following November and stayed at Vicarage Road for more than ten years, playing for the Hornets in the 1984 FA Cup final.

BORN: Selby, 10.12.53. GAMES: 17. GOALS: 0.
OTHER CLUBS: Brighton and Hove Albion *on loan* (0, 0); Millwall *on loan* 73/4 (1, 0); Brentford *on loan* 73/4-74/5 (62, 0); Watford 76/7-86/7 (211, 1); Grimsby Town 87/8-92/3 (183, 0); Northampton Town 93/94 (16, 0); Grimsby Town (0, 0); Lincoln City 94/5 (7, 0).

1971/72-1975/76

RAY LEWINGTON

To escape from what was the Second Division a side needs a player who can win the ball in midfield, and that was the role Ray Lewington performed for the Blues as they gained promotion on a tide of youthful enthusiasm in 1976/77. The red-haired terrier didn't miss a match and it was the platform provided by his biting tackles which allowed the more sophisticated talents of Ray Wilkins and Garry Stanley to flourish. The crucial game against Luton on Easter Saturday saw him at his best: he worked tirelessly throughout to give Chelsea control of the middle of the pitch, and crowned a stirring performance when he robbed Jimmy Husband and fed Steve Finnieston, who did the rest.

In the First Division the following season Lewington was unable to make the same impact, perhaps because he lacked the pace required at the higher level, and he was left out of the side for long spells. When Danny Blanchflower succeeded Ken Shellito in December 1978, he soon made up his mind that he had no use for what the chunky midfielder had to offer, and Ray was allowed to try his luck in Canada.

The rest of his career was spent in the lower divisions, including a successful spell as Fulham's player-manager, but he never quite recaptured the form he had produced under the influence of Eddie McCreadie.

BORN: Lambeth, 7.9.56. GAMES: 87 (5). GOALS: 4.
OTHER CLUBS: Vancouver Whitecaps; Wimbledon 79/80 (23, 0); Fulham 79/80-84/5 (174, 20) and 86/7-89/90 (60, 1); Sheffield United 85/6 (36, 0). MANAGER: Fulham (86-90).

1975/76-1978/79

JOHN PHILLIPS

Having been signed from Aston Villa for £25,000 to replace the injured Tommy Hughes as Peter Bonetti's deputy at the beginning of the season, 19-year-old John Phillips looked set to play in the 1971 European Cup-Winners' Cup final as Chelsea's first-choice goalkeeper. His chance to impress had come earlier than expected when the England international was sidelined for two months by a combination of a shoulder injury and pneumonia, but the ambitious youngster had seized it decisively, demonstrating courage, a safe pair of hands and growing poise as the Blues maintained a position in the top four and won through to the Athens final.

Had Dave Sexton shown faith in the highly motivated teenager at this crucial point, he might well have fulfilled the hopes raised by an assured performance in a rousing home win against Leeds and matured into a top-class performer. Instead Peter Bonetti was recalled and, while the cup was won, an opportunity was lost.

Although 'Sticks' made 31 appearances over the next two seasons, he was firmly cast in the role of understudy until New Year's Day 1974, when his rival was a victim of the purge that followed four successive defeats. He made a brilliant penalty save in the third round of the Cup against QPR four days later and, apart from two brief spells when the more experienced man was preferred, held the place for the next 18 months. However, he received scant protection from a porous defence and his form declined together with his confidence as the team slid ingloriously towards the drop.

A serious ankle injury meant that Phillips missed the start of the 1975/76 campaign, and thereafter he had only occasional spells in the first team. By the time he finally moved on to Brighton in March 1980 the cool certainty which had created such an impression nine years earlier had become little more than a memory.

BORN: Shrewsbury, 7.7.51.
GAMES: 149. GOALS: 0.
HONOURS: 4 Wales caps (73-77).
OTHER CLUBS: Shrewsbury Town 68/9-69/70 (51, 0); Aston Villa 69/70 (15, 0); Crewe Alexandra *on loan* 79/80 (6, 0); Brighton and Hove Albion 80/1 (1, 0); Charlton Athletic 81/2 (2, 0); Crystal Palace (0, 0).

1970/71-1978/79

GRAHAM WILKINS

Although his Chelsea first-team career spanned no fewer than ten seasons, Graham Wilkins made just 137 League appearances for the Blues and he was never certain of a place in the side. At his best the diminutive full-back was an accomplished performer, but competition from Gary Locke restricted his opportunities on the right flank, where he was more comfortable, and consistency always proved elusive.

Having made his senior debut as a 17-year-old on Boxing Day 1972, Graham had to wait until the following October for a second chance and his progress was interrupted when he broke his left leg at Old Trafford a week later. It took him some time to recover from that setback but he managed to establish himself at left-back in Eddie McCreadie's promotion-winning team in 1976/77, only to lose his place to John Sparrow in the closing weeks of the season.

While he was inevitably overshadowed by his gifted younger brother Ray, Graham had considerable natural ability and liked to play his way out of tight situations whenever possible. He looked impressive when moving forward with the ball but lacked composure and his defensive shortcomings were cruelly exposed on more than one occasion during the Blues' unhappy two-year sojourn in the First Division, most notably at Maine Road in November 1977 when he was run ragged by Manchester City's Peter Barnes and eventually sent off after his desperate attempts to halt the flying winger had incurred the displeasure of the referee.

Graham's approach was generally rather less aggressive, which led some simple-minded members of the Stamford Bridge crowd to question his commitment, but he could be a dogged defender, as he had demonstrated when he contained John Robertson of Nottingham Forest a few weeks earlier. However, his confidence was gradually eroded over the years and he became increasingly uncertain. The arrival of Dennis Rofe in February 1980 ended his chances of winning a regular place in the Blues' first team but he remained at the Bridge for two more, largely unproductive, seasons before moving to Brentford in the summer of 1982.

BORN: Hillingdon, 28.6.55.
GAMES: 148 (1). GOALS: 1.
OTHER CLUBS: Brentford 82/3-83/4 (38, 0);
Southend United *on loan* 83/4 (3, 0).

1972/73-1981/82

STEVE FINNIESTON

Every successful side needs at least one of its forwards to find the net regularly and Steve Finnieston will be remembered as the man who scored 24 League goals in 39 matches as Eddie McCreadie's energetic young side returned the Blues to the First Division. They included three penalties, a few gifts and plenty of close-range efforts, including the winner volleyed past an advancing 'keeper from eight yards in the vital home game against Nottingham Forest in April; but a reliable finisher who would punish the sort of mistakes that Second Division defences tend to make was precisely what McCreadie had been looking for when, in some desperation, he recalled the Edinburgh-born striker midway through the previous season. 'Jock', who had never doubted his ability to score goals, made no secret of the fact that he felt the opportunity was overdue, and responded by proving his point five times in a dozen appearances.

Although the strong and determined target man could shield the ball and lay it off to colleagues effectively – if not always very stylishly – and worked to improve other aspects of his game, it was his hunger for goals and coolness in the box that made him so important to the side. Finnieston rounded off the triumphant promotion season with a hat-trick in the last match against Hull but missed four months of the following campaign with Achilles tendon trouble, and when he returned – with a characteristic goal, banged home from a rebound, in the third round Cup win against Liverpool – a lot of the old sharpness seemed to have disappeared. However, when he was sold to Sheffield United for £90,000 that May, it confirmed the suspicion that many people at Stamford Bridge had never really believed in him and sadly another injury which forced Steve to give up League football denied him the chance to prove them wrong.

BORN: Edinburgh, 30.11.54.
GAMES: 86 (4). GOALS: 37.
OTHER CLUBS: Cardiff City *on loan* 74/5 (9, 2);
Sheffield United 78/9 (23, 4).

1974/75-1977/78

KEN SWAIN

Although he subsequently enjoyed a long and distinguished career, winning Championship and European Cup medals with Aston Villa and continuing to play League football regularly until he was 39, Ken Swain's stay at Chelsea was relatively unspectacular and his contribution to the Blues' promotion in 1977 largely unremarked. Most of the plaudits went to players whose talent was destined to fade after a brief period in full blossom, while the unassuming Merseysider just kept on getting better.

This was only to be expected, perhaps, since Ken had come late to professional football, qualifying as a schoolteacher before moving to Stamford Bridge from Wycombe Wanderers in August 1973. A winger who was at home on either flank, he made a handful of senior appearances the following spring without making any lasting impact, but was not among the 25 players called into first-team action as the Blues lurched towards relegation in 1974/75. He was given another chance to prove his worth the following season and the injury which sadly ended Ian Hutchinson's career allowed the 24-year-old to establish himself as a striker in the closing months of the campaign.

The promising partnership he had formed with Steve Finnieston continued to develop as Eddie McCreadie's side set the pace at the top of the Second Division table the following winter, but Ken's thoughtful distribution, neat ball control and dogged persistence could not disguise the fact that, with only 13 goals in 36 League appearances, he was a profligate finisher, and Tommy Langley was preferred for the run-in.

The following August Ken Shellito announced that he intended to use Swain in midfield, feeling that his intelligent reading of the game would be put to better use in a deeper role, and the switch was immediately justified when the former winger capped an influential display at Old Trafford with a flighted centre that gave Bill Garner the winning goal. Ken continued to operate as a provider until November 1978 when, with the Blues struggling, he was dropped and asked for a transfer. Shortly afterwards he moved to Villa Park in a £100,000 deal – and discovered that his best position was full-back.

BORN: Birkenhead, 28.1.52.
GAMES: 127 (5). GOALS: 29.
OTHER CLUBS: Aston Villa 78/9-82/3 (148, 4);
Nottingham Forest 82/3-84/5 (112, 2);
Portsmouth 85/6-87/8 (113, 0); West Bromwich Albion *on loan* 87/8 (7, 1);
Crewe Alexandra 88/9-91/2 (126, 1).
MANAGER: Grimsby Town (97).

1973/74-1978/79

BILL GARNER

A powerfully built, old-fashioned centre-forward, dangerous in the air but less happy when the ball was on the ground, Bill Garner was signed to provide Dave Sexton with an attacking option denied him by Ian Hutchinson's continuing fitness problems, but found difficulty in adapting to the demands of First Division football following his £100,000 move from humble Southend in September 1972. He was ineligible for League Cup ties, having played against the Blues in an early round of the competition, and this, combined with a series of minor injuries of the kind that were to dog him throughout his career with Chelsea, prevented him from staking an early claim to a regular first-team place.

His best performances that season were reserved for the FA Cup, two goals against Ipswich in round four – both with his feet – suggesting that the tall striker was progressing nicely, although an ugly clash with the Sheffield Wednesday captain in the next round at Hillsborough which resulted in both men being sent off revealed a suspect temperament. His heading prowess troubled the Arsenal defence in the quarter-final replay, creating a goal for Peter Houseman, but it was not enough to save the game.

Much of the following campaign was lost as a result of an unpleasant viral illness, and the remainder of Bill's stay at Stamford Bridge proved disheartening. Two thumping headers against QPR in February 1974 confirmed that he could still pose a considerable threat but, in common with Steve Kember and Chris Garland, he was a victim of inconsistent team selection, Sexton appearing to have little clear idea of the type of side he was attempting to construct to succeed his cup-winning teams. However, while they joined Keith Weller at Leicester when the Blues went down, Garner remained for another three, largely fruitless seasons, before joining Cambridge United on a free transfer in November 1978.

BORN: Leicester, 14.12.47.
GAMES: 105 (14). GOALS: 36.
OTHER CLUBS: Notts County 66/7 (2, 0);
Southend United 69/70-72/3 (102, 41);
Cambridge United 78/9-79/80 (24, 3); Brentford 83/4 (3, 1).

1972/73-1978/79

GARY LOCKE

Following his League debut in September 1972, Gary Locke was Chelsea's first-choice right-back for almost a decade, but his career was plagued by a succession of injuries which gradually took their toll on his startling acceleration and drew much of the sting from his game. Only twice was he able to make more than 32 League appearances in a season, and the rich potential he had shown when he first broke into the side was never quite fulfilled.

Dave Sexton considered Locke's promise to be so exceptional that he was prepared to accept Crystal Palace's offer for the man in possession of the number two shirt, Paddy Mulligan, before the willowy 18-year-old had so much as kicked a ball in senior football, and his faith was rewarded when the England youth international performed impressively at Coventry the following Saturday. He seemed to have little difficulty in adapting to the demands of the First Division but at the end of March he suffered the first of the injuries that were to interrupt his progress, dislocating his right shoulder playing in goal in a practice match and missing the rest of the season. However, he had performed with admirable poise and assurance and quickly re-established himself in the first team the following autumn, winning the Player of the Year Trophy awarded by the Supporters Club.

Gary acknowledged that the Chelsea youth team manager, Ken Shellito, had been a major influence on his game and his polished displays certainly evoked memories of his distinguished predecessor. He had been well schooled in the mysteries of the full-back's art, his sound positional play and acute tactical awareness allowing him to dictate terms to the winger facing him. Elegant and composed, he timed his tackles with rare delicacy and as he gained experience he matured into a solid and reliable defender. Coming forward, Locke used the ball intelligently and his penetrating runs down the right wing in support of the attack regularly brought the Stamford Bridge crowd to life. A surging 50-yard burst which took him past three defenders deep into enemy territory and ended with a measured centre that offered an irresistible invitation to Ian Hutchinson in a 3-1 win against Birmingham in September 1973 was typical of his dashing, enterprising style.

Gary's consistently reliable form shone out like a beacon during the Blues' dismal slide towards relegation in 1974/75 and he was an ever-present member of the side which regained Chelsea's place in the First Division with such exuberance two years later. Although only 22 himself, he was more experienced than most of his team-mates and, as the tension which gripped Eddie McCreadie communicated itself to his young squad, his calming influence was invaluable.

Locke dislocated his troublesome right shoulder once again that summer and made only 18 League appearances the following season, while an ankle injury restricted him to just eight games in 1978/79, and it is tempting to conclude that Chelsea's stay in the First Division might have beeen rather more rewarding had they been able to call upon his services more often. A serious back problem in 1980 that threatened to cut short his career added to the tally of matches he had been forced to miss, and as the years went by the attacking forays became rarer and less effective. Inevitably, some of Gary's sprinting speed had been lost and he was no longer quite the formidable force he had once been.

When John Neal signed Joey Jones it was, in part, a reluctant acknowledgement that Locke's best days were behind him and, following a loan period, he was allowed to join Crystal Palace in February 1983. He stayed at Selhurst Park for four seasons, subsequently moving to New Zealand.

BORN: Kingsbury, 12.7.54.
GAMES: 315 (2). GOALS: 4.
OTHER CLUBS: Crystal Palace 82/3-85/6 (84, 1);
Napier City Rovers, New Zealand.

1972/73-1982/83

BRIAN BASON

Brian Bason appeared to be establishing himself in Eddie McCreadie's promotion-chasing team when he suffered a double fracture of the right shin in the 20th minute of a League Cup tie with Arsenal at Highbury in October 1976. Although he made a full recovery and was able to demonstrate his fitness with Vancouver Whitecaps that summer, there was little prospect of him breaking back into the side and, after spending a month on loan with Plymouth Argyle, he was transferred to the West Country club in January 1978.

A busy, industrious midfielder who generally played wide on the right, Bason made his first-team debut soon after his 17th birthday in a 2-1 defeat at Sheffield United in September 1972 and appeared in three further matches that season without placing any pressure on the men he had stood in for. His next appearance came more than two years later against Carlisle in the autumn of 1975 and although he did well, scoring with a thunderous drive, it was not enough to keep him in the side for long.

However, when he returned in 1976/77 in place of the injured Ian Britton, he gave the team a useful extra dimension, creating a number of goals, and looked set to stay until that fateful clash with Sammy Nelson.

BORN: Epsom, 3.9.55. GAMES: 20 (2). GOALS: 1.
OTHER CLUBS: Vancouver Whitecaps;
Plymouth Argyle 77/8-80/1 (129, 10);
Crystal Palace 80/1-81/2 (27, 0); Portsmouth *on loan* 81/2 (9, 0);
Reading 82/3 (41, 0).

1972/73-1976/77

DAVID STRIDE

When David Stride made his League debut at Birmingham in September 1978, it was already apparent that Chelsea would find it difficult to hang on to their place in the First Division, although few foresaw the humiliation that was to come. A total of 31 players were used during the season and frequent team changes were made in an unavailing effort to head off the inevitable, but in these unpromising circumstances the 20-year-old succeeded in making the left-back position his own.

A former winger, Stride was happiest when advancing down the flank in support of his attack but was developing into a sound defender when his run of 33 successive appearances was ended by a nasty head injury after ten minutes of the home game against Middlesbrough in April. He was taken to hospital where he was found to have suffered concussion and a hairline fracture of the skull, and missed the four matches that remained.

David had performed resourcefully in a side woefully short of confidence, but at the start of the following season Graham Wilkins was preferred and, with the club keen to reduce its playing staff to more manageable proportions, the former reserve team captain was sold to an American club, Memphis Rogues, in November 1979.

BORN: Lymington, 14.3.58. GAMES: 37. GOALS: 0.
OTHER CLUBS: Memphis Rogues; Minnesota Kicks;
Jacksonville Tea Men; Millwall 82/3-83/4 (55, 3);
Leyton Orient 84/5 (29, 0).

1978/79-1979/80

IAN BRITTON

Standing alongside the mighty figure of Micky Droy, little Ian Britton looked like a sturdily built schoolboy, but during the course of a Chelsea first-team career spanning ten seasons the bustling midfielder proved conclusively that size isn't everything. He was only 5ft 5in tall and weighed just 9½ stone, but his tenacity enabled him to hold his own against opponents who, almost without exception, towered over him.

Ian had his first run in the side in the spring of 1973, but it was only when Ron Suart and Eddie McCreadie committed themselves to a youth policy in 1974/75 that his unspectacular promise showed signs of developing into something more than that. He played a leading role in a creditable 2-2 draw at Anfield in March and the following season he showed admirable consistency in an ever-changing team as the Blues came to terms with the shock of relegation. The key to the competitive Scot's game was a willingness to run for 90 minutes, allied to neat passing and the skill to beat an opponent. Playing on the left of midfield, he was one of the cornerstones of the promotion-winning team of 1976/77, his busy, purposeful style complementing the rather more eye-catching talents of Ray Wilkins.

Like most of his colleagues, Ian found the First Division something of an ordeal and his confidence took quite a battering, with the result that he became increasingly reluctant to attempt anything positive when in possession, preferring to play the safe ball to a colleague behind him. Back in Division Two, Britton made 41 League appearances as Chelsea came close to an immediate return under Geoff Hurst, but he gradually slipped from favour over the next two seasons, and in the summer of 1982 he was transferred to Dundee United, subsequently returning to England to play for Blackpool and Burnley.

BORN: Dundee, 19.5.54.
GAMES: 279 (10). GOALS: 34.
OTHER CLUBS: Dundee United;
Blackpool 83/4-85/6 (106, 15);
Burnley 86/7-88/9 (108, 10).

1972/73-1981/82

RAY WILKINS

For four seasons Ray Wilkins was hailed as Chelsea's saviour, the inspirational boy-genius who was going to guide the Blues away from the dark shadows cast by the threat of bankruptcy to the promised land of renewed success on the field. It was an intolerable burden for any one player to shoulder, no matter how outstanding his talent, and it was inevitable that the gifted midfielder would eventually sink beneath its weight.

Having made a handful of first-team appearances in 1973/74, Ray seemed to have established himself in the side the following season, his maturity and ice-cool nerve catching the eye in a sterling performance at Anfield in March, but four weeks later Ron Suart turned to his most experienced players in an effort to halt the Blues' alarming slide and Wilkins was out. However, when Eddie McCreadie took over as manager prior to the crucial match at White Hart Lane that would effectively decide whether the club returned to the Second Division after an interval of 12 years, he placed his faith in youth. Ray was recalled and, astonishingly, the 18-year-old was made captain. A born leader, he handled the pressure with remarkable assurance, and seemed to feel no embarrassment at chivying or encouraging men ten years his senior, but Spurs won the match and Chelsea went down.

The following season, as McCreadie searched frantically for a winning combination, 'Butch' was the fulcrum of the team, constantly involved and seeking to dictate every aspect of the game. His touch deserted him for a while but he recovered his form in time to win his first international cap against Italy in New York in May, embarking on what would prove to be a long and distinguished England career.

Ray confirmed his class in 1976/77, leading from the front in every game as the Blues stormed to promotion on a tide of emotion. Playing just behind the strikers, he had the freedom to exploit his creativity to the full, although the ploy proved less effective in the second half of the season when teams playing against Chelsea for the second time attempted to shackle him. Stylish and assured, the precocious midfield general produced a series of imperious displays illuminated by his remarkable awareness and pinpoint 40-yard passes. Even his greatest admirers would hesitate to describe Ray as quick or aggressive and he lacked the sharpness to go past an opponent, but his astute reading of the game and immaculate distribution enabled him to take command of matches as effectively as any scurrying workaholic. The perfectly angled through-ball that gave Tommy Langley the goal at Molineux which clinched promotion was typical, and he scored a few beauties as well, including a 25-yard volley in a 4-0 win against Sheffield United that dipped and swerved.

With Ken Shellito replacing McCreadie, Wilkins reverted to a more orthodox role the following winter but did not make the expected impression, partly because of a persistent groin strain that looked likely to end his season prematurely. However, his continuing value to the side was demonstrated when he returned for the last few matches to steer the Blues to safety after they had begun to drift into trouble during his absence.

Ray rarely produced his best form in 1978/79 and it is probably no coincidence that Chelsea spent most of the campaign propping up the table. Transfer speculation filled the back pages and he admitted that he was no longer enjoying his football. He was relieved of the captaincy by Danny Blanchflower in February but it was a season when nothing went right and he seemed to lose confidence as one defeat followed another. When the Blues were relegated it was inevitable that he would leave and he eventually rejoined Dave Sexton at Old Trafford, Manchester United paying £875,000 for his signature.

BORN: Hillingdon, 14.9.56.
GAMES: 193 (5). GOALS: 34.
HONOURS: 84 England caps (76-86).
OTHER CLUBS: Manchester United 79/80-83/4 (160, 7);
AC Milan; Paris St Germain; Glasgow Rangers;
Queens Park Rangers 89/90-93/4 (154, 7) and 94/5-96/7 (21, 0);
Crystal Palace 94/5 (1, 0); Wycombe Wanderers 96/7 (1, 0); Hibernian;
Millwall 96/7 (3, 0); Leyton Orient 96/7 (3, 0).
MANAGER: Queens Park Rangers (94-9); Fulham (97-8).

1973/74-1978/79

GARRY STANLEY

The comparisons with Bobby Charlton may have been a little fanciful, but there were certainly occasions during Chelsea's high-energy assault on the Second Division in 1976/77 when Garry Stanley showed at least as much promise as his highly rated colleague Ray Wilkins. However, while the England international went on to justify many of the extravagant claims made on his behalf during the course of that exciting season, the remainder of Stanley's career was to be something of an anti-climax.

At the age of 22, the midfielder was older than most of his team-mates, yet he had only made his debut at the start of the previous term, having sat on the bench without being called upon no fewer than eight times prior to that. The first question marks arose when, after a few indifferent games, he was left out of the side for the promotion run-in – because, Eddie McCreadie explained, the pressure was affecting him. But by that stage his powerful running on the right flank and neat, incisive passing had played a major part in bringing a return to the big time within the Blues' grasp. Strong and determined, 'Starsky' was also useful in the air and possessed a tremendous shot – the hardest in the country according to his manager – which brought him a memorable goal against Charlton at the Bridge in November.

Stanley had just a dozen games to measure himself against the best at the start of the 1977/78 season before a serious groin injury ruled him out until the following August and, although he played regularly on his return, the exuberance which had distinguished his performances two years earlier was no longer seen, as the status which had been fought for so passionately was surrendered with only token resistance. After spending the summer in America, Garry was transferred to Everton, but the fire which had made him effective had seemingly been extinguished.

BORN: Burton, 4.3.54.
GAMES: 115 (5). GOALS: 15.
OTHER CLUBS: Fort Lauderdale Strikers;
Everton 79/80-80/1 (52, 1); Swansea City 81/2-83/4 (72, 4);
Portsmouth 83/4-85/6 (47, 1); Wichita Wings;
Bristol City 88/9 (10, 0).

1975/76-1978/79

STEVE WICKS

It is seldom a good idea to return to the scene of past triumphs and Steve Wicks's second spell at Stamford Bridge could scarcely have been more disheartening. The powerfully built centre-half was signed from Queens Park Rangers for £470,000 – the biggest fee Chelsea had ever paid – in July 1986, seven years after he had been transferred to Derby County, but the new season was just three games old when John Hollins decided to revert to the established pairing of McLaughlin and Pates at the centre of the defence, leaving the 29-year-old to make occasional appearances as an understudy.

An injury to Pates gave Steve a chance to establish himself at the start of 1987/88, but he was soon sidelined by a serious back problem which required surgery and, despite making a courageous comeback and playing a characteristically determined role in the Blues' desperate struggle to avoid a return to Division Two, he was forced to announce his retirement in August 1988, when he was reportedly on the verge of joining Tottenham.

It was a sad end to an itinerant career that had begun when Ron Suart gave him his League debut against Ipswich in March 1975. The flaxen-haired giant was recalled to the first team when John Dempsey twisted his knee that December, and made spectacular progress, emerging as one of the key members of Eddie McCreadie's promotion-winning side the following season. Tall and strong, Wicks was rarely troubled when the ball was in the air and his tackling was resolute, but it was his mature professionalism that was most impressive, with a steady, assured display in an entertaining draw against Nottingham Forest at the City Ground in November outstanding.

The youngster's lack of experience was exposed when he faced First Division opposition the following winter but he learned quickly, benefiting from the presence of Micky Droy alongside him, and was developing into a highly accomplished defender when Danny Blanchflower agreed to let him move to the Baseball Ground in January 1979 to help finance his team rebuilding plans.

BORN: Reading, 3.10.56.
GAMES: 163 (1). GOALS: 8.
OTHER CLUBS: Derby County 78/9-79/80 (24, 0);
Queens Park Rangers 79/80-80/1 (73, 0) and 81/2-85/6 (116, 6);
Crystal Palace 81/2 (14 , 1).
MANAGER: Scarborough (93-94).

1974/75-1978/79 & 1986/87-1987/88

DUNCAN McKENZIE

Chelsea's first major signing for four years demonstrated a faith in the value of gifted, crowd-pleasing forwards that was entirely in keeping with the club's colourful traditions; unhappily in this instance that faith proved to be misplaced. After a period of severe financial stringency, Duncan McKenzie was bought from Everton for £165,000 in September 1978 in the hope that, as well as adding a much-needed cutting edge to the Blues' attack, he would bring some self-belief to a side whose confidence had been visibly draining away over the previous 12 months.

An individual in a game increasingly dominated by the collective approach, he scored twice in his first three matches, producing glimpses of the audacity that had enchanted his admirers in the past as well as an appetite for the ball that some of his former managers might have viewed with a cynical eye. However, even the most talented forward is dependent upon the support and service he receives and, for all his apparent self-assurance, Duncan soon became as demoralised as his colleagues.

As the battle against the drop became more hopeless, he came to seem a costly irrelevance, a forlorn attempt to revive past glories amid present squalor, and in March he quietly moved on to Blackburn for less than half of what had been paid six months earlier.

BORN: Grimsby, 10.6.50. GAMES: 16. GOALS: 4.
OTHER CLUBS: Nottingham Forest 69/70-73/4 (111, 41);
Mansfield Town *on loan* 69/70 (10, 3) and 72/3 (6, 7);
Leeds United 74/5-75/6 (66, 27); Anderlecht; Everton 76/7-
77/8 (48, 14); Blackburn Rovers 78/9-80/1 (74, 16);
Tulsa Roughnecks; Chicago Sting; Hong Kong.

1978/79

JOHN SPARROW

When John Sparrow broke into the Chelsea side at the age of 16 in March 1974, it seemed that the club's wonderfully productive youth scheme had unearthed a natural successor to Eddie McCreadie, whose career was drawing to a close amid persistent fitness problems; but during the seven years he spent in contention for a first-team place, the East Ender never played more than a dozen League games in a season and, like many of his contemporaries, his early promise gradually faded away together with his self-belief.

Sparrow's lack of experience was exploited on a number of occasions during the Blues' melancholy slide into the Second Division, notably in the decisive defeat at White Hart Lane in April 1975, and this early exposure to the harsh realities of life at the bottom probably hindered the England youth international's progress. He was impressive coming forward, as he demonstrated when his centre gave Peter Houseman a goal on his debut, and possessed a dangerous long throw, but despite a useful turn of speed and firm tackle his defending was not sufficiently reliable to win him a regular place.

John did not have the best of luck with injuries and, with the arrival of Dennis Rofe finally ending his hopes of establishing himself, he moved on to Exeter City in January 1981.

BORN: Bethnal Green, 3.6.57.
GAMES: 68 (6). GOALS: 2.
OTHER CLUBS: Millwall *on loan* 78/9 (7, 0);
Exeter City 80/1-82/3 (63, 3).

1973/74-1979/80

EAMONN BANNON

It was entirely characteristic of the somewhat romantic approach that Danny Blanchflower brought to the daunting task he faced that, when the departure of Ken Swain and Steve Wicks gave him the means to bring new players to Stamford Bridge, he opted to pay Hearts £200,000 for the services of Eamonn Bannon. A manager with a more conventional background would surely have preferred to recruit a battle-hardened veteran to bring organisation and resilience to a demoralised side, but the Irishman wanted to see his team play its way out of trouble.

The 20-year-old midfielder was certainly gifted, with the traditional Scottish talent for running with the ball and then threading through an imaginative pass. His stylish performances during the second half of the season made the ordeal of Chelsea's long-suffering supporters more bearable, but he was not able to bring about the transformation in the club's fortunes that the desperate situation demanded.

It was a pretty harrowing introduction to English football for the youngster and early the following season, with Geoff Hurst having moved into the manager's office, he became unsettled and decided to return to Scotland. His outstanding performances for Dundee United over the next few seasons confirmed his ability and made many of the Blues' fans regret that he hadn't come south in more favourable circumstances.

BORN: Edinburgh, 18.4.58.
GAMES: 27. GOALS: 1.
HONOURS: 11 Scotland caps (79-86).
OTHER CLUBS: Heart of Midlothian (twice);
Dundee United; Hibernian.

1978/79-1979/80

MICKY NUTTON

It looked as though Chelsea had discovered a defender of real promise when 19-year-old Micky Nutton combined with John Sitton to blot out the Liverpool attack at Stamford Bridge in March 1979. Micky had made just six previous first-team appearances (enough to make him a veteran compared with his colleague, who was playing only his second League game) but showed great composure, even finding time to go upfield and hit the post with a thumping header. However, some bad luck with injuries and stiff competition from Gary Chivers and Colin Pates meant that, despite his clear ability, the elegant centre-back was never able to command a regular first-team place.

Very quick but lacking authority in the air, Nutton was at his most effective when paired with Micky Droy in the middle of the defence, although he occasionally found himself at full-back or in midfield. He was comfortable in possession and his deceptive stride was the springboard of many attacks, but he was possibly a little too relaxed to prosper in the non-stop bustle of Second Division football.

As time went on, Micky appeared to lose his way and, after spending a month on loan at Reading, he was allowed to join Millwall in March 1983. However, that youthful potential was sadly never fully realised.

BORN: St John's Wood, 3.10.59.
GAMES: 81 (2). GOALS: 0.
OTHER CLUBS: Reading *on loan* 82/3 (6, 0);
Millwall 82/3-85/6 (82, 4).

1978/79-1982/83

COLIN VILJOEN

Like Colin Lee and Dennis Rofe, Colin Viljoen was signed by Geoff Hurst in the second half of 1979/80 in the hope that his experience and composure would help Chelsea clinch promotion, but the aristocratic midfielder appeared to find it difficult to adapt to the bustling style of Second Division football. Viljoen was an intelligent player whose measured passing could open up defences, but during his time with the Blues he only rarely produced the form that had made him such an influential member of the stylish Ipswich side of the early seventies. Nevertheless he remained a model professional who thought deeply about the game and was happy to offer advice to his younger colleagues.

The former England international's commanding performance at home to Shrewsbury in January 1981, when he was recalled after a four-month absence, suggested that the years had not eroded his talent, but his stay in the side was to be brief. The following winter, with John Neal now in charge, Colin appeared to have established himself at last and he played a large part in a memorable League Cup win over Southampton, but when injury sidelined him for several weeks he was unable to get back into the team and that summer he was released. It was a disappointing end to a distinguished League career.

BORN: Johannesburg, South Africa, 20.6.48.
GAMES: 22 (1). GOALS: 0.
HONOURS: 2 England caps (75).
OTHER CLUBS: South Transvaal;
Ipswich Town 66/7-77/8 (305, 45);
Manchester City 78/9-79/80 (27, 0).

1979/80-1981/82

TREVOR AYLOTT

After Trevor Aylott's first two matches for Chelsea it looked as though he might be the answer to Ken Shellito's prayers. Prior to the visit of Bristol City in October 1977 the team had failed to score in four matches and had managed only seven goals all season, prompting the anxious manager to invite the big, burly 19-year-old from Bermondsey to show that he could do what Bill Garner couldn't. Aylott battled away gamely, and his 55th-minute header from Charlie Cooke's beautifully weighted cross was enough to win the points.

Confidence soaring, the fans' new hero followed this up with an eager and aggressive performance against the League leaders, Nottingham Forest, at Stamford Bridge the following Saturday, thumping the only goal of the game past Peter Shilton after a powerful run. However, as the glow of this impressive beginning faded, Trevor's technical limitations became apparent and when no further goals followed Shellito looked elsewhere for the solution to his problems.

The heavyweight striker played another 13 games in 1978/79, but the hunger that had put him in the headlines a year earlier was missing and he failed to find the net. After five further appearances he was sold to Barnsley in November 1979 and began his extensive and generally fruitful travels.

BORN: Bermondsey, 26.11.57. GAMES: 29 (3). GOALS: 2.
OTHER CLUBS: Barnsley 79/80-81/2 (96, 26);
Millwall 82/3 (32, 5); Luton Town 82/3-83/4 (32, 10);
Crystal Palace 84/5-85/6 (53, 12); Barnsley *on loan* 85/6 (9, 0);
AFC Bournemouth 86/7-90/1 (147, 27);
Birmingham City 90/1-91/2 (27, 0); Oxford United 91/2 (37, 6);
Gillingham 92/3 (10, 2).

1977/78-1979/80

PETAR BOROTA

Petar Borota believed that, as a professional footballer, it was part of his job to entertain the people who paid to watch him, a heretical philosophy which led reporters to damn him with the tag 'eccentric'. The extrovert Yugoslav's colourful personality made him enormously popular with Chelsea's supporters, but in the press box his willingness to dash from his penalty area to clear the ball was held to embody unsound Continental attitudes towards goalkeeping. Nevertheless, the Player of the Year trophies he received in each of his two full seasons in the first team were evidence that at his best he was a spectacular but reliable performer.

Communication with his team-mates was not a problem, as he had a fair command of English, but his unpredictability was sometimes a little unsettling for his colleagues. In a cup-tie at Southampton, for example, he came out of the box and, instead of kicking the ball into the stand, back-heeled it to an astonished Micky Droy, explaining that he wanted to liven up the crowd as no goals had been scored.

Borota's adventurous style occasionally proved costly, as in a game against Orient when he completely missed the ball after another valiant sally beyond the 18-yard line, allowing the on rushing forward to score, but such errors were rare and he more than compensated for them with his outstanding shot-stopping. In 1980/81 his imposing physique, considerable agility and conspicuous bravery enabled him to break Peter Bonetti's club record of 16 League clean sheets in a season – and in the home game against Cardiff he went upfield for a corner in a memorable attempt to remedy a shortage of goals at the other end of the pitch.

A warm, likeable man, Petar was displaced by Steve Francis in November 1981 and the following summer John Neal allowed him to join Brentford, but his committed efforts will be remembered with gratitude by the people he put first – the fans.

BORN: Belgrade, Yugoslavia, 5.3.52.
GAMES: 114. GOALS: 0.
HONOURS: 14 Yugoslavia caps.
OTHER CLUBS: Belgrade Sporting; Partizan Belgrade;
Brentford (0, 0); Benfica; FC Porto.

1978/79-1981/82

CLIVE WALKER

Exciting, adventurous, unpredictable and hopelessly inconsistent, Clive Walker was the sort of player who is adored by the fans but makes exasperated managers yearn for some more secure form of employment. When the circumstances were right, the flying winger was capable of transforming a game single-handedly, but there were other days – too many – when he was largely ineffective.

Clive made his first appearance in the headlines when he scored twice at Molineux in December 1977, and became the darling of the Shed with a match-winning performance against Liverpool in the third round of the FA Cup a month later. The first of his two goals in Chelsea's epic 4-2 victory was typical of his thrillingly uncomplicated approach. Receiving the ball back from a team-mate after he had taken a throw-in, he sprinted past a bemused Joey Jones and hit a swerving shot into the top left-hand corner of the net from an acute angle.

After that game the European Champions' goalkeeper, Ray Clemence, suggested that Walker would find it increasingly difficult to make the same sort of impact as opponents became more familiar with his game, and to some extent that judgement was to be borne out in the years that followed. However, there was no denying the buzz of expectation that went round the ground whenever the flaxen-haired outside-left gained possession and set off towards goal.

Clive's ability to redeem even the most hopeless cause was never seen more clearly than when he came on as a substitute against Bolton Wanderers in October 1978 with 20 minutes remaining. The Blues were trailing 3-0 but the funereal mood of the crowd was replaced by mounting frenzy as the dashing 21-year-old's electrifying running inspired an irresistible fight-back, which was completed when his driven cross was sliced into his own net by the unfortunate Sam Allardyce to give Chelsea a victory that had been unthinkable before Walker was called from the bench.

Geoff Hurst sought to capitalise on Clive's startling pace and willingness to shoot at every opportunity by playing him in the centre of the attack, a strategy which yielded a rich harvest of spectacular goals, including a typical individual effort in a 4-0 win against Newcastle in January 1980. Employed in this role, he saw plenty of the ball and was less likely to fade from the game than when he was restricted to the flanks, and once he had broken clear of the defence in pursuit of a long through-pass, no one was going to catch him.

There were times when Walker seemed to be a luxury Chelsea could not afford in their reduced circumstances, and in John Neal's first two seasons in charge at the Bridge he was not certain of a place in an ever-changing team. However, the 25-yard drive at Bolton in May 1983 that spared the club the ignominy of Third Division football was a timely reminder that he could still conjure a goal out of nothing, and in the opening weeks of the following season he played as well as he had at any time in his career, scoring four times in eight appearances.

It seemed that the positive mood created by Neal's astute transfer dealings during the summer had given Clive renewed self-belief, but a broken jaw meant that the revival was sadly brief. Pat Nevin's rapid emergence prevented him from reclaiming his place on his return to fitness and in July he decided to make a fresh start at Roker Park, returning a few months later to score the goals that took Sunderland to the Milk Cup final at the Blues' expense.

BORN: Oxford, 26.5.57.
GAMES: 191 (33). GOALS: 65.
OTHER CLUBS: Sunderland 84/5-85/6 (50, 10);
Queens Park Rangers 85/6-86/7 (21, 1);
Fulham 87/8-89/90 (109, 29);
Brighton and Hove Albion 90/1-92/3 (106, 8).

1976/77-1983/84

GARY CHIVERS

It is always frustrating when a player fails to exploit his natural gifts, and there is no doubt that, had his talent been harnessed properly, Gary Chivers could have made a greater impact on the game than he has. Like his contemporaries Micky Nutton and Colin Pates, his best position was alongside the centre-half, although he filled in enthusiastically at full-back or in midfield on occasion.

Chelsea were already condemned to relegation to the Second Division when Gary made his first-team bow in April 1979, but the following season he was a regular member of Geoff Hurst's promotion-chasing team. He was not particularly strong in the air and would perhaps have benefited from a little more pace, but by the autumn of 1980 he had developed into one of the best young defenders in the Second Division. His inspirational displays were an influential factor in a sequence of eight wins in nine games that put the Blues firmly in contention for promotion, and a splendid goal in a 6-0 victory against Newcastle at Stamford Bridge was a fitting reward for an outstanding performance.

Always cool and unflustered, Chivers generally tried to play his way out of tight situations and Hurst encouraged his attacking instincts, but that relaxed style could help explain why he has not achieved the success that his first couple of years in League football led many people to expect. There were times when he seemed to lack urgency, and it is tempting to conclude that if Gary had shown more ambition and pushed himself harder he would have been more likely to maintain his early progress.

Instead, his form slumped over the next two seasons as Chelsea plumbed the depths of mediocrity, and he was not always sure of a place in the starting line-up. In the summer of 1983 John Neal decided that there was no room for him in his revamped team and he was allowed to join Swansea City.

BORN: Stockwell, 15.5.60.
GAMES: 143 (5). GOALS: 4.
OTHER CLUBS: Swansea City 83/4 (10, 0);
Queens Park Rangers 84/5-86/7 (60, 0); Watford 87/8 (14, 0);
Brighton and Hove Albion 87/8-92/3 (217, 13); AFC Bournemouth 93/4-94/5 (31, 2).

1978/79-1982/83

PHIL DRIVER

Geoff Hurst bought Phil Driver because he felt that the best way to overcome the well-organised defences of teams visiting Stamford Bridge was to get behind them on the flanks and, while Peter Rhoades-Brown and Clive Walker could perform this role on the left, he had no one to play on the right wing. Pencil-slim, with long, fragile-looking limbs, Driver played a starring role in the demolition of Newcastle in October 1980, his centres creating two of Colin Lee's three goals, but he found consistency hard to achieve and was often employed as a substitute, his arrival more than once sparking a dramatic improvement in the Blues' fortunes.

Direct and speedy, Phil was at his best when running at defenders, and his exciting style inevitably made him popular with Chelsea's dwindling support. An injury to Walker gave him an early opportunity to force his way into John Neal's team the following autumn and he did well, scoring three goals in as many games. Then, however, the former non-League player suffered serious damage to his knee at Cambridge which kept him out for the rest of the season. In 1982/83 he started another nine matches but was unable to rediscover his earlier sparkle and that summer he returned to Wimbledon before dropping out of League football.

BORN: Huddersfield, 10.8.59.
GAMES: 25 (21). GOALS: 4
OTHER CLUBS: Wimbledon 78/9-80/1 (16, 3)
and 83/4-84/5 (4, 0).

1980/81-1982/83

ALAN MAYES

Much was expected of Alan Mayes when he joined Chelsea from Third Division Swindon Town in December 1980. His goalscoring feats had attracted considerable publicity and the Stamford Bridge faithful hoped that his prowess in the penalty area would ensure that the club's promotion challenge did not falter. Unhappily, the 27-year-old striker was unable to give the fans what they wanted and, in their frustration at the almost total inability to put the ball in the net which wrecked the Blues' season, they turned on him.

Mayes certainly missed a few chances but the main reason for his lack of success was that he had come into a team whose self-belief was swiftly evaporating. He was a small, neat forward who liked the ball played in accurately to his feet so that he could twist and turn to lose his marker, but during his two and a half seasons at the Bridge he was obliged to survive on a diet of optimistic high balls that were of little use to a player of his physique or style. A determined and resilient character, Alan was able to savour a few moments of triumph such as his pair of well-taken goals against Leicester in March 1982, but in 1982/83 he was displaced by new recruits and that summer he became one of a number of players to move on as John Neal wielded the new broom with vigour.

BORN: Edmonton, 11.12.53.
GAMES: 71 (5). GOALS: 24.
OTHER CLUBS: Queens Park Rangers (0, 0);
Watford 74/5-78/9 (133, 31);
Northampton Town *on loan* 75/6 (10, 4);
Swindon Town 78/9-80/1 (89, 38) and 83/4-84/5 (62, 27);
Carlisle United 85/6 (10, 2); Newport County *on loan* 85/6 (3, 1);
Blackpool 86/7 (13, 6).

1980/81-1982/83

STEVE FRANCIS

Steve Francis seemed to have a long and distinguished career at Stamford Bridge ahead of him when he became Chelsea's first-choice 'keeper at the age of 17. He had shown remarkable maturity on his debut in a League Cup tie at Southampton and John Neal had no hesitation in turning to him a few weeks later when his patience with Petar Borota's erratic displays became exhausted. The youngster performed with impressive consistency and his exemplary handling indicated an exceptional natural talent.

However, Steve was a quiet, reserved lad and his lack of assertiveness on the pitch hindered his progress. The following season was a demoralising one for the Blues and, with the team slipping down the table, the young 'keeper's confidence was gradually eroded. After making 73 consecutive appearances he was replaced, albeit briefly, by Bob Iles, and that summer Eddie Niedzwiecki was recruited from Wrexham.

Francis now found himself in the role of understudy, but when the Welshman suffered a serious injury in March 1986 he failed to make the most of his opportunity, conceding 14 goals in four games (four of them in the Full Members' Cup final). That misfortune prompted John Hollins to look elsewhere, but Steve has enjoyed better luck since moving to Reading in February 1987.

BORN: Billericay, 29.5.64.
GAMES: 88. GOALS: 0.
HONOURS: Full Members' Cup 85/6.
OTHER CLUBS: Reading 86/7-92/3 (216, 0);
Huddersfield Town 93/4- (183, 0).

1981/82-1985/86

DENNIS ROFE

Dennis Rofe was a perky, lively character with a huge amount of experience and it was these qualities as much as his ability as a left-back that prompted Geoff Hurst to sign him from Leicester City in February 1980 in an effort to consolidate Chelsea's promotion challenge. Aggressive and determined, the 29-year-old defender was a good organiser with a professional attitude to the game that some of his colleagues appeared to lack, and Hurst acknowledged the value of his influence by making him captain the following season.

By this stage of his career Rofe was perhaps a little short of pace, but he remained a rugged tackler with a good left foot who attacked enterprisingly. It took him a while to settle at Stamford Bridge, but towards the end of the 1980/81 campaign he began to produce the sort of form that had made him such a respected performer for more than a decade, with a polished display at home to Bolton standing out.

Dennis made 54 successive appearances after his arrival but when he limped out of a match against Charlton in September 1981 with a groin injury, his tenure in the first team was effectively at an end. He was unable to regain his place from Chris Hutchings and that summer he was allowed to move on to Southampton, where he subsequently embarked on a coaching career.

BORN: Epping, 1.6.50.
GAMES: 61 (2). GOALS: 0.
OTHER CLUBS: Leyton Orient 67/8-72/3 (171, 6);
Leicester City 72/3-79/80 (290, 6);
Southampton 82/3-83/4 (20, 0).
MANAGER: Bristol Rovers (92).

1979/80-1981/82

TOMMY LANGLEY

If international caps were awarded solely on the basis of effort and determination, Tommy Langley would have ended up with a cupboardful. However, the hard-working striker had the misfortune to establish himself in the Chelsea first team just as the Blues were setting out on what would prove to be a demoralising two-year stay in the First Division, and although he continued to show the boyish enthusiasm which had endeared him to the fans when he made his League debut as a bustling 16-year-old in November 1974, his game did not develop sufficiently for him to make a lasting impression at the highest level.

The England youth international had to wait until the closing weeks of the 1976/77 campaign before he was given much of a run in the team, replacing Ken Swain as Steve Finnieston's partner. He proved himself by running onto Ray Wilkins's pass at Molineux and shooting home off a post to clinch promotion, and was a regular the following season, emerging as top scorer with 13 goals from 46 appearances. The spirited youngster put the seemingly limitless energy that had earned him the nickname 'Lungs' to good use, constantly chasing lost causes and harrying defenders, but the highlights of his season were a splendid goal in a League victory over Liverpool at the Bridge and a hat-trick in a 5-4 win against Birmingham.

Tommy invariably put everything he had into his football – not least when acting as emergency 'keeper – and his eagerness meant that his finishing was not always as clinical as it might have been, but despite not being a great header of the ball he claimed more than a third of the meagre total of 44 League goals the Blues managed as they finished bottom of the table in 1978/79.

However, there were signs during the valiant promotion chase the following winter that he had ceased to make progress, tireless grafting almost becoming an end in itself, and in August 1980 he decided to switch to Queens Park Rangers. Geoff Hurst was sorry to see him go and the fee of £425,000 was an indication of the reputation he had built up, but he was unable to rediscover the momentum he had lost and became one of football's wanderers.

BORN: Lambeth, 8.2.58.
GAMES: 139 (13). GOALS: 43.
OTHER CLUBS: Queens Park Rangers 80/1 (25, 8);
Crystal Palace 80/1-82/3 (59, 8); AEK Athens; Coventry City 83/4 (2, 0);
Wolverhampton Wanderers 84/5 (23, 4); Aldershot *on loan* 84/5 (16, 4);
South China, Hong Kong; Aldershot 86/7-87/8 (81, 21); Exeter City 88/9 (21, 2).

1974/75-1979/80

PETER RHOADES-BROWN

Peter Rhoades-Brown was most effective when operating as a traditional left-winger and it was in this role that he first established himself in the side in the autumn of 1980. His pace and good close control usually enabled him to get the better of his marker and his accurate centres produced a stream of goals such as Colin Lee's equaliser against Preston at Stamford Bridge and Mike Fillery's diving header at Bolton. However, the youngster was unable to maintain this sparkling standard in the second half of the season as the Blues mysteriously forgot how to score.

When John Neal took over in the manager's office he asked 'PRB' to drop back into midfield. He was now expected to shuttle up and down the left flank, denying opponents space, but it was a game that was alien to him. He had plenty of stamina and had succeeded in making himself more aggressive, but he was not a natural defender and all too often his efforts to win the ball ended in clumsy or ill-timed tackles that incurred the referee's displeasure.

Peter was never able to achieve consistency and his crossing, in particular, tended to be erratic – perhaps because his evident enthusiasm was inclined to get the better of him. His finishing was also disappointing, but Chelsea fans will never forget his goal in a fifth round FA Cup tie against Liverpool when he ran with the ball from the halfway line before shooting coolly past Bruce Grobbelaar.

Hard-working and dependable, Rhoades-Brown appeared to lose confidence in his talent, and when the arrival of Mickey Thomas in January 1984 virtually ended his chances of regular first-team football he was allowed to move to Oxford. He played his part in his new club's climb from the Third Division to the First, but sadly fitness problems brought this popular player's career to a premature end.

BORN: Hampton, 2.1.62.
GAMES: 97 (12). GOALS: 5.
OTHER CLUBS: Oxford United 83/4-88/9 (112, 13).

1979/80-1983/84

CHRIS HUTCHINGS

Chris Hutchings was working as a bricklayer when
Geoff Hurst brought him to Stamford Bridge from Harrow
Borough of the Berger Isthmian League in July 1980. The 23-
year-old made a handful of appearances in midfield that season,
scoring the winning goal on his League debut at Cardiff in
October eight minutes after replacing the injured Mike Fillery,
but his real opportunity came when Dennis Rofe succumbed to
a groin injury against Charlton the following September.
Chris took over at left-back for the visit of Norwich the
following Saturday and quickly made the position his own.

This was a difficult period for the Blues, the heroic fifth round
FA Cup win against Liverpool in 1982 providing the only relief
from the prevailing gloom, but Hutchings performed with
admirable consistency in unpromising circumstances.
A conscientious defender who used the ball sensibly and enjoyed
getting forward at every opportunity, he was a member of John
Neal's rebuilt team at the start of 1983/84, scoring against Derby
on the opening day, but was unable to regain his place from
Joey Jones after dropping out with a head injury. In November
he was allowed to join Brighton, but he had proved himself as a
League player and can have had few regrets about his
decision to lay aside the pointing trowel.

BORN: Winchester, 5.7.57.
GAMES: 97 (4). GOALS: 3.
OTHER CLUBS: Brighton and Hove Albion 83/4-87/8 (153, 4);
Huddersfield Town 87/8-89/90 (110, 10); Walsall 90/1 (40, 0);
Rotherham United 91/2-93/4 (78, 4).

1980/81-1983/84

KEVIN HALES

After making eight first-team appearances in 1979/80,
Kevin Hales was in the wilderness for more than a year before
John Neal restored him to the starting line-up in November
1981. Second chances are no more common in football than
they are elsewhere, and the 20-year-old midfielder did not waste
his opportunity to persuade the new manager he deserved a
regular place. In 14 appearances he was on the losing side only
once, and his industrious and enthusiastic displays on the right
flank – typified by a home game against Sheffield Wednesday
in which he scored a splendid goal – made a significant
contribution to a marked improvement in the Blues' results
which saw them reach the FA Cup quarter-finals.

Small and slight, Hales occasionally appeared a little
lightweight and may have lacked the sharpness to thrive at the
highest level, but he was developing into a neat and reliable
performer when his progress was cruelly interrupted by a serious
knee injury sustained at Barnsley in March. He fought
back courageously and returned to the side the following
January, but the confidence that had been forming the previous
season had inevitably disappeared. That summer he moved
on to Orient and gave the East London club dependable
service for a decade.

BORN: Dartford, 13.1.61.
GAMES: 25 (2). GOALS: 2.
OTHER CLUBS: Leyton Orient 83/4-92/3 (300, 23).

1979/80-1982/83

BRYAN ROBSON

The signing of 'Pop' Robson from Carlisle in August 1982 marked the beginning of the extensive rebuilding that was clearly essential if the Blues were to regain what their supporters regarded as their rightful place among the country's leading clubs. The hugely experienced striker had been a consistent goalscorer throughout a long and eventful career, but at the age of 36 his best days as a player were inevitably behind him. However, while his stay in the Chelsea first team seemed likely to be a short one, John Neal was confident that the example of his professionalism would help transform the spirit at the club.

Robson demonstrated the value of his cool finishing with an 87th-minute winner in the first match of the season at Cambridge but was unable to reproduce the neat, busy football which, together with his predator's eye for goal, had made him a popular hero at Newcastle and West Ham. In mid-September 'Pop' gave way to David Speedie and he made only a handful of appearances thereafter, a foot injury restricting his chances. After rejoining Carlisle on loan for a spell he was transferred to Sunderland in the summer, having failed to make the impact at Stamford Bridge that Neal had hoped for.

BORN: Sunderland, 11.11.45. GAMES: 12 (5). GOALS: 5.
OTHER CLUBS: Newcastle United 64/5-70/1 (206, 82);
West Ham United 70/1-73/4 (120, 47) and 76/7-78/9 (107, 47);
Sunderland 74/5-76/7 (90, 34), 79/80-80/1 (52, 23)
and 83/4 (12, 3); Carlisle United 80/1-81/2 (48, 21)
and 84/5-85/6 (13, 1); Carlisle United *on loan* 82/3 (11, 4).

1982/83

PAUL CANOVILLE

When he was in the mood, Paul Canoville could transform a game. That was never seen more clearly than in the fifth round Milk Cup replay at Hillsborough in January 1985, when he came on for the injured Colin Lee at half-time with the Blues three goals down and inspired an irresistible fight-back. The tall, leggy winger scored with his first touch, after about ten seconds, and his second goal appeared to have put Chelsea into the semi-finals, only for Wednesday to make it 4-4 from the penalty spot in the dying seconds.

A natural athlete with pace and great stamina, Canoville demonstrated his rich potential during the desperate battle against relegation in the closing weeks of 1982/83 and looked set to build on the foothold he had gained in the side the following season. His exciting, unpredictable style soon had the morons who had jeered him when he first appeared in the team singing his praises, but he was infuriatingly inconsistent and a hat-trick against Swansea ironically served as a reminder that his finishing generally lacked composure.

The arrival of Mickey Thomas in January blocked Paul's progress and thereafter his exuberant skills were seen to best effect when he was used as a substitute. In August 1986 he was transferred to Reading, having started just five matches the previous season, but injury sadly prevented him from proving his worth at Elm Park.

BORN: Hillingdon, 4.3.62. GAMES: 67 (36). GOALS: 15.
OTHER CLUBS: Reading 86/7-87/8 (16, 4).

1981/82-1985/86

MIKE FILLERY

Nothing is more certain to promote groans among the devotees of pure football than the tendency of some League managers to stress the importance of 'commitment', 'effort' and 'competitiveness', while omitting to mention the desirability of being able to pass the ball to a player wearing the same colour shirt; but it cannot be denied that if Mike Fillery had possessed these mundane qualities in greater abundance, his outstanding natural talent would have made him one of the most highly regarded creative midfield players in the country. Instead, dispiritingly, his gifts were largely wasted.

Fillery's nonchalant, languid manner infuriated those members of the dwindling Stamford Bridge crowd who had never learned to appreciate the finer things in life and even his most devoted admirers were regularly driven to despair by his dis-appearance for long periods from games that his ability should have allowed him to dominate. He was an established member of the Chelsea first team for four seasons, having had his first taste of senior football during the closing weeks of the wretched drift towards relegation in 1978/79, but consistency proved elusive. The hurly-burly of Second Division football was scarcely suited to his champagne style but, like his friend Gary Chivers, he appeared to lack drive and motivation.

Mike's cultured left foot was capable of great delicacy, the superb swerving free-kick that gave the Blues the lead in the sixth round FA Cup tie against Spurs in March 1982 being the best-remembered example, but could also hit the ball with startling power, as a screaming 35-yard match-winner at Orient in 1980/81 confirmed. In addition, the stylish midfielder had good close control and used possession intelligently, while his healthy scoring record included a number of well-judged headers.

John Neal kept faith with Fillery even when his influence declined alarmingly during the miserable 1982/83 season, but that summer he was transferred to Queens Park Rangers, where he impressed for a while before his career once again appeared to run out of steam, partly as a result of fitness problems.

BORN: Mitcham, 17.9.60.
GAMES: 176 (5). GOALS: 41.
OTHER CLUBS: Queens Park Rangers 83/4-86/7 (97, 9);
Portsmouth 87/8-90/1 (67, 6); Oldham Athletic 90/1 (2, 0); Millwall *on loan* 90/1 (1, 0);
Torquay United *on loan* 91/2 (4, 0).

1978/79-1982/83

TONY McANDREW

Tony McAndrew's Chelsea career was wrecked by injury when it had scarcely begun. A robust, combative midfielder who could also play in the centre of the defence, he had been John Neal's captain at Middlesbrough and was brought to Stamford Bridge in September 1982 to add resilience and determination to a side conspicuously lacking those fundamental qualities. However, after he had made just nine appearances he was laid low by a nasty back problem which required surgery.

During a lengthy and painful fight to regain fitness Tony demonstrated the courage and professionalism that Neal had hoped would benefit the club on the field, but at the start of the following season he was unable to force his way into the dramatically reconstructed side. He was recalled in December and when John Hollins stood down he took over as captain, which suggested that Neal felt he still had a major contribution to make, but he was unable to recapture his old drive, the injury appearing to have taken its toll on his mobility.

McAndrew demonstrated the value of experience by assuming the role of penalty-taker, coolly solving what had become an exasperating problem, but when everyone was fit he returned to the sidelines and the following September he returned to Ayresome Park as part of the deal that brought Darren Wood to London.

BORN: Glasgow, 11.4.56.
GAMES: 23. GOALS: 4.
OTHER CLUBS: Middlesbrough 73/4-81/2 (247, 13) and 84/5-85/6 (66, 2);
Darlington 88/9 (11, 0); Hartlepool United 88/9 (4, 0).

1982/83-1983/84

GORDON DAVIES

Gordon Davies was a schoolteacher until he joined Fulham from Merthyr Tydfil, but in his six full seasons at Craven Cottage he earned a reputation as an outstanding marksman. Then in November 1984 Chelsea gave him the chance he had been waiting for to prove himself in the First Division.

'Ivor' knew that he would not find it easy to force his way into the team, but he was given an early opportunity to stake his claim when David Speedie missed three games through suspension shortly after his arrival. Judged purely as a goalscorer, Davies could scarcely have done better, heading home a Pat Nevin cross on his debut at Hillsborough and following that up two weeks later with a hat-trick in a 4-3 win at Goodison that was a model of cool finishing.

Small and quick, Gordon was an opportunist who tended to disappear from games until a half-chance came along, and in terms of overall contribution to the team he could not replace Speedie, who returned to the starting line-up after two games on the bench. There were further openings for the cheerful Welsh international later in the season when 'Speedo' was again absent through suspension, but he was never more than an understudy and the following October, now aged 30, he decided to make a fresh start with Manchester City.

BORN: Merthyr Tydfil, 8.8.55.
GAMES: 13 (2). GOALS: 6.
HONOURS: 16 Wales caps (79-86).
OTHER CLUBS: Fulham 77/8-84/5 (247, 114) and 86/7-90/1 (147, 45); Manchester City 85/6-86/7 (31, 9);
Wrexham 91/2 (22, 4). MANAGER: Tornado, Norway.

1984/85-1985/86

JOEY JONES

The arrival of Joey Jones from Wrexham in October 1982 did much to disperse the dark clouds that had gathered over Stamford Bridge. Fans who had lost all hope that the club would ever shake off the shabby mediocrity that had engulfed it found themselves cheering enthusiastically in response to the effervescent Welsh international's defiant clenched fist or cheery thumbs-up. His positive attitude lifted spirits in the dressing room in equally dramatic fashion and by the end of the season a team which had seemed to be prostrated by self-pity had summoned sufficient pride to scramble clear of relegation. It was exactly the response John Neal had hoped for when he signed the former Liverpool full-back, whose career he had launched during his time in charge at the Racecourse Ground.

Although Jones had quickly become Chelsea's first-choice number two, it had taken him some time to discover his touch. He could not be described as a polished defender and his distribution was often disappointing, but his uncompromising tackling, total commitment and refusal to concede the possibility of defeat until the final whistle ensured that he was adored by the lads in the Shed, who came to think of him as one of their own. The following season Joey switched to the left and played a leading part in Chelsea's successful pursuit of the Second Division Championship, but the signing of Doug Rougvie that summer relegated him to the role of understudy. He made a total of 21 appearances in all four defensive positions in 1984/85, but when John Hollins became manager it was decided that the absences from training that were the inevitable consequence of Joey's reluctance to move to the southeast were no longer acceptable. In August 1985 he was sold to Huddersfield, to the regret of all those who remembered the part he had played in inspiring Chelsea's revival.

BORN: Llandudno, 4.3.55.
GAMES: 89 (2). GOALS: 2.
HONOURS: Second Division Championship 83/4. 72 Wales caps (75-86).
OTHER CLUBS: Wrexham 72/3-74/5 (98, 2), 78/9-82/3 (146, 6) and 87/8-91/2 (132, 11);
Liverpool 75/6-77/8 (72, 3); Huddersfield Town 85/6-86/7 (68, 3).

1982/83-1984/85

COLIN PATES

When it was revealed in October 1988 that Colin Pates had moved to Charlton on loan with a view to a permanent transfer, many Chelsea fans greeted the news with disbelief. Although he was only 27, the polished defender had come to seem an indispensable part of the Stamford Bridge scene over the previous nine years. Changes to the playing staff during that period had been as unceasing as alterations to the club's change strip, but Pates had survived the repeated purges and it had somehow been taken for granted that he would remain with the Blues for the rest of his career.

Colin made his first-team debut as a gangling 18-year-old centre-half in a remarkable 7-3 win at Orient in November 1979 and Micky Droy's frequent absences through injury meant that he had plenty of opportunity to demonstrate his ability over the next couple of seasons, but he was not really sufficiently dominant when the ball was in the air to develop into a top-class number five. The appointment of John Neal prompted an upturn in the youngster's fortunes and he played in every League game in 1981/82, establishing himself as Droy's regular partner at the back before moving forward into midfield in the second half of the season when a spate of serious injuries depleted the squad.

As Neal acknowledged, Pates had by no means been born to the role, as he lacked mobility and his distribution was no more than adequate, but he threw himself into the task in characteristically wholehearted style, and was one of the few players to emerge with credit from the Blues' inglorious struggle to stave off relegation to Division Three the following season, invariably giving his all whatever position he was asked to fill.

Colin's efforts were sufficient to earn him a place alongside Joe McLaughlin in the centre of the defence when Neal's dramatically reshaped team was revealed at the start of the next campaign and they proved to be a well-matched pair, the Scot dealing with most of the high balls while Pates, more composed and rather more constructive, tidied up the loose ends. They provided a solid foundation for the Blues' successful assault on the Second Division Championship, steadily gaining confidence and conceding less than a goal a game.

Although he was one of the youngest members of the side, 'Sharky' was handed the captaincy towards the end of the season and seemed to thrive on the additional responsibility, producing a series of assured, authoritative displays as the club chased honours over the next two years. Calm and professional yet aggressive in the tackle, Colin had matured into a solid, reliable defender who read the game well and used the ball thoughtfully whenever circumstances permitted, his commanding display in a 3-1 win against Liverpool in December 1984 confirming that he had become one of the best young centre-backs in the country.

However, disharmony in the dressing room was beginning to undermine the Blues' performances and, after an unhappy season during which he had had to overcome a challenge for his place from new signing Steve Wicks, Colin surrendered the skipper's armband at the beginning of 1987/88. A cartilage operation sidelined him until mid-October and he managed only 17 League appearances that season, although he was recalled for the vital game against Charlton and the tense play-off matches.

At the start of the new season Pates was back in favour and, with Joe McLaughlin out of the side, he became established as Graham Roberts's partner in the middle of the back four. But then came the phone call from Charlton manager Lennie Lawrence and Bobby Campbell's unexpected decision to accept his offer of £400,000 for a player who still had a lot to offer at Stamford Bridge . . .

BORN: Carshalton, 10.8.61.
GAMES: 345 (1). GOALS: 10.
HONOURS: Second Division Championship 83/4; Full Members' Cup 85/6.
OTHER CLUBS: Charlton Athletic 88/9-89/90 (38, 0);
Arsenal 89/90-92/3 (21, 0);
Brighton and Hove Albion *on loan* 90/1 (17, 0);
Brighton and Hove Albion 93/4-94/5 (50, 0).

1979/80-1988/89

DOUG ROUGVIE

During eight seasons with Aberdeen Doug Rougvie had won two Scottish League Championship medals, three Scottish Cup winner's medals and a Scottish cap, and had been a member of the European Cup-Winners' Cup-winning side in 1983, so when he joined Chelsea in a £150,000 deal in August 1984 there seemed to be no doubt about his class. The 28-year-old defender had been signed to replace Joey Jones at left-back and his arrival was regarded as an indication that the Blues would not be content simply to make up the numbers in the First Division.

Ferocious in the tackle and strong in the air, Dougie soon took over the Welshman's role as the Stamford Bridge folk-hero, his rampaging style endearing him to the fans. He was a robust, battling player, quick to lose his temper but with an equally ready smile, who always seemed to bring passion and enthusiasm to his football. However, his performances during his three years with the Blues were disappointing, his impulsiveness making him vulnerable whenever forwards ran at him with the ball, a weakness that became painfully apparent at White Hart Lane that November when Tottenham's elusive winger, John Chiedozie, tormented him mercilessly.

Dougie seemed to be unable to adapt to the demands of English football and in the second half of the season he was displaced by Keith Dublin. Although he fought his way back into the side at the beginning of 1985/86, he then lost his place once again and was rarely a first choice thereafter. However, he proved a valuable stand-in, his height making him particularly effective when taking the place of one of the regular centre-backs, and he performed with his usual commitment whenever called upon. Nevertheless it was clear that he had no part to play in John Hollins's long-term plans and in the summer of 1987 he was transferred to Brighton.

BORN: Ballingry, 24.5.56.
GAMES: 100. GOALS: 3.
HONOURS: Full Members' Cup 85/6. 1 Scotland cap (83).
OTHER CLUBS: Aberdeen; Brighton and Hove Albion 87/8 (35, 2);
Shrewsbury Town 88/9 (21, 3); Fulham 88/9 (18, 1);
Dunfermline Athletic.

1984/85-1986/87

COLIN LEE

Once Bill Garner had dropped out of the first-team reckoning, Chelsea found themselves without a big, traditional centre-forward and it was to rectify this weakness in his promotion-chasing squad that Geoff Hurst signed Colin Lee from Tottenham in January 1980. The athletic striker was prevented from making an immediate impact by a persistent hamstring problem but the first few months of the following season saw Lee at his most effective. By the end of November he had scored no fewer than 14 times, his ability 'upstairs' ensuring that the service provided from the flanks was turned into goals, but that golden spell was forgotten when the Blues failed to find the net in all but three of their last 22 League matches.

John Neal's wholesale rebuilding in the summer of 1983 gave new impetus to Lee's career and, in his role as the link between the attack and midfield, he showed skill and subtlety as well as strength. A stirring 5-3 win at Fulham demonstrated the potential of his partnership with Kerry Dixon, but illness unluckily cost Colin his place and in his absence David Speedie established himself as the rampaging number nine's provider.

Wholehearted and professional, Lee fought back from this setback by slotting in at right-back when John Hollins bowed out; his power in the air and composure made a major contribution to Chelsea's march to the Second Division Championship, but the arrival of Darren Wood that autumn cast renewed doubt over his future. A series of niggling injuries hampered Colin over the next couple of years and he was rarely certain of a first-team place. Two goals when standing in for Dixon in the 1986 Full Members' Cup final and a match-winning pass to Colin West against Arsenal the following season confirmed that the talent was still there but his troublesome hamstrings were continuing to bother him and in July 1987 he moved to Brentford to pursue his interest in coaching.

BORN: Torquay, 12.6.56.
GAMES: 200 (23). GOALS: 41.
HONOURS: Second Division Championship 83/4; Full Members' Cup 85/6.
OTHER CLUBS: Bristol City; Hereford United *on loan* 74/5 (9, 0);
Torquay United 76/7-77/8 (35, 14); Tottenham Hotspur 77/8-79/80 (62, 18); Brentford 87/8-88/9 (24, 1).
MANAGER: Watford (90).

1979/80-1986/87

JOHN BUMSTEAD

For thirteen seasons a succession of Chelsea managers knew that they could rely on John Bumstead to do a solid job of work for them. The embodiment of selfless professionalism, the industrious midfielder would produce the same performance, week in, week out, with the consistency of a carefully maintained machine – totally dependable, and therefore easily taken for granted.

A career dedicated to stifling the talents of more gifted players began when John was given his first-team debut at Leeds in November 1978, the tenacious 19-year-old rarely straying more than a couple of yards from the side of Tony Currie throughout the game. It was a difficult time for a youngster to try and make his mark: Chelsea were second from bottom in the First Division and within weeks Ken Shellito had been replaced as manager by Danny Blanchflower. The following season Geoff Hurst succeeded the amiable Ulsterman and under his tutelage John's career blossomed. He was quite outstanding as the Blues mounted an exciting promotion charge but a tackle from behind against Shrewsbury in February left him with a dislocated ankle, and during his ten-week absence the Blues' assault faltered.

It took Bumstead a long time to recover his bite but his battling displays during John Neal's first two seasons at Stamford Bridge confirmed that the dogged Londoner possessed the sort of spirit that was going to be needed if Chelsea were to restore their faded fortunes. A quiet, modest man who carried out the task assigned to him without fuss and seemingly without emotion, John was a highly effective destroyer, as difficult to shake off as a dog with its jaws clamped round a postman's leg, but there was more to his game than that. He passed the ball tidily and made a valuable contribution as a goalscorer, a stunning 35-yard drive at the Valley in November 1981 demonstrating that he had a superb shot which he used all too rarely.

When Neal's reconstructed side was revealed at the start of 1983/84, John was paired with Nigel Spackman in the engine room and performed with his usual understated efficiency, although a number of well-struck goals from free-kicks ensured that his efforts were not totally overlooked. When back trouble sidelined him for a month he had difficulty dislodging Tony McAndrew, but he was recalled towards the end of the campaign and shared in the Blues' thrilling Championship triumph.

Bumstead's committed style meant he collected injuries with disheartening regularity but he remained a member of Chelsea's first-choice line-up until 1988/89, when it seemed that he might be leaving Stamford Bridge. However, the departure of Darren Wood gave him the chance to reclaim his place and he had the satisfaction of scoring the goal against Leeds that clinched another Second Division Championship medal, turning the ball past Mervyn Day from close range after good work by Kerry Dixon.

John started the following season on the substitute's bench – his ability to fill in at right-back or in the middle of the defence made him a useful player to have in reserve – but once again he fought back to prove that the passing years had not diminished his effectiveness. He made only a handful of appearances in 1990/91, but when Aston Villa visited the Bridge in November he shackled David Platt in the same relentless style that he had subdued Tony Currie more than a decade earlier. At the end of the campaign, with his 33rd birthday in sight, this unassuming and highly regarded professional was given a free transfer and joined Charlton, serving the Valiants dependably for two years before back problems forced his retirement in 1993.

BORN: Rotherhithe, 27.11.58.
GAMES: 379 (30). GOALS: 44.
HONOURS: Second Division Championship 83/4, 88/9;
Full Members' Cup 85/6, 89/90.
OTHER CLUBS: Charlton Athletic 91/2-92/3 (56, 3).

1978/79-1990/91

MICKEY THOMAS

For the match at Derby on 14 January 1984 John Neal made two changes to his side which transformed Chelsea from exciting but unpredictable promotion hopefuls into worthy Second Division Champions: Colin Lee came in for John Hollins at right-back; and, decisively, Mickey Thomas, who had recently arrived from Stoke City, took over the number eleven shirt from the orthodox left-wingers who had previously occupied it. A player of prodigious energy and boundless enthusiasm, the 29-year-old Welsh international did the work of two men, combining the roles of industrious midfielder and enterprising outside-left in one all-action package, and the Blues remained undefeated for the rest of the season.

Since his departure from Old Trafford in August 1981, Thomas had somehow lost his way and his reputation had inevitably suffered, but during his season and a half in the Chelsea team he was a model of consistency, becoming a favourite of the fans, just as John Neal (who had guided his career in its formative years at Wrexham) had predicted. He made an immediate impact with an influential performance and two well-taken goals on his home debut against the leaders, Sheffield Wednesday, and continued to play a leading role in the Stamford Bridge revival the following season, despite some bad luck with injuries. Once again Mickey responded to the challenge presented by the Owls' combative style, this time in the Milk Cup, and his irresistible displays in the three matches needed to settle the tie typified the indomitable spirit that carried the Blues into the semi-finals.

When John Hollins succeeded Neal that summer he signed Jerry Murphy, followed a few weeks later by Mick Hazard. Thomas, who missed the start of the season with a broken jaw, evidently had no place in his vision of the club's future and was sold to West Bromwich Albion in September – to the dismay of those who had taken the mercurial Welshman to their hearts.

BORN: Newtown, 7.7.54.
GAMES: 53 (1). GOALS: 11.
HONOURS: Second Division Championship 83/4. 51 Wales caps (76-86).
OTHER CLUBS: Wrexham 71/2-78/9 (230, 33) and 91/2-92/3 (34, 2); Manchester United 78/9-80/1 (90, 11); Everton 81/2 (10, 0); Brighton and Hove Albion 81/2 (20, 0); Stoke City 82/3-83/4 (57, 14) and 89/90-90/1 (46, 7); West Bromwich Albion 85/6 (20, 0); Derby County *on loan* 85/6 (9, 0); Wichita Wings; Shrewsbury Town 88/9 (40, 1); Leeds United 89/90 (3, 0).

1983/84-1984/85

EDDIE NIEDZWIECKI

If a team is to achieve sustained success, a dependable goalkeeper is essential. The signing of Eddie Niedzwiecki from Third Division Wrexham in June 1983 played an important part in Chelsea's return to the limelight over the next three years and the injury which tragically cut short his career was surely one reason the Blues' sojourn in the First Division proved to be surprisingly brief.

The Welshman with the Polish name grew in confidence during his first season at Stamford Bridge and was soon dominating his penalty area, coming for crosses with authority and calling decisively, but it was his bravery and agility that made Niedzwiecki exceptional. Both were called upon in a Milk Cup replay at Craven Cottage in November 1985: Fulham deserved to win comfortably but he stopped everything that was thrown at him and a Dixon goal at the other end was enough to put Chelsea through.

Only the brilliance of Everton's Neville Southall prevented Eddie winning a string of Welsh caps before the fateful night in March 1986 when his left knee was badly damaged in a League game against Queens Park Rangers. Major surgery was required but he battled his way back to fitness with characteristic courage and returned to League action at Aston Villa in November. He was not able to move with his old freedom, however, and after a dozen more appearances he was back in hospital. He returned to the side at the start of the following season and seemed to be approaching his best when the knee let him down once again against Oxford in October. This time there was to be no comeback.

Eddie faced his new challenge with the determination that had made him so popular with Chelsea's supporters and threw himself into a career in management. After a season and a half learning the trade in charge of the Blues' youth side he moved to Reading as Ian Porterfield's assistant, and returned to Stamford Bridge when the Scot succeeded Bobby Campbell in 1991. He has become a valued member of the Blues' management team, and is currently the club's specialist goalkeeping coach.

BORN: Bangor, 3.5.59.
GAMES: 175. GOALS: 0.
HONOURS: Second Division Championship 83/4.
2 Wales caps (85-87).
OTHER CLUBS: Wrexham 77/8-82/3 (111, 0).

1983/84-1987/88

DAVID SPEEDIE

A fire burned within David Speedie that made him abrasive, argumentative – and a player of rare inspiration. He had come up the hard way, earning his living at the bottom of a coal mine for ten months before Barnsley gave him a contract, and the ferocity with which the little striker celebrated his goals gave the impression that he had a point to prove to those who had doubted him as a youngster. A relentless competitor, he thrived on conflict, and his unfailing belligerence made him a hero of the Stamford Bridge crowd, which was still chanting his name with affection when he returned with Coventry City more than three years after his departure.

Signed by John Neal from Darlington for £80,000 in May 1982, Speedie won a regular first-team place after scoring twice on his debut against Oldham in September, his courage and tenacity bringing some much-needed zest to a team chronically short of confidence. He found himself relegated to the bench when Neal's rebuilt side was unveiled at the start of the following season, but he seized the opportunity presented by an illness which sidelined Colin Lee with characteristic determination, and rapidly became a pivotal member of the side which won the Second Division Championship in electrifying style and went on to challenge for further honours over the next two years.

Although he was only 5ft 6½in tall, 'Speedo' was an outstanding header of the ball, his timing and sheer ebullience enabling him to outjump defenders who towered over him. The first of his three goals in the Full Members' Cup final against Manchester City at Wembley in 1986 was typical, but in general his finishing lacked the ruthlessness expected of a top marksman. Always eager to get behind the defence, Dave was caught offside with frustrating regularity and when he did succeed in breaking clear with only the goalkeeper to beat he often appeared indecisive; but he could be highly effective at close range, as he demonstrated when he coolly lobbed a last-minute equaliser past Arsenal's John Lukic at Stamford Bridge in January 1985.

A dependable target man, Speedie frequently dropped back into midfield to find space and much of his best work was done there, shielding the ball, turning and laying it precisely into the path of Mickey Thomas or Pat Nevin as they surged towards goal. He supplied Kerry Dixon with many of his openings and they came to be regarded as one of the most dangerous pairings in English football, Dixon's speed and strength complementing his partner's fine close control and eye for a penetrating through-ball.

Never one to keep his feelings to himself, Dave reacted venomously if an opponent was so rash as to try to intimidate him, and team-mates who failed to deliver the ball in the way he required could expect to receive a tongue-lashing, as could referees whose interpretation of incidents on the field was at variance with the fiery Yorkshireman's. His ceaseless aggression earned him a string of bookings, and as a consequence he was regularly unavailable for selection, which did little to endear him to his employers . . .

The industrious striker won his first international cap for Scotland in May 1985 but the rich promise the Blues had shown since their return to the First Division was to remain unfulfilled. Amid the turmoil that engulfed the club in 1986/87, Speedie's form slumped and it seemed that, once again, Chelsea had found it impossible to sustain a working relationship with a volatile but enormously gifted player. He made just 22 League appearances that season and was sold to Coventry City for £750,000 in July, subsequently moving to Liverpool in February 1991 to add a little zip to the Anfield giants' annual title challenge.

BORN: Glenrothes, 20.2.60.
GAMES: 197 (8). GOALS: 64.
HONOURS: Second Division Championship 83/4; Full Members' Cup 85/6.
10 Scotland caps (85-89).
OTHER CLUBS: Barnsley 78/9-79/80 (23, 0); Darlington 80/1-81/2 (88, 21);
Coventry City 87/8-90/1 (122, 31); Liverpool 90/1 (12, 6);
Blackburn Rovers 91/2 (36, 23); Southampton 92/3 (11, 0);
Birmingham City *on loan* 92/3 (10, 2); West Bromwich Albion *on loan* 92/3 (7, 2);
West Ham United *on loan* 92/3 (11, 4); Leicester City 93/4 (37, 12).

1982/83-1986/87

KERRY DIXON

There were times when Kerry Dixon looked pedestrian, even lethargic, but when he had the goal in his sights he was instantly transformed. A superbly athletic striker, he seemed to live for the satisfaction of putting the ball in the net and his dashing exploits inevitably made him the hero of the Stamford Bridge faithful.

Kerry was signed from Reading in August 1983 as part of John Neal's extensive rebuilding plans and began to repay the £175,000 fee at once with two goals on the opening day of the season. He would never be the most elegant of players and at first he looked a little cumbersome, but he finished the campaign as the Second Division's leading scorer.

The big number nine was fortunate that the players around him complemented his single-minded style so well. He was majestic in the air and thrived on a seemingly unending supply of inch-perfect crosses from Pat Nevin on the right flank, like the one from which he headed the goal at Grimsby that clinched the Championship. However, his greatest asset was his blistering pace, and he quickly established a partnership with David Speedie that was to become one of the most respected in the country, the fiery Yorkshireman's selfless work ensuring that his partner had plenty of enticing through-balls to run onto. Strange as it might seem, Dixon was not an outstanding finisher – his record from the penalty spot was abysmal – but his splendid anticipation meant that he could afford to be profligate.

Kerry earned his first full international caps during the summer tour of North America in 1985, but his career suffered a major blow when he sustained torn stomach muscles in a fourth round FA Cup tie against Liverpool the following January. He missed only a handful of matches but he was hampered by the injury for some time and many observers concluded that it must have had a permanent effect on him since he was never to find goals so easy to come by again. However, it should be remembered that the exciting team Neal had assembled was starting to disintegrate, with the result that Kerry was no longer getting the reliable service he needed.

Two splendid goals at Old Trafford earned Dixon a place in the England party for the 1986 World Cup, but the next two seasons proved largely frustrating and in the early part of 1988 it seemed that he was likely to join Arsenal or West Ham in a £1 million transfer. In the event he stayed at Stamford Bridge and his 25 goals were a major factor in the Blues' storming Second Division Championship triumph in 1988/89.

Dixon had never been a player who wasted too much energy chasing hopeless causes but under the influence of Bobby Campbell his game developed and he became much more of a creator, using his pace and enormously improved close control to go past defenders on the flanks. His overall contribution was greater than ever but his effectiveness as a marksman was inevitably compromised. He scored regularly on the Blues' return to the First Division, but over the next couple of years the flow gradually dried up once more. The electrifying pace had begun to fade and once again the supply of ammunition was fitful at best. It was clear that a move would be in the interests of all concerned and in July 1992 Dixon was transferred to Southampton for £575,000. Bobby Tambling's scoring record which had been his target for so long would remain unbroken, but Kerry left behind him a store of golden memories which Chelsea fans will cherish for many years to come.

BORN: Luton, 24.7.61.
GAMES: 413 (7). GOALS: 193.
HONOURS: Second Division Championship 83/4, 88/9;
Full Members' Cup 89/90.
8 England caps (85-86).
OTHER CLUBS: Tottenham Hotspur (0, 0);
Reading 80/1-82/3 (116, 51); Southampton 92/3 (9, 2);
Luton Town *on loan* 92/3 (17, 3); Luton Town 93/4-94/5 (58, 16);
Millwall 94/5-95/6 (31, 9); Watford 95/6 (11, 0); Doncaster Rovers 96/7 (16, 3).
MANAGER: Doncaster Rovers.

1983/84-1991/92

NIGEL SPACKMAN

When Nigel Spackman returned to Stamford Bridge in September 1992 he was a different player from the one who had been transferred to Liverpool more than five years earlier. The non-stop running had been replaced by a more measured, thoughtful approach, reflecting the lessons he had learned during his successful spell at Anfield and the experience he had gained with Glasgow Rangers. However, some things hadn't changed: his presence in midfield was every bit as influential as it had been in the eighties and, as before, his slightly laboured, meticulous style ensured that his invaluable contribution did not always receive the acknowledgement it deserved.

Having come into the professional game relatively late, Nigel was originally signed from Third Division Bournemouth for £40,000 in the summer of 1983 as part of John Neal's extensive rebuilding programme. He helped set the tone for the new era at the club with a goal on his debut in a 5-0 win. Nigel had the stamina to run all day and his midfield partnership with John Bumstead, another player with seemingly inexhaustible reserves of energy, was a key element in the team's direct style. A doughty tackler, 'Spackers' was a formidable ball-winner and his passing, while seldom ambitious, was painstaking in its accuracy. Although he possessed a powerful shot, a Spackman goal was a rare event, but he invariably showed enterprise and intelligence when the opportunity arose to break forward in search of an opening.

Nigel missed only two games as the Blues stormed to the Second Division title and was an ever-present the following season, which saw Neal's side maintain its spectacular progress. A thoughtful, purposeful player, he had little difficulty in adapting to the demands of top-flight football, as he demonstrated with a magnificent performance at White Hart Lane in November. He totally overshadowed his immediate adversary, Glenn Hoddle, and in the last twenty minutes took command of the middle of the pitch as Spurs wilted in the face of his ceaseless harrying.

Spackman's determination and professionalism typified the spirit of the new Chelsea, but when John Hollins moved into the manager's office in the summer of 1985 his place in the team became less secure. There were persistent stories that he was unsettled, and in February 1987 he was allowed to join Liverpool in a £400,000 deal.

Nigel's second spell at Chelsea was initially cruelly frustrating. After just six appearances he was sidelined by a career-threatening back problem, and although he bravely turned out in the last two games of the season it was 14 months before he had recovered sufficiently to make a serious first-team comeback. He managed only a handful of outings in 1993/94 but enjoyed an uninterrupted period of pre-season training prior to the following campaign and succeeded in wresting the role of the defensive midfielder sitting in front of the back four from Eddie Newton. It was a task the new-model Spackman was well equipped to perform, because while his tackling was as authoritative as ever his reading of the game had naturally improved. No longer required to dash all over the pitch, he could be king of his small kingdom, winning the ball and playing a simple pass to a colleague in the Anfield tradition. Nigel's versatility proved invaluable when UEFA's restriction on foreign players prompted Hoddle – now Chelsea's manager – to use him at centre-back alongside Erland Johnsen in Vienna in the Cup-Winners' Cup, his anticipation and composure ensuring that he was seldom troubled despite his shortage of pace, but his finest hour came in the home leg of the quarter-final against Bruges, when he was simply inspirational.

Confirming his return to fitness, Nigel made a total of 48 starts that season, earning himself a new one-year contract, but in 1995/96 Newton returned to favour and Spackman was seen in the first team less often. In the summer, at the age of 35, he was given a free transfer and joined Sheffield United as player-coach, subsequently taking over as manager at Bramall Lane.

BORN: Romsey, 2.12.60.
GAMES: 254 (13). GOALS: 14.
HONOURS: Second Division Championship 83/4; Full Members' Cup 85/6.
OTHER CLUBS: AFC Bournemouth 80/1-82/3 (119, 10); Liverpool 86/7-88/9 (51, 0);
Queens Park Rangers 88/9-89/90 (29, 1); Glasgow Rangers;
Sheffield United 96/7 (23, 0).
MANAGER: Sheffield United (97-98).

1983/84-1986/87 & 1992/93-1995/96

PAT NEVIN

It is an accepted part of football wisdom that small, tricky wingers with delicate skills are like the decorations on a Christmas tree: pretty to look at but of no practical value, and apt to disintegrate when anyone touches them. However, that unflattering comparison could not be applied to Pat Nevin during his five seasons at Stamford Bridge. The artistry that made the tiny Scottish sorcerer the idol of the terraces was put to work, harnessed to the needs of the team, and he was rarely guilty of self-indulgence. Intelligent and hard-working, he became Chelsea's most dependable source of goal-scoring opportunities, and a key member of a rousing side that looked set to challenge the best.

Signed from Clyde of the Scottish First Division for £95,000 in May 1983, Nevin was not in the starting line-up when John Neal's remodelled side was unveiled at the beginning of the new season, but when he made his first-team debut as a substitute in a Milk Cup tie against Gillingham in September it was immediately apparent that he possessed breathtaking ball control allied to delightful audacity. He didn't miss a game for the rest of the season and it is a measure of his contribution to the Blues' exhilarating Second Division Championship triumph that the manager's most frequently repeated tactical advice to his men was a simple exhortation to 'give it to Pat'.

Nevin seemed to be able to hold the ball for ever, even when he was surrounded by opponents bent on taking it from him, and a mesmerising 80-yard dribble against Newcastle in November reinforced the impression that he could beat defenders as he pleased. Although he usually played on the right, he was equally at home on his left foot and a fruitful ploy was to cut inside, drawing the centre-back, before slipping the ball through for the rampaging Dixon to run onto. Pat also contributed 14 valuable goals that season, the best of them an exquisite, curling free-kick that helped the Blues to a 6-1 win against Swansea in December.

The 'wee man' maintained his high standards in the First Division the following winter. His looping, curling crosses played invitingly into the box from near the corner flag provided Kerry Dixon and David Speedie with a steady stream of chances, but it was Pat's remarkable awareness that was most impressive. Just when it seemed that he was weaving his way into an impenetrable maze, he would release the ball with the precision of a rapier thrust, just as he did to make Chelsea's third and fourth goals in the epic 4-4 draw at Hillsborough in the Milk Cup.

The thoughtful Scot, a devotee of obscure rock bands and Russian literature, was inevitably subjected to some wild tackling but he had an uncanny ability to ride even the most agricultural assault and was certainly not lacking in courage. However, as time went by he became less effective. He won his first Scottish cap against Romania in March 1986 but as Chelsea lost their way he saw less of the ball and was usually closely marked, often by two or three men. He continued to work diligently for the side but became an increasingly forlorn figure, waiting in vain for the service he needed if he was to make an impression.

It was therefore no surprise that, when defeat at the hands of Middlesbrough in the play-offs in May 1988 consigned Chelsea to the Second Division once more, Nevin exercised his right to move on and joined Everton, a transfer tribunal setting the fee at £925,000. Shortly afterwards Bobby Campbell signed Peter Nicholas and Graham Roberts to give the side the hard-edged pragmatism it had undeniably lacked, but they could scarcely be expected to replace this peerless entertainer and goal-maker in the hearts of the Stamford Bridge faithful.

BORN: Glasgow, 6.9.63.
GAMES: 237 (5). GOALS: 45.
HONOURS: Second Division Championship 83/4; Full Members' Cup 85/6.
28 Scotland caps (86-96).
OTHER CLUBS: Clyde; Everton 88/9-91/2 (109, 16);
Tranmere Rovers *on loan* 91/2 (8, 0);
Tranmere Rovers 92/3-96/7 (193, 30); Kilmarnock.

1983/84-1987/88

KEITH DUBLIN

Whether racing forward from left-back to link with the attack or testing his pace against some speedy winger, Keith Dublin moved with the lithe grace of a natural athlete. A cultured player who always tried to use the ball constructively, the composed England youth international's tackling was crisp and decisive, yet somehow his defending lacked authority, perhaps because his confidence in his exceptional sprinting ability had led him to neglect the niceties of positional play as a youngster.

Having made his debut in the final home game of the triumphant 1983/84 season only to miss the Championship decider at Grimsby through injury, Keith was given his First Division baptism after the Milk Cup semi-final defeat in March 1985 and showed great promise, his polished display against Spurs earning rave reviews. After a three-month spell in the first team the following winter, he finally won possession of the number three shirt from Doug Rougvie in 1986/87, forming an impressive partnership with Steve Clarke in the second half of the campaign. However, the signing of Clive Wilson and Tony Dorigo made it clear that John Hollins had lost faith in Dublin and in August 1987 he joined the growing colony of Stamford Bridge exiles at Brighton.

BORN: High Wycombe, 29.1.66.
GAMES: 66 (2). GOALS: 0.
HONOURS: Full Members' Cup 85/6.
OTHER CLUBS: Brighton and Hove Albion 87/8-89/90 (132, 5); Watford 90/1-93/4 (168, 2); Southend United 94/5- (165, 7).

1983/84-1986/87

KEITH JONES

Keith Jones appeared to have all the qualities required by the modern midfielder. He could win the ball in the tackle and use it effectively, either playing a simple pass to a nearby colleague or a more ambitious defence-splitter, and wasn't afraid to get into the box and score a few himself.

The England youth international looked like winning a regular place in the side in the autumn of 1984 with a series of thoughtful performances, the best of which was against Manchester City in the Milk Cup, when he notched up his fourth goal in ten full appearances after pouncing on Paul Canoville's mishit shot. However, when an aggressive Manchester United side put him under pressure a few weeks later, Keith was unable to impose himself on the game and was replaced at half-time by David Speedie. That chastening experience took its toll on his fragile confidence and he returned to the shadows for the next 18 months, playing only occasionally.

In 1986/87 'KJ' was given an extended run which represented his make-or-break opportunity, but in an ever-changing side he failed to produce his best form and it became clear that he had little future at Stamford Bridge. The following September he was transferred to Brentford, where he emerged as one of the most influential midfield generals in the lower divisions before moving to Southend.

BORN: Dulwich, 14.10.65.
GAMES: 57 (12). GOALS: 10.
OTHER CLUBS: Brentford 87/8-91/2 (169, 13); Southend United 91/2-94/5 (90, 11); Charlton Athletic 94/5- (119, 4).

1982/83-1986/87

DALE JASPER

Dale Jasper's natural ability was highly regarded in the Chelsea dressing room and John Neal was convinced that he would play an important part in the club's future, but a sequence of misfortunes prevented him from translating that talent into a regular first-team place. Cool and elegant, he made his League debut at centre-half, emerging with credit as the Blues salvaged a point with three goals in the last six minutes at Cardiff in March 1984, and confirmed his adaptability by playing at left-back in the 1-0 win at Grimsby which clinched the Second Division title.

However, Dale's best position was in midfield and that is where he started the following season, showing considerable promise until a foot injury allowed John Bumstead to regain his place. His next opportunity came when he was called from the bench to replace Joe McLaughlin after 11 minutes of the first leg of the Milk Cup semi-final against Sunderland in February, but it was not Chelsea's night and the 21-year-old conceded two unlucky penalties which were to prove decisive. It was a setback from which Jasper's career never really recovered. He made only one full appearance in 1985/86 and before the season was out the club had reluctantly taken the decision to give him a free transfer. Unhappily, his spells with Brighton and Crewe brought him little better fortune.

BORN: Croydon, 14.1.64.
GAMES: 13 (2). GOALS: 0.
OTHER CLUBS: Brighton and Hove Albion 86/7-87/8 (49, 6); Crewe Alexandra 88/9-91/2 (111, 2).

1983/84-1985/86

TONY GODDEN

It is a fact of football life that one man's misfortune represents another's opportunity. After ten seasons with West Bromwich Albion during which he had had his fair share of ups and downs, Tony Godden was signed on loan following Eddie Niedzwiecki's injury in March 1986 to provide cover for the Welshman's deputy, Steve Francis. However, when the goals-against tally started mounting alarmingly, Godden was given a chance to relaunch his career with the team that was fourth in the First Division. His authority and experience helped steady the ship and the transfer was made permanent that summer.

Tony had the ability to be a match-winning goalkeeper, as he demonstrated at Old Trafford in September when he saved two penalties to ensure that Kerry Dixon's second-minute goal was enough to give the Blues the points. However, there were other days when he looked less convincing, although it should be said that the protection he was given was sometimes scanty.

Godden's efforts to make himself an indispensable part of the Chelsea team were ultimately undermined by illness and injury. With Roger Freestone arriving to understudy Niedzwiecki, he was no longer needed at Stamford Bridge and was allowed to join Birmingham in July 1987, but he had done a valuable job for the club at a difficult time.

BORN: Gillingham, 2.8.55. GAMES: 38. GOALS: 0.
OTHER CLUBS: West Bromwich Albion 76/7-85/6 (267, 0); Preston North End *on loan* (0, 0); Luton Town *on loan* 82/3 (12, 0); Walsall *on loan* 83/4 (19, 0); Birmingham City 87/8-88/9 (29, 0); Bury *on loan* 88/9 (1, 0); Sheffield Wednesday *on loan* (0, 0); Peterborough United 89/90 (24, 0).

1985/86-1986/87

GORDON DURIE

There are few more stirring sights in football than that of a big, powerful forward heading straight for goal, defying the burly defenders who stand in his path to stop him. When he was at the pinnacle of his form, Gordon Durie looked utterly irresistible, a potent combination of pace and surprising delicacy leaving opponents helpless in his wake, but his dramatic, uncompromising style inevitably exacted its dues. The muscular Scot was injured with heartbreaking regularity and, in the end, it came to seem that his spells in the first team were little more than brief interludes between extended periods on the treatment table.

It took Gordon a little time to make his mark at Stamford Bridge following his £380,000 move from Hibernian at the end of 1985/86. He started the new campaign on the flank but that proved to be one of John Hollins's less successful ideas and after three games the new arrival was relegated to the substitute's bench. A knee operation interrupted his progress and the only real highlight of a frustrating first season in London was a rousing display against Aston Villa in the FA Cup.

The departure of David Speedie that summer allowed Gordon to prove his worth in the middle of the attack, a flurry of goals at the start of the campaign earning him his first full Scottish cap. The knee trouble that sidelined him for three months was a major factor in the Blues' wretched slide towards relegation, but in the long term his career may well have benefited from a season of Second Division football. Durie relished the space he was given by weaker defences and his confidence visibly blossomed. He developed a streak of arrogance that made him all the more effective, and his five goals at Walsall in January were plundered with a crowd-pleasing swagger.

Largely as a result of his continuing fitness problems, Gordon was infuriatingly inconsistent, but when the mood took him he could win games single-handedly. He was essentially a lone raider and his partnership with Kerry Dixon never really fulfilled its obvious potential. The Scot had a thunderous shot – as he demonstrated when he rifled a quite unstoppable free-kick past Liverpool's Bruce Grobbelaar in December 1989 – and was sometimes tempted to go for glory when a measured pass to a colleague would have resulted in a clear-cut opening. Often spurning the simple chances that came his way, he scored a number of magnificent individual goals, with a classically direct effort in a 6-4 win at the Baseball Ground the following season typifying his rousing style. Receiving the ball from a Dave Beasant throw near the halfway line, Gordon set off towards the Derby goal in characteristically single-minded fashion, swept into the penalty area, then bamboozled a couple of hapless defenders before steering his shot past Peter Shilton.

A recurrent groin problem restricted 'Juke Box' to 14 League appearances in 1989/90 but his late-season form gained him a place in the Scottish party for the World Cup in Italy, and the following campaign was probably the best of his five-year stay at Stamford Bridge. Injuries handicapped him once again but his powerful running always posed a threat and against Manchester United he scored a goal that was truly breathtaking, battering the ball past Les Sealey after the Reds' back four had retreated in the face of his onslaught.

It had been reported for some time that Gordon was keen to move back to Scotland so that he and his wife could be closer to their families, so it was no real surprise when he was involved in a £2.2 million transfer on the eve of the following season. However, the fans who had once idolised the charismatic striker made no attempt to conceal their bitterness when it was announced that he was moving no further north than White Hart Lane.

BORN: Paisley, 6.12.65.
GAMES: 145 (8). GOALS: 63.
HONOURS: Second Division Championship 88/9; Full Members' Cup 89/90.
39 Scotland caps (87-).
OTHER CLUBS: East Fife; Hibernian;
Tottenham Hotspur 91/2-93/4 (58, 11); Glasgow Rangers.

1985/86-1990/91

DEREK JOHNSTONE

ROBERT ISAAC

DUNCAN SHEARER

DEREK JOHNSTONE 1983/84-1984/85

Forward. BORN: Dundee, 4.11.53.
GAMES: 1 (3). GOALS: 0.
HONOURS: 14 Scotland caps (73-79).
OTHER CLUBS: Glasgow Rangers (twice);
Dundee United *on loan*. MANAGER: Partick Thistle.

TERRY HOWARD 1984/85-1986/87

Full-back. BORN: Stepney, 26.2.66.
GAMES: 6. GOALS: 0.
OTHER CLUBS: Crystal Palace *on loan* 85/6 (4, 0);
Chester City *on loan* 86/7 (2, 0); Leyton Orient 86/7-94/5 (328, 31);
Wycombe Wanderers 94/5-95/6 (59, 2).

ROBERT ISAAC 1984/85-1986/87

Defender. BORN: Hackney, 30.11.65.
GAMES: 13. GOALS: 0.
OTHER CLUBS: Brighton and Hove Albion 86/7-88/9 (30, 0).

JOHN MILLAR 1985/86-1986/87

Full-back. BORN: Coatbridge, 8.12.66.
GAMES: 11. GOALS: 0.
OTHER CLUBS: Hamilton Academical *on loan*;
Northampton Town *on loan* 86/7 (1, 0);
Blackburn Rovers 87/8-90/1 (126, 2); Heart of Midlothian;
Raith Rovers.

DUNCAN SHEARER 1985/86

Forward. BORN: Fort William, 28.8.62.
GAMES: 2. GOALS: 1.
HONOURS: 7 Scotland caps (94-95).
OTHER CLUBS: Huddersfield Town 85/6-87/8 (83, 38);
Swindon Town 88/9-91/2 (159, 78);
Blackburn Rovers 91/2 (6, 1); Aberdeen;
Inverness Caledonian Thistle.

LES FRIDGE 1985/86

Goalkeeper. BORN: Inverness, 27.8.68.
GAMES: 1. GOALS: 0.
OTHER CLUBS: St Mirren; Clyde; Raith Rovers; Dundalk.

TERRY HOWARD

JOHN MILLAR

LES FRIDGE

JOHN McNAUGHT

JOHN COADY

MICKY BODLEY

JOHN McNAUGHT 1985/86-1987/88

Midfielder. BORN: Glasgow, 19.6.64.
GAMES: 12 (1). GOALS: 2.
OTHER CLUBS: Hamilton Academical; Partick Thistle.

COLIN WEST 1986/87-1987/88

Forward. BORN: Middlesbrough, 19.9.67.
GAMES: 8 (8). GOALS: 4.
OTHER CLUBS: Partick Thistle *on loan*;
Swansea City *on loan* 88/9 (14, 3); Dundee; Hartlepool United
93/4 (36, 5).

JOHN COADY 1986/87-1987/88

Full-back/midfielder. BORN: Dublin, 25.8.60.
GAMES: 10 (9). GOALS: 3.
OTHER CLUBS: Shamrock Rovers; Derry City.

BILLY DODDS 1986/87-1988/89

Forward. BORN: New Cumnock, 5.2.69.
GAMES: 0 (5). GOALS: 0.
HONOURS: 4 Scotland caps (96-97).
OTHER CLUBS: Partick Thistle *on loan*; Dundee; St Johnstone;
Aberdeen.

MICKY BODLEY 1987/88

Central defender. BORN: Hayes, 14.9.67.
GAMES: 8. GOALS: 1.
OTHER CLUBS: Northampton Town 88/9 (20, 0);
Barnet 91/2-92/3 (69, 3); Southend United 93/4-95/6 (67, 2);
Gillingham *on loan* 94/5 (7, 0); Birmingham City *on loan* 94/5 (3, 0);
Peterborough United 96/7- (62, 1).

PERRY DIGWEED 1987/88

Goalkeeper. BORN: Westminster, 26.10.59.
GAMES: 3 (*on loan* from Brighton and Hove Albion). GOALS: 0.
OTHER CLUBS: Fulham 76/7-80/1 (15, 0);
Brighton and Hove Albion 80/1-92/3 (179, 0);
West Bromwich Albion *on loan* (0, 0);
Charlton Athletic *on loan* (0, 0);
Newcastle United *on loan* (0, 0); Wimbledon *on loan* (0, 0);
Wimbledon (0, 0); Watford 93/4-94/5 (29, 0).

COLIN WEST

BILLY DODDS

PERRY DIGWEED

DARREN WOOD

During his four and a half seasons at Stamford Bridge, Darren Wood maintained the standard he had achieved with admirable consistency and was seldom out of the first team for long. A hard-working, adaptable player with the ingrained pragmatism of a true Yorkshireman, he offered a model of professionalism at a time when the Blues' fortunes were fluctuating with the unpredictability of the Stock Exchange, but the suspicion remains that he was capable of rather more.

A £50,000 signing from Middlesbrough in September 1984, Darren had gained considerable experience during a brief but eventful senior career at Ayresome Park, and the 20-year-old's glowing reputation suggested that he would have little difficulty in establishing himself as the Blues' first-choice right-back at the expense of Colin Lee. However, it was not until the following autumn that he earned a secure place in the side, and although he played his part in the Blues' many achievements that season, it was clear that, like so many modern full-backs, he was more impressive coming forward than in defence. Enthusiastic and energetic, he used the ball intelligently and relished every opportunity to attack, but although his tackling had bite he often looked uncertain when faced by a tricky winger.

The arrival of Steve Clarke from St Mirren in January 1987 appeared to cast a deep shadow over Wood's future, but after four games as substitute he was recalled in midfield and revelled in his new role, working tirelessly and throwing himself into every challenge with quite awe-inspiring bravery. Showing an aggression that had previously seemed alien to him, Darren continued to impress during Chelsea's feckless slide into Division Two in 1987/88, and a cartilage operation which caused him to miss the last few weeks of the season undoubtedly hindered the Blues' struggle for survival.

Wood returned to the fray with his passion undiminished and it was a considerable surprise when he was transferred to Sheffield Wednesday in January 1989. Unhappily, his return to Yorkshire was to be blighted by injuries.

BORN: Scarborough, 9.6.64.
GAMES: 167 (11). GOALS: 4.
HONOURS: Second Division Championship 88/9; Full Members' Cup 85/6.
OTHER CLUBS: Middlesbrough 81/2-84/5 (101, 6);
Sheffield Wednesday 88/9-89/90 (11, 0).

1984/85-1988/89

JERRY MURPHY

Jerry Murphy became John Hollins's first signing when he joined Chelsea from Crystal Palace on a free transfer in August 1985. He had been a member of Terry Venables's exciting young side in the late seventies and made more than 200 appearances during the course of nine seasons at Selhurst Park, but terrible luck with injuries prevented him from winning a regular first-team place at Stamford Bridge.

Murphy made an encouraging start to his career with the Blues, playing in the first seven matches of the new campaign on the left of midfield and impressing on his home debut against Coventry. His calm and measured style was easily mistaken for a lack of urgency but, although he was a little short of pace, his perceptive and accurate passing promised to give the side a more cultured look. The London-born Irish international then lost his place through injury but he played his part in a richly merited 1-1 draw at Anfield on his return to the side in November.

Competition from Kevin McAllister and Mick Hazard restricted Jerry's opportunities during the remainder of the campaign, and during the next two seasons he made just 13 appearances, fitness problems continuing to frustrate his efforts to establish himself. He left the club in the summer of 1988 and dropped out of League football, no doubt wondering what he had done to deserve such misfortune.

BORN: Stepney, 23.9.59.
GAMES: 39. GOALS: 3
HONOURS: 3 Ireland caps.
OTHER CLUBS: Crystal Palace 76/7-84/5 (229, 20).

1985/86-1987/88

ROY WEGERLE

The road that led Roy Wegerle to Stamford Bridge was unusually tortuous. Born in South Africa, he went to college in America and became a professional with the Tampa Bay Rowdies (who were managed by Rodney Marsh, the former Queens Park Rangers star) but was unable to pursue his career in Europe until his father discovered that he was entitled to a West German passport. He finally signed for Chelsea in June 1986, having spent two months with the Blues 'on trial' the previous season.

Roy could do things with the ball that took the breath away, but never succeeded in harnessing his abundant skill to the needs of the team, with the result that he made only occasional appearances, often as a substitute. He usually played on the wing or in midfield, but his ability to lose his marker would surely have been employed to greater effect in a central striking role. He confirmed his talent with a magnificent goal in the third round of the FA Cup at Derby in January 1988, running from the halfway line before beating Peter Shilton, but when Bobby Campbell succeeded John Hollins he quickly decided that he had no use for Roy's intermittent inventiveness. That summer he was sold to Luton for £75,000 but by December 1989 he had made such startling progress that QPR paid £1 million to take him to Loftus Road . . .

BORN: Johannesburg, South Africa, 19.3.64.
GAMES: 18 (10). GOALS: 4. HONOURS: 35 USA caps.
OTHER CLUBS: Tampa Bay Rowdies;
Swindon Town *on loan* 87/8 (7, 1); Luton Town 88/9-89/90 (45, 10); Queens Park Rangers 89/90-91/2 (75, 29); Blackburn Rovers 91/2-92/3 (34, 6); Coventry City 92/3-94/5 (53, 9).

1986/87-1987/88

MICK HAZARD

Mick Hazard was something of an anachronism in modern English football: a cultured midfield general who relied upon his audacious skills to justify his selection. He would do his best to 'close down' opponents and win the ball, but he was often a helpless civilian in the war of attrition which has come to dominate the middle of the pitch in so many matches. That didn't worry the purists among Chelsea's supporters, however, who appreciated that one moment of magic from the little maestro might be enough to win a game. Hazard could create space for himself with such ease that his lack of pace was seldom a handicap, and his thoughtful distribution was capable of prising open even the most securely locked defence, the beautifully disguised pass which presented Kevin Wilson with his second goal at White Hart Lane in September 1989 typifying his subtlety.

Mick's arrival at Stamford Bridge in September 1985 from Tottenham appeared to indicate that John Hollins intended to modify the direct style that had brought the Blues such success over the previous two seasons in favour of a more considered build-up, yet during his four and a half years with the club Hazard was never certain of a place in the starting line-up. This was partly because he rarely received the steady supply of possession he needed to thrive, but it must be admitted that he was apt to disappear from the game for long periods, seemingly unable to get involved. He was often at his most effective as a substitute, and hardly ever stamped his authority on a game for the full 90 minutes.

Hazard made just four appearances during the Blues' irresistible surge to the Second Division title in 1988/89, but seemed to be back in favour the following autumn. However, he had been unsettled for some time and, having been consigned to the reserves once more following the crashing defeats by Wimbledon and Queens Park Rangers that put an end to any thoughts of a serious challenge for the Championship by Bobby Campbell's men, he decided to try his luck with Second Division Portsmouth.

BORN: Sunderland, 5.2.60.
GAMES: 94 (9). GOALS: 12.
HONOURS: Full Members' Cup 85/6.
OTHER CLUBS: Tottenham Hotspur 79/80-85/6 (91, 13)
and 93/4-94/5 (28, 2); Portsmouth 89/90 (8, 1);
Swindon Town 90/1-93/4 (119, 17).

1985/86-1989/90

CLIVE WILSON

When he was running at defences, Clive Wilson looked irresistible. Nimble and well balanced, he was blessed with pace and the sort of tantalising ball skills that put a smile on the faces of the fans, but all too often he would take the easy option and pass the responsibility for opening a way to goal to a colleague. It was partly a question of tactics, no doubt. Clive was generally employed on the left of midfield and was not free to push forward without heed of the consequences, but his stay at Stamford Bridge would surely have proved more rewarding had he placed greater faith in his exceptional natural talent.

Wilson was signed from Manchester City in March 1987 but it was agreed that he would remain at Maine Road on loan for the rest of the season to help City's unavailing battle against relegation. He made a bright start to his Chelsea career, his cool head and thoughtful distribution attracting favourable comment, but before long the Blues were sliding down the table with gathering momentum and by mid-January Clive had been consigned to the substitute's bench.

Equally at home in the centre of midfield, Wilson was nothing if not versatile. Many of his appearances for his previous club had been at left-back, and when Tony Dorigo was sidelined at the start of the following campaign the cheerful Mancunian was the obvious deputy. His assured, enterprising performances suggested that he would benefit from a permanent switch to the number three shirt, but with Dorigo fit again he had to resume his frustrating fight for a place in midfield. Consistency remained elusive and he played only a supporting role in the Blues' march to the Second Division Championship.

Clive started just a dozen League games in 1989/90, but a vibrant display when he came on as a substitute at Loftus Road in December provided a reminder of his ability to terrorise defences when in the mood. Although he remained a valuable member of Bobby Campbell's squad, he wanted regular first-team football and in the summer, resisting attempts to persuade him to sign a new contract, he joined Queens Park Rangers for £450,000.

BORN: Manchester, 13.11.61.
GAMES: 85 (18). GOALS: 5.
HONOURS: Second Division Championship 88/9; Full Members' Cup 89/90.
OTHER CLUBS: Manchester City 81/2-86/7 (109, 9);
Chester City *on loan* 82/3 (21, 2);
Queens Park Rangers 90/1-94/5 (172, 12); Tottenham Hotspur 95/6- (70, 1).

1987/88-1989/90

JOE McLAUGHLIN

While the Stamford Bridge faithful were savouring the skills of Nevin, Speedie and Dixon, Joe McLaughlin was getting on with the job . . . coolly, professionally, dependably – and largely unnoticed. He was Chelsea's first-choice centre-half throughout his six years with the club and his importance to the side was only too apparent whenever he was sidelined by injury, but he seldom received the recognition his doughty efforts deserved.

The athletic Scot was signed from Morton for £95,000 during John Neal's spectacular swoop on some of the less well illuminated corners of British football in the summer of 1983 and immediately formed an impressive partnership in the centre of the defence with Colin Pates, missing just one game as the Blues stormed to the Second Division title. Although he was not the tallest of number fives, his timing and determination meant that he was rarely troubled in the air, while his fearless tackling and mobility ensured that forwards enjoyed little respite when the ball was on the floor.

When Peter Withe scored twice in a 4-2 defeat at Aston Villa in September 1984, it seemed that 'Big Joe' might find life in the top flight more difficult, but those fears proved unfounded and by the spring he had made such progress that the experienced striker posed little threat in the return fixture at the Bridge. McLaughlin was appointed captain at the start of 1987/88, but these were difficult times for the Blues and the burdens of office appeared to affect his form. He had always favoured a 'safety first' approach but now his distribution became decidedly erratic and, with the crowd turning on him, he surrendered the armband to Graham Roberts in August 1988. He bounced back with characteristic courage to win his second Division Two Championship medal but had decided that he needed a change of environment and was allowed to join Charlton in a £600,000 deal in the summer of 1989.

BORN: Greenock, 2.6.60.
GAMES: 268. GOALS: 7.
HONOURS: Second Division Championship 83/4, 88/9; Full Members' Cup 85/6.
OTHER CLUBS: Morton; Charlton Athletic 89/90 (31, 0);
Watford 90/1-91/2 (46, 2); Falkirk; Hibernian.

1983/84-1988/89

GRAHAM ROBERTS

Graham Roberts was 29 when he joined Chelsea from Glasgow Rangers in August 1988, but his greying hair, rugged features and aura of total self-assurance gave him the air of a battle-hardened veteran who did not expect to be unduly troubled by the callow conscripts facing him. Bobby Campbell signed him in the hope that, together with Peter Nicholas, who had arrived from Aberdeen five days earlier, he would give the Blues the resilience and aggression that would be required if they were to gain promotion at the first attempt, and the £475,000 transfer fee proved to be money well spent.

'Robbo' was a born leader and it seemed natural that he should assume both the captaincy and the ticklish role of penalty-taker, a task he performed with such aplomb that 12 of his 15 League goals came from the spot. He didn't miss a game during Chelsea's record-breaking march to the Second Division Championship, imperiously conducting operations from his position at centre-back, and if his progress around the pitch was decidedly stately, his reading of the game was so good that he was rarely inconvenienced. The former England international's tackling was ferocious and he seemed to relish his 'hard man' image, putting the eager young heroes who tried to fluster him in their place with disdain.

Roberts was joined by David Lee and Ken Monkou in a three-man central defensive unit the following season and at first the new tactics worked splendidly, the Blues leading the table after 13 matches. But then Campbell's assistant, Ian Porterfield, moved to Reading, Roberts joined the coaching staff and suddenly huge holes started appearing at the back, although the relationship between these three circumstances is uncertain. Within a few weeks Graham had resigned his new post and requested a transfer. He remained with the club until November 1990, when he joined West Bromwich Albion, but did not play in the first team again, to the dismay of the fans who had seen him as the symbol of a new beginning.

BORN: Southampton, 3.7.59.
GAMES: 83. GOALS: 22.
HONOURS: Second Division Championship 88/9.
6 England caps (83-84).
OTHER CLUBS: Portsmouth (0, 0);
Tottenham Hotspur 80/1-86/7 (209, 23);
Glasgow Rangers; West Bromwich Albion 90/1-91/2 (39, 6).

1988/89-1989/90

TONY DORIGO

Inevitably there were those stern critics who preferred to dwell on Tony Dorigo's shortcomings. Lamenting the continuing porosity of the Blues' rearguard, they maintained that the stylish left-back was not a sound defender; he lacked aggression, and his fondness for attack meant that his true responsibilities were sometimes neglected. However, such mean-spirited criticism was not typical. Most Chelsea fans were only too well aware that they were enjoying a rare privilege: the sight of a player out of the very top drawer wearing a blue shirt.

Dorigo had an unusual background, to say the least. An Australian who retained a rich Antipodean accent that would have seemed more natural at Lord's or the Oval, he had travelled to England as a teenager to build a career with Aston Villa, the only club which had deigned to reply to his letter asking for a trial. When Villa were relegated at the end of 1986/87, the ambitious youngster decided to move on, joining Chelsea in a £475,000 deal, but his first season at Stamford Bridge was to prove no less disappointing.

Tony lost no time in demonstrating his class. He possessed electrifying pace that enabled him to win the ball with the delicacy of a pickpocket when others might have had to rely on smash and grab tactics, and his cultured partnership with Steve Clarke seemed certain to banish memories of the Blues' perennial weakness at full-back. Dorigo was occasionally caught out of position – generally after one of his thrilling forays upfield had come to nought – but, like a Grand Prix car slicing through the rush-hour traffic, he was usually able to overhaul his hapless opponent and dispossess him. The 22-year-old's immaculate performances caught the imagination of the Stamford Bridge crowd and he was voted the fans' Player of the Year, but it was a season when little went right for Chelsea and once again he was faced with the unattractive prospect of Second Division football.

A groin injury prevented Dorigo from earning his first full England cap during the European Championships that summer and caused him to miss the start of the new season, but of greater concern to the Chelsea management was his desire to leave Stamford Bridge in order to safeguard his international prospects. Tony made three written transfer requests but Bobby Campbell was adamant that he would not be allowed to go, and in April Dorigo announced that he was prepared to honour his four-year contract. By that time the Blues were on the threshold of the First Division, and the polished defender had played a starring role in their triumph.

Tony was simply majestic when he was coming forward with the ball, his speed and close control taking him past defenders with apparent ease. He produced a steady stream of inviting crosses from the left flank and scored a number of important goals, none better than a superb individual effort against Manchester City at Maine Road in March 1989 when he collected the ball in his own half and raced into the City penalty area before rounding the 'keeper and stroking it home. He was also a master of the flighted free-kick, as he demonstrated with the superbly placed strike that won the ZDS Cup final against Middlesbrough at Wembley in 1990.

Stuart Pearce's consistency meant that Dorigo's international ambitions remained largely unfulfilled but he finally won his first full cap in December 1989 and deputised for the Nottingham Forest stalwart when England met Italy to decide third place in the 1990 World Cup. However, during the course of the following season it gradually became clear that, despite Chelsea's efforts to keep him at the Bridge, he would not be staying when his contract expired in the summer. He eventually opted for Leeds United, a transfer tribunal setting the fee at £1.3 million. No amount of cash could adequately compensate the Blues for the loss of a player of Dorigo's quality, and the fans' gloom was intensified when their former favourite helped the Yorkshire club to the Championship.

BORN: Melbourne, Australia, 31.12.65.
GAMES: 180. GOALS: 12.
HONOURS: Second Division Championship 88/9; Full Members' Cup 89/90.
15 England caps (89-93).
OTHER CLUBS: Aston Villa 83/4-86/7 (111, 1); Leeds United 91/2-96/7 (171, 5); Torino.

1987/88-1990/91

KEN MONKOU

Few Continental players have adapted to the special demands of English football more effectively than Ken Monkou. The tall Dutchman was quick to appreciate that the enterprising style that immediately endeared him to the Stamford Bridge crowd was less likely to find favour with the coaching staff nursing their anxiety on the touchline, and he tightened up his natural game to emerge as one of the most dependable central defenders in the country.

Signed from Feyenoord for the bargain-basement fee of £100,000 in March 1989, Monkou was given time to settle into his new surroundings and when he made his full debut at the start of the following season it was in a five-man defence that had apparently been devised to give free rein to his creative abilities. With Graham Roberts and David Lee available to cover him, Ken was given a licence to drive forward in search of an opening and his slightly ungainly, long-legged forays soon had the terraces roaring with approval. For a while the Blues were riding high in the table, but this glimpse of foreign exoticism – a flash of rich colour amid the West London grime – was not destined to last.

In the new year Ken settled down to form a steady partnership with Erland Johnsen in a conventional back four and now it was his defensive abilities that caught the eye. Tall and athletic, he was exceptional in the air and his tackling had bite and authority. He became the first black player to be voted the fans' Player of the Year and the following season the combination of Dutch panache with the homely virtues of Wimbledon-born Jason Cundy gave the Blues' rearguard a reassuringly solid look, Monkou's inspirational display against Manchester United at Stamford Bridge typifying his commanding form.

The arrival of Paul Elliott increased the competition for places in 1991/92 and after a few shaky performances – notably a nightmare against Everton – Ken was the odd man out. An attempt to use him at left-back proved unsuccessful and in August 1992 the popular Dutchman moved on to Southampton in search of a fresh challenge.

BORN: Necare, Surinam, 29.11.64.
GAMES: 117 (2). GOALS: 2.
HONOURS: Full Members' Cup 89/90.
OTHER CLUBS: Feyenoord;
Southampton 92/3- (176, 9).

1988/89-1991/92

KEVIN McALLISTER

An old-fashioned winger who looked truly comfortable only when the ball was at his feet and he could run at his full-back, Kevin McAllister made valiant efforts to conform to the mould imposed by modern football. Scurrying up and down the right flank like an eager schoolboy, the tiny Scot strove courageously to involve himself in the frantic midfield battle but most of the time he found himself excluded from the action, almost as if the bigger boys had refused to let him join in their game.

Signed from Falkirk by John Neal shortly before he handed over the reins to John Hollins, Kevin spent his first three seasons at Stamford Bridge in the shadow of Pat Nevin, and his first-team opportunities were frustratingly limited. He played in the Full Members' Cup final at Wembley in March 1986, but that seemed likely to be the highlight of his Chelsea career when he started the 1987/88 season on a weekly contract and ended it back at Falkirk on loan.

However, the departure of Nevin that summer presented McAllister with an open door and, after some initial hesitation, he strode through it, earning a regular place in the side that swept irresistibly to the Second Division Championship. Kevin may have lacked his compatriot's extensive repertoire of ball skills and exceptional vision, but his persistence and spirit made him quite a handful, as he showed against Hull when he surged outside two defenders before sending over a high centre which was despatched with relish by Kerry Dixon.

However, McAllister's evident enthusiasm sometimes resulted in over-excitement, to the detriment of his finishing and final ball into the box, and he found himself back on the substitute's bench in the first half of the following season. He regained his place at Christmas, but rarely made much impression on the well-organised defences he faced in the First Division and spent long spells ineffectually chasing shadows. His confidence visibly fading, Kevin made only a handful of appearances in 1990/91 and returned to Falkirk that summer for a fee of £225,000.

BORN: Falkirk, 8.11.62.
GAMES: 101 (39). GOALS: 13.
HONOURS: Second Division Championship 88/9;
Full Members' Cup 85/6, 89/90.
OTHER CLUBS: Falkirk (twice); Falkirk *on loan*; Hibernian.

1985/86-1990/91

ROGER FREESTONE

It takes time for a goalkeeper to ripen to full maturity. Roger Freestone was thrown into battle before he was ready to meet the challenge and his career has suffered as a result.

Signed from Newport County for £90,000 in March 1987, the young Welshman played in the last few games of the season after injury had sidelined Tony Godden and found himself promoted to first-choice when Eddie Niedzwiecki was confined to the treatment room by a recurrence of his knee injury the following autumn. A strapping six-footer, Freestone displayed superb reactions and impressive agility, but he was rather less convincing when the ball was crossed into the penalty area and his positioning occasionally revealed his inexperience. His recall coincided with a disastrous slump in the Blues' form, and after he had made 15 League appearances behind a wobbling defence without collecting a single win bonus, John Hollins turned in desperation to Perry Digweed.

New signing Kevin Hitchcock's fitness problems gave Freestone another chance in 1988/89, but his confidence had taken a battering and he rarely looked assured or commanding. Although Chelsea were enjoying an impressive unbeaten run, Bobby Campbell decided to recruit Dave Beasant in January and Freestone found himself out in the cold, eventually moving to Swansea City in September 1991.

BORN: Caerleon, 19.8.68. GAMES: 53. GOALS: 0.
HONOURS: Second Division Championship 88/9.
OTHER CLUBS: Newport County 86/7 (13, 0);
Swansea City *on loan* 89/90 (14, 0); Hereford United *on loan* 89/90 (8, 0); Swansea City 91/2- (312, 3).

1986/87-1988/89

JASON CUNDY

During his two seasons in the Chelsea first team Jason Cundy became a firm favourite with the Stamford Bridge crowd and the club's decision to sell him to Tottenham prompted a wave of angry protests. The burly centre-back was not a player of great delicacy or refinement but he threw himself into every tackle with undisguised relish, and it was this air of playing for the hell of it, as if he were a Sunday morning footballer testing his mettle with his mates, that made him so popular.

Jason was not far short of his 21st birthday when he was finally given his League debut in September 1990, but he soon made up for lost time, earning a regular place alongside Ken Monkou in the second half of the season. He was still a bit raw and clumsy-looking, but he had a physique that brooked no argument and covered the ground with impressive speed for such a big man. A defiant performance in the Rumbelows Cup quarter-final replay confirmed that Cundy was developing into a defender to be respected, but a series of frustrating injuries prevented him from maintaining his progress the following autumn. Fit once more, he regained his place in the new year and his partnership with Paul Elliott was a key factor in the Blues' dogged progress to the quarter-final of the FA Cup, but when defeat at Roker Park effectively ended Chelsea's season Ian Porterfield decided to make changes to his squad, and on transfer deadline day Cundy moved to Spurs on loan in anticipation of the completion of an £800,000 deal in the summer.

BORN: Tooting, 12.11.69. GAMES: 56 (1). GOALS: 2.
OTHER CLUBS: Tottenham Hotspur 91/2-95/6 (26, 1);
Crystal Palace *on loan* 95/6 (4, 0); Bristol City *on loan* 96/7 (6, 1); Ipswich Town 96/7- (54, 5).

1990/91-1991/92

PETER NICHOLAS

When Peter Nicholas moved on to Watford in March 1991, he could look back with considerable satisfaction on the job he had done for Chelsea during his two and a half years at Stamford Bridge.
The experienced midfielder had arrived from Aberdeen on the eve of the 1988/89 season and, together with Graham Roberts, the other seasoned campaigner recruited from Scottish football by Bobby Campbell to give the side extra bite and composure, had steered the Blues to the Second Division title by a comfortable margin.

A highly encouraging start to the following campaign suggested that the Welsh international's robust pragmatism would prove equally effective among football's aristocracy, but he was never really accepted by the fans, who grudgingly acknowledged the value of his professionalism but reserved their affection for players with rather more verve and dash. Although 'Nicho' was primarily a ball-winner, he was capable of producing passes of exquisite delicacy, such as the perfectly weighted through-ball that presented Kevin McAllister with a goal in a 4-0 win against Sheffield Wednesday in August, and his flighted corners created a number of goalscoring opportunities. Unfortunately, a lack of mobility hampered his efforts and his distribution was sometimes frustratingly wayward, failings that made him the target of the spiteful jeers of a section of the crowd.

Resolute and courageous, Peter succeeded Graham Roberts as captain and became only the second Chelsea skipper to lift a trophy at Wembley in peacetime when Middlesbrough were defeated in the Full Members' Cup final in March 1990. However, when Campbell decided to give youth its chance at Old Trafford the following autumn it was clear that, at the age of 31, Nicholas had no place in his long-term plans and, his task complete, the former Crystal Palace star made the journey to Vicarage Road to help the Hornets in their fight against relegation.

BORN: Newport, 10.11.59.
GAMES: 92 (1). GOALS: 2.
HONOURS: Second Division Championship 88/9; Full Members' Cup 89/90.
73 Wales caps (79-91).
OTHER CLUBS: Crystal Palace 77/8-80/1 (127, 7) and 83/4-84/5 (47, 7);
Arsenal 80/1-82/3 (60, 1); Luton Town 84/5-86/7 (102, 1);
Aberdeen; Watford 90/1-91/2 (40, 1).

1988/89-1990/91

ALAN DICKENS

If ever confirmation were needed that in modern football simple ability is no guarantee of success, it is provided by the dizzying plunge in the fortunes of Alan Dickens during his four seasons at Stamford Bridge. A cultured midfielder whose forte was the acutely angled through-ball, he was signed from newly relegated West Ham in August 1989 to add some guile to a side which had taken a fairly direct route to the Second Division title. A transfer tribunal set the fee at £635,000, the second-highest Chelsea had ever paid, but the move to West London seemed to rob him of the poise and assurance that had distinguished his performances for the Hammers.

With the Blues riding high in the table, Alan held his place until mid-December, even though he often found himself a spectator as the action swirled frantically around him, but after three heavy defeats he was out. He languished on the fringes of the first team for more than a year, but his professionalism and loyalty remained irreproachable and when he was finally recalled he battled away with the grim determination of a man aware that he belonged to a species facing extinction. However, Dickens never seemed to have the space he needed to exploit his unquestioned skill, largely because he lacked acceleration, and the arrival of Vinnie Jones early the following season marked the end of his chances at the Bridge. After another year in the shadows Alan was given a free transfer, joining Brentford in February 1993.

BORN: Plaistow, 3.9.64.
GAMES: 46 (9). GOALS: 4.
OTHER CLUBS: West Ham United 82/3-88/9 (192, 23); West Bromwich Albion *on loan* 92/3 (3, 1); Brentford 92/3 (15, 1); Colchester United 93/4 (32, 3).

1989/90-1991/92

DAMIAN MATTHEW

It is tempting to speculate how Damian Matthew might have fared had he been born twenty years earlier. A cultured play-maker who liked to hold the ball and assess his options before finding his man with a carefully weighted pass, he cut a forlorn figure amid the relentless bustle of the modern game. His undisputed talent proved sufficient to earn him a stack of England under-21 caps but it was glimpsed only intermittently during his irregular first-team outings at club level. Denied the time and space he needed if he was to be effective, Damian was seldom able to dictate the pattern of play and his valiant efforts to turn himself into a midfield workhorse were largely unavailing.

Matthew had his first taste of the frenzied pace of top-flight football alongside Graham Stuart in April 1990 but was given only one realistic opportunity to come to terms with it – a run of six successive matches the following season. He helped the Blues to a famous victory over an otherwise undefeated Arsenal side and a memorable Rumbelows Cup triumph at White Hart Lane but dropped out of contention after an ineffectual display in the first leg of the semi-final. A long-term injury sidelined him for much of the following campaign, and when he was restored to the side at the start of 1992/93 he lost his place to Eddie Newton after just two matches. A little surprisingly, the switch to a more cultured style of football following the appointment of Glenn Hoddle made no difference to Damian's fading fortunes and, having reached the end of the road at Stamford Bridge, he decided to make a fresh start with Crystal Palace.

BORN: Islington, 23.9.70. GAMES: 19 (8). GOALS: 0.
OTHER CLUBS: Luton Town *on loan* 92/3 (5, 0); Crystal Palace 93/4-95/6 (24, 1); Bristol Rovers *on loan* 95/6 (8, 0); Burnley 96/7- (59, 7).

1989/90-1992/93

DAVE BEASANT

A goalkeeper's mistakes are almost always costly and there is little he can do to redeem himself: perfection is included in the job description. When the assured form that had earned Dave Beasant international recognition deserted him, he found himself in a downward spiral from which there was no escape.

Beasant joined the Blues from Newcastle in January 1989 for £725,000 – a club record – to reinforce a promotion drive that had already built up seemingly irresistible momentum. Famed for his habit of dribbling out of his penalty area before launching a thunderous kick down the field, Dave could not truthfully be described as a stylist, his goalkeeping resembling the unruly mop of hair that crowned his mighty frame, but the courage with which he would dive in among the flailing boots to retrieve a ball he had only parried at the first attempt could not be faulted. For a year or so he made a valuable contribution to the Blues' success, pulling off a string of match-winning saves with spectacular agility, but then the goals started to flow, his confidence leaked away and the muttering began.

A cracked bone in a finger ended an uninterrupted run of senior appearances stretching back nine years in the autumn of 1990, and the following season a series of niggling injuries allowed Kevin Hitchcock to mount a serious challenge for the goalkeeper's jersey. Dave's increasingly erratic performances drew mounting hostility from the unsympathetic Stamford Bridge crowd, and when he gifted Norwich victory in September 1992 Ian Porterfield made it clear that the big goalkeeper would have to find himself alternative employment. Beasant had spells on loan at Grimsby and Wolves, but ironically it was to be the manager who departed rather than the player he had castigated.

When David Webb took over he promptly recalled the former Wimbledon stalwart to the first team and Beasant repaid the new manager's faith with a number of valiant displays. However, he rarely looked entirely at ease and before the season was out he had been replaced by Dmitri Kharine. An unfortunate incident involving a bottle of salad cream that left him with a nasty foot injury denied Dave the chance to stake a claim for a place in Glenn Hoddle's team at the start of the following season and in November 1993 he was transferred to Southampton.

BORN: Willesden, 20.3.59.
GAMES: 157. GOALS: 0.
HONOURS: Second Division Championship 88/9; Full Members' Cup 89/90. 2 England caps (89).
OTHER CLUBS: Wimbledon 79/80-87/8 (340, 0); Newcastle United 88/9 (20, 0); Grimsby Town on loan 92/3 (6, 0); Wolverhampton Wanderers on loan 92/3 (4, 0); Southampton 93/4-96/7 (88, 0); Nottingham Forest 97/8- (41, 0).

1988/89-1992/93

VINNIE JONES

There was the Vinnie Jones of popular legend: the tattooed, shaven-headed monster created by the sensation-hungry press, a wild, vicious degenerate who revelled in violence and regarded a football match as an opportunity to settle old scores and open some new ones; and then there was the Vinnie that the Stamford Bridge crowd came to adore: a strong, aggressive midfielder with more talent than his critics were prepared to admit who always gave the punters their money's worth.

From the moment he completed his £575,000 transfer from Sheffield United in August 1991 it was clear that Vinnie's drive and competitiveness would have a significant role to play in Ian Porterfield's rebuilding plans. Exhorting his colleagues to greater efforts with a clenched fist, offering advice and encouragement to his younger team-mates, his influence on the pitch was invaluable and he struck up an immediate rapport with the fans, who warmed to his cheerful defiance and refusal to concede a thing.

Tall and muscular, the former hod-carrier was a formidable tackler and his forbidding presence in front of the back four gave Andy Townsend the freedom to get forward and threaten defences. Vinnie's uncompromising lunges were occasionally a source of embarrassment to his more faint-hearted admirers, and his abrasive style inevitably reaped a harvest of bookings. His absence from the FA Cup quarter-final against Sunderland through suspension was to prove costly, but it would be wrong to lose sight of his creative contribution, since to the surprise of many he turned out to be a more than capable passer of the ball.

Vinnie's height posed a threat at every set piece and his long throws produced a string of goalscoring opportunities, but his best all-round performance came at Anfield in February when his thunderous 25-yard volley helped the Blues to a memorable triumph. Jones could not truthfully be described as an elegant or subtle player but he was undeniably effective, and it was therefore a considerable surprise when he was transferred to Wimbledon the following September, Porterfield apparently feeling that Nigel Spackman could perform the same role with rather more finesse.

BORN: Watford, 5.1.65.
GAMES: 52. GOALS: 7.
HONOURS: 9 Wales caps (94-97).
OTHER CLUBS: Wimbledon 86/7-88/9 (77, 9) and 92/3-97/8 (177, 12);
Leeds United 89/90-90/1 (46, 5); Sheffield United 90/1-91/2 (35, 2);
Queens Park Rangers 97/8- (7, 1).

1991/92-1992/93

PAUL ELLIOTT

Ian Porterfield's efforts to build a Chelsea side capable of challenging for honours suffered a savage blow when Paul Elliott was carried from the pitch at Anfield in September 1992 following a sickening collision with Liverpool's Dean Saunders. The towering centre-half had suffered severe damage to the ligaments of his right knee that would ultimately end his career and his commanding presence would be sorely missed in the years that followed.

Chelsea had been trailing Paul for some time when they finally clinched the £1.4 million deal with Celtic that brought him back to London in July 1991, and it was soon apparent that he would lend poise and authority to a defence that had been woefully inconsistent for too long. His height, imposing physique and impressive athleticism enabled him to dominate the penalty area and he was quite superb in the air, attacking the ball with confidence and aggression.

Cool under pressure, Elliott's tackling was crisp and decisive, and his performance against Sheffield United in the FA Cup was nothing less than heroic as he dealt calmly with everything the Yorkshiremen could throw at him. His measured distribution reflected the experience he had gained during his time in Italy, where defenders are expected to be able to use the ball constructively, and he could be equally effective at the opposite end of the pitch, as he demonstrated on his Chelsea debut against Wimbledon, when he scored the Blues' first goal of the season with a thumping header from a Dennis Wise corner.

Resolute and defiant, the big defender was regularly to be seen encouraging his team-mates with a clenched fist, and he quickly became a firm favourite with the Stamford Bridge crowd. The following season he was joined in the middle of the back four by Mal Donaghy and it seemed that the Blues had a solid foundation on which to build a winning team, but then came the fateful clash at Anfield.

A thoughtful, compassionate man, Paul fought courageously to regain his fitness for a year and a half, but shortly before Chelsea's appearance in the 1994 FA Cup Final he was forced to announce his retirement.

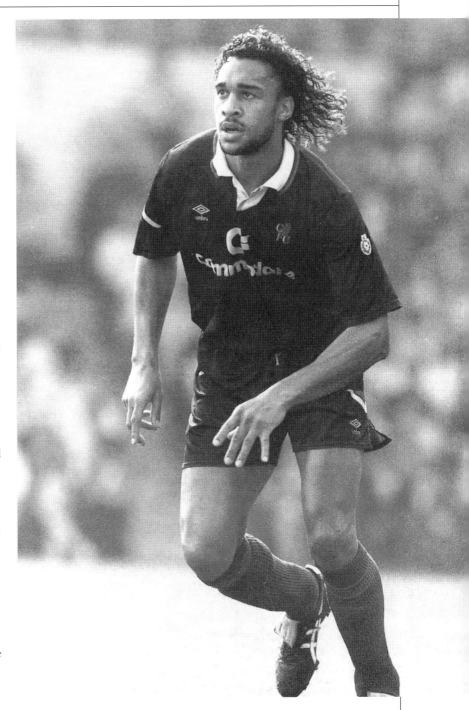

BORN: Lewisham, 18.3.64.
GAMES: 54. GOALS: 3.
OTHER CLUBS: Charlton Athletic 81/2-82/3 (63, 1); Luton Town 82/3-85/6 (66, 4); Aston Villa 85/6-86/7 (57, 7); Pisa; Glasgow Celtic.

1991/92-1992/93

GARETH HALL

When he ran onto the pitch to make his senior debut at Plough Lane in May 1987, Gareth Hall's immediate ambition was clear: he wanted to be Chelsea's first-choice right-back; and to achieve that he would have to dislodge the man in possession, Steve Clarke. Over the years that followed, as managers came and went and every other face in the dressing room changed, Gareth fought doggedly to break the Scot's grip on the position but in the end he was forced to concede that the battle to establish himself had been lost and attempt to revive his moribund career elsewhere.

Gareth may not have possessed Clarke's natual ability but he made full use of the gifts that had been bestowed upon him. He was a solid, reliable defender whose unfailing enthusiasm more than made up for any shortcomings in technique but was a little short of pace and lacked the inventiveness to pose much of a threat when going forward.

Following that first outing at Wimbledon, Hall made occasional appearances as an understudy in 1987/88, his robust displays earning him the first of his nine Welsh caps, but he produced his best performances in the play-off semi-finals against Blackburn, where he proved to be a very effective midfield ball-winner. He had a decent run at right-back the following season when Clarke was injured, but the real breakthrough came in February 1990 when he finally managed to secure a regular place in the side at his rival's expense. Gareth remained the first choice for much of the following campaign but Ian Porterfield, who succeeded Bobby Campbell in the summer of 1991, preferred Clarke, prompting Hall to ask for a move.

Steve's injury problems allowed Gareth to fight back and in 1992/93, having started the season on the left, he appeared to have regained the upper hand until a suspension gave the Scot the chance to prove his pedigree to new manager David Webb. Hall reverted to midfield briefly but following the appointment of Glenn Hoddle he was never more than a short-term stand-in. With the arrival of Dan Petrescu increasing the competition for places, Hall finally brought down the curtain on a Chelsea first-team career that had spanned ten seasons, joining Sunderland in January 1996 after a spell on loan.

BORN: Croydon, 20.3.69.
GAMES: 148 (23). GOALS: 5.
HONOURS: Second Division Championship 88/9; Full Members' Cup 89/90. 9 Wales caps (88-92).
OTHER CLUBS: Sunderland 95/6-97/8 (49, 0); Brentford *on loan* 97/8 (6, 0).

1986/87-1995/96

KEVIN WILSON

Kevin Wilson was a busy, industrious striker with neat control and a sharp eye for a half-chance, but even his greatest admirers would have to concede that he lacked the explosive virtuosity of Gordon Durie, his rival for a place alongside Kerry Dixon in the Blues' attack. As a result, for most of his stay at Stamford Bridge the Northern Ireland international was cast in a supporting role, moving to centre-stage only when one of the big-name stars was indisposed.

A £335,000 signing from Ipswich in June 1987, Kevin started his Chelsea career on the substitute's bench and Christmas was looming by the time he had scored his first goal for his new club. His confidence had gradually leaked away and for a time it seemed that even the basic skills were beyond his desperate grasp, but the following season he was to make an influential contribution to the Blues' irresistible assault on the Second Division Championship. Once Dixon and Durie had renewed their injury-blighted partnership in attack, Wilson was switched to midfield and his eager foraging, initially on the right flank, then on the left, helped ensure that his better-known colleagues were supplied with a steady flow of chances.

The Scot's absence for much of 1989/90 allowed Wilson to renew his credentials as a striker. The first of his two goals in a splendid 4-1 win at White Hart Lane confirmed his opportunism, the second the coolness of his finishing, but it was his deft touch and the composure with which he linked with the players around him that really caught the eye. With Durie restored to full vigour 'Willo' reverted to midfield, but the opening weeks of the following season presented another opportunity to try his luck up front and he responded in style, with five goals in eight outings.

Thereafter Wilson dropped out of the reckoning but his rival's departure in the summer of 1991 presented him with the chance to earn a secure first-team place that he had been waiting for for so long. When he failed to deliver the goods Ian Porterfield turned to Clive Allen, and on transfer deadline day Kevin joined Notts County to boost their fight against relegation.

BORN: Banbury, 18.4.61.
GAMES: 155 (36). GOALS: 55.
HONOURS: Second Division Championship 88/9; Full Members' Cup 89/90.
42 Northern Ireland caps (87-95).
OTHER CLUBS: Derby County 79/80-84/5 (122, 30);
Ipswich Town 84/5-86/7 (98, 34); Notts County 91/2-93/4 (69, 3); Bradford City *on loan* 93/4 (5, 0);
Walsall 94/5-96/7 (125, 38); Northampton Town 97/8- (9, 0).

1987/88-1991/92

ANDY TOWNSEND

English football possesses any number of players who can win the ball in midfield and deny their opponents space. A handful of them are capable of opening up a defence with a precisely weighted pass, but those who also have the drive and mobility to get forward and score goals are as rare as winning Lottery tickets – so it is easy to understand why, at his peak, Andy Townsend was so highly regarded by his fellow professionals.

Townsend joined the Blues in the summer of 1990, a transfer fee of £1.2 million having been agreed with Norwich City before he boosted his growing reputation with some stirring performances for the Republic of Ireland in the World Cup finals in Italy (he qualified for Jack Charlton's cosmopolitan team through his grandmother). After a quiet start he enjoyed a splendid first season at Stamford Bridge, his tigerish tackling and powerful running making him a firm favourite with the fans, who voted him their Player of the Year.

A fierce competitor who always seemed to enjoy his football as much as he had when he was playing as a part-timer with Welling United and Weymouth, Andy was an instinctive leader, constantly encouraging and advising the men around him. His infectious enthusiasm and bubbly personality proved an invaluable influence in the dressing room, and when Peter Nicholas dropped out of the side it was natural that he should take over the captaincy. One criticism that could possibly be made was that Townsend appeared to reserve his best performances for the big occasion, but it would be fairer to say that he responded to the passionate atmosphere generated by a large crowd.

When he was in the mood, Andy was capable of totally dominating the middle of the pitch. A real terrier who allowed his adversary no peace, he covered a huge amount of ground during the course of a match and used the ball with precision and imagination, although his right foot was by no means a match for his left. He also possessed a thunderous shot – which he made too little use of – but the most exciting part of his game was his surging bursts towards goal, his strength carrying him past defenders who were seemingly powerless to stop him. Perhaps the greatest testimony to Townsend's ability was the way he totally overshadowed Paul Gascoigne in the Rumbelows Cup quarter-final replay at White Hart Lane in 1991, scoring the first goal when he ran onto a flick from Kerry Dixon then presenting the big striker with the second when his well-struck drive came back off a post.

Andy made a flying start to the following season, scoring five goals before the end of September, one of them a quite superb 30-yard screamer at Queens Park Rangers. The arrival of Vinnie Jones to stand guard in front of the defence gave him the freedom to press forward more often, but he was struggling with a groin injury and it eventually became impossible to delay surgery any longer. He was out of action for just five weeks – which says much for his determination – but never quite recaptured the fizz he had shown before the lay-off.

Townsend was back to his best in 1992/93, with a brilliant individual goal against Crystal Palace in the quarter-final of the Coca-Cola Cup adding weight to the extravagant claims that there was no more effective midfielder in Europe. However, it was not enough to win the tie and Andy's evident dismay was understandable. He clearly found it intensely frustrating that, despite his immense personal contribution, he was not a member of a winning side and speculation grew that he would welcome a move to another club in order to improve his chances of gaining his first domestic honour. Chelsea were understandably reluctant to weaken their team by losing such an influential player but new manager Glenn Hoddle came to the conclusion that there was nothing to be gained by forcing him to stay and Townsend was allowed to join Aston Villa in July 1993. The fee – £2.1 million – was a substantial one for a player entering his thirties, but his energy and zest would be sadly missed.

BORN: Maidstone, 23.7.63.
GAMES: 138. GOALS: 19.
HONOURS: 70 Ireland caps.
OTHER CLUBS: Southampton 84/5-87/8 (83, 5); Norwich City 88/9-89/90 (71, 8); Aston Villa 93/4-97/8 (131, 8); Middlesbrough 97/8- (37, 2).

1990/91-1992/93

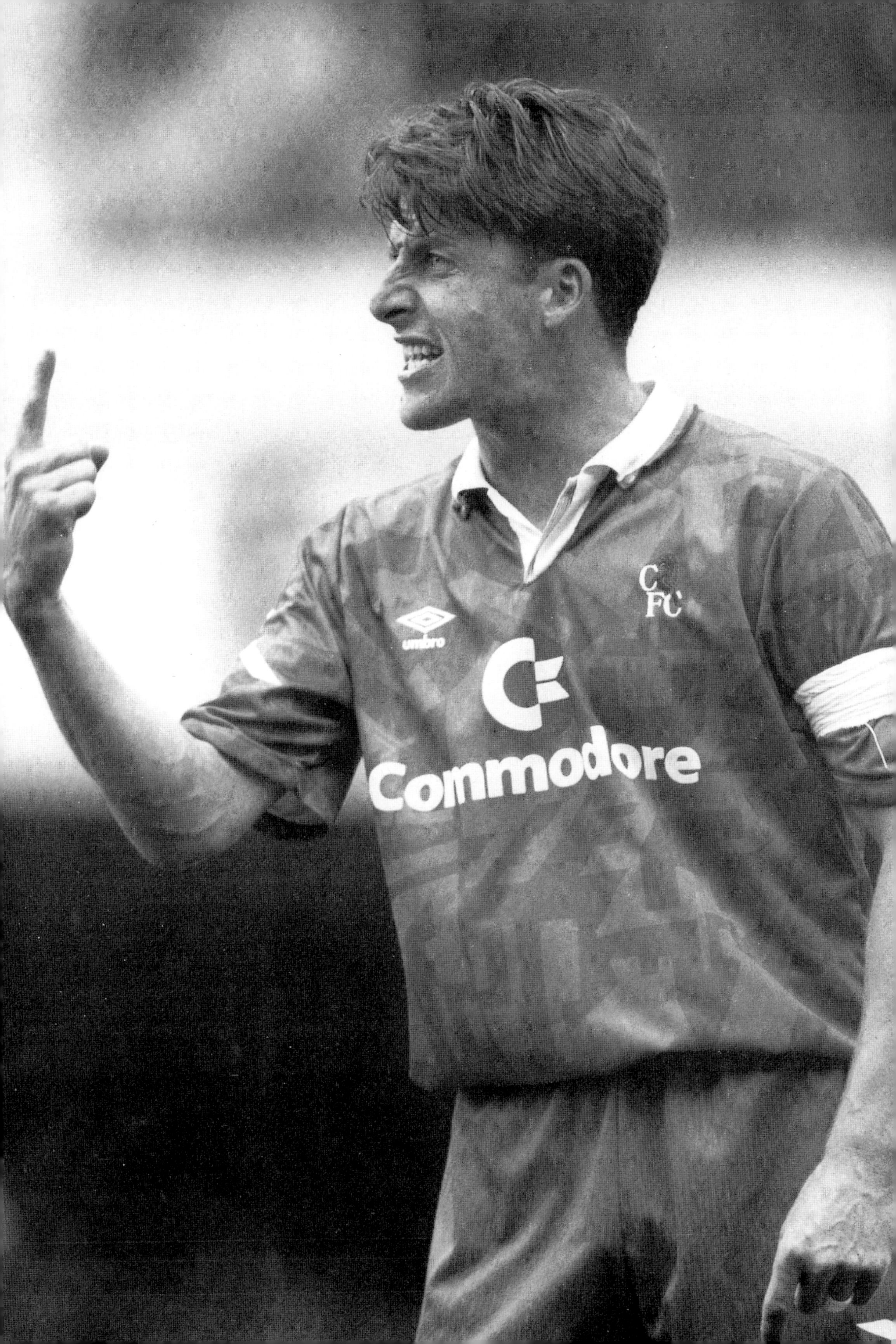
CFC
umbro
Commodore

TOM BOYD

Replacing a player of the class of Tony Dorigo was never going to be easy, but it would be fair to say that during his eight months at Stamford Bridge Tom Boyd failed to make much of an impression. The timing of his move from Motherwell probably didn't help: the completion of the Scottish international's £800,000 transfer was delayed to allow him to lead the Fir Park club to victory in the Scottish Cup final, and by the time he reported for pre-season training with Chelsea the Blues had a new manager.

The first indication of Ian Porterfield's doubts about Boyd's effectiveness at left-back came when Tom started the opening game of the season in midfield. That experiment was short-lived and he quickly settled down in a conventional role on the left of the back four, but it seemed significant that when the manager wanted to make a tactical substitution it was often the number three board that was held aloft.

Boyd was a neat, tidy player who used the ball sensibly, but there was no area of the game at which he excelled: he was not particularly quick or aggressive, and he certainly lacked Dorigo's attacking flair. It looked as though he might have been happier on the right flank but Chelsea were already well provided for in that position, and when an injury to Kerry Dixon left the Blues in urgent need of a big centre-forward Porterfield lost no time in agreeing an exchange deal involving Celtic's Tony Cascarino.

BORN: Glasgow, 24.11.65.
GAMES: 31 (1). GOALS: 0.
HONOURS: 53 Scotland caps (90-).
OTHER CLUBS: Motherwell;
Glasgow Celtic.

1991/92

CLIVE ALLEN

Clive Allen was the wrong side of thirty when he arrived at Stamford Bridge in December 1991 and largely barren spells with Bordeaux and Manchester City had tarnished the reputation for deadly finishing he had earned at Tottenham, but over the next four months the well-travelled striker confirmed that goalscoring is a gift that time cannot erode. The £250,000 deal that had brought the nomad back to London was hailed as the bargain of the season, but then, just as suddenly as he had appeared, he was gone . . .

Clive had never had too much pace and chasing long through-balls was not really his game, but he was certainly quick-witted and his sharp reactions, anticipation and immaculate control made him a constant threat in the penalty box. A spectacular volley against Everton in the fourth round of the Cup will linger in the memory of all those who witnessed it, but when Sheffield United came to the Bridge in the next round Clive showed that he was more than a goalscorer, holding the ball and laying it off with the finesse of a master craftsman. A typical close-range effort against Sunderland opened the way to the semi-finals, but then Allen seemed to fall from favour. When defeat in the replay at Roker Park had effectively ended the Blues' season, Ian Porterfield decided to prune his squad in preparation for further signings in the summer and on transfer deadline day Clive was sold to West Ham.

BORN: Stepney, 20.5.61. GAMES: 22 (2). GOALS: 9.
HONOURS: 5 England caps (84-88).
OTHER CLUBS: Queens Park Rangers 78/9-79/80 (49, 32) and 81/2-83/4 (87, 40); Arsenal (0, 0); Crystal Palace 80/1 (25, 9); Tottenham Hotspur 84/5-87/8 (105, 60); Bordeaux; Manchester City 89/90-91/2 (53, 16); West Ham United 91/2- 93/4 (38, 17); Millwall 93/4 (12, 0); Carlisle United 95/6 (3, 0).

1991/92

TONY CASCARINO

After frustrating spells at Aston Villa and Celtic, Tony Cascarino had something to prove when he moved to Stamford Bridge in a swap deal involving Tom Boyd in February 1992. Sadly, the big striker was to be dogged by a succession of injuries during his two and a half seasons with the Blues and never really managed to recapture the swashbuckling form he had shown in his Millwall days.

A traditional, big-hearted centre-forward, Tony was at his most effective when the ball was in the air, and if he received the service he needed – accurate crosses to the far post from the wings – he could threaten any defence. On the floor, he sometimes looked a little cumbersome but he was a capable target man and, on occasion, a crisp finisher.

Two goals from 13 starts during the remainder of 1991/92 represented an unspectacular start to Cascarino's Chelsea career and summer knee surgery followed by a second operation ruled him out for the first half of the next campaign. Fit again, he made a valuable contribution to the Blues' fight to stave off the threat of relegation under David Webb and looked sharp and purposeful at the start of the following season, only for injury to sideline him once more. Tony returned in time for the FA Cup semi-final against Luton and had a hand in both goals, but after making an appearance as a substitute in the final he was given a free transfer. He opted to move to France and enjoyed considerable success, confirming that, when he was fully fit, he remained a more than useful performer.

BORN: St Paul's Cray, 1.9.62.
GAMES: 39 (6). GOALS: 8.
HONOURS: 76 Ireland caps.
OTHER CLUBS: Gillingham 81/2-86/7 (219, 78); Millwall 87/8-89/90 (105, 42); Aston Villa 89/90-90/1 (46, 11); Glasgow Celtic; Marseille; Nancy.

1991/92-1993/94

MICK HARFORD

An abrasive, awkward centre-forward, all sharp edges and aggression, Mick Harford was 33 when he joined the Blues from newly relegated Luton on the eve of the 1992/93 season, so there was never any doubt that his stay at Stamford Bridge would be relatively brief. In the event, the lugubrious Wearsider was a Chelsea player for just eight months, but during that time he confirmed that he had forgotten none of the lessons he had learned during a long and honourable career in the number nine shirt.

Although Mick was justly famed for his ability with his head, it was the deftness with which he controlled the ball before bringing the midfield men into the game that was most impressive. He was not the quickest of movers but he had the strength to resist the attentions of the eager youths attempting to contain him and, to the surprise of many, he proved to be a clinical finisher, a spectacular 25-yard drive on his debut against Oldham paving the way for a steady stream of well-taken goals in the first half of the season.

Harford was suspended for three matches in December, his combative style having earned him a flurry of yellow cards, and then he picked up a calf injury. When he returned to the side the bite that had helped Chelsea climb the table before Christmas had gone and, with the Blues' season in ruins, the former England international was sold to Sunderland shortly before transfer deadline day. But it had been fun while it lasted.

BORN: Sunderland, 12.2.59. GAMES: 33 (1). GOALS: 11.
HONOURS: 2 England caps (88).
OTHER CLUBS: Lincoln City 77/8-80/1 (115, 41);
Newcastle United 80/1 (19, 4); Bristol City 81/2 (30, 11);
Birmingham City 81/2-84/5 (92, 25);
Luton Town 84/5-89/90 (139, 57) and 91/2 (29, 12);
Derby County 89/90-91/2 (58, 15); Sunderland 92/3 (11, 2);
Coventry City 93/4 (1, 1); Wimbledon 94/5-96/7 (61, 9).

1992/93

DAVID LEE

It has often seemed that David Lee would be better suited to Continental football than to the relentless bustle of the English game. A tall, somewhat ungainly defender who likes to come forward with the ball and switch play with a pinpoint crossfield pass, he is ideally equipped to operate as a libero but lacks the pace and aggression expected of a traditional centre-back. Disappointingly, despite the wind of change that has swept through Stamford Bridge in recent years, his undoubted ability has continued to go to waste.

Having been confined to a supporting role during the Blues' Second Division Championship triumph in 1988/89, David started the following season alongside Graham Roberts and Ken Monkou in a five-man defence and his assured displays quickly earned rave reviews, but shortly before Christmas the bubble burst and he spent the second half of the campaign on the bench. His career stagnated for two years but Paul Elliott's appalling injury in September 1992 presented him with another chance and he enjoyed a good run as Frank Sinclair's partner in a conventional back four. Following a disastrous sequence of results, however, Ian Porterfield was replaced by David Webb and, with a watertight defence taking priority over freewheeling creativity, Lee was dropped.

The appointment of Glenn Hoddle looked likely to revive his prospects but his most telling contribution over the next two seasons was to be as a midfield ball-winner in the closing weeks of 1994/95. When Hoddle decided to return to a back three the following season Ruud Gullit was signed to play as the 'free' defender, but after a few weeks the Dutchman was sidelined by injury and Lee was finally allowed to show what he could do in his favourite position. He quickly became the fulcrum of the defence, confirming that he had lost none of his confidence, vision or passing ability, but the team managed just one Premiership clean sheet in the last three months of the season and in the summer Frank Leboeuf was recruited to fill the role. Injury was heaped upon insult when David suffered a broken leg in his first Premiership start of 1996/97 against Tottenham in October, and although he has made a full recovery he has been unable to force his way back into the first-team reckoning.

BORN: Kingswood, 26.11.69.
GAMES: 148 (46). GOALS: 10.
HONOURS: Second Division Championship 88/9; Full Members' Cup 89/90.
OTHER CLUBS: Reading *on loan* 91/2 (5, 5);
Plymouth Argyle *on loan* 91/2 (9, 1); Sheffield United *on loan* 97/8 (5, 0).

1988/89-

GRAHAM STUART

Despite his obvious ability, it took time for Graham Stuart to come to terms with the demands of first-team football. Then, just as his talent was beginning to blossom, he decided to move on, allowing another club to reap the benefit of his long apprenticeship at Stamford Bridge.

Quick and well balanced with good close control, Graham was at his most effective when running at opponents, as he demonstrated with a magnificent goal against Sheffield Wednesday at Hillsborough in August 1992, when he carried the ball half the length of the pitch before jinking his way past two bewildered defenders and coolly slipping it beyond Chris Woods. As a result, most of his appearances were made wide on the right of midfield but the virtuosity with which he created space for himself was not always matched by the accuracy of his ball to the men in the middle and he was also prone to fade out of games for long periods.

Having scored on his debut in April 1990, Graham was recalled to the side the following November and although he never had a shirt to call his own he missed only a handful of games thereafter. However, the 20-year-old was troubled for much of the season by what proved to be a stress fracture of the shin and he sat out the first three months of the following campaign while the problem was sorted out. A splendid performance against Nottingham Forest in November suggested that, despite his slight build, he might be most effective in a central striking role, but in the event the only goal he managed all season was a brilliant individual effort against Sheffield United in the fifth round of the FA Cup.

Fully fit once more, 'Bobby' (the nickname was a constant reminder that he is a graduate of the FA School of Excellence established during Bobby Robson's reign as England manager) earned a regular place in 1992/93 and as the season progressed he became increasingly influential, seeing a lot of the ball and scoring a healthy ration of goals. It seemed that he would play an important role in Chelsea's future but, despite Glenn Hoddle's appointment in the summer of 1993, Stuart opted to continue his career elsewhere, joining Everton on the eve of the new season with a tribunal setting the initial fee at £850,000.

BORN: Tooting, 24.10.70.
GAMES: 89 (21). GOALS: 18.
OTHER CLUBS: Everton 94/4-97/8 (136, 22); Sheffield United 97/8- (28, 5).

1989/90-1992/93

ROBERT FLECK

The purchase of Robert Fleck from Norwich for £2.1 million – a club record – proved to be an expensive mistake. When he arrived at Stamford Bridge shortly before the start of the 1992/93 season, Blues' fans blithely anticipated a flurry of goals like the magnificent strike that had reduced them to stunned silence nine months earlier. However, Robert had never been a prolific marksman and for all his dogged efforts he was unable to produce the goals that had been expected. Before the season was out he had been branded a failure and discarded, but he would surely have enjoyed greater success if Chelsea had been willing to change their style to suit him. He was at his most dangerous when he could run onto a through-ball down the middle or along the flanks, allowing him to exploit his pace and strength, but during his time with the Blues he rarely received the service he needed.

Fleck's Chelsea career began encouragingly enough, despite the worrying shortage of goals. Always enthusiastic and hard-working, he helped create numerous chances for others, although his unselfish contribution did not always receive the recognition it deserved. He formed an effective striking partnership with Mick Harford, who found the net regularly, but when the veteran centre-forward was injured Fleck was left to carry the burden alone. The honeymoon was over and as the Blues' season collapsed the Scot found himself relegated to the bench for a while. He persevered but his confidence had drained away and before long new manager David Webb had turned to John Spencer.

Fleck made a handful of appearances the following season but Glenn Hoddle's commitment to a passing game meant that his chances of rehabilitating himself were always likely to be limited and the only first-team football he played in 1994/95 was during a loan spell at Bristol City. Always popular with the fans, Robert continued to work hard in the reserves and in September 1995 he was finally released from his ordeal, rejoining Norwich for around a third of the fee Chelsea had paid.

BORN: Glasgow, 11.8.65.
GAMES: 35 (3). GOALS: 3.
HONOURS: 4 Scotland caps (90-91).
OTHER CLUBS: Partick Thistle;
Glasgow Rangers; Norwich City 87/8-91/2 (143, 40)
and 95/6-97/8 (104, 16); Reading 97/8- (5, 0).

1992/93-1993/94

GAVIN PEACOCK

Gavin Peacock was the standard-bearer for the Glenn Hoddle era at Stamford Bridge. Signed from Newcastle shortly after Hoddle's arrival, he was a £1.25 million replacement for Andy Townsend, who had made it clear he wanted to move on. Gavin was a dedicated, conscientious professional whose personal values and commitment to success mirrored those of the new manager. As an inventive, stylish player, he played an influential role in the revolution that saw Chelsea close the gap that separated them from the game's elite.

Gavin started the new season in a five-man midfield but before long he moved up front, scoring the only goal in a superb home win against Manchester United. However, he was most effective playing behind the two strikers and he was to make this position his own after Hoddle had switched to a diamond formation in midfield. Although he was a bit short of pace, he had the knack of timing his run into the penalty area perfectly and was surprisingly dangerous in the air for a player of 5ft 9in. He scored six goals during the Blues' run to the FA Cup final, including a stunning volley against Wolves in the quarter-final and a brace in the semi-final, but there was more to his game than goals. His close control was excellent and he had the ability to spin past his marker, while his perceptive passing, often subtly disguised, was a delight.

The goals did not flow so freely in 1994/95, partly because Gavin spent much of the season on the left of midfield, where his curling crosses, often delivered with little backlift, created a number of opportunities. He remained a key member of the side, and with Dennis Wise out of action in the second half of the campaign, he took over the captain's armband. The following season, however, with the arrival of Ruud Gullit and a return to the sweeper system, Gavin's position came under threat and after Christmas, he regularly found himself on the substitutes' bench. Once the Dutchman had succeeded Hoddle as manager, Gavin found himself out of the picture altogether and in December, after a month-long loan, he returned to Queens Park Rangers, the club where he had started his career.

BORN: Welling, 18.11.67.
GAMES: 119 (15). GOALS: 27.
OTHER CLUBS: Queens Park Rangers 86/7-87/8 (17, 1) and 96/7- (66, 14);
Gillingham 87/8-88/9 (70, 11);
AFC Bournemouth 89/90-90/1 (56, 8);
Newcastle United 90/1-92/3 (105, 35).

1993/94-1995/96

JOHN SPENCER

John Spencer never quite achieved that elusive consistency needed to stay at the top, and as a result, his place in the Blues' side was never guaranteed. However, there is no doubt that at his best he was a true match-winner.

John joined Chelsea on the eve of 1992/93 from Rangers, where he had been unable to establish himself in the first team, but had to wait until the following January before he was given his full debut. In the closing weeks of the season, following the appointment of David Webb, the Scottish striker managed to displace Robert Fleck, but after the opening game of Glenn Hoddle's first season as manager, he was back in the reserves. He made an impressive return after Christmas, however, forming an unlikely partnership with Chelsea's other pocket battleship, Mark Stein, as the Blues reached Wembley.

Although he was only 5ft 6in tall, John had a big heart and allowed defenders no respite. An exuberant, confident character, he worked tirelessly, regularly coming deep to link up with the men in midfield. However, it was his sharpness in and around the box that mattered most, his cool finishing and powerful shot giving him a very respectable scoring record.

John consolidated his position during the first half of 1994/95, averaging a goal every other game, and his brilliant effort in Vienna, when he ran with the ball from deep in his own half before tucking it past the 'keeper, must rank as one of the most memorable in Chelsea's recent history. He won his first international cap shortly afterwards but in the New Year he was asked to drop back into midfield. He seemed admirably suited to the position, but he did not enjoy playing there and the experiment was abandoned.

The following season was probably Spencer's best, despite persistent hamstring problems. Profiting from the strength, skill and awareness of Mark Hughes, he was a regular goalscorer, and in the summer he represented Scotland in Euro '96. However, the signing of Gianluca Vialli meant that first team openings became very limited and, unwilling to accept his role within Ruud Gullit's squad system, he completed a £2.5 million transfer to Queens Park Rangers in November 1996.

BORN: Glasgow, 11.9.70.
GAMES: 100 (37). GOALS: 43.
HONOURS: 14 Scotland caps (94-97).
OTHER CLUBS: Rangers; Morton *on loan*; Lai Sun, Hong Kong *on loan*;
Queens Park Rangers 96/7-97/8 (48, 22); Everton *on loan* 97/8 (6, 0).

1992/93-1996/97

ANDY DOW

Andy Dow became Glenn Hoddle's first signing for Chelsea when he joined the Blues from Dundee in the summer of 1993. Recruited on the recommendation of Graham Rix, Hoddle's recently appointed youth team coach, who had played alongside him the previous season, he seemed well suited to the role of left-wing-back in the new manager's preferred tactical system. Sadly, the quiet Scot was unable to capitalise on his golden opportunity and his stay at Stamford Bridge proved largely frustrating.

Following a difficult baptism on the opening day of the season, Andy had a run in the side in the autumn and played in the splendid home wins against Manchester United and Liverpool. He had a sweet left foot and crossed the ball well but he was a little short of pace and lacked the trickery to beat a man and make space for himself. He was very much an attacking player, and his positioning often looked suspect when he was called upon to defend.

By the time he was recalled after a spell out of the side, Hoddle had reverted to a back four, and playing as a conventional full-back, Dow's defensive frailties were particularly apparent. Having been omitted again, he was given another chance at Anfield but following a disappointing display he dropped out of the first-team reckoning. He made just one more appearance in two years before returning to Scotland with Hibernian in March 1996.

BORN: Dundee, 7.2.73.
GAMES: 17 (1). GOALS: 0.
OTHER CLUBS: Dundee; Bradford City *on loan* 94/5 (5, 0); Hibernian.

1993/94-1995/96

MAL DONAGHY

Mal Donaghy was fast approaching his 35th birthday when Ian Porterfield brought him to Stamford Bridge from Manchester United on the eve of the 1992/93 season, but the Northern Ireland international proved to be such a tower of strength that he retained his place in the starting line-up long after the manager who had signed him had departed.

Donaghy started the campaign alongside Paul Elliott in the middle of the back four – an indication of Porterfield's laudable desire to play constructive football from the back, for Mal was not a man to kick the ball just anywhere – and produced a series of immaculate displays. He then switched to left-back, where he performed with equal assurance, his reading of the game more than compensating for his lack of sprinting speed. Elegant and unhurried in his every action, the former Luton stalwart provided invaluable guidance to the youngsters who played alongside him, and the opportunity to learn from such a craftsman can only have advanced their football education.

At the start of the following season Mal was handed yet another role, playing as a defensive midfielder in front of the back three. His principal task was to provide cover when new player-manager Glenn Hoddle made his forays out of defence, and he proved quietly effective. When the tactical revolution was put on hold, Donaghy soon slipped out of the first-team reckoning and at the end of the season he was released.

BORN: Belfast, 13.9.57.
GAMES: 72 (6). GOALS: 3.
HONOURS: 91 Northern Ireland caps (80-94).
OTHER CLUBS: Luton Town 78/9-88/9 (410, 16); Manchester United 88/9-91/2 (89, 0); Luton Town *on loan* 89/90 (5, 0).

1992/93-1993/94

ANTHONY BARNESS

When Anthony Barness agreed to join the Blues from Charlton in September 1992, he had every reason to suppose that the move would advance his career. In the event, his four-year stay at Stamford Bridge proved a cruel disappointment, and when it was over he found himself back where he had started.

Signed when he was still only 19 as a long-term prospect, Anthony made two appearances during his first season with the club but following the appointment of Glenn Hoddle he slipped to the back of the first-team queue. A traditional, defensive full-back who lacked the pace to hare down the wings and send over crosses, he did not possess the attacking instincts required to play as a wing-back in the new manager's chosen formation.

His chance to impress came in 1994/95, when he played 11 games in succession in a conventional back four. Although naturally right-footed, 'Barney' was equally comfortable on the left and that was where he found an opening before switching to the opposite flank. While he was a neat, composed defender, he was sometimes a little casual and that proved to be his undoing when his lack of assertiveness cost a couple of goals in a defeat at Norwich. That was the end of his run in the side and, apart from a solitary Coca-Cola Cup match the following season, the end of his Chelsea first-team career. In August 1996 he returned to Charlton to begin again.

BORN: Lewisham, 25.2.73.
GAMES: 16 (3). GOALS: 0. OTHER CLUBS: Charlton Athletic 91/2-92/3 (27, 1) and 96/7- (74, 3); Middlesbrough *on loan* (0, 0); Southend United *on loan* 95/6 (5, 0).

1992/93-1995/96

DARREN BARNARD

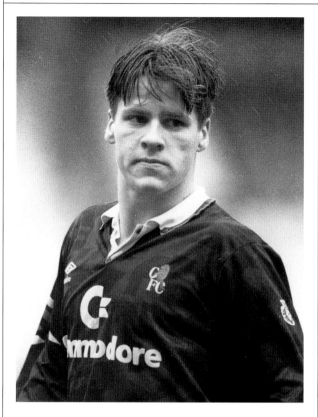

Consistently outstanding in the reserves, Darren Barnard was never given the extended run in the Chelsea first team that might have allowed him to reproduce that form on a bigger stage.

Darren arrived at Stamford Bridge as an awestruck 18-year-old in the summer of 1990, having impressed with his performances for non-League Wokingham, but had to wait nearly two years before he was considered ready for his senior debut. A natural winger, he had a fine left foot and earned top marks from the Blues' coaching staff for his powerful shooting and tantalising crosses, his only obvious weakness being a lack of real sprinting speed. He started eight games in 1992/93, all wide on the left, but following the arrival of Glenn Hoddle he was forced to prove his adaptability, filling in at wing-back and full-back as well as on the left of a midfield diamond during the new manager's first season. Barnard played his part in the FA Cup semi-final victory over Luton at Wembley, coming on as a first-half substitute, and seemed to have established himself as a valued squad member. However, with the signing of Scott Minto and David Rocastle adding to the fierce competition for places on the flanks, he found himself out in the cold, and in October 1995 he moved on to Bristol City.

BORN: Rinteln, Germany, 30.11.71.
GAMES: 20 (13). GOALS: 2.
HONOURS: 1 Wales cap (98-).
OTHER CLUBS: Reading *on loan* 94/5 (4, 0); Bristol City 95/6-96/7 (78, 15); Barnsley 97/8- (35, 2).

1991/92-1993/94

MARK STEIN

Mark Stein had one commodity to offer, the most valuable in the game: goals. A deadly finisher in the penalty area, he contributed little outside it and when the harvest failed he soon found himself surplus to requirements.

Mark had enjoyed a bumper crop during his time at Stoke and it took several weeks for Glenn Hoddle to persuade the Potteries club to part with their prize asset. The £1.5 million deal was completed in October 1993 but at first, try as he might, Mark was unable to deliver the goods. Then, after a seven-game famine, he found the net with a subtle lob in a 3-1 defeat at Southampton and over the next few weeks he couldn't stop scoring. In all he rattled up 12 goals in 14 games, setting a new Premiership record by scoring in seven successive matches along the way.

A tiny, childlike figure, Mark was an economical marksman who was content to roll the ball into the net without unnecessary power or flourishes. With his confidence soaring, he was single minded in his pursuit of goals and prepared to try his luck from any angle. He found space intelligently and was most effective when he could run onto a pass, allowing him to use his pace to get ahead of defenders, but his first touch was not so impressive and when the ball was played to his feet he was occasionally embarrassed.

Mark's golden age came to an end when he injured his ankle at Old Trafford in March and although he returned in time to play in the FA Cup final he needed surgery in the summer to cure the problem. He was eventually able to return to action in December and quickly re-established himself, scoring 11 goals in 26 starts, but his lethargic demeanour and lack of obvious passion meant that he never won the hearts of the Stamford Bridge crowd. With competition for places increasing with the arrival of Mark Hughes, Stein's goalscoring touch deserted him in the opening weeks of 1995/96 and he quickly dropped out of the first-team squad. A proposed return to Stoke the following season fell through and he remained at Stamford Bridge, his talents wasted, until the closing weeks of 1997/98 when a free transfer finally released him from his dispiriting ordeal.

BORN: Cape Town, South Africa, 29.1.66.
GAMES: 57 (6). GOALS: 25.
OTHER CLUBS: Luton Town 83/4-87/8 (54, 19); Aldershot *on loan* 85/6 (2, 1);
Queens Park Rangers 88/9-89/90 (33, 4); Oxford United 89/90-91/2 (82, 18);
Stoke City 91/2-93/4 (94, 50); Stoke City *on loan* 96/7 (11, 4);
Ipswich Town *on loan* 97/8 (7, 2); AFC Bournemouth *on loan* 97/8 (11, 4).

1993/94-1995/96

DAVID HOPKIN

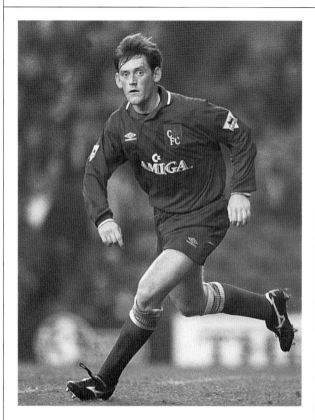

Watching his performances for Chelsea, few Blues supporters could have foreseen that David Hopkin would become a Scottish international and earn himself a £3.25 million move to Leeds United, all within two years of leaving Stamford Bridge. When David joined Chelsea from Morton in September 1992 for a rather more modest £300,000, he was regarded as a natural right-winger whose game was all about running at defenders and getting in crosses, and it was in this position that he made his first League appearances for the Blues the following February. However, the arrival of Glenn Hoddle that summer meant that Hopkin was obliged to reinvent himself as a midfield player, since the new manager had no use for the traditional attacking winger.

A powerfully built six-footer, David made sporadic appearances over the next two seasons, occasionally filling in as a makeshift striker, but never looked comfortable away from the touchline. As befitted his red hair, he was energetic and aggressive, sometimes trying too hard in his efforts to impress when he might have done better to rely on his natural abilities. In the summer of 1995 Hoddle sold him to Crystal Palace for £850,000 and he was presumably as surprised as anyone at the way Hopkin was to flourish – playing in midfield – during his two seasons at Selhurst Park.

BORN: Greenock, 21.8.70.
GAMES: 24 (22). GOALS: 1.
HONOURS: 4 Scotland caps (97).
OTHER CLUBS: Morton; Crystal Palace 95/6-96/7 (83, 21);
Leeds United 97/8- (25, 1).

1992/93-1994/95

NEIL SHIPPERLEY

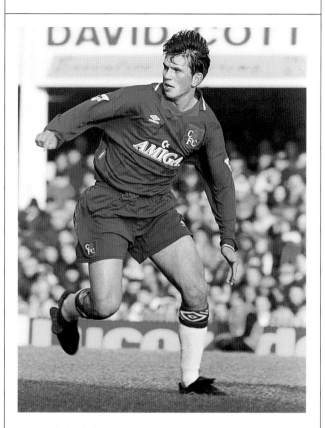

It was difficult for a couple of seasoned campaigners like Tony Cascarino and Mick Harford to take the place of Kerry Dixon in the hearts of the Chelsea faithful. But for a time it looked as though young Neil Shipperley just might.

A big, bustling centre-forward, Neil was a prolific marksman in youth and reserve football and confirmed his potential with a goal on his full first-team debut at the end of 1992/93. Still only 18, he continued his rapid progress under the tutelage of Glenn Hoddle, quickly making himself a favourite of the Stamford Bridge crowd with a series of wholehearted displays, crowned by a spectacular winner against Liverpool. His inevitable lack of experience was very apparent and he sometimes looked painfully naive, failing to see openings and wasting his energy chasing hopeless causes. However, for a man of his size he displayed a neat touch, although his goalscoring record didn't reflect his ability.

Neil was displaced by John Spencer after Christmas and was never a regular thereafter. On his occasional outings he appeared to have lost some of his old sharpness and mobility and when Southampton made an offer of £1.2 million for him in January 1995, Hoddle accepted it, leaving the Blues' fans searching for a new hero.

BORN: Chatham, 30.10.74.
GAMES: 35 (13). GOALS: 9.
OTHER CLUBS: Watford *on loan* 94/5 (6, 1); Southampton 94/5-96/7 (66, 12); Crystal Palace 96/7- (58, 19).

1992/93-1994/95

GLENN HODDLE

When Glenn Hoddle arrived at Stamford Bridge as player-manager in the summer of 1993, he had reached an age when most footballers already hung up their boots. Inevitably, he was not as fit as he had been in his prime and a career-threatening knee injury which had kept him out of the game for 18 months had also taken its toll. Nevertheless, his performances over the next two seasons left Chelsea fans in no doubt that this legend of the game was still one of the most gifted players English football had ever seen.

Keen to give his new charges an example of the cultured style he wanted to introduce, Glenn played in each of the Blues' first 17 matches. He had adopted the 3-5-2 formation he had employed at his previous club, Swindon, and once again filled the key role of the spare defender himself. His total confidence in his mastery of the ball meant that he had time to consider the options open to him when he was in possession and a buzz went round the ground whenever he surged forward to initiate an attack, but it was hard to avoid the conclusion that such an outstanding creative talent would have been employed to greater effect further forward.

Hoddle was forced to abandon his plans when he was sidelined by injury for three months and he started only a handful of games thereafter. However, he continued to make telling contributions as a substitute, this time in a more influential midfield role, notably against Wolves in an FA Cup quarter-final in 1994. The superb ball control, the vision, the inch-perfect passing and the sheer class that had been the trademark of his glory days remained undimmed by the passage of time and it was a testament to his enduring ability that he was never adequately replaced when he was missing.

Glenn bowed out in majestic style against Arsenal in the final game of 1994/95, setting up the first goal with a beautifully disguised pass and dominating proceedings with the easy mastery of a conjuror. He left the field to a standing ovation, and the Chelsea supporters in the crowd were left to rue the fact that he had spent the best years of his glittering career at Tottenham and Monaco rather than Stamford Bridge.

BORN: Hayes, 27.10.57.
GAMES: 22 (17). GOALS: 1.
HONOURS: 53 England caps (79-88).
OTHER CLUBS: Tottenham Hotspur 75/6-86/7 (377, 88); Monaco; Swindon Town 91/2-92/3 (64, 1).
MANAGER: Swindon Town (91-93); Chelsea (93-96); England (96-).

1993/94-1994/95

DMITRI KHARINE

Prior to rupturing a knee ligament for the second time in his career at Sheffield Wednesday in September 1996 Dmitri Kharine was regarded as one of the Premiership's top goalkeepers. Since coming to Stamford Bridge from CSKA Moscow nearly four years earlier, the Russian international had earned a reputation as an exceptional shot-stopper whose athleticism and agility would not have disgraced an Olympic gymnast. The injury kept him out of action for more than a year and although he returned to the Chelsea goal on a part-time basis in the closing weeks of 1997/98 it remains to be seen whether he will be able to regain his position as the Blues' number one 'keeper.

Although Dmitri made his Chelsea debut not long after completing his £400,000 move to London in December 1992, it was not until the start of Glenn Hoddle's reign that he finally established himself in the side. Invariably clad in tracksuit bottoms, he received scant protection from a somewhat disorganised defence and pulled off a string of crucial saves as the Blues dragged themselves away from the relegation zone, none more spectacular than a flying leap to deny Rob Lee at Newcastle in April. However, he proved somewhat reluctant to come off his line for crosses, never really dominating his goalmouth, and in the absence of a truly authoritative centre-half that proved to be a significant shortcoming. Like most continental goalkeepers, he tended to punch the ball rather than catching it, and he clearly had little appetite for the robust challenges permitted by English referees, but he gradually became accustomed to the unfamiliar tempo and tactics of the British game and, with his command of the language slowly improving, his understanding with his defenders looked rather more secure.

Having missed only a couple of games in 1993/94, Dmitri briefly lost his place to Kevin Hitchcock after injuring his shoulder in February 1995 and spent much of the second half of 1995/96 on the bench after picking up a knock in the third round of the Cup against Newcastle. Nevertheless, he was Ruud Gullit's first choice at the start of the following season and looked in fine form until suffering the injury at Hillsborough that sadly put his career on hold. All Chelsea fans will hope that the best is yet to come.

BORN: Moscow, Russia, 16.8.68.
GAMES: 141. GOALS: 0.
HONOURS: 36 Russia/USSR/CIS caps.
OTHER CLUBS: Torpedo Moscow; Dynamo Moscow; CSKA Moscow.

1992/93-

KEVIN HITCHCOCK

For most of his ten years at Stamford Bridge Kevin Hitchcock has been Chelsea's number two goalkeeper. It is an unglamorous but vitally important role, and one he performs with exemplary professionalism. Loyal, cheerful and enthusiastic, he accepts his lot uncomplainingly, and it is only bad luck with injuries, together with a question mark over his consistency, that has prevented him from making the position his own.

Signed from Mansfield in March 1988 only hours before the transfer deadline to halt the Blues' slide towards relegation, Kevin made an immediate impact, his commanding presence giving confidence to a shell-shocked defence, but the following season a series of injuries denied him the chance to build on that bright beginning. By the time he had recovered, Dave Beasant had arrived to reinforce Chelsea's promotion drive. Kevin made a total of seven appearances in three years but in 1991/92 it was the former Wimbledon hero's turn to suffer fitness problems and Hitchcock enjoyed several spells in the team, making a vital penalty save in the fourth round of the FA Cup against Everton.

When Ian Porterfield finally lost patience with Beasant's increasing fallibility the following autumn, Kevin seized his opportunity with a string of fine performances, proving himself to be brave and agile and an exceptional shot-stopper. He has always been less secure when the ball is crossed into the goalmouth, however, and a misjudgement in David Webb's first game in charge was to prove costly. Beasant was recalled once more and at the start of the next campaign new manager Glenn Hoddle opted for Dmitri Kharine, who had been signed the previous December. Back in the shadows for 18 months, Kevin re-emerged to make some crucial saves in the Cup-Winners' Cup quarter-final first leg in Bruges in February 1995 and enjoyed another extended run in 1995/96, helping the Blues reach the FA Cup semi-final. Untimely injuries allowed Frode Grodas to establish himself when Kharine was sidelined the following season and since the Russian's return to fitness Kevin has come to be regarded as a full-time substitute, happy to be involved and ready to prove himself once more if the opportunity presents itself.

BORN: Custom House, 5.10.62.
GAMES: 129 (3). GOALS: 0.
HONOURS: FA Cup 96/7; Coca-Cola Cup 97/8; European Cup-Winners' Cup 97/8.
OTHER CLUBS: Nottingham Forest (0, 0); Mansfield Town 83/4-87/8 (182, 0);
Northampton Town *on loan* 90/1 (17, 0); West Ham United *on loan* (0, 0).

1987/88-

SCOTT MINTO

For much of his time at Stamford Bridge Scott Minto was dogged by injuries and illness, and it was only during what was to be his last season as a Chelsea player that he began to produce the form that had prompted Glenn Hoddle to sign him from Charlton in the summer of 1994.

Scott's arrival was seen as the long-overdue solution to the Blues' perennial weakness at left-back, but an achilles tendon problem prevented him from making his Chelsea League debut until mid-November. Although he managed a total of 27 starts that season, he was unable to build up any real momentum and always looked slightly ill at ease in his new surroundings.

Scott missed a large part of the following campaign with an ankle injury, and it was not until the autumn of 1996 that he was finally able to earn a regular first-team place. His old sharpness gradually returned and as his confidence and understanding with his team-mates grew, he became increasingly impressive. Happiest when pushing forward down the flank, he had the pace to get behind defences and the skill to dummy his way past an opponent, although his forays too often promised rather more than they delivered. His five goals were a welcome bonus, but the Blues' FA Cup triumph over Middlesbrough was to be his last game for the club. Unable to agree terms for a new contract, in the summer he opted to join Portuguese giants Benfica on a free transfer.

BORN: Bromborough, 6.8.71.
GAMES: 70 (2). GOALS: 5.
HONOURS: FA Cup 96/7.
OTHER CLUBS: Charlton Athletic 88/9-93/4 (180, 7); Benfica.

1994/95-1996/97

JAKOB KJELDBJERG

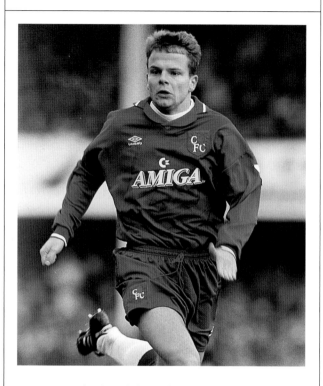

Fate was not kind to Jakob Kjeldbjerg. Having adapted well to the demands of the Premiership after a hesitant beginning, the affable Dane was struck by a heartbreaking series of injuries that would ultimately end his career.

Signed by Glenn Hoddle from Silkeborg shortly after the start of the 1993/94 season, the big central defender took a little time to come to terms with the rough and tumble that remains an essential part of English football, allowing forwards dwarfed by his towering 6ft 3in frame to get the better of him. He was left out of the side for a while after Christmas, but returned to form an effective partnership with Erland Johnsen as the Blues reached the FA Cup final for the first time in more than twenty years. Good in the air, Jakob was surprisingly quick for a man of his size but there were occasions when he was caught unawares, revealing his relative lack of experience at the top level.

The two Scandinavians remained the twin pillars of the Chelsea defence the following season but in an FA Cup tie at Millwall in January Jakob dislocated his shoulder. No sooner had he returned to action than he tore a hamstring and in December, while working his way back to fitness after a problem with his left knee, he sustained damage to his right knee that would force him to retire from football a year later. He was just 27, and there is no doubt that Blues fans had yet to see the best of him.

BORN: Frederiks, Denmark, 21.10.69.
GAMES: 65 (1). GOALS: 2.
HONOURS: 14 Denmark caps.
OTHER CLUBS: Holstebro; Viborg; Silkeborg.

1993/94-1994/95

PAUL FURLONG

Although Chelsea paid a club record fee to bring Paul Furlong to Stamford Bridge in May 1994, the athletic striker remained unproven at the top level. Now 25, he had spent a single inconclusive season in the old First Division with Coventry City, who had signed him from non-League Enfield, but the Midlanders had then sold him to Watford for £250,000. Paul had impressed during his two years at Vicarage Road, but when Glenn Hoddle agreed to pay £2.3 million to secure his services he was investing in the player's potential rather than acquiring the finished article. Burdened by his hefty price tag and the expectations of supporters desperate for success, Paul was unable to reproduce his training-ground performances when it mattered, and his potential was to remain unfulfilled.

'Furs' made a flying start to his Chelsea career, scoring on his debut and notching a total of five goals in his first ten appearances. Quick and strong, he was comfortable with the ball on either foot and possessed impressive control for a six-footer. He was a cool finisher and good in the air as well, although there were times when it seemed he was not making as much use of his imposing physique as he might have done.

Paul suffered a serious setback when he sustained a damaged hamstring in late October. It kept him out for six weeks and when he returned he seemed to have lost some of his earlier sharpness. With the goals drying up, he came under pressure from the Stamford Bridge crowd, which misinterpreted a loss of confidence as a lack of heart, but he silenced the doubters with a terrific performance in the home leg of the Cup-Winners' Cup quarter-final against Bruges, scoring one goal and making the other as the Blues stormed to a famous victory.

Furlong finished the season in rampaging style with five goals in as many games and seemed sure to play a key role the following season, but the arrival of Mark Hughes meant that he was competing with Mark Stein and John Spencer for a place as the Welsh international's foil. He made irregular appearances and seldom recaptured his best form. In the summer he moved on to Birmingham City for an initial fee of £1.5 million.

BORN: Wood Green, 1.10.68.
GAMES: 59 (26). GOALS: 17.
OTHER CLUBS: Coventry City 91/2 (37, 4); Watford 92/3-93/4 (79, 37); Birmingham City 96/7- (68, 25).

1994/95-1995/96

DAVE MITCHELL

MICHAEL GILKES

IAN PEARCE

NICK COLGAN

JOE ALLON

STEVE LIVINGSTONE

GRAHAM RIX

DAVE MITCHELL 1988/89-1990/91

Forward. BORN: Glasgow, 13.6.62.
GAMES: 8. GOALS: 0.
HONOURS: Australia caps.
OTHER CLUBS: Rangers; Eintracht Frankfurt; Feyenoord; NEC
Nijmegen *on loan*; Newcastle United *on loan* 90/1 (2, 1);
Swindon Town 91/2-92/3 (68, 16); Altay Izmir;
Millwall 93/4-94/5 (55, 15)

JOE ALLON 1991/92-1992/93

Forward. BORN: Gateshead, 12.11.66.
GAMES: 4 (14). GOALS: 3.
OTHER CLUBS: Newcastle United 84/5-86/7 (9, 2);
Swansea City 87/8-88/9 (34, 11); Hartlepool United 88/9-90/1 (112,
50) and 95/6- (56, 19); Port Vale *on loan* 91/2 (6, 0);
Brentford 92/3-93/4 (45, 19); Southend United *on loan* 93/4 (3, 0); Port
Vale 93/4-94/5 (23, 9); Lincoln City 95/6 (4, 0).

MICHAEL GILKES 1991/92

Winger. BORN: Hackney, 20.7.65.
GAMES: 0 (2) (*on loan* from Reading). GOALS: 0.
OTHER CLUBS: Reading 84/5-96/7 (393, 43);
Southampton *on loan* 91/2 (6, 0); Wolverhampton Wanderers 96/7- (8, 1).

STEVE LIVINGSTONE 1992/93

Forward. BORN: Middlesbrough, 8.9.69.
GAMES: 0 (1). GOALS: 0.
OTHER CLUBS: Coventry City 86/7-90/1 (31, 5); Blackburn Rovers
90/1-92/3 (30, 10); Port Vale *on loan* 93/4 (5, 0);
Grimsby Town 93/4- (171, 33).

IAN PEARCE 1990/91-1992/93

Central defender/forward. BORN: Bury St Edmunds, 7.5.74.
GAMES: 0 (5). GOALS: 0.
OTHER CLUBS: Blackburn Rovers 93/4-97/8 (62, 2);
West Ham United 97/8- (30, 1).

GRAHAM RIX 1994/95

Midfielder. BORN: Doncaster, 23.10.57.
GAMES: 1 (3). GOALS: 0.
HONOURS: 17 England caps (80-84).
OTHER CLUBS: Arsenal 76/7-87/8 (351, 41); Brentford *on loan* 87/8
(6, 0); Caen; Le Havre; Dundee.

NICK COLGAN 1996/97-

Goalkeeper. BORN: Drogheda, Ireland, 19.9.73.
GAMES: 1. GOALS: 0.
OTHER CLUBS: Crewe Alexandra *on loan* (0, 0); Grimsby Town *on
loan* (0, 0); Millwall *on loan* (0, 0); Brentford *on loan* 97/8 (5, 0);
Reading *on loan* 97/8 (5, 0);

GERRY PEYTON

GERRY PEYTON 1992/93

Goalkeeper. BORN: Birmingham, 20.5.56.
GAMES: 0 (1) (*on loan* from Everton). GOALS: 0.
HONOURS: 33 Ireland caps.
OTHER CLUBS: Burnley 75/6-76/7 (30, 0);
Fulham 76/7-85/6 (345, 0); Southend United *on loan* 83/4 (10, 0);
AFC Bournemouth 86/7-90/1 (202, 0); Everton (0, 0);
Bolton Wanderers *on loan* 91/2 (1, 0); Norwich City *on loan* (0, 0);
Brentford 92/3 (19, 0); West Ham United (0, 0).

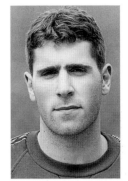

JOE SHEERIN

JOE SHEERIN 1996/97-

Forward. BORN: Hammersmith, 1.2.79.
GAMES: 0 (1). GOALS: 0.

NEIL CLEMENT 1996/97-

Full-back. BORN: Reading, 3.10.78.
GAMES: 1. GOALS: 0.

NEIL CLEMENT

PAUL PARKER 1996/97

Defender. BORN: West Ham, 4.4.64.
GAMES: 1 (3). GOALS: 0. HONOURS: 19 England caps (89-94).
OTHER CLUBS: Fulham 80/1-86/7 (153, 2); Queens Park Rangers
87/8-90/1 (125, 1); Manchester United 91/2-95/6 (105, 1); Derby
County 96/7 (4, 0); Sheffield United 96/7 (10, 0); Fulham 96/7 (3, 0);
Sunderland (0, 0).

PAUL PARKER

CRAIG FORREST 1996/97

Goalkeeper. BORN: Vancouver, Canada, 20.9.67.
GAMES: 2 (1) (*on loan* from Ipswich Town). GOALS: 0.
HONOURS: Canada caps.
OTHER CLUBS: Colchester United *on loan* 87/8 (11, 0); Ipswich
Town 88/9-96/7 (263, 0); West Ham United 97/8- (13, 0).

STEVE HAMPSHIRE

STEVE HAMPSHIRE 1997/98-

Midfielder. BORN: Edinburgh, 17.10.79.
GAMES: 0 (1). GOALS: 0.

CRAIG FORREST

NICK CRITTENDEN 1997/98-

Winger/wing-back. BORN: Bracknell, 11.11.78.
GAMES: 1 (2). GOALS: 0.

JON HARLEY 1997/98-

Midfielder. BORN: Maidstone, 26.9.79.
GAMES: 3. GOALS: 0.

JON HARLEY

NICK CRITTENDEN

FRANK SINCLAIR

During a Chelsea first-team career that has now spanned eight seasons, Frank Sinclair has seen off the challenge of many rivals who have arguably possessed greater natural talent. In that time he has filled a bewildering array of defensive roles but the tenacity with which he has held onto his first-team place is a testament to his wholehearted enthusiasm, commitment and versatility.

Although he is right-footed, Frank was introduced to senior football at left-back, Bobby Campbell giving him a brief run in the side in April 1991. But when he finally established himself in the team in 1992/93, it was at centre-back, following the injury that ended Paul Elliott's career. Although, at 5ft 9in, he was often shorter than the forwards he faced, he was rarely outjumped. His positional play was sometimes suspect but his lightning pace usually got him out of trouble and by the end of the season, he had become a firm favourite of the Stamford Bridge crowd.

Frank remained a first-team regular under Glenn Hoddle, usually playing in the middle of the defence although he was at left-back once again when he had the misfortune to concede a hotly disputed penalty in the 1994 FA Cup final. If his distribution was not always of the standard the new manager wished to see, his determined tackling could not be faulted, although he was sometimes let down by lapses in concentration. The boisterous Londoner missed much of 1995/96 due to a recurrent shin problem and was also sidelined for the first half of the following season, but when Michael Duberry was ruled out by injury, Frank was ready to step into the breach. For the Cup semi-final against Wimbledon he was switched to right-back in order to reinforce the defence and stayed there in 1997/98. The improvement in his passing and ball skills under the influence of Ruud Gullit was remarkable and with his confidence blossoming, Frank was invited to play for the Jamaican national side. There seems no doubt that, despite the continuing influx of foreign imports, there will be a place for him in the Chelsea team for many seasons to come.

BORN: Lambeth, 3.12.71.
GAMES: 210 (7). GOALS: 13.
HONOURS: FA Cup 96/7; Coca-Cola Cup 97/8. 5 Jamaica caps.
OTHER CLUBS: West Bromwich Albion *on loan* 91/2 (6, 1).

1990/91 -

EDDIE NEWTON

Eddie Newton does not fit the stereotype of the midfield ball-winner; from the stands he appears to be the epitome of cool sophistication, the antithesis of the fire-breathing hard men who usually fill the role. However, he is a doughty tackler with the stamina to run all day, and it is an indication of the importance of his contribution to the Blues' recent successes that he is sorely missed when he is ruled out by injury, as he has been all too often in the last few seasons.

Having gained some much-needed experience during a spell on loan at Cardiff in 1991/92, Eddie was given his Chelsea debut in the final game of the season at Everton, scoring a spectacular goal after coming on as a substitute. The following season the Londoner was rarely out of the side, demonstrating his versatility by filling in on the right flank and at left-back before settling down as Andy Townsend's partner in the middle of the pitch. It was during Glenn Hoddle's first season in charge at Stamford Bridge that Eddie discovered what has come to be regarded as his natural position, playing at the base of a midfield diamond. It is a role that suits him well.

Although he covers a huge amount of ground during a game, he lacks the pace to surge forward and play one-twos with his strikers. But sitting in front of the centre-backs like a hungry spider, he breaks up the opposition's attacking movements and keeps things ticking over with the kind of meticulous short passes that leave opponents frustratedly chasing shadows.

Nigel Spackman's fine form in 1994/95 meant that Eddie had to fight for his place in the team but he was playing some of the best football of his career when he broke his right leg in a collision with Kevin Hitchcock in February 1996. Although he made a full recovery he has since been troubled by a never-ending sequence of serious injuries and has yet to rediscover his best form. Nevertheless, he has helped the Blues to three major cup triumphs and, while he seldom receives the credit he deserves, he remains a key member of Gianluca Vialli's squad.

BORN: Hammersmith, 13.12.71.
GAMES: 180 (25). GOALS: 10.
HONOURS: FA Cup 96/7; Coca-Cola Cup 97/8; European Cup-Winners' Cup 97/8.
OTHER CLUBS: Cardiff City *on loan* 91/2 (18, 4).

1991/92-

TERRY PHELAN

The basis of Terry Phelan's game was his startling pace. Signed from Manchester City to provide attacking options on the left when Scott Minto was ruled out by injury, the former Wimbledon full-back perhaps lacked the guile or ball skills to thread his way through a defence but his speed posed a threat that was hard to contain. However, his sprinting ability was achieved at a price and for much of his stay at Stamford Bridge he was troubled by fitness problems.

In fact, Terry was carrying a hamstring strain when he joined the Blues in November 1995 and he suffered a recurrence shortly after making his belated Chelsea debut. He returned to the side for the FA Cup third round match against Newcastle and immediately proved how effective he could be, sending over a beautiful curling cross that was headed home by Mark Hughes to give the Blues the lead. The Irish international was sometimes guilty of squandering the openings he created but he remained a fixture in the side until the semi-final against Manchester United, when he suffered a thigh injury shortly after half-time. Unwisely, it was decided that he should to run the problem off but by the time he had left the field, United had scored twice.

Terry suffered more niggling injuries the following season and was unable to reclaim his place in the team. Within days of making his first start of the campaign at the end of December, he was sold to Everton at a profit of £100,000.

BORN: Manchester, 16.3.67.
GAMES: 21 (3). GOALS: 0.
HONOURS: 38 Ireland caps.
OTHER CLUBS: Leeds United 85/6 (14, 0); Swansea City 86/7 (45, 0); Wimbledon 87/8-91/2 (159, 1); Manchester City 92/3-95/6 (103, 1); Everton 96/7- (24, 0).

1995/96-1996/97

DAVID ROCASTLE

David Rocastle was only 27 when he joined Chelsea from Manchester City in August 1994 but in retrospect it seems clear that the flame that had burned so brightly during his glory days at Arsenal, which saw him win two League Championship medals and 14 England caps, had already been extinguished.

Highly regarded by his team-mates, 'Rocky' started the first 22 games of the season, usually on the right flank, and invariably gave everything he had, but there were times when the game seemed to pass him by. When in possession, he tended to over-elaborate, trying to dribble his way out of tight situations when a simple pass might have been more effective. He might perhaps have been happier in the middle of the pitch. He lost his place in November and although he returned later in the season, producing a stirring display against Bruges in the Cup-Winners' Cup at Stamford Bridge, he was regularly replaced before the game was over. It transpired that he had been handicapped by a problem with his toe and he underwent surgery in the summer to correct it. He made a brief return to the side the following October in a 3-0 defeat at Blackburn but a foot injury sustained shortly afterwards ruled him out for much of the remainder of the season. Unhappily, David was unable to force his way back into the first-team reckoning and he saw out the balance of his four-year contract in the reserves, where he offered generous assistance to the youngsters playing alongside him.

BORN: Lewisham, 2.5.67.
GAMES: 37 (3). GOALS: 2.
HONOURS: 14 England caps (88-92).
OTHER CLUBS: Arsenal 85/6-91/2 (218, 24); Leeds United 92/3-93/4 (25, 2); Manchester City 93/4 (21, 2); Norwich City on loan 96/7 (11, 0); Hull City on loan 97/8 (9, 1).

1994/95-1995/96

ERLAND JOHNSEN

Erland Johnsen was much the same player when he left Chelsea in the summer of 1997 as he had been when he arrived nearly eight years earlier: a tough, uncompromising central defender who relished the physical side of the game and invariably gave his all.

It is difficult to explain, therefore, why the big Norwegian's fortunes should have fluctuated so dramatically during his long stay at Stamford Bridge.

Recruited from Bayern Munich in December 1989, Erland quickly forged an effective defensive partnership with Ken Monkou, his wholehearted performances confirming that he was well suited to English football as the Blues finished fifth. However, at the start of the following season, he was dropped after two games and over the next two and a half years he was to make just a dozen first-team starts. A Chelsea career that seemed to be drifting towards an ignominious conclusion was unexpectedly revived when David Webb succeeded Ian Porterfield in February 1993 and promptly restored Johnsen to the side. Good in the air and quick for his size, the red-haired centre-back proved to be a tower of strength, winning the ball and clearing it in the no-nonsense style demanded by the new manager.

Erland had to prove himself once more at the start of Glenn Hoddle's reign but in the second half of the season he was a permanent fixture in the middle of the back four, adding some much-needed strength and aggression to the side as the Blues dragged themselves out of the relegation zone. With Hoddle's encouragement, he became increasingly accomplished on the ball, playing within his limitations and seldom wasting possession. Resolute and unflappable, Johnsen enjoyed his best season in 1994/95, playing an influential role as the Blues reached the semi-finals of the Cup-Winners' Cup, but once a suspension had forced him out of the team the following December he was unable to re-establish himself, apart from a brief spell at the start of 1996/97. Always popular with the fans, Erland was to make a telling contribution to Chelsea's FA Cup triumph, helping subdue Wimbledon's muscular attack in the semi-final, but he had already made up his mind to return to Norway and at the end of the season he joined Rosenborg on a free transfer.

BORN: Fredrikstad, Norway, 5.4.67.
GAMES: 170 (13). GOALS: 1.
HONOURS: 24 Norway caps.
OTHER CLUBS: Moss FK; Bayern Munich; Rosenborg.

1989/90-1996/97

STEVE CLARKE

Even by the standards of an era when few footballers seem to stay with one club for very long, Stamford Bridge has seen a remarkable turnover of players in the last decade or so. But while the revolving door has continued to spin, Steve Clarke has resolutely stayed put. The fact that the Scot has remained with the Blues for 11 years is obviously a testament both to his loyalty and to his abundant talent, but it is his adaptability that has ultimately been the decisive factor that has enabled him to survive a period of endless change.

When he came to Stamford Bridge from St Mirren in January 1987 Steve was a buccaneering right-back who looked very stylish when he was on the attack but was less secure when he was obliged to defend. After a couple of games at centre-back, he quickly established himself in the side in place of Darren Wood, and his form during the Blues' inept slide towards relegation the following season was sufficiently impressive for him to earn international recognition, although, to the bewilderment of all Chelsea fans, it would be some time before he added to his haul of five full caps. The sight of the tall, classy defender driving forward, exchanging passes with a team-mate and racing into the penalty area was electrifying, although it must be admitted that his attacking forays frequently ended in frustration as he sent his cross into the crowd or dragged his shot wide of the target.

Having played a leading role in the Blues' Second Division Championship triumph in 1988/89, Steve continued to impress as Bobby Campbell's side made a successful return to the top flight, but there were clouds on the horizon. A back injury sustained during training with the Scottish squad in preparation for the World Cup cost him his place in the Chelsea team, which ended his hopes of going to Italy. Indignant at the frustration of his international ambitions, he asked for a transfer but after nine months on the list he agreed to put the past behind him and try to force his way back into the side. The arrival of Ian Porterfield in the summer of 1991 gave him the chance to make a new start and he responded brilliantly, adding a new defensive authority to his undiminished attacking flair, only for a hernia operation to ruin his season. A similar injury allowed Gareth Hall to displace him once more in 1992/93, but he was restored to the side by David Webb and with the arrival of Glenn Hoddle his talent was finally given long-overdue recognition.

Making full use of all his accumulated experience, Steve had developed into an accomplished defender, strong, aggressive and pacy, and his outstanding form received proper acknowledgement when he was restored to the Scotland team and voted Chelsea's Player of the Year. Now a model of consistency, he maintained his high standards in 1994/95, but the arrival of Dan Petrescu in the wake of Hoddle's decision to reintroduce his favoured 3-5-2 system seemed to spell the end of his first-team chances at Stamford Bridge. However, before long Clarke had found a way back, playing as a marker on the left of the back three, and performed with such cool assurance, despite being on the 'wrong' flank, that it looked as though he had spent his whole career there. Biding his time before making a biting tackle, then playing a simple pass to a colleague, he was quite superb and retained the role until Ruud Gullit switched to a conventional back four for the 1997 FA Cup semi-final against Wimbledon, in which he played at left-back. He joined Frank Leboeuf in the middle of the defence for the final, and in 1997/98, now a veteran of 34, he remained a valued member of the Blues' squad, filling in wherever he was required. Steve has proved his resilience on many occasions in the past, and it would be foolish to bet against his adding to the honours that have deservedly come his way towards the end of his career.

BORN: Saltcoats, 29.8.63.
GAMES: 406 (14). GOALS: 10.
HONOURS: Second Division Championship 88/9; FA Cup 96/7; Coca-Cola Cup 97/8; European Cup Winners' Cup 97/8; 6 Scotland caps (87-94).
OTHER CLUBS: St Mirren.

1986/87-

DENNIS WISE

Few of Chelsea's big-money signings have provided better value for money than Dennis Wise. The £1.6 million the Blues paid to prise the bubbly Londoner away from Wimbledon established a new club record, but his inspirational example and unquenchable spirit, coupled with a technical finesse that seldom receives proper acknowledgement, have been crucial to Chelsea's successes in the 1990s. After a testing start to his Stamford Bridge career he has become so closely identified with the club that no Chelsea team seems complete without the little cockney terrier.

Wise has undergone a remarkable transformation during his years with the Blues. When he moved to Stamford Bridge in the summer of 1990 he was a feisty 23-year-old winger. A spectacular performance against Derby on the opening day of the season suggested that he would be a real crowd-pleaser, and the unrealistic expectations raised by that memorable home debut were to prove something of a burden over the next couple of years. Dennis has never had the pace to go past his full-back on the outside in the style of a traditional winger but, given half a yard, he will play the ball into the penalty area with the deadly accuracy of a laser guided missile, curling it around the defender facing him with the minimum of backlift, even when off balance. Always busy and inventive, he immediately became the Blues' most creative player, his superbly flighted dead-ball kicks invariably putting defenders under pressure, and at the end of his first season at Stamford Bridge he made his international debut in a European Championship qualifying match in Turkey.

Significantly, Dennis produced his best performances during Ian Porterfield's spell in charge when he was employed in midfield, operating immediately behind the strikers in a free role that allowed him to see plenty of the ball and make full use of his perceptive passing, and following the arrival of Glenn Hoddle in the summer of 1994 he was to develop into one of the most accomplished midfielders in the country. An eager, cheerful character with the grin of a cheeky schoolboy, Dennis has enormous stamina and is capable of running all day, chasing and covering remorselessly. He tackles with great spirit but his enthusiasm sometimes gets the better of him and regular absences from the side through suspension have come to seem inevitable. He has a fiery temper which sometimes leads him to act foolishly but, deprived of his natural aggression, he would not be half the player he is. With the departure of Andy Townsend, Hoddle handed him the captain's armband and he seemed to benefit from the added responsibility, learning to keep his volatile temperament under better control.

Following the Blues' appearance in the 1994 FA Cup final Dennis was recalled to the England side after an absence of three years, but he suffered a considerable setback when he tore a thigh muscle that December, an injury which sidelined him for much of the rest of the season. During his long absence, the Blues' fortunes nosedived, confirming once more just how much they had come to rely upon their influential skipper. It took Dennis a while to regain full fitness and it was not until 1996/97 that he rediscovered his best form. Playing further infield since the decision to revert to 3-5-2, he was the team's mainspring, winning the ball and playing a simple pass to a colleague and fittingly became the first Chelsea captain since Ron Harris to lift a major trophy when the Blues won the FA Cup.

In 1997/98 Dennis scaled new heights, revelling in the opportunity to play alongside world-class players after carrying much of the creative burden single handedly during the early part of his Chelsea career. Fitness problems took some of the wind out of his sails in the second half of the season and as usual he was sorely missed whenever he was sidelined. Still the loveable rogue, he is now in his thirties but he continues to mature as a player and seems sure to remain an essential part of the Stamford Bridge scene for several years yet.

BORN: Kensington, 16.12.66.
GAMES:308 (7). GOALS: 61.
HONOURS: European Cup-Winners' Cup 97/8; FA Cup 96/7; Coca-Cola Cup 97/8.
5 England Caps (91).
OTHER CLUBS: Wimbledon 84/5-89/90 (135, 27).

1990/91-

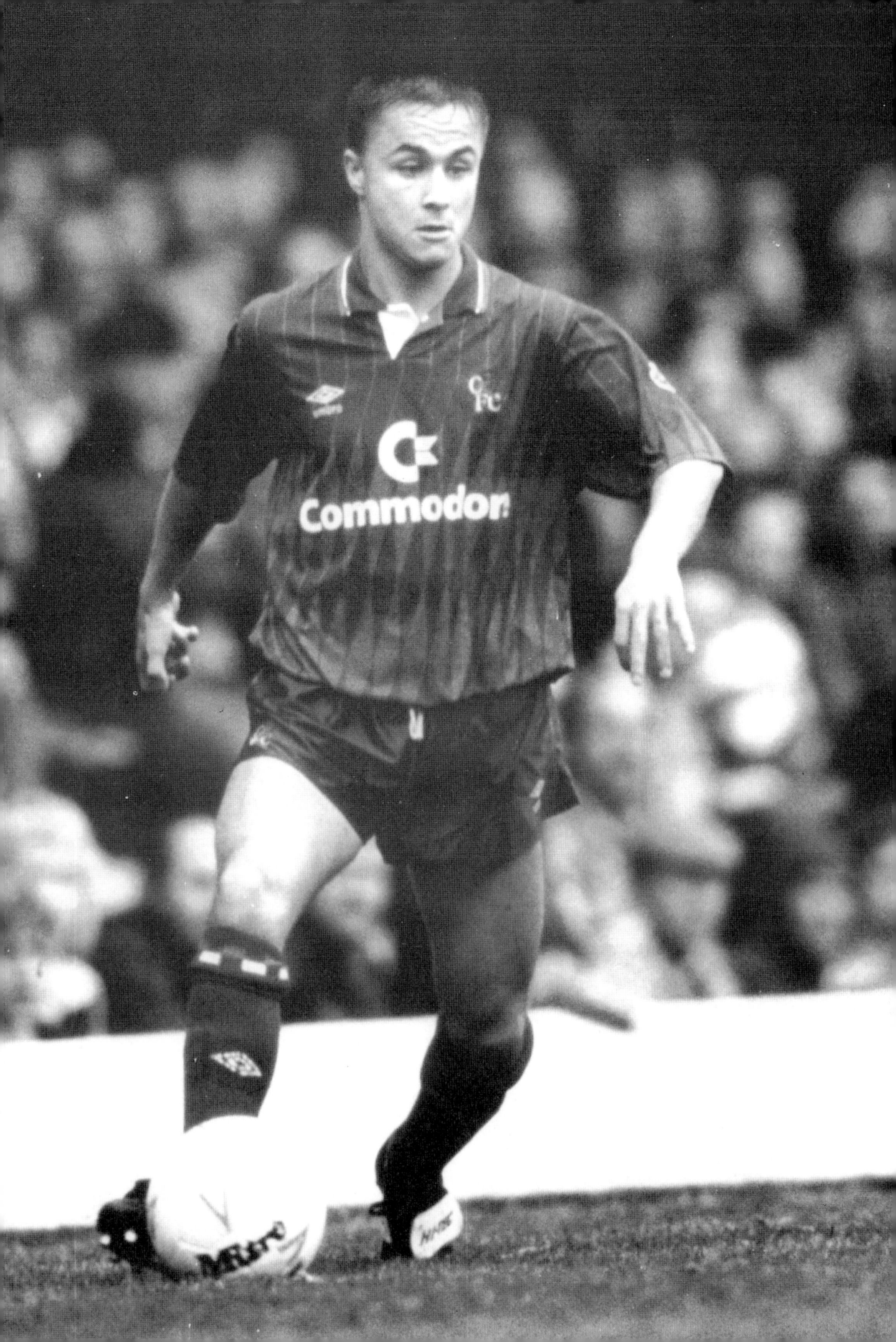
Commodore

RUUD GULLIT

The 1995/96 season will be recalled with a warm glow of nostalgia by Chelsea fans for many years to come. The club won no trophies and could finish no higher than 11th in the Premiership, but the Blues' line-up was regularly graced by one of the undisputed all-time greats of world football: Ruud Gullit. Although there was naturally much brave talk when the dreadlocked Dutchman was persuaded to move to Stamford Bridge on a free transfer at the end of his contract with Sampdoria, even the most sanguine observer could scarcely have foreseen the full extent of his impact on English football. Quite apart from his mesmerising skill on the pitch, he possessed an aura of sophistication and style that would help forge the game's current fashionable image.

Although Gullit had made his name as a free-wheeling attacker, Glenn Hoddle recruited him with the intention of employing him as a libero, but while the former AC Milan star's imperious surges out of defence electrified the Stamford Bridge crowd he showed little enthusiasm for regaining his position when possession was lost. When he returned to the side shortly before Christmas after a month-long injury lay-off he was switched to midfield and became much more influential, frequently dominating the game with his vision, pinpoint passing and powerful running. Although Ruud was now 33 and had suffered serious knee injuries during his time in Italy, he remained a superb natural athlete, combining surprising strength with a devasting change of pace, but it was his air of unshakeable confidence and the breathtaking close control with which he played his way out of tight corners that sent the fans into raptures.

When he succeeded Hoddle in the summer of 1996, Ruud's playing career inevitably suffered. Having been sidelined by knee trouble for much of the first half of 1996/97, he was quite majestic when he stood in for Frank Leboeuf over Christmas but he stepped aside once the Frenchman was available again. In March he suffered a broken ankle, and although he made occasional appearances the following season, usually at centre-back, he never really recaptured his old sharpness. When he finally left the club in controversial circumstances in February 1998, Chelsea's stunned supporters could at least console themselves with their memories of his fantastic first season in London.

BORN: Amsterdam, Netherlands, 1.9.62.
GAMES: 50 (14). GOALS: 7.
HONOURS: 65 Netherlands caps.
OTHER CLUBS: Haarlem; Feyenoord; PSV Eindhoven; AC Milan (twice); Sampdoria (twice).
MANAGER: 96-98.

1995/96-1997/98

ANDY MYERS

Since scoring on his full debut a month before his 18th birthday, Andy Myers has not made the progress many had anticipated. This has largely been the result of a heartbreaking catalogue of injuries but to some extent, he has also been the victim of his own commendable versatility.

At the time of his League baptism against Liverpool in October 1991, Andy was regarded as a midfielder but his real breakthrough came later that season when he was given a run at left-back following the departure of Tom Boyd. His positional play was understandably suspect, reflecting his lack of previous experience in the role, but his grit and determination carried him through and he seemed set to challenge for a regular first-team place in 1992/93.

Unhappily, he sustained a serious ankle injury in a pre-season friendly which was to trouble him for more than two years and missed much of the following campaign after breaking a bone in his foot. Once he had regained full fitness, new recruit Scott Minto's regular absences allowed him a number of opportunities but while Andy was an effective defender, he was less impressive when coming forward.

It was only when he was employed on the left of the back three in place of the suspended Erland Johnsen in December 1995 that Myers was finally able to establish himself in the team and, although he lacks the height to be dominant in the air, this is probably his best position. Immensely strong and blessed with plenty of pace, he is a fierce competitor and his tackles carry real bite. After a few weeks he was ruled out by a hamstring injury but he returned towards the end of the campaign to resume his successful partnership with Michael Duberry and David Lee.

Andy was used as a wing-back at the start of the following season but another fitness setback allowed Minto to press his claims and since then Myers has made only a handful of appearances, many of them as a conventional centre-back. There is no doubt that he has the ability to make the grade in the Premiership but he is now 24 and it may be that he will have to look elsewhere for first-team football.

BORN: Isleworth, 3.11.73.
GAMES: 88 (14). GOALS: 2.
HONOURS: FA Cup 96/7; European Cup-Winners' Cup 97/8.

1990/91 -

MARK HUGHES

Although Mark Hughes was nearly 32 when he joined Chelsea from Manchester United in the summer of 1995, he had been a pivotal member of the United side that had just finished second in the Premier League and his appetite for the game appeared undiminished. The fee of £1.5 million undoubtedly represented good business for the Manchester club but many United supporters continue to believe that the talismanic Welshman was sold prematurely. Whatever the truth of that may be, there is no doubt that the Reds' loss has been Chelsea's gain.

Mark remains an outstanding target man, perhaps the best in English football. He has immaculate control and immense strength, allowing him to kill the ball immediately, keep possession while colleagues move forward to support him and lay it off to them no matter how closely marked he might be. After so long with one of the biggest clubs in Europe, it understandably took Mark a while to find his feet at Stamford Bridge. At first, some of his new team-mates tended to aim the ball towards his head, hoping that he would get a flick-on, but they quickly came to realise that he is much more effective if the ball is played accurately to his feet or chest. With the arrival of Dan Petrescu and Terry Phelan, he had players on the flanks providing an outlet for him as Kanchelskis and Giggs had done and Chelsea began to produce some of the most fluent attacking football they had managed in years.

Mark has never been a record-setting marksman and his tally of 12 goals in 39 appearances in his first season with the Blues was in keeping with his career average. He rarely seems to score simple goals but his strength means that he is a threat whenever the ball is crossed to the far post. Spectacular volleys and bicycle kicks are his acknowledged speciality, and he cemented his relationship with the Stamford Bridge crowd with a glorious effort from 20 yards against Southampton in his third home match. However, it was the FA Cup semi-final against his old club that provided what must surely have been his most satisfying moment of the season: taking a long pass with a defender at his back with characteristic deftness, the lionhearted striker turned and bulldozed his way past two opponents before sending over a lovely flighted cross which Ruud Gullit despatched into the net with a powerful header amid a flurry of dreadlocks.

At the start of the following season 'Sparky' was paired with Gianluca Vialli but the chemistry wasn't right and by mid-December he had managed only two goals. When Gianfranco Zola joined him up front, however, the pair struck up an immediate rapport. Mark hit the target five times in the FA Cup alone and deservedly collected the fourth winner's medal of his career, his finest hour coming in the fourth-round tie against Liverpool at Stamford Bridge when he joined the fray as a half-time substitute and immediately transformed a match that had appeared lost, adding an urgency and aggression to the Blues' attack that had previously been missing.

Although he is softly spoken and self-effacing in post-match interviews, Mark is a fearsome competitor on the pitch. No defender enjoys facing him and some of his challenges are a throwback to an earlier, less genteel era, but in fairness it should be said that he takes a lot more punishment than he metes out and routinely shrugs off injuries that would make most of us faint.

In 1997/98 Mark was less sure of a spot in the Blues' starting line-up as first Gullit and then Vialli rotated their squads, but whenever he was called upon he continued to trouble defences and the superbly placed volley against Vicenza that clinched a place in the Cup-Winners' Cup final typified his relish for the big occasion. He was left on the bench in Stockholm and there was speculation that he would be returning north in the summer. Mark has become a Stamford Bridge folk-hero over the last three seasons and the memories of his stirring exploits for the Blues will endure for many years to come.

BORN: Wrexham, 1.11.63.
GAMES: 108 (14). GOALS: 38.
HONOURS: FA Cup 96/7; Coca-Cola Cup 97/8; European Cup-Winners' Cup 97/8.
66 Wales caps (84-97).
OTHER CLUBS: Manchester United 83/4-85/6 (89, 37) and 88/9-94/5 (256, 82);
Barcelona; Bayern Munich *on loan*.

1995/96-

DAN PETRESCU

Many highly regarded players owe much of their success to the physical attributes, such as strength, height and pace, that give them an edge over their opponents, but Dan Petrescu has followed a different route to the top. The Romanian international's achievements are the product of immaculate technique, guile and the mental acuity of a chess grandmaster.

Dan was signed from Sheffield Wednesday in November 1995 to play at right-wing-back in the 3-5-2 formation favoured by Glenn Hoddle, who had been pursuing him since the summer as part of his effort to assemble the players needed to make the system effective. There was a delay in completing his £2.3 million move to Stamford Bridge because of difficulties arising from the routine medical, but he soon became a key member of Chelsea's increasingly cosmopolitan squad.

It quickly became apparent that Dan is essentially a midfielder rather than a pacy overlapping full-back. His running off the ball reflects his pin-sharp awareness, allowing him to find space deep in enemy territory, as Wimbledon discovered to their cost in the FA Cup quarter-final replay a few months after his arrival. He has instantaneous control, dancing feet and an extensive repertoire of feints and tricks that make him hard to contain, but it is his eye for the match-winning through-ball that is his greatest asset, typified by the superbly weighted pass that gave Gianluca Vialli his first goal against Liverpool in the Cup in 1997.

Dan could not be described as a combative player, so it was not difficult to understand Ruud Gullit's decision to use a conventional back four against Wimbledon in the semi-final, freeing Petrescu of most defensive responsibilities and allowing him to concentrate on what he does best. He remained on the right of midfield in 1997/98, enabling him to chalk up seven goals before Christmas, but there were signs that Ruud was becoming frustrated by his tendency to disappear from games. It is a problem Vialli will need to address, but there is no doubt that when he is in on form, the Romanian is a purist's delight.

BORN: Bucharest, Romania, 22.12.67.
GAMES: 113 (2). GOALS: 15.
HONOURS: FA Cup 96/7; Coca-Cola Cup 97/8; European Cup-Winners' Cup 97/8. 67 Romania caps.
OTHER CLUBS: Steaua Bucharest; FC Olt *on loan*; Foggia; Genoa; Sheffield Wednesday 94/5-95/6 (37, 3).

1995/96-

CRAIG BURLEY

In an era of increasingly frantic transfer activity, it is easy for clubs to take for granted the players they have nurtured themselves. Craig Burley became an established Scottish international during his time at Stamford Bridge but was less sure of his place in the Chelsea side, and it sometimes seemed that he might have been appreciated a little more if he had been signed from another club for a hefty fee instead of emerging from the Blues' own youth nursery.

A tall, cultured midfielder, Craig made his debut as a substitute in April 1991 but had only a handful of senior outings over the next couple of seasons. Following injury problems in the second half of 1992/93, he was overlooked by new manager Glenn Hoddle at the start of the following campaign and seemed set to join Coventry until the deal fell through. However, with Chelsea slipping down the table, he was given his chance after Christmas and the 22-year-old played a starring role as the Blues eased away from relegation and reached the FA Cup final. Operating on the right of the midfield diamond, Burley scored some memorable goals from long range, with a blazing left-foot volley at Anfield the pick of the bunch, and used the ball intelligently. An all-rounder who worked hard, tackled with determination and ran at defences, committing opponents, before opening them up with a telling pass, he seemed ideally suited to the 'pass and move' game Hoddle favoured but over the next couple of seasons, partly because of injuries, he was in and out of the side, despite winning his first full caps in the summer of 1995.

Generally employed as a wing-back at international level, Craig performed dependably in a variety of roles for the Blues, his adaptability reflecting an astute football brain, but he was happiest in the middle of the pitch, pulling the strings. Under Ruud Gullit, he was seldom out of the team and was extremely unfortunate to play no part in the 1997 FA Cup final. Uncertain of his long-term prospects, he declined to sign a new contract and Chelsea, unwilling to see him depart on a free transfer at the end of his existing deal, reluctantly sold him to Celtic for £2.5 million in the summer.

BORN: Cumnock, 24.9.71.
GAMES: 105 (32). GOALS: 11.
HONOURS: 23 Scotland caps (95-).
OTHER CLUBS: Celtic.

1990/91-1996/97

ROBERTO DI MATTEO

In the early stages of his Chelsea career, it looked as though Roberto Di Matteo was finding the transition from Serie A to the Premiership something of a culture shock. The game tended to pass him by and the Italian international, a £4.9 million signing from Lazio in the summer of 1996, appeared a little bewildered by the frenzy all around him. However, he soon adjusted to the relentless pace of the English game and after two seasons at Stamford Bridge has become one of the most accomplished midfielders in the country.

In Italy, Roberto was regarded as a defensive player and he began his first season in London as a midfield anchorman, but it was not until he was given a more attacking role shortly before Christmas that he began to fulfil the expectations aroused by that large transfer fee. Despite the image of cool sophistication created by his good looks and languid gait, he has proved to be a feisty competitor who is happy to trade tackles with the Premiership's numerous hard men. His accurate passing, unhurried but always purposeful, even under pressure, has become a key element in the Blues' cultured style, but he is most impressive when he changes up a gear and drives forward, accelerating smoothly past stranded defenders. He has a keen eye for the killer through-ball but it is Roberto's venomous shooting with either foot that has made him a favourite of the Stamford Bridge crowd. The dipping 30-yard drive that set the Blues on the way to victory after just 43 seconds in the 1997 FA Cup final has earned him a lasting place in the pantheon of Chelsea heroes.

Roberto is now so much a part of the Stamford Bridge scene that it is easy to forget those early struggles. In 1997/98 he was asked to play in a variety of midfield roles to meet the needs of the team and did so with characteristic professionalism. A real enthusiast, he always gives the impression of enjoying his football and his ready smile has cemented his popularity with fans and team-mates alike. He is only 28 and there is no doubt that he will be a key figure in Chelsea's pursuit of honours in the years ahead.

BORN: Schaffhausen, Switzerland, 29.5.70.
GAMES: 84 (3). GOALS: 19.
HONOURS: FA Cup 96/7; Coca-Cola Cup 97/8; European Cup-Winners' Cup 97/8. 31 Italy caps.
OTHER CLUBS: Schaffhausen; FC Zurich; Aarau; Lazio.

1996/97-

GIANLUCA VIALLI

Since joining the Blues on a free transfer from Juventus shortly after captaining the Turin side to victory in the final of the 1996 European Champions' Cup, Gianluca Vialli has experienced as many sudden reversals of fortune as the hero of a Victorian novel. But through it all, in good times and bad alike, the charismatic Italian striker has maintained a quiet professionalism that has helped make him one of the most popular players Chelsea have ever had.

Although he was 32 at the start of his first season at Stamford Bridge, Gianluca remained a player of absolute world class. However, niggling injuries that had interrupted his summer training meant that the Italian veteran was not as fit as he would have wished and his partnership with Mark Hughes was not the immediate success that many had anticipated. He averaged a goal every other game during the first four months of the season, but after a hamstring injury had sidelined him for three weeks he was unable to force his way back into the team and spent most of the second half of the campaign on the substitutes' bench.

It seemed certain that a token appearance in the closing moments of the FA Cup final would mark the end of Vialli's Chelsea career but he was still at Stamford Bridge at the start of the following season and, with no injury problems this time, he looked much fitter and hungrier than he had 12 months before. For all his superstar status, he is a very industrious player who works tirelessly to put defenders under pressure. He has inevitably lost some of his old sharpness but he is full of tricks and flicks and remains a deadly finisher who will punish the slightest lapse. With Tore Andre Flo adding to the strength of the Blues' squad, Gianluca's first-team appearances were still infrequent but his goalscoring record was hugely impressive.

By the time he was appointed manager in February 1998, he had notched up 15 goals in 21 appearances, eight of them as a substitute. Revelling in his new role, he then produced his best performances for the club, leading by example, with his valiant display against Vicenza providing a poignant reminder of the talent that had so often been allowed to go to waste during Ruud Gullit's reign.

BORN: Cremona, Italy, 9.7.64.
GAMES: 49 (18). GOALS: 30.
HONOURS: FA Cup 96/7; European Cup-Winners' Cup 97/8. 59 Italy caps.
OTHER CLUBS: Cremonese; Sampdoria; Juventus.
MANAGER: Chelsea (98-).

1996/97-

DANNY GRANVILLE

PAUL HUGHES

It is an indication of the strength of the current Chelsea squad that a young player like Danny Granville is not merely unable to secure a regular first-team berth but is arguably third in line for his preferred position. An adventurous left-back who can also play as a marker in a back three, Danny joined the Blues from Cambridge United shortly before the transfer deadline in March 1997, the clubs agreeing an initial fee of £300,000. He made three starts before the end of the season and looked highly impressive, confirming his potential as an attacking player by creating a goal for Mark Hughes against Leicester with a jinking run and a superb curling cross.

A fine performance in the Charity Shield at the start of the following season suggested that, with new signing Celestine Babayaro injured, Granville would be given a chance to make the position his own, but on the eve of the opening fixture at Coventry Graeme Le Saux was brought in, dashing the 22-year-old's hopes. Danny was recalled for the Cup-Winners' Cup match against Slovan Bratislava at Stamford Bridge and eased the Blues' anxiety with a crucial goal after a piece of brilliant improvisation, but it was not enough to retain his place. He had few opportunities to impress thereafter but he has a bright future. A willowy six-footer, he is a solid defender, with pace, composure and a decisive tackle, and once he forces his way into the Blues' starting line-up he will be difficult to dislodge.

BORN: Islington, 19.1.75.
GAMES: 18 (7). GOALS: 1.
HONOURS: European Cup-Winners' Cup 97/8.
OTHER CLUBS: Cambridge United 93/4-96/7 (99, 7).

Paul Hughes was haunted by dreadful luck with injuries during his formative years at Stamford Bridge and, although he has yet to make the transition from promising youngster to fully-fledged first-team regular, it says much for his talent and determination that he has progressed as far as he has. Having finally put his fitness problems behind him, the gifted midfielder was called from the substitutes' bench to make his Premiership bow against Derby in January 1997 and marked the occasion with one of the goals of the season. Picking the ball up in the middle of the pitch, the 20-year-old surged downfield, exchanging passes with Roberto Di Matteo and Mark Hughes as he went, before coolly tucking the ball past the stranded 'keeper.

Paul went on to make nine starts during the remainder of the campaign, his encouraging form denying Craig Burley a place in Ruud Gullit's side for the FA Cup quarter-final at Portsmouth. However, while the lanky Londoner plays with style and passes the ball imaginatively, he looks somewhat ponderous at times and perhaps needs to add a little urgency to his game if he is to fulfil his potential.

Unable to force his way into the starting line-up at the beginning of 1997/98, Paul was rather surprisingly employed at right-back when Frank Sinclair was suspended but the experiment ended unhappily after a run of five games. Since then, he has had little chance to add to his experience, but his ability is obvious and it should be remembered that he has overcome greater setbacks in the past.

BORN: Hammersmith, 19.4.76.
GAMES: 15 (8). GOALS: 2.

1996/97-

1996/97-

MARK NICHOLLS

If Mark Nicholls eventually establishes himself in the Chelsea team, it will be because of his attitude as much as his innate talents. A slim, wiry figure, he does not possess the extravagant skills of his better-known team-mates but he is armed with an unshakeable self-belief that ensures he exploits his relatively modest gifts to the full.

As a youth team player, Mark was an out-and-out goalscorer, a cool finisher with an instinct for the half-chance inside the penalty area who contributed little outside it, but he is a bit short of pace, a critical weakness at the top level. In addition, he lacks the physique to win the ball in the air or act as a target man and his Premiership debut at Leicester in October 1996, when he was replaced at half-time, offered little encouragement.

When he returned to the side at the end of the season he was employed in midfield and that is where he made most of his occasional appearances in 1997/98. Although few of his performances have been particularly eye-catching, Mark is a dogged, hard-working player with good close control who does an effective, if easily overlooked, job for the team. He also retains an eye for goal, as he demonstrated with two fine poacher's efforts after coming on as a substitute against Coventry. Mark will have to maintain his steady progress if he is to make the grade at Stamford Bridge, but there is no doubt that he will be giving it his best shot.

BORN: Hillingdon, 30.5.77.
GAMES: 14 (20). GOALS: 3.
HONOURS: European Cup-Winners' Cup 97/8.

1996/97-

JODY MORRIS

With the influx of overseas signings in recent years, it has become increasingly difficult for players emerging from the Blues' youth scheme to make their mark at Stamford Bridge. However, if any of the current crop of young pretenders is to follow in the footsteps of Tambling, Osgood and Wilkins it will surely be Jody Morris, the brightest prospect the club has produced in many years.

Jody has made only sporadic first-team appearances since Glenn Hoddle gave him his debut as a substitute in February 1996, a couple of months after his 17th birthday, but the diminutive midfielder's ability is apparent every time he plays. Although he is only 5ft 5in tall and inevitably lacks the pace and power of the men facing him, he has excellent technique and a sharp football brain, looks comfortable in possession and passes the ball with imagination and finesse.

Having made a handful of senior starts in the opening weeks of 1996/97, Jody suffered an ankle injury that disrupted his season and fell behind Paul Hughes in the midfield pecking order. The following season he was held back by further fitness problems but when he returned to the side in the spring he was noticeably stronger and more assertive than before. His performance against Vicenza at Stamford Bridge confirmed that he now has the maturity as well as the talent to cope in any company, and if he makes the most of his opportunities there is no reason why he should not develop into one of the country's top midfielders.

BORN: Hammersmith, 22.12.78.
GAMES: 19 (11). GOALS: 3.
HONOURS: European Cup-Winners' Cup 97/8.

1995/96-

MICHAEL DUBERRY

Although it is Chelsea's foreign legion of high-profile international stars who are understandably the focus of media attention, the one player at Stamford Bridge who has become truly indispensable is Michael Duberry. The young Londoner may not possess the dazzling skills of Zola or Gallic poise of Leboeuf, but since the departure of Erland Johnsen in the summer of 1997 he has been the only experienced defender in the large Blues' squad with the height and strength to meet the physical challenge posed by the Premiership's more robust strikers on equal terms.

Michael made his first-team debut as an 18-year-old in May 1994 but had to wait 18 months for his next opportunity. Recalled at short notice from Bournemouth, where he had been on loan, after Frank Sinclair was ruled out by shin problems, he was immediately thrown into action on the right of the back three and performed so impressively that he proved impossible to dislodge. He is an outstanding natural athlete, combining a powerful physique with real sprinting speed, and although, at 6ft 1in, he is not as tall as some players in his position he is seldom beaten in the air. In those early days his lack of experience was sometimes apparent, but he more than held his own and his thrilling surges down the right flank were guaranteed to bring the Stamford Bridge crowd to life.

A wholehearted player who tackles with ferocious commitment, 'Doobs' suffered a potentially devastating setback when he sustained a ruptured achilles tendon in January 1997, ending his season and causing him to miss the Blues' FA Cup triumph. Happily, he made a speedy recovery and was recalled to the colours three weeks into the new campaign to subdue Wimbledon's combative attack at Selhurst Park. Another nasty ankle injury halted his progress shortly afterwards, but as soon as he had recovered he was back in the firing line to face Everton's Duncan Ferguson, confirming his importance to the team. Michael makes occasional errors and perhaps needs to work on his distribution and reading of the game, but he is only 22 and if he maintains his spectacular progress there is no reason why he should not join his illustrious team-mates in international football.

BORN: Enfield, 14.10.75.
GAMES: 80 (2). GOALS: 3.
HONOURS: Coca-Cola Cup 97/8; European Cup-Winners' Cup 97/8.
OTHER CLUBS: AFC Bournemouth *on loan* 95/6 (7, 0).

1993/94-

FRANK LEBOEUF

Frank Leboeuf raises defending to an art form. While most centre-backs rely on their physical strength the French international is elegance personified. Deceptively quick, he reads the game brilliantly, allowing him to make countless interceptions during the course of a match, and when he has to make a tackle he does so with clinical precision and immaculate timing. Sometimes, however, there is no substitute for power and aggression, and on those occasions Frank can be found wanting.

A £2.5 million signing from Strasbourg in the summer of 1996, Leboeuf was recruited to play as the libero in the 3-5-2 formation Ruud Gullit had inherited from Glenn Hoddle, a role that allowed him to make full use of his creative abilities. With two markers playing alongside him, Frank had the freedom to bring the ball out of defence, regularly pushing upfield to provide an extra attacker in open play, but it was his relaxed, perceptive distribution that made him such an instant success. His vision is outstanding, and his beautifully flighted long passes from the back have created a string of stunningly simple goals like Gianluca Vialli's memorable effort at Old Trafford in November 1996, or Mark Hughes' FA Cup quarter-final goal at Portsmouth later that season. Leboeuf also has a thunderous shot which he is not afraid to use and has proved to be a rock-steady penalty-taker.

At first Frank struggled to cope with the barrage of high balls into the penalty area that characterises English football but he gradually improved that aspect of his game and when he was asked to play as a conventional centre-back against Wimbledon in the semi-final he was seldom troubled, prompting Gullit to retain a back four in 1997/98. Frank's opportunities to come forward were inevitably restricted but his passing remained majestic and he looked increasingly solid in defence, particularly when he was paired with Michael Duberry, whose aerial dominance makes him the ideal foil for the urbane Frenchman. Despite his air of cool certainty, Frank wears his heart on his sleeve and enjoys a warm rapport with the Stamford Bridge crowd, who have been quick to appreciate the sheer class of a defender who is a master of his craft.

BORN: Marseille, France, 22.1.68.
GAMES: 81. GOALS: 13.
HONOURS: FA Cup 96/7; Coca-Cola Cup 97/8; European Cup-Winners' Cup 97/8. 12 France caps.
OTHER CLUBS: Hyeres; Meaux; Laval; Racing Club Strasbourg.

1996/97-

GIANFRANCO ZOLA

Gianfranco Zola made an enormous impact on English football during his first part-season at Stamford Bridge following his £4.5 million move from Parma in November 1996 and was fittingly voted the football writers' Footballer of the Year, becoming the first Chelsea player to win this prestigious award. The tiny Sardinian striker is a supreme professional, who works tirelessly to perfect his mesmerising skills, yet he plays with the simple enjoyment and enthusiasm of a schoolboy. He is a perfectionist whose frustration when he makes a mistake is as readily apparent as his delight when things go well, but most importantly he is a man of great humility and dignity who, for all his dazzling repertoire of tricks, remains the embodiment of sportsmanship.

Gianfranco's arrival at Stamford Bridge was an irrefutable indication of Chelsea's new-found determination to challenge for the Premiership title. He was a current Italian international with 26 caps to his credit who, at 30, was still at the peak of his career. A dead-ball specialist, Zola took immediate responsibility for all the Blues' corners and free-kicks and created a memorable goal for Gianluca Vialli on his home debut but, playing on the right of midfield, he found it difficult to involve himself in the game, although his sheer class was obvious enough. However, against West Ham on the Saturday before Christmas, with Vialli sidelined by injury, Gianfranco moved up front to partner Mark Hughes and looked a different player. Involved in the thick of the action, the Italian maestro could use his captivating ball skills where it mattered and scored a brilliant individual goal, running at Hammers hard-man Julian Dicks and leaving him totally bewildered before driving the ball past Ludek Miklosko.

The pair complement each other ideally, the Welshman's strength and aggression creating space for the Italian, who is ideally equipped to exploit it to the full. Zola has extraordinary close control and outstanding balance, enabling him to wriggle his way out of almost any situation, even though he noticeably favours his right foot. Even when he is running with the ball at full pace, he has the ability to stop and turn on a sixpence, as he demonstrated with his superb goal in the FA Cup semi-final against Wimbledon, one of the best as well as one of the most important in Chelsea history. He has impressive awareness and times his runs into space superbly as well as passing the ball with precision and imagination. For a small man he shoots with remarkable power and his tally of 12 goals in 29 starts was more than respectable for a player who tends to come deep or move to the flanks to collect the ball before taking on defences.

If Gianfranco has a weakness it is a tendency to disappear from matches. In the FA Cup final, for example, his contribution was relatively modest, but in characteristic fashion he popped up from nowhere to flick Dan Petrescu's overhit cross back into the path of Eddie Newton for the crucial second goal.

In 1997/98 Gianfranco was rarely as effective as he had been the season before, perhaps because defenders were now familiar with the threat he presented and marked him more tightly, and he occasionally found himself out of the side as first Ruud Gullit and then Gianluca Vialli rotated their large squads. Strange as it may seem, the brilliant Italian appeared to lose confidence and sometimes looked an anonymous, slightly forlorn figure, although he continued to work hard for the team. He produced one of his best performances of the season in the Cup-Winners' Cup semi-final second leg against Vicenza, scoring a fine headed goal, and there is no doubt that he remains a match-winner. Immensely popular with the Stamford Bridge crowd, Gianfranco may never rediscover the spellbinding form that captivated football fans up and down the country during the second half of 1996/97, when he also scored a superb goal for Italy at Wembley, but Chelsea supporters will long cherish their memories of his first season in London and his contribution to the Blues' FA Cup win.

BORN: Oliena, Sardinia, Italy, 5.7.66.
GAMES: 64 (6). GOALS: 24.
HONOURS: FA Cup 96/7; Coca-Cola Cup 97/8; European Cup-Winners' Cup 97/8.
35 Italy caps.
OTHER CLUBS: Nuorese; Torres; Napoli; Parma.

1996/97-

FRODE GRODAS

When Frode Grodas joined the Blues from Lillestrom – initially on a three-month loan – in September 1996 he can scarcely have imagined that he would end the season with an appearance in the FA Cup final. The Norwegian international was signed to reinforce a squad depleted by Dmitri Kharine's serious knee injury but an unhappy debut in a 3-1 home defeat at the hands of Blackpool in the Coca-Cola Cup suggested that it might take him a little time to acclimatise.

When his next opportunity came along, as a result of an elbow problem that ruled out the Russian's acknowledged deputy, Kevin Hitchcock, Frode was better prepared and did well enough to be given a two-and-a-half-year contract. Tall and powerfully built, he got down impressively for such a big man and his bravery was unquestioned but he proved a little vulnerable to speculative shots from distance and when a run of five matches without defeat ended at Nottingham Forest Kevin was recalled.

A month later the luckless Hitchcock was sidelined once again and this time Grodas held his place for the rest of the season. Despite his height he was a little suspect on crosses and his head-long rushes from goal occasionally proved ill judged, but as his confidence grew he became increasingly authoritative. Having withstood Wimbledon's bombardment in the FA Cup semi-final, he made a crucial stop at Wembley, but during the summer Ruud Gullit signed Ed de Goey and the popular Norwegian, no longer wanted at Stamford Bridge, eventually moved on to Spurs in search of first-team football.

BORN: Volda, Norway, 24.10.64. GAMES: 26 (1). GOALS: 0.
HONOURS: FA Cup 96/7. 36 Norway caps.
OTHER CLUBS: Sogndal; Lillestrom; Tottenham Hotspur 97/8- (0, 0).

1996/97

ED DE GOEY

Ed de Goey is not the most stylish goalkeeper in the Premiership. Immensely tall and quite heavily built, he does not move with the lithe athleticism of many of his peers, but after a difficult start to his Chelsea career the saturnine Dutchman succeeded in regaining the confidence of the Stamford Bridge crowd and made a decisive contribution to the Blues' successes in 1997/98.

The Dutch international, signed from Feyenoord for £2.25 million in the summer of 1997 when it became apparent that Dmitri Kharine would not be ready to return to action at the start of the new season, understandably took a little time to adjust to the hurly-burly of English football. Despite his height and powerful physique, he was reluctant to come off his line and when he did so he usually opted to punch the ball instead of making a clean catch.

However, as the season progressed Ed became increasingly impressive. He gets down surprisingly well for a man of his size and although he will never be the tidiest of goalkeepers he is certainly a highly capable shot-stopper. His saves at Arsenal in the first leg of the Coca-Cola Cup semi-final were to prove vital and his performances against Real Betis in Seville and in Vicenza were crucial to Chelsea's progress in the Cup-Winners' Cup. Although he reluctantly stood aside for Kharine in a number of Premiership games in the closing weeks of the season, he was recalled for the big cup matches and his position as Chelsea's number one 'keeper appears unassailable.

BORN: Gouda, Netherlands, 20.12.66.
GAMES: 42 (0). GOALS: 0.
HONOURS: Coca-Cola Cup 97/8; European Cup Winners' Cup 97/8; 30 Netherlands caps.
OTHER CLUBS: Sparta Rotterdam; Feyenoord.

1997/98-

BERNARD LAMBOURDE

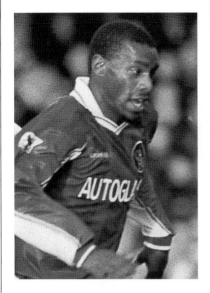

Bernard Lambourde's first season at Stamford Bridge following his £1.5 million move from Bordeaux in the summer of 1997 was largely frustrating. The big Frenchman had spent most of his career playing as a central defender but when he made his belated Chelsea debut – at Old Trafford, of all places – in September, having recovered from a niggling pre-season hip injury, he was employed as a defensive midfielder, a role he had seldom filled before. He acquitted himself well, impressing with his athleticism, determined tackling and cool distribution, but his hopes of establishing himself in the team in his preferred position suffered a major setback at Anfield eleven days later when, standing in for the suspended Frank Leboeuf, he was sent off with just 25 minutes played after collecting two yellow cards with clumsy challenges.

After that dispiriting experience, Bernard had only one brief spell in the first team, a run of four games in midfield in January. His powerful running and perceptive passing again showed real potential, but it seems that he needs to increase his contribution if he is to be more than a squad player.

BORN: Pointe à Pitre, Guadeloupe, 11.5.71.
GAMES: 9 (4). GOALS: 0.
OTHER CLUBS: Cannes; Angers *on loan*; Bordeaux.

1997/98-

CELESTINE BABAYARO

A £2.25 million signing from Anderlecht, Celestine Babayaro was only 18 when he joined the Blues in the summer of 1997 but he was already an established international. He had been a member of the strong Nigerian team that had won the Olympic tournament in Atlanta a year earlier, but he has unfortunately had little chance to show what he can do since coming to London.

Equally at home anywhere on the left flank, 'Baba' missed the start of the season after suffering a stress fracture of a bone in his foot. He eventually made his Premiership bow at home to Leicester in October, playing at left-back, and immediately won over the Stamford Bridge crowd, which was delighted by his speed, inventiveness and sheer exuberance. He looked set to establish a formidable left-wing partnership with Graeme Le Saux but at Tottenham in December Celestine suffered a recurrence of his foot injury. Surgery was required and by the time he had recovered the season was almost over, but the ebullient Nigerian is likely to provide Chelsea fans with rich entertainment for many years to come.

BORN: Kaduna, Nigeria, 29.8.78.
GAMES: 11 (2). GOALS: 0.
HONOURS: 6 Nigeria caps.
OTHER CLUBS: Anderlecht.

1997/98-

LAURENT CHARVET

A right-wing-back who is also comfortable on the right of midfield, Laurent Charvet came to Stamford Bridge on loan from Cannes in January 1998 to increase the options available to Ruud Gullit at a time when he was evidently considering making a return to the 3-5-2 formation he had abandoned towards the end of the previous season in an effort to reverse the puzzling slump in the Blues' fortunes.

Laurent was thrown into action almost immediately as a second-half substitute in the first leg of the Coca-Cola Cup semi-final at Highbury and emerged with credit. He started the next two matches but after Gullit had been replaced by Gianluca Vialli his opportunities were strictly rationed. When selected, however, he did well, creating a favourable impression with his pace and energy. The Frenchman is good in the air and scored a fine headed goal against West Ham, adding a superb half-volley to his tally against Leeds a few weeks later. Laurent seems well suited to English football and if his move to Chelsea is made permanent he will be a more than useful addition to the Blues' squad.

BORN: Béziers, France, 8.5.73.
GAMES: 7 (6). GOALS: 2.
HONOURS: European Cup-Winners' Cup 97/8.
OTHER CLUBS: Cannes.

1997/98-

TORE ANDRE FLO

There must have been times during his first season at Stamford Bridge following his transfer from Brann Bergen in the summer of 1997 when Tore Andre Flo wondered what more he had to do to win a regular place in the Chelsea side. The lanky Norwegian striker confirmed his abundant potential with a number of highly impressive performances and scored some outstanding goals but figured in the starting line-up for fewer than half of the Blues' matches.

It took his new team-mates a while to appreciate that, although Tore Andre is well over 6ft tall, he has far more to offer than just his height and prefers the ball to be played to him on the ground. Quick and mobile, he has excellent close control and is particularly dangerous when he is running at defenders from the flanks, as he demonstrated with two superb individual goals against Real Betis in Seville, which effectively clinched Chelsea's place in the Cup-Winners' Cup semi-finals. He proved to be a cool finisher but despite a fine goalscoring record, including a memorable hat-trick against Spurs at White Hart Lane in December comprising a header, a fierce drive and a delicate chip, he was unable to produce his best form with sufficient consistency to establish himself in the Blues' star-studded team. However, the Norwegian international has time on his side and looks sure to be a key figure in the Chelsea attack long after Hughes, Vialli and Zola have brought down the curtain on their playing careers.

BORN: Stryn, Norway, 15.6.73.
GAMES: 23 (21). GOALS: 15.
HONOURS: Coca-Cola Cup 97/8; European Cup-Winners' Cup 97/8. 23 Norway caps.
OTHER CLUBS: Stryn Sogndal; Tromso; Brann Bergen.

1997/98-

GUSTAVO POYET

A sickening knee injury ruined Gustavo Poyet's first season as a Chelsea player but the form he displayed before he was sidelined and the courage with which he fought his way back to fitness suggest that the South American midfielder will play an influential role in the Blues' pursuit of honours in 1998/99 and beyond.

A tall, powerfully built Uruguayan international, Gustavo came to Stamford Bridge on a free transfer from Real Zaragoza as part of Chelsea's ambitious team-building efforts in the summer of 1997. Playing on the left flank, he made an impressive start to the season, his poised, unhurried style concealing a fierce competitiveness. His height proved particularly valuable: not only did he win the ball in the air in midfield, he also posed a potent threat at corners, as he confirmed with the winning goal against Newcastle at the end of September.

Sadly a couple of weeks later Gustavo ruptured a cruciate ligament in his right knee, an injury which was expected to rule him out for the rest of the season. With characteristic determination, however, the amiable Uruguayan made a remarkable recovery and was back in the Blues' starting line-up for the second leg of the Cup-Winners' Cup semi-final against Vicenza at Stamford Bridge, marking his return with the vital first goal. It was a reminder of just how much Chelsea had missed him during his long absence and an encouraging indication of the contribution he can be expected to make now that he is fit once again.

BORN: Montevideo, Uruguay, 15.11.67.
GAMES: 15 (3). GOALS: 5.
HONOURS: European Cup-Winners' Cup 97/8. 27 Uruguay caps.
OTHER CLUBS: River Plate; Grenoble; Bellavista; Real Zaragoza.

1997/98-

GRAEME LE SAUX

It was apparent when Chelsea sold Graeme Le Saux to Blackburn Rovers shortly before the transfer deadline in March 1993 that they were losing a player of immense promise. The valuation agreed by the clubs was a knock-down £700,000 and the fact that little-known striker Steve Livingstone had been signed in part-exchange merely reinforced the feeling among Blues fans that the Lancashire club had got the better deal, a view that was emphatically vindicated when Chelsea paid £5 million to bring the Channel Islander back to Stamford Bridge on the eve of the 1997/98 season.

'Bergerac' came into the professional game later than most, joining the Blues from Jersey club St Paul's as a fresh-faced 19-year-old in December 1987. He had to wait another two years for his first senior start and it was not until 1990/91 that he began to figure regularly in the first team. He mostly played wide on the left of midfield, where his electrifying pace and direct running posed a constant threat, a scintillating display against Spurs in the Rumbelows Cup providing ample evidence of his ability to open up defences. His inexperience was obvious, a wayward final pass sometimes marring all that had gone before, but his sheer verve made him difficult to contain. Although he continued to forage tirelessly, Graeme's form the following season was generally less spectacular. After missing the start of 1992/93 following an ankle injury he found it impossible to regain his place and, with his career having lost its early momentum, he was allowed to move north.

During his Chelsea days Graeme had appeared reluctant to switch to left-back, despite a number of impressive performances there, but at Blackburn he was to be employed almost exclusively in that role. Under the tutelage of Kenny Dalglish he finally fulfilled his potential, helping Rovers to the League title and becoming an England international. However, a horrendous ankle injury sustained in December 1995 ruled him out for nearly a year and since returning to London he has struggled to produce his best form. Although he still comes forward with great panache, he looks a little vulnerable when he is facing a quick, skilful forward, and it seems likely that, once Celestine Babayaro has recovered from his injury problems, Graeme will settle down in his old role on the left of midfield.

BORN: Jersey, 17.10.68.
GAMES: 133 (21). GOALS: 12.
HONOURS: Coca-Cola Cup 97/8. 23 England caps (94-).
OTHER CLUBS: Blackburn Rovers 92/3-96/7 (129, 7).

1988/89-1992/93 & 1997/98-

TED DRAKE   MANAGER: MAY 1952-SEPTEMBER 1961

No Chelsea manager has refashioned the club more dramatically than Ted Drake. A fearless, rampaging centre-forward with Arsenal and England before the war, he succeeded Billy Birrell at Stamford Bridge in the summer of 1952 after serving a five-year apprenticeship at Reading. Determined that the Blues should at last fulfil their obvious potential and cease to be a team of big-name stars whose whole was invariably less than the sum of its parts, he abolished the club's old-established emblem, the Pensioner – putting an end to one of music hall's more enduring jokes – and called on the supporters to be more partisan. Aiming to build a side with the courage and spirit that had characterised his own playing career, Drake signed a number of players from the Third Division and recruited others from amateur football, and their success in the top flight was to be a remarkable vindication of his judgement. In Ted's first season in charge, the Blues finished 19th, as they had 12 months earlier, but the changes he had made gradually took effect and in 1954/55 Chelsea won the League Championship.

The following campaign proved to be a sorry anti-climax and, with a number of players apparently past their best, Drake started to dismantle his title-winning team – prematurely, in the view of some observers. A genial Hampshireman with a sunny, idealistic view of the game, Ted now placed his faith in a youth policy and filled the side with the gifted youngsters emerging from the club's Juniors. There were days when Drake's Ducklings showed enormous promise, but too many fresh-faced teenagers had been thrown in at the deep end together and heartbreaking inconsistency was the predictable consequence. The seasoned players he signed to hasten his young charges' progress failed to make the expected contribution and there were suggestions that discipline at Stamford Bridge had become lax. The incomparable genius of Jimmy Greaves ensured that enough goals were scored to counter-balance the torrent conceded by a leaky defence, but when the little maestro moved to Italy in the summer of 1961 disaster was inevitable. After a discouraging start to the new season, the Chelsea directors decided that change was essential and after nine years Drake was relieved of his position.

TOMMY DOCHERTY   MANAGER: JANUARY 1962-OCTOBER 1967

Tommy Docherty's passion and steely determination brought Chelsea agonisingly close to sustained success, but his turbulent reign was attended by unceasing conflict. He came to Stamford Bridge as a coach in February 1961 after a distinguished playing career with Preston, Arsenal and Scotland, but made a handful of first-team appearances the following season as the Blues slipped perilously down the table. When the decision was taken to replace Ted Drake, Docherty was put in charge of team affairs with the title of chief coach, and his self-confident, aggressive manner impressed the directors sufficiently for him to be appointed manager in January.

Nothing could be done to prevent relegation but Docherty lost no time in reshaping the playing staff, dispensing with the services of a number of stalwarts who had served the club well for many years. His remodelled team, built around the latest crop of youngsters to emerge from the Chelsea youth scheme, swept to promotion at the first attempt, eventually scraping into the First Division on goal average after the Big Freeze had interrupted their imperious progress. The Doc's fire and drive were superbly complemented by the tactical astuteness of his coach, Dave Sexton, and the exciting young team they had created became famed for fast, exciting football, based on non-stop running with the full-backs overlapping at every opportunity.

However, Docherty's Diamonds never quite fulfilled their potential. In 1964/65 they chased an unprecedented treble but only the League Cup was won, and an incident at Blackpool when eight players were sent home in disgrace after breaking a curfew seemed to poison the atmosphere in the dressing room. The following season the Blues reached the semi-finals of the FA Cup for the second season in succession and the semi-final of the Fairs Cup, but controversy was never far away and four leading players departed in quick succession. Doc's tough stance seemed to have been vindicated when the Blues led the First Division the following autumn, but then Peter Osgood broke his leg, and although Chelsea finally reached the FA Cup final, the old sparkle had gone. A disastrous start to the new campaign suggested that morale was at a low ebb, and when Docherty was suspended by the FA as a result of a dispute with a referee during a summer tour to Bermuda his departure from Stamford Bridge became inevitable.

DAVE SEXTON MANAGER: OCTOBER 1967-OCTOBER 1974

It now appears a little ironic that Dave Sexton should have been the players' choice to succeed Tommy Docherty. He had given up his position as Chelsea coach in January 1965 to manage Leyton Orient, and subsequently worked as a coach at Fulham and Arsenal before returning to Stamford Bridge. He would become the most successful manager in Chelsea's chequered history, but his relationship with his star players was never comfortable, and it seems clear that he would have been more effective had he been relieved of responsibility for matters such as contracts and discipline, and left to concentrate on the coaching at which he excelled.

The Blues advanced up the table in purposeful fashion following Sexton's appointment, finishing in sixth place, and the players he signed fitted in well. The frantic intensity of the Docherty days had gone for ever but the team played with style and spirit, and in 1969/70 they looked a match for any side in the country, winning the FA Cup and taking third place in the League. The following season brought the European Cup-Winners' Cup to Stamford Bridge and in 1971/72 the Blues reached their third Cup final in successive seasons, but Sexton's previously sure touch in the transfer market appeared to have deserted him. He signed a number of players without seeming to have a clear idea of the role he wanted them to fill and endless team changes gave the impression of a loss of direction.

A quiet, scholarly man who thought deeply about the game and rarely betrayed any emotion, Sexton appeared to have lost the respect of some of his players and the Blues' increasing inconsistency pointed to problems behind the scenes. There were persistent reports that he was engaged in a battle of wills with Alan Hudson and Peter Osgood and matters came to a head when the two stars were dropped in January 1974. Hudson was soon on his way but the board's reluctance to part with the popular stiker apparently prompted Dave to offer his resignation before the directors reluctantly gave him their backing. Osgood was sold, but Chelsea slipped to 17th place in the final table and, with the financial burden imposed by the building of a new stand making success on the field imperative, a disappointing start to the following season resulted in Sexton's dismissal.

RON SUART MANAGER: OCTOBER 1974-APRIL 1975

The task that faced Ron Suart when he replaced Dave Sexton could scarcely have been more daunting. Chelsea were haunted by the prospect of relegation, star players had left, morale was low and there was no money available for replacements. Suart was liked and respected, having been the club's assistant manager for seven years, and had the experience gained during nine seasons in charge at Blackpool to fall back on, but it was a situation where a fire-breathing evangelist was needed rather than a competent administrator.

An improvement in the atmosphere at the club was immediately apparent and Suart introduced a few of the talented youngsters who represented the Blues' hope for the future, but despite one or two encouraging performances, it was quickly apparent that he was no miracle-worker. The threat of relegation grew ever more real and in desperation the directors turned to Eddie McCreadie, with Suart moving 'upstairs'. He remained with the club until 1983, subsequently joining Wimbledon as chief scout.

EDDIE McCREADIE MANAGER: APRIL 1975-JULY 1977

Eddie McCreadie appeared to regard the task of managing Chelsea as a personal crusade to save the club from oblivion. He had just three games in which to stave off the threat of relegation when he was put in charge of team affairs and he responded to the challenge with the courage and defiance that had characterised his long and distinguished career as the Blues' left-back, dropping a number of his former team-mates and making 18-year-old Ray Wilkins captain.

Despite the new manager's bold gamble, the Blues went down and a massive financial crisis threatened to overwhelm the club. No money was available for transfers but Chelsea had to start winning if they were to survive. A fiery, passionate character who seemed to have based his management style on that of his old sparring partner, Tommy Docherty, McCreadie suffered agonies of frustration as his young team failed to perform. He built them up with extravagant praise and knocked them down with savage criticism until at last he found the winning blend. The following season they raced to promotion playing exciting, flowing football that brought the crowds flocking back to Stamford Bridge. McCreadie had achieved mission impossible. There seemed to be every reason to take him seriously when he declared that his exuberant young team was going to take the First Division by storm, but in July, outraged at the board's lack of appreciation for his efforts, he walked out and embarked on a new life in America.

KEN SHELLITO MANAGER: JULY 1977-DECEMBER 1978

As the manager of Chelsea's youth team, Ken Shellito had been responsible for the development of many of the young players who had regained the Blues' place in the First Division in such stirring fashion in 1977, and when Eddie McCreadie walked out he must have seemed the obvious candidate to take over. Philosophical and unfailingly cheerful, Ken was a very different personality from his old full-back partner and favoured a more measured, controlled style of football, but too many of the players at his disposal proved unequal to the challenge.

Ken strove mightily to keep the ship afloat and 16th place in the final table represented a creditable achievement. The introduction of Clive Walker prompted a flurry of goals, and a rousing Cup win against Liverpool pointed to a brighter future, but the following season Chelsea looked certain to go down almost from the first day of the campaign and after a humiliating farce when the directors flirted with Miljan Miljanic, the celebrated Yugoslav coach, Ken resigned. It was a sorry end to Shellito's long association with the club he had served with such distinction, but at least he had the satisfaction of knowing that no one could have tried harder.

DANNY BLANCHFLOWER MANAGER: DECEMBER 1978-SEPTEMBER 1979

Danny Blanchflower was an idealist who longed to restore beauty and style to a game that had been defaced by cynicism and the win at all costs mentality. Since the end of his outstanding playing career with Tottenham his only involvement with professional football (apart from some journalism) had been as the part-time manager of the Northern Ireland team, so his appointment represented a brave gamble, to say the least. He encouraged the Chelsea players to enjoy themselves and attempted to liberate them from the shackles imposed by traditional coaching methods, but they seemed to lack the technique and imagination to put their new manager's ideas into effect.

Despite one or two inspired signings, the Blues showed no signs of clawing their way clear of relegation, and when the start of the following season brought no improvement Danny accepted that fine words were no substitute for success on the field, and departed.

GEOFF HURST MANAGER: OCTOBER 1979-APRIL 1981

Geoff Hurst was very nearly an extremely successful Chelsea manager. The former West Ham star and hero of England's 1966 World Cup victory came to Stamford Bridge in the summer of 1979 to act as Danny Blanchflower's first-team coach, and when the amiable Ulsterman departed he took over, initially as a caretaker. With Bobby Gould acting as his assistant, Hurst succeeded in getting the best out of the players he had inherited, but the experienced men he signed failed to make the expected impact and defensive shortcomings ultimately caused the Blues to miss out on promotion on goal difference.

The following autumn saw another stirring drive towards the top of the table. Often playing with two out-and-out wingers, Hurst's side produced some thrilling football but they were then afflicted by a mysterious inability to put the ball in the net, failing to score in all but three of their League matches from the start of December. Brimming self-belief quickly gave way to abject despair, and before the season was out Chelsea were once again looking for a new manager. However, most fans felt that a little more patience might well have seen the Hurst/Gould partnership put the club back on the right path.

JOHN NEAL MANAGER: MAY 1981-JUNE 1985

John Neal was the first manager with previous experience at another League club to be given the job at Stamford Bridge since Ron Suart, and his record at Wrexham and Middlesbrough suggested that he was likely to enjoy rather more success than the hopefuls who had tried their hand before him. His first season in charge brought little satisfaction apart from an exciting run to the FA Cup quarter-finals but, with the support of the club's ambitious new chairman, Ken Bates, Neal then set about restoring the Blues' fortunes. Determined to add resilience and drive to a side that had seemingly lost much of its heart, he recruited a number of seasoned professionals and the example they offered would prove invaluable.

Chelsea narrowly escaped relegation to Division Three in 1982/83, but that summer Neal signed seven new players and his rebuilt team stormed to the Second Division Championship, playing the most attractive football seen at Stamford Bridge for a decade, combining flair with energy and a steely determination to succeed. The club had seemingly been reborn and amid great optimism the Blues went on to finish sixth in the First Division the following season, but it was then decided that Neal, who had undergone heart surgery the previous summer, should make way for John Hollins. Neal was given a place on the board but that arrangement was not destined to last and his association with the club he had done so much to revive was soon severed altogether.

JOHN HOLLINS   MANAGER: JUNE 1985-MARCH 1988

When John Hollins moved into the manager's office in the summer of 1985, success seemed guaranteed. As a coach, he had made an influential contribution to Chelsea's recent resurrection, and the young team John Neal had brought together had shown enormous potential.

Hollins lost no time in imposing his own ideas on the successful set-up he had inherited, tightening discipline and replacing the Blues' high-octane style with a more measured approach. Chelsea remained in touch with the leading bunch until Easter but injuries to Kerry Dixon and Eddie Niedzwiecki seemed to tear the heart out of the side and at Christmas Chelsea were firmly rooted at the bottom of the table. The tabloid press mounted a campaign of unprecedented viciousness in an effort to force the personable young manager out of his job and there were unending stories of dressing-room unrest, but John showed commendable courage and, with the steadfast support of the chairman, guided the team back to a respectable position.

Substantial changes to the playing staff during the summer appeared to put the club back on course, but then Niedzwiecki was injured again and the Blues' season collapsed. The press set to work once more and after four months without a League win a change became inevitable. Once again a lack of previous experience in the hot seat had seen a Chelsea manager ill-equipped for his task.

BOBBY CAMPBELL   MANAGER: MAY 1988-MAY 1991

Bobby Campbell put Chelsea back on an even keel after three seasons of turmoil, but he never really seemed likely to lead them to a secure place among football's elite. He was brought to Stamford Bridge by Ken Bates to act as John Hollins's first-team coach and when Hollins departed he took over as manager. He could not prevent the Blues from going down but the improvement in team spirit after his appointment was obvious.

The cheerful Liverpudlian adopted a pragmatic approach to the task in hand and his judgement was vindicated when Graham Roberts and Peter Nicholas, the two battle-scarred veterans he had signed during the summer, led the Blues to a crushing Second Division Championship triumph. Campbell had not enjoyed too much success during his previous spells as a manager at Fulham and Portsmouth but when Chelsea briefly topped the First Division table the following autumn playing cultured, flowing football it seemed that the decision to appoint him had been inspired.

The Blues finished the season in fifth place and the arrival of Andy Townsend and Dennis Wise in the summer suggested that they could expect to challenge for honours in 1990/91, but the team failed to fulfil their obvious potential and after a bitterly disappointing defeat at the hands of Sheffield Wednesday in the Rumbelows Cup semi-final it became clear that Chelsea would look elsewhere.

IAN PORTERFIELD   MANAGER: JUNE 1991-FEBRUARY 1993

Despite frantic transfer activity, Ian Porterfield never seemed to have the squad he wanted during his brief spell as Chelsea manager and it was hardly surprising therefore that success remained elusive. A thoughtful Scot who had proved his worth at Sheffield United and Aberdeen, he was not top of the club's short-list when the decision was taken to appoint a new manager, but he had made a favourable impression when he spent 16 months at Stamford Bridge as Bobby Campbell's assistant and seemed to have a real feeling for the club.

The Blues reached the FA Cup quarter-finals during his first season at the helm but 14th place in the final League table was a disappointment. Porterfield proved to be an astute bargain-hunter but Tony Dorigo and Gordon Durie were never adequately replaced and the loss of Paul Elliott through injury the following autumn was a serious setback. Ian encouraged his young side to play attractive, constructive football and by Christmas they were in a position to challenge for the title, but defeats in the Coca-Cola Cup quarter-final and FA Cup third round within a week left their season in tatters. Confidence evaporated with alarming speed and after two months without a win Porterfield was shown the door.

DAVID WEBB   MANAGER: FEBRUARY 1993-MAY 1993

Like some jobbing plumber called out to plug a leak, David Webb was summoned back to Stamford Bridge to halt the Blues' ignominious slide towards the relegation zone. He had achieved creditable results with meagre resources at Bournemouth, Torquay and Southend and received a warm welcome from the Stamford Bridge crowd, who remembered him as the swashbuckling defender whose goal had won the Cup in 1970.

With his engaging mixture of breezy amiability and steely determination, Webb succeeded in restoring the spirit and pride that had seemingly been lacking, but insisted on a dour, utilitarian style of football that did not please the purists. He succeeded in hauling the club to mid-table respectability but – somewhat surprisingly – at the end of the season it was announced that his three-month contract had not been extended.

GLENN HODDLE MANAGER: JUNE 1993-MAY 1996

The appointment of Glenn Hoddle marked the beginning of a new era at Stamford Bridge. Although the Blues never finished higher than 11th in the League during his three-year reign, his efforts to banish complacency and create the infrastructure associated with a top club did much to lay the foundations for Chelsea's subsequent success.

Glenn had served his managerial apprenticeship at Swindon, but his football philosophy had been shaped during his spell with Monaco, whose cerebral coach, Arsène Wenger, had had a profound influence on his thinking. As a result, Continental attitudes towards diet and fitness were introduced at Stamford Bridge long before they became *de rigueur* in England.

From the outset, Hoddle made it clear that he wanted to see his team play thoughtful, constructive football, but he was soon forced to compromise his ideals and tailor his tactics to the abilities of the players he had available. Midway through his first season in charge, the Blues looked like strong candidates for relegation but after a switch to a more robust style of play they hauled themselves up to 14th place, an appearance in the FA Cup final helping to disguise the team's shortcomings. That steady progress was maintained during the first half of 1994/95, but much of the momentum was lost when an injury to Dennis Wise left the side bereft of leadership and invention.

Glenn had made a number of forays into the transfer market in an attempt to strengthen his squad but few of his signings had a lasting impact and it was not until his third season at Stamford Bridge that he succeeded in assembling the players he needed to make his preferred 3-5-2 formation effective. Disappointingly, he decided to leave the club with the massive job he had begun far from complete in order to take over as coach of the England team. The real value of the work he had put in would become apparent only after his departure.

RUUD GULLIT MANAGER: MAY 1996-FEBRUARY 1998

Ruud Gullit stepped into management with such assurance and panache that it is easy to forget that the decision to appoint him as Glenn Hoddle's successor represented something of a leap in the dark. While his tactical acumen and natural authority were beyond dispute, he had no previous experience in the role and his knowledge of English football was inevitably limited. Ruud performed his duties in his own inimitable fashion and undoubtedly leant heavily on the other members of the Chelsea management team, but the Dutchman's status as one of the giants of world football, disdain for mediocrity and boundless self-belief were to be key factors in the Stamford Bridge renaissance.

In Gullit's first season at the helm the Blues lifted the FA Cup, their first major trophy in 26 years, and finished sixth in the Premiership, their highest placing since 1989/90. While it is true that the squad at his disposal was probably the strongest in the club's history, there is no doubt that he deployed his forces with boldness and imagination. Every tactical change he made seemed to come off, and if some of the players disliked the way he rotated his squad to keep everyone on their toes it was hard to argue with the system's effectiveness.

Smiling serenely as he sat on the bench, Ruud always gave the impression that he had all the answers and he retained his magic touch well into the following season. The squad had been further reinforced and the Blues were looking like serious Championship challengers. However, a loss of form in December and January presented Gullit with his first real test, and when he overplayed his hand in contract negotiations the club opted to look elsewhere. A golden age had come to a sudden and frustratingly premature end, but the memories would last a lifetime.

GIANLUCA VIALLI MANAGER: FEBRUARY 1998-

The challenge facing Gianluca Vialli when he dramatically exchanged his role as a high-profile Supersub for the responsibilities of management – combined with the opportunity to make the starting eleven rather more often – could scarcely have been more daunting, yet within three months he had guided Chelsea to victory in the finals of the Coca-Cola Cup and the Cup-Winners' Cup. Of course, much of the credit for those triumphs belongs to Ruud Gullit, who had brought the team together, but it cannot be denied that under Vialli the Blues showed a passion and determination to finish the job that were not always apparent during his adored predecessor's period in charge.

Immensely popular with his team-mates, Gianluca led from the front, inspiring the Blues to unforgettable semi-final victories against Arsenal and Vicenza at Stamford Bridge. It must be admitted, however, that they were much less impressive in many routine League matches when there was not so much at stake. Vialli has proved that he can lift his players for the big occasion, but it remains to be seen whether he can coax similar performances from them with the sort of consistency that will be required if the club's Championship ambitions are to be fulfilled.

PLAYERS' STATISTICS

Player	Season	LEAGUE			FA CUP			LEAGUE CUP			FULL MEMBERS' CUP			EUROPE			TOTAL		
		App	Sub	Gl	App	Sub	Gl	App	Sub	Gl	App	Sub	Gl	App	Sub	Gl	App	Sub	Gl
Allen C	1991	15	(1)	7	4	(1)	2	0		0	3		0	0		0	22	(2)	9
Allon J	91-92	3	(11)	2	0		0	0	(2)	0	1	(1)	1	0		0	4	(14)	3
Anderton S	58-61	76		2	3		0	1		0	0		0	2		0	82		2
Aylott T	77-79	26	(3)	2	1		0	2		0	0		0	0		0	29	(3)	2
Babayaro C	97-	8		0	0		0	1	(1)	0	0		0	2	(1)	0	11	(2)	0
Baldwin T	66-74	182	(5)	74	21		5	14	(3)	6	0		0	11	(3)	7	228	(11)	92
Bannon E	78-79	25		1	0		0	2		0	0		0	0		0	27		1
Barnard D	91-93	18	(11)	2	1	(1)	0	1	(1)	0	0		0	0		0	20	(13)	2
Barness A	92-95	12	(2)	0	0		0	2		0	0		0	2	(1)	0	16	(3)	0
Barron J	1965	1		0	0		0	0		0	0		0	0		0	1		0
Bason B	72-76	18	(1)	1	0		0	2	(1)	0	0		0	0		0	20	(2)	1
Beasant D	88-92	133		0	5		0	11		0	8		0	0		0	157		0
Birchenall A	67-69	74	(1)	20	10		3	7		3	0		0	4		2	95	(1)	28
Block M	57-61	37		6	2		0	0		0	0		0	1		0	40		6
Blunstone F	52-63	317		47	24		4	3		2	0		0	2		0	346		53
Bodley M	1987	6		1	0		0	1		0	1		0	0		0	8		1
Bolland G	1961	2		0	0		0	0		0	0		0	0		0	2		0
Bonetti P	59-78	600		0	57		0	45		0	0		0	26		0	728		0
Borota P	78-81	107		0	2		0	5		0	0		0	0		0	114		0
Boyd T	1991	22	(1)	0	2		0	2		0	5		0	0		0	31	(1)	0
Boyle J	64-73	188	(10)	10	24	(1)	0	21		1	0		0	20	(2)	1	253	(13)	12
Brabrook P	54-61	251		47	12		4	4		4	0		0	3		2	270		57
Bradbury T	60-61	29		1	0		0	0		0	0		0	0		0	29		1
Bridges B	58-65	174	(2)	80	17		9	5		3	0		0	7		1	203	(2)	93
Britton I	72-81	253	(10)	33	15		0	11		1	0		0	0		0	279	(10)	34
Brolly M	72-73	7	(1)	1	1		0	0		0	0		0	0		0	8	(1)	1
Brooks J	59-60	46		6	2		0	4		1	0		0	0		0	52		7
Brown D	63-64	10		1	1		0	2		1	0		0	0		0	13		2
Bumstead J	78-90	318	(24)	38	20	(1)	3	29	(5)	1	12		2	0		0	379	(30)	44
Burley C	90-96	85	(28)	7	12	(4)	4	5		0	2		0	1		0	105	(32)	11
Butler D	61-62	18		0	0		0	0		0	0		0	0		0	18		0
Butler G	1967	8	(1)	0	0		0	0		0	0		0	0		0	8	(1)	0
Canoville P	81-85	53	(26)	11	2	(3)	1	12	(6)	3	0	(1)	0	0		0	67	(36)	15
Cascarino T	91-93	35	(5)	8	3	(1)	0	1		0	0		0	0		0	39	(6)	8
Charvet L	97-	7	(4)	2	0		0	0	(1)	0	0		0	0	(1)	0	7	(6)	2
Chivers G	78-82	128	(5)	4	7		0	8		0	0		0	0		0	143	(5)	4
Clare J	1980	0	(1)	0	0		0	0		0	0		0	0		0	0	(1)	0
Clarke S	86-	325	(9)	7	34	(2)	1	24	(2)	1	12		1	11	(1)	0	406	(14)	10
Clement N	96-	1		0	0		0	0		0	0		0	0		0	1		0
Cliss D	57-61	24		1	0		0	0		0	0		0	0		0	24		1
Coady J	86-87	9	(7)	2	0		0	0	(1)	0	1	(1)	1	0		0	10	(9)	3
Colgan N	96-	1		0	0		0	0		0	0		0	0		0	1		0
Cooke C	65-72	204	(8)	15	28	(1)	3	18	(1)	3	0		0	17		1	267	(10)	22
	& 73-77	85	(2)	7	4	(1)	0	4		1	0		0	0		0	93	(3)	8
Crittenden	97-	0	(2)	0	0		0	1		0	0		0	0		0	1	(2)	0
Crowther S	58-60	51		0	4		0	1		0	0		0	2		0	58		0
Cundy J	90-91	40	(1)	2	6		0	6		0	4		0	0		0	56	(1)	2
Davies G	84-85	11	(2)	6	2		0	0		0	0		0	0		0	13	(2)	6
de Goey E	97-	28		0	1		0	4		0	0		0	9		0	42		0
Dempsey J	68-75	161	(4)	4	15	(1)	2	15	(2)	0	0		0	9		1	200	(7)	7
Dickens A	89-91	39	(9)	1	0		0	3		0	4		3	0		0	46	(9)	4
Digweed P	1987	3		0	0		0	0		0	0		0	0		0	3		0
Di Matteo R	96-	61	(3)	11	8		2	7		3	0		0	8		3	84	(3)	19
Dixon K	83-91	335	(4)	148	18	(2)	8	40	(1)	25	20		12	0		0	413	(7)	193
Docherty J	1978	2	(1)	0	0		0	0		0	0		0	0		0	2	(1)	0
Docherty T	1961	4		0	0		0	0		0	0		0	0		0	4		0
Dodds B	86-88	0	(3)	0	0		0	0		0	0	(2)	0	0		0	0	(5)	0
Donaghy M	92-93	63	(5)	3	1	(1)	0	8		0	0		0	0		0	72	(6)	3
Dorigo T	87-90	149		11	4		0	14		0	13		1	0		0	180		12
Dow A	93-95	14	(1)	0	1		0	2		0	0		0	0		0	17	(6)	0
Driver P	80-82	25	(19)	4	0	(1)	0	0	(1)	0	0		0	0		0	25	(21)	4
Droy M	70-84	263	(9)	13	21		4	17	(2)	2	0		0	1		0	302	(11)	19
Duberry M	93-	59	(2)	1	10		2	5		0	0		0	6		0	80	(2)	3
Dublin K	83-86	50	(1)	0	5		0	6		0	5	(1)	0	0		0	66	(2)	0
Dunn J	62-65	13		0	3		0	0		0	0		0	0		0	16		0
Durie G	85-90	119	(8)	54	6		1	11		7	9		1	0		0	145	(8)	63
Elliott P	91-92	42		3	5		0	2		0	5		0	0		0	54		3
Elmes T	1980	2	(2)	0	0		0	0		0	0		0	0		0	2	(2)	0
Evans B	1960	32		0	1		0	4		1	0		0	0		0	37		1
Falco M	1982	3		0	0		0	0		0	0		0	0		0	3		0
Fascione J	64-68	22	(7)	1	0		0	3		0	0		0	2		0	27	(7)	1
Feely P	70-72	4	(1)	2	0		0	0		0	0		0	0		0	4	(1)	2
Fillery M	78-82	156	(5)	32	11		3	9		6	0		0	0		0	176	(5)	41
Finnieston S	74-77	78	(2)	34	4	(2)	1	4		2	0		0	0		0	86	(4)	37
Fleck R	92-93	35	(5)	3	1		0	7		1	0		0	0		0	43	(5)	4
Francis S	81-85	71		0	10		0	6		0	1		0	0		0	88		0
Freestone R	86-88	42		0	3		0	2		0	6		0	0		0	53		0

Player	Season	LEAGUE			FA CUP			LEAGUE CUP			FULL MEMBERS' CUP			EUROPE			TOTAL		
		App	Sub	Gl	App	Sub	Gl	App	Sub	Gl	App	Sub	Gl	App	Sub	Gl	App	Sub	Gl
Flo TA	97-	16	(18)	11	1		0	3	(1)	2	0		0	3	(2)	2	23	(21)	15
Forrest C	1996	2	(1)	0	0		0	0		0	0		0	0		0	2	(1)	0
Furlong P	94-95	44	(20)	13	5	(5)	1	3		0	0	(1)	0	7		3	59	(26)	17
Godden T	85-86	34		0	1		0	2		0	1		0	0		0	38		0
Graham G	64-66	72		35	11		3	8		5	0		0	11		3	102		46
Granville D	96-	12	(6)	0	0		0	3		0	0		0	3	(1)	1	18	(7)	1
Greaves J	57-60	157		124	7		3	2		2	0		0	3		3	169		132
Grodas F	1996	20	(1)	0	5		0	1		0	0		0	0		0	26	(1)	0
Gullit R	95-97	37	(12)	4	7	(1)	3	6	(1)	0	0		0	0		0	50	(14)	7
Hales K	79-82	18	(2)	2	7		0	0		0	0		0	0		0	25	(2)	2
Hall G	86-95	122	(19)	4	6		0	12	(1)	0	7	(2)	1	1	(1)	0	148	(23)	5
Hamilton I	1966	3	(2)	2	0		0	0		0	0		0	0		0	3	(2)	2
Hampshire S	97-	0		0	0		0	0	(1)	0	0		0	0		0	0	(1)	0
Harford M	1992	27	(1)	9	1		0	5		2	0		0	0		0	33	(1)	11
Harley J	97-	3		0	0		0	0		0	0		0	0		0	3		0
Harmer T	62-63	8		1	0		0	1		0	0		0	0		0	9		1
Harris A	60-64	70		0	4		0	6		1	0		0	0		0	80		1
	& 65-66	12	(2)	0	3	(1)	0	1	(1)	0	0		0	2		0	18	(4)	0
Harris R	61-79	646	(9)	13	64		0	46	(2)	0	0		0	27		1	783	(11)	14
Harrison M	56-62	61		8	0		0	0		0	0		0	3		1	64		9
Hateley T	1966	26	(1)	6	6		3	0		0	0		0	0		0	32	(1)	9
Hay D	74-78	107	(1)	2	6	(1)	0	5		1	0		0	0		0	118	(2)	3
Hazard M	85-89	78	(3)	9	4	(2)	1	7	(3)	1	5	(1)	1	0		0	94	(9)	12
Hinton M	63-74	257	(8)	3	30	(3)	0	22	(3)	0	0		0	18	(2)	1	327	(16)	4
Hitchcock K	87-	94	(3)	0	14		0	12		0	5		0	4		0	129	(3)	0
Hoddle G	93-94	19	(12)	1	0	(2)	0	3		0	0		0	0	(3)	0	22	(17)	1
Hollins J	63-74	436		47	50		4	43		7	0		0	27		5	556		63
	& 1983	29		1	1		0	5		0	0		0	0		0	35		1
Hopkin D	92-94	21	(19)	1	3	(2)	0	0	(1)	0	0		0	0		0	24	(22)	1
Houseman P	63-74	252	(17)	20	25		10	32	(1)	4	0		0	15		5	324	(18)	39
Houston S	67-70	6	(3)	0	3		0	1	(1)	0	0		0	0		0	10	(4)	0
Howard T	84-86	6		0	0		0	0		0	0		0	0		0	6		0
Hudson A	68-73	144	(1)	10	14		0	16		2	0		0	13		2	187	(1)	14
Hughes M	95-	88	(7)	25	13	(1)	9	7	(3)	3	0		0	0	(3)	1	108	(14)	38
Hughes P	96-	13	(8)	2	1		0	0		0	0		0	1		0	15	(8)	2
Hughes T	66-69	11		0	0		0	0		0	0		0	0		0	11		0
Hutchings C	80-83	83	(4)	3	7		0	7		0	0		0	0		0	97	(4)	3
Hutchinson I	68-75	112	(7)	44	11		6	10		4	0		0	3		3	136	(7)	57
Iles B	78-82	14		0	0		0	0		0	0		0	0		0	14		0
Isaac R	84-86	9		0	0		0	2		0	2		0	0		0	13		0
Jasper D	83-85	10		0	0		0	3	(1)	0	0	(1)	0	0		0	13	(2)	0
Johnsen E	89-96	135	(10)	1	16	(3)	0	7		0	4		0	8		0	170	(13)	1
Johnson G	78-80	16	(3)	9	1	(1)	0	1		0	0		0	0		0	18	(4)	9
Johnstone D	83-84	1	(3)	0	0		0	0		0	0		0	0		0	1	(3)	0
Jones J	82-84	76	(2)	2	5		0	8		0	0		0	0		0	89	(2)	2
Jones K	82-86	43	(9)	7	1		0	9	(2)	3	4	(1)	0	0		0	57	(12)	10
Jones V	91-92	42		4	4		1	1		0	5		2	0		0	52		7
Kember S	71-74	125	(5)	13	10	(1)	0	9		2	0		0	0		0	144	(6)	15
Kevan D	1962	7		1	0		0	0		0	0		0	0		0	7		1
Kharine D	92-	117		0	12		0	8		0	0		0	4		0	141		0
Kirkup J	65-67	48	(5)	2	6	(2)	0	3		0	0		0	5		0	62	(7)	2
Kjeldbjerg J	93-94	52		2	6	(1)	0	6		0	0		0	1		0	65	(1)	2
Knox T	62-64	20		0	0		0	1		0	0		0	0		0	21		0
Lambourde B	97-	5	(2)	0	0		0	3		0	0		0	1	(2)	0	9	(4)	0
Langley T	74-79	129	(13)	40	6		2	4		1	0		0	0		0	139	(13)	43
Leboeuf F	96-	58		11	8		1	6		0	0		0	9		1	81		13
Lee C	79-86	167	(18)	36	12		2	20	(4)	1	1	(1)	2	0		0	200	(23)	41
Lee D	88-	119	(32)	11	10	(4)	0	13	(8)	1	5	(1)	1	1	(1)	0	148	(46)	13
Le Saux G	88-92	77	(13)	8	7	(1)	0	7	(6)	1	8	(1)	0	0		0	99	(21)	9
	& 97-	26		1	1		1	4		1	0		0	3		0	34		3
Lewington R	75-78	80	(5)	4	4		0	3		0	0		0	0		0	87	(5)	4
Livesey C	59-60	39		17	2		1	1		0	0		0	0		0	42		18
Livingstone S	1992	0	(1)	0	0		0	0		0	0		0	0		0	0	(1)	0
Lloyd B	66-68	8	(2)	0	0		0	0		0	0		0	0		0	8	(2)	0
Locke G	72-82	270	(2)	3	24		1	21		0	0		0	0		0	315	(2)	4
Luke G	1966	1		0	0		0	0		0	0		0	0		0	1		0
McAllister K	85-90	78	(31)	7	3	(2)	1	9	(2)	2	11	(4)	3	0		0	101	(39)	13
McAndrew T	82-83	20		4	1		0	2		0	0		0	0		0	23		4
McCalliog J	64-65	7		2	0		0	5		1	0		0	0		0	12		3
McCreadie E	62-73	327	(4)	4	41		0	21	(1)	1	0		0	16		0	405	(5)	5
McKenzie D	1978	15		4	1		0	0		0	0		0	0		0	16		4
McLaughlin J	83-88	224		5	9		0	23		1	12		1	0		0	268		7
McMillan P	1967	1		0	0		0	0		0	0		0	0		0	1		0
McNally E	61-63	9		0	0		0	0		0	0		0	0		0	9		0
McNaught J	85-87	9	(1)	2	0		0	3		0	0		0	0		0	12	(1)	2
Malcolm A	1961	27		1	1		0	0		0	0		0	0		0	28		1
Matthew D	89-92	13	(8)	0	0		0	5		0	1		0	0		0	19	(8)	0
Matthews R	56-60	135		0	9		0	1		0	0		0	3		0	148		0
Maybank T	74-76	28		6	4		0	0		0	0		0	0		0	32		6
Mayes A	80-82	61	(5)	19	9		5	1		0	0		0	0		0	71	(5)	24
Minto S	94-96	53	(1)	4	9		0	3		1	0		0	5	(1)	0	70	(2)	5

Player	Season	LEAGUE App	Sub	Gl	FA CUP App	Sub	Gl	LEAGUE CUP App	Sub	Gl	FULL MEMBERS' CUP App	Sub	Gl	EUROPE App	Sub	Gl	TOTAL App	Sub	Gl
Morris J	95-	15	(10)	1	0		0	3		2	0		0	1	(1)	0	19	(11)	3
Myers A	90-	73	(10)	2	9	(1)	0	2	(1)	0	1		0	3	(2)	0	88	(14)	2
Newton E	91-	138	(20)	8	16	(2)	1	15	(2)	1	0		0	11	(1)	0	180	(25)	10
Nicholls M	96-	11	(16)	3	1		0	2	(2)	0	0		0	0	(2)	0	14	(20)	3
Niedzwiecki E	83-87	136		0	8		0	25		0	6		0	0		0	175		0
Nutton M	78-82	77	(2)	0	3		0	1		0	0		0	0		0	81	(2)	0
Ord T	1972	3		1	0		0	0		0	0		0	0		0	3		1
O'Rourke J	1963	0		0	0		0	1		0	0		0	0		0	1		0
Osgood P	64-73	276	(3)	103	33		19	30		10	0		0	25	(1)	16	364	(4)	148
	& 78-79	10		2	1		0	0		0	0		0	0		0	11		2
Parker P	1996	1	(3)	0	0		0	0		0	0		0	0		0	1	(3)	0
Pates C	79-88	284	(1)	10	20		0	32		0	9		0	0		0	345	(1)	10
Peacock G	93-95	92	(11)	17	14	(4)	9	6		1	0		0	7		0	119	(15)	27
Pearce I	90-92	0	(4)	0	0		0	0		0	0	(1)	0	0		0	0	(5)	0
Petrescu D	95-	87	(2)	10	14		1	5		2	0		0	7		2	113	(2)	15
Peyton G	1992	0	(1)	0	0		0	0		0	0		0	0		0	0	(1)	0
Phelan T	95-96	13	(2)	0	8		0	0	(1)	0	0		0	0		0	21	(3)	0
Phillips J	70-78	125		0	11		0	9		0	0		0	4		0	149		0
Pinner M	1961	1		0	0		0	0		0	0		0	0		0	1		0
Potrac T	1971	1		0	0		0	0		0	0		0	0		0	1		0
Poyet G	97-	11	(3)	4	0		0	0		0	0		0	4		1	15	(3)	5
Rhoades-Brown P	79-83	86	(10)	4	7	(2)	1	4		0	0		0	0		0	97	(12)	5
Rix G	1994	0	(1)	0	0		0	0		0	0		0	1	(2)	0	1	(3)	0
Roberts G	88-89	70		18	4		0	3		1	6		3	0		0	83		22
Robson B	1982	11	(4)	3	0		0	1	(1)	2	0		0	0		0	12	(5)	5
Robson T	1965	6	(1)	0	0		0	0		0	0		0	0		0	6	(1)	0
Rocastle D	94-95	27	(2)	0	0		0	3		1	0		0	7	(1)	1	37	(3)	2
Rofe D	79-81	58	(1)	0	1	(1)	0	2		0	0		0	0		0	61	(2)	0
Rougvie D	84-86	74		3	4		0	16		0	6		0	0		0	100		3
Scott M	57-61	97		0	5		0	0		0	0		0	2		0	104		0
Shaw C	1961	1		0	0		0	0		0	0		0	0		0	1		0
Shearer D	1985	2		1	0		0	0		0	0		0	0		0	2		1
Sheerin J	96-	0	(1)	0	0		0	0		0	0		0	0		0	0	(1)	0
Shellito K	58-65	114		2	4		0	1		0	0		0	4		0	123		2
Sherwood S	71-75	16		0	0		0	1		0	0		0	0		0	17		0
Shipperley N	92-94	26	(11)	7	3		1	4	(2)	1	0		0	2		0	35	(13)	9
Sillett J	56-61	93		0	5		0	2		1	0		0	2		0	102		1
Sillett P	53-61	260		29	20		2	3		2	0		0	4		1	287		34
Sinclair B	1964	1		0	0		0	0		0	0		0	0		0	1		0
Sinclair F	90-	163	(6)	7	18		1	17	(1)	2	0		0	12		3	210	(7)	13
Sissons J	1974	10	(1)	0	1		0	1		0	0		0	0		0	12	(1)	0
Sitton J	78-79	11	(2)	0	0		0	1		0	0		0	0		0	12	(2)	0
Smart J	1964	1		0	0		0	0		0	0		0	0		0	1		0
Smethurst D	70-71	14		4	0		0	1		0	0		0	3	(1)	1	18	(1)	5
Sorrell D	61-63	3		0	1		1	0		0	0		0	0		0	4		1
Spackman N	83-86	139	(2)	12	8		1	22	(1)	0	7		1	0		0	176	(3)	14
	& 92-95	60	(7)	0	6	(3)	0	5		0	0		0	7		0	78	(10)	0
Sparrow J	73-79	63	(6)	2	2		0	3		0	0		0	0		0	68	(6)	2
Speedie D	82-86	155	(7)	47	12		5	23	(1)	7	7		5	0		0	197	(8)	64
Spencer J	92-96	75	(28)	36	16	(4)	4	5	(4)	2	0		0	4	(1)	1	100	(37)	43
Stanley G	75-78	105	(4)	15	4	(1)	0	6		0	0		0	0		0	115	(5)	15
Stein M	93-95	46	(4)	21	9		2	0	(1)	0	0		0	2	(1)	2	57	(6)	25
Stepney A	1966	1		0	0		0	0		0	0		0	0		0	1		0
Stride D	78-79	35		0	1		0	1		0	0		0	0		0	37		0
Stuart G	89-92	70	(17)	14	5	(2)	1	11		2	3	(2)	1	0		0	89	(21)	18
Swain K	73-78	114	(5)	26	7		2	6		1	0		0	0		0	127	(5)	29
Tambling B	58-69	298	(4)	164	36		25	18		10	0		0	14		3	366	(4)	202
Thomas M	83-84	43	(1)	9	3		0	7		2	0		0	0		0	53	(1)	11
Thomson J	65-67	33	(6)	1	5	(1)	0	0		0	0		0	2		0	40	(7)	1
Tindall R	55-61	160		68	9		2	3		0	0		0	2		0	174		70
Townsend A	90-92	110		12	7		0	17		7	4		0	0		0	138		19
Upton F	61-64	74		3	8		0	4		0	0		0	0		0	86		3
Venables T	59-65	202		26	19		1	8		1	0		0	8		3	237		31
Vialli G	96-	37	(12)	20	1	(5)	4	3	(1)	0	0		0	8		6	49	(18)	30
Viljoen C	79-81	19	(1)	0	0		0	3		0	0		0	0		0	22	(1)	0
Waldron C	1967	9		0	0		0	1		0	0		0	0		0	10		0
Walker C	76-83	168	(30)	60	14	(2)	3	9	(1)	2	0		0	0		0	191	(33)	65
Watson I	62-64	5		1	1		0	3		0	0		0	0		0	9		1
Webb D	67-73	230		21	23		6	27		3	0		0	18		3	298		33
Wegerle R	86-87	15	(8)	3	1	(1)	1	0		0	2	(1)	0	0		0	18	(10)	4
Weller K	70-71	34	(4)	14	3		0	3		1	0		0	8	(1)	0	48	(5)	15
West C	86-87	8	(8)	4	0		0	0		0	0		0	0		0	8	(8)	4
Whiffen K	1966	1		0	0		0	0		0	0		0	0		0	1		0
Wicks S	74-78	117	(1)	5	6		2	3		0	0		0	0		0	126	(1)	7
	& 86-87	34		1	2		0	1		0	0		0	0		0	37		1
Wilkins G	72-81	136	(1)	1	5		0	7		0	0		0	0		0	148	(1)	1
Wilkins R	73-78	176	(3)	30	11	(1)	2	6	(1)	2	0		0	0		0	193	(5)	34
Williams P	1982	1		0	0		0	0		0	0		0	0		0	1		0
Wilson C	87-89	71	(13)	5	4		0	3	(3)	0	7	(2)	0	0		0	85	(18)	5
Wilson K	87-91	126	(29)	44	7	(1)	1	10	(2)	4	12	(4)	6	0		0	155	(36)	55
Wise D	90-	237	(7)	46	25		6	27		6	5		2	14		1	308	(7)	61

Player	Season	LEAGUE			FA CUP			LEAGUE CUP			FULL MEMBERS' CUP			EUROPE			TOTAL		
		App	Sub	Gl	App	Sub	Gl	App	Sub	Gl	App	Sub	Gl	App	Sub	Gl	App	Sub	Gl
Wood D	84-88	134	(10)	3	9		0	11		0	13	(1)	1	0		0	**167**	(11)	**4**
Wosahlo R	1966	0	(1)	0	0		0	0		0	0		0	0		0	**0**	(1)	**0**
Young A	61-66	20		0	2		1	1		0	0		0	3		0	**26**		**1**
Zola G	96-	45	(5)	16	8		4	4		0	0		0	7	(1)	4	**64**	(6)	**24**

Dates shown indicate first years of each season. Thus 58-61 means 1958/59 to 1961/62. A single entry indicates one season only; eg 1965 refers to 1965/66. The figures quoted under League include the play-off matches in 1987/88.

Gianfranco Zola scoring the winning goal in the 1998 Cup-Winners' Cup final versus VfB Stuttgart.

C000144740

AA

walking in the
Peak District

First published 2008

Produced by AA Publishing
© Automobile Association Developments Limited 2008

All rights reserved. No part of this publication may be reproduced, stored in a retrieval system, or transmitted in any form or by any means – electronic, photocopying, recording or otherwise – unless the written permission of the publishers has been obtained beforehand.

Published by AA Publishing (a trading name of Automobile Association Developments Limited, whose registered office is Fanum House, Basing View, Basingstoke, Hampshire RG21 4EA; registered number 1878835)

Visit the AA Publishing website at www.theAA.com/travel

 This product includes mapping data licensed from Ordnance Survey® with the permission of the Controller of Her Majesty's Stationery Office.
© Crown copyright 2008. All rights reserved. Licence number 100021153

ISBN-13: 978-0-7495-5872-7

A CIP catalogue record for this book is available from the British Library.

The contents of this book are believed correct at the time of printing. Nevertheless, the publishers cannot be held responsible for any errors or omissions or for changes in the details given in this book or for the consequences of any reliance on the information it provides. This does not affect your statutory rights. We have tried to ensure accuracy in this book, but things do change and we would be grateful if readers would advise us of any inaccuracies they may encounter.

We have taken all reasonable steps to ensure that these walks are safe and achievable by walkers with a realistic level of fitness. However, all outdoor activities involve a degree of risk and the publishers accept no responsibility for any injuries caused to readers whilst following these walks. For more advice on walking safely see page 112.

Some of these routes may appear in other AA walks books.

Researched and written by John Morrison, Andrew McCloy, John Gillham, Hugh Taylor and Moira McCrossan
Field-checked and updated 2007 by Andrew McCloy

Managing Editor: David Popey
Senior Editor: Sue Lambert
Layout and Design: Tracey Butler
Image Manipulation and Internal Repro: Sarah Montgomery
Series Design: Liz Baldin at Bookwork Creative Associates for AA Publishing
Cartography provided by the Mapping Services Department of AA Publishing

A03624

Repro by Keenes Group, Andover
Printed by Leo Paper Group in China

PAGES 2–3: *Countryside near the Roaches, Peak District National Park*
RIGHT: *The rocky escarpment of Kinder Downfall, Derbyshire*
PAGES 6: *A climber on Kinder Downfall with Kinder Reservoir in the distance*

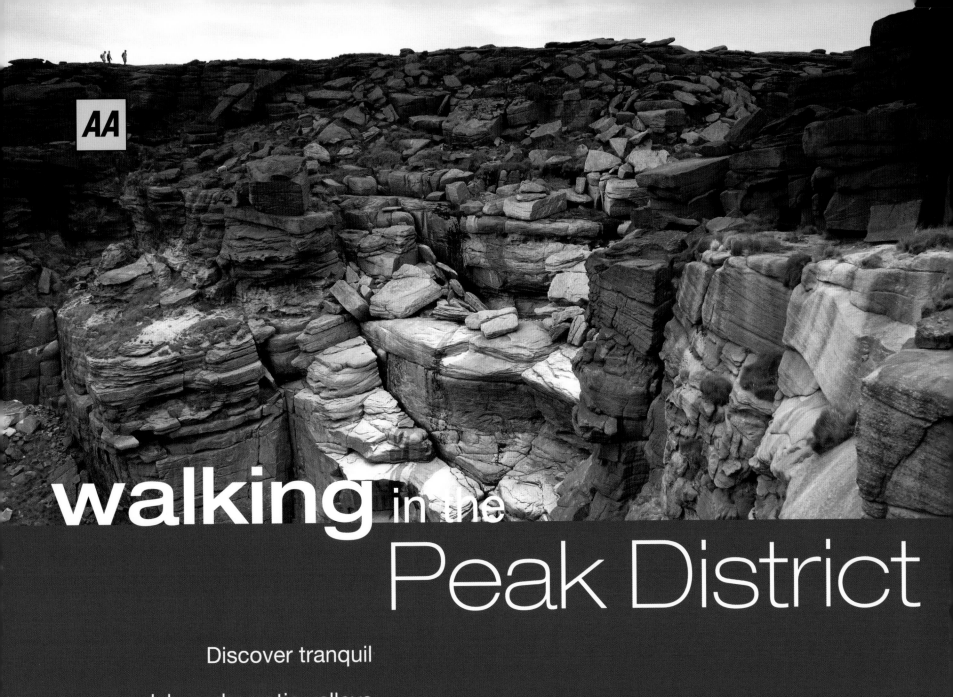

walking in the Peak District

Discover tranquil

lakes, dramatic valleys

and beautiful uplands

Contents

This superb selection of walks introduces the themes and characters that define the beautiful landscape of Peak District.

A Walk to White Nancy Above Bollington 12

Hunt for Wild Boar in Macclesfield Forest 16

Lud's Church and the Roaches 20

Combs Reservoir and Across Dickie's Meadow 26

In the Footsteps of the Trespass 31

Along the Colne Valley 36

Peak Practice 42

Pilsbury Castle and the Upper Dove Valley 46

Ghosts of Miller's Dale 50

Dovedale: Ivory Spires and Wooded Splendour 56

A Taste of the Last of the Summer Wine 60

Marching Roads and Battlefields 66

A High Ridge and Lost Villages at Ladybower 72

Through Monsal Dale, the Valley of the Gods 78

Skeletons from the Past 84

On the Edge at Stanage 88

Chatsworth Park and Gardens 92

Bradfield and the Dale Dike Dam Disaster 98

Scaling the Heights of Abraham 102

Climbing up to Crich in Search of Cardale 108

Introducing the Peak District

The Peak District sits at the base of the Pennines, with one foot in the North and one in the Midlands. At its northern tip, the high moorlands merge seemlessly into the South Pennine massif dividing Yorkshire and Lancashire. In the south the graceful River Dove sparkles out of the limestone landscape, dividing Derbyshire and Staffordshire. Between these two contrasting images lies the Peak District National Park, a backyard playground for the city dwellers of the East and North Midlands, South and West Yorkshire and Greater Manchester. Surely nowhere else in Britain offers so great a contrast in landscapes, to so many people, in such a relatively small area. The Peak District National Park was the first National Park to be established in England (in 1951) and protects 542 square miles (1,404sq km) of this precious environment.

Plateau

But you shouldn't expect to find any mountain peaks in this beautiful upland. The name comes from the Old English 'peac' which describes a knoll or hill. With a few notable exceptions, the heights are predominantly plateau-like, carved with deep valleys which give a sense of elevation to the various edges and occasional summits bold enough to lift their contours above the rest. Best-loved among these are the conical elevations of Shutlingsloe, Shining Tor, Chrome Hill and Parkhouse Hill and you can be forgiven for assuming that the region took its name from their magnificent pointed crests.

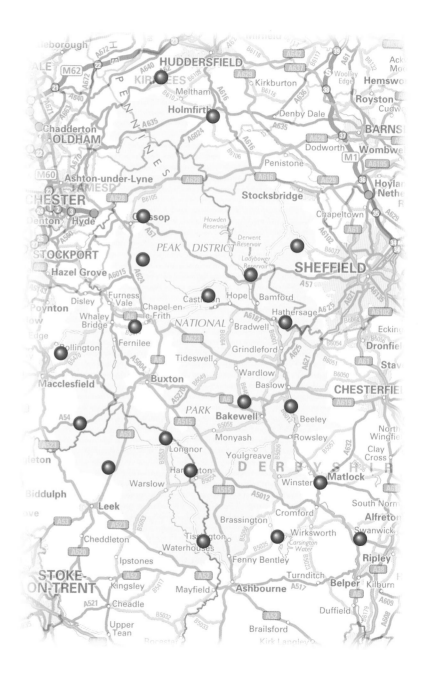

Dark Peak

The northern area is known as the Dark Peak. It's one of brooding moorlands, green valleys and many reservoirs. From the gritstone outcrops and peaty morasses tumble well-fed streams. The abundance of water drew the industrialists of the surrounding conurbations and virtually all the valleys except Edale boast a reservoir, or often several. You'll see this as you walk around the moorland fringes of West and South Yorkshire, in the Holme Valley and around Bradfield. From Glossop, Hayfield, Longdendale and Chinley on the western side each valley seems to have been dammed in turn. The most dramatic is the upper Derwent Valley, where villages were removed and vast acres of poor farmland flooded to make a series of breathtaking waterscapes. With its tales of mass trespass and pioneering access agreements, this is the heartland of the English rambling tradition. But the walking here can be harder than it is in the limestone dales to the south. The weather can quickly take a dramatic turn for the worse, even on a sunny day, and navigation can become more problematic as the moors are engulfed in impenetrable cloud. The highest points of Kinder and Bleaklow surpass 2,000ft (610m) and heavy snowfall is not uncommon in the winter months.

White Peak

Gentler walking can be found in the southern half of the district. The White Peak takes its name from the limestone which dominates the scenery. Here you will find tiny valleys carved into the plateau, Lathkill Dale, Monsal Dale, Mill Dale and Wolfscote Dale. Perhaps the most famous is Dovedale, chaperoning the River Dove through a landscape of bizarre rock pinnacles and caves steeped in mythology. The River Manifold too, cuts a dramatic gorge, flanked by limestone crags and mysterious chasms. You'll find many pretty villages here as well – Tissington, Hartington, Youlgreave and Ashford in the Water

– fine places to take afternoon tea or relax in a friendly pub. The Derwent Valley momentarily opens out, south of Baslow, making space for the parklands surrounding Chatsworth House. Here the Duke of Devonshire's palatial home sits in a splendid green vale, with gritstone edges to the east and limestone dales to the west.

Gritstone Fringe

Fingers of gritstone surround the White Peak, giving Cheshire and Staffordshire a valuable moorland fringe and lingering in the east so that even Chesterfield can catch a piece in the delightful Linacre Valley. From Crich Stand the defiant heights look out over much plainer territory. You can follow a gritstone trail along the serene edges overlooking Bollington and Macclesfield, or linger around the shores of Tittesworth Reservoir, or the rocky towers of the Roaches. On these quiet heights it seems barely credible that a third of England's population lives less than one hour's drive away.

Industrial Relics

Industry has always tried to tame this landscape, but somehow the remains of the mills, lead mines, quarries and railways have blended in to add to its romance. Certainly the easy access afforded to walkers by trails on former railway trackbeds has added greatly to the Peak District's charm. Where steam trains once wound their tedious course through Monsal Dale or across the limestone plateau, so the modern walker can now stride in confidence on the Tissington, High Peak and Monsal trails. Before the railways it was the 'Jaggers' with their trains of packhorses who crossed these hills. Now you can follow their routes over high moors and through lonely dale heads, perhaps with a hint of gratitude for their eye for an easy gradient and a well-placed bridge. They carried salt and coal through this beautiful landscape long before anyone considered it to be one worth preserving.

Beyond the National Park

Beyond the national park, the Midland plain reaches up to capture the towns and villages of South Derbyshire. Here you will find a very different walking experience, in the parkland of great houses such as Melbourne, Markeaton, Osmaston, Shirley and Calke Abbey. But don't overlook it. The character of the landscape may be very different from that of the Peak District proper, but for many its warm brick-built buildings will provide a welcome contrast to the ubiquitous stone of its northern neighbours.

The Walks

These walks represent a snapshot of the opportunities available to those prepared to muddy their feet and stray off the beaten path. From high points to low, light to dark you'll find the Peak District has a lot more to offer the walker than tea shops and show caves. It is hoped that the walks in this book inspire you to return to the many delights of the Peak District again and again.

RIGHT: A track on Mam Tor near Castleton, site of an Iron Age fort

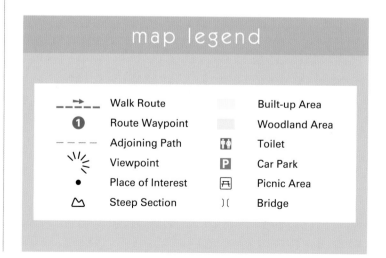

map legend

⇢	Walk Route		Built-up Area
❶	Route Waypoint		Woodland Area
– – –	Adjoining Path	🚻	Toilet
☀	Viewpoint	🅿	Car Park
•	Place of Interest	⊟	Picnic Area
⌂	Steep Section	)(	Bridge

Information Panels
An information panel for each walk shows its relative difficulty, the distance and total amount of ascent. An indication of the gradients you will encounter is shown by the rating ▲▲▲▲ (no steep slopes) to ▲▲▲▲ (several very steep slopes). The minimum time suggested for the walk is for reasonably fit walkers and doesn't allow for stops.

Suggested Maps
Each walk has a suggested Ordnance Survey Explorer map.

Start Points
The start of each walk is given as a six-figure grid reference prefixed by two letters indicating which 100-km square of the National Grid it refers to. You'll find more information on grid references on most Ordnance Survey maps.

Dogs
We have tried to give dog owners useful advice about the dog friendliness of each walk. Please respect other countryside users. Keep your dog under control, especially around livestock, and obey local bylaws and other dog-related notices.

Car Parking
Many of the car parks suggested are public, but occasionally you may find you have to park on the roadside or in a lay-by. Please be considerate when you leave your car, ensuring that access roads or gates are not blocked and that other vehicles can pass safely.

Maps
Each walk in this book is accompanied by a map based on Ordnance Survey information. The scale of these maps varies from walk to walk.

Exploring a short but scenic ridge,

with a strange landmark, above

the leafy town of Bollington.

A Walk to White Nancy Above Bollington

Bollington lies just outside the far western edge of the Peak District National Park, but it continues to attract walkers and sightseers due in part to the short but inviting ridge of Kerridge Hill that overlooks the small Cheshire town. However it's not just the superb views that will hold your attention, but also the curiously shaped monument at the far northern tip of the hill.

ABOVE: The houses and mills of Bollington
LEFT: The White Nancy monument on the
Gritstone Trail overlooking Bollington

Striking Monument

Visible from below, and for some distance around for that matter since it stands at 920ft (280m) above sea level, White Nancy is a round stone construction that was built by the local Gaskell family in 1820 to commemorate the Battle of Waterloo. It was originally an open shelter with a stone table and benches, and was presumably a popular spot for picnics, but gradual decay and occasional vandalism led to it being bricked up, and now the building has no discernible door or windows. Nor does it bear any plaque or information panel, and most striking of all it is painted bright white. In terms of shape it resembles a large bell, or perhaps a giant chess pawn, with a large base that tapers into an odd little point. As for its name – the most entertaining version suggests that Nancy was the name of one of the eight horses that pulled the heavy stone table to the summit when the tower was built. Beacons are still lit next to it to mark special occasions.

Stone Quarries

For all its scenic qualities the lower western slopes of Kerridge Hill are still quarried, although it's not visible on the walk until you reach the main summit ridge. The dressed stone is used for roofing slates and paving slabs and originally it was removed via narrow boats on the Macclesfield Canal that also served the mills and factories that once dotted the Bollington area. For a while, shallow pits in the hill even yielded enough coal to supply the local engine houses, as steam power replaced water power during the Industrial Revolution's relentless advance. But inevitably your eye will be drawn to sights further afield, and if the weather is clear there will be good views across Macclesfield and the Cheshire Plain to the Mersey Estuary, the urban sprawl of Greater Manchester, as well as the long, high outline of the Pennines away to the north. Meanwhile White Nancy continues to sit impassively, a fittingly ambiguous monument to a past era when people felt compelled to mark the winning of a great overseas battle by building a picnic shelter on top of a small hill in Cheshire.

1 The walk starts towards the top of Lord Street (which Church Street leads into) where it turns sharply right at the top of a steep hill. Go along Cow Lane, a cul-de-sac, and through the gate at the far end. Take the upper of two field paths, heading half right across the sloping field on the right. Aim for the gate and cattle grid at the far left top corner of the field.

2 Turn left on to an open farm track and follow this all the way down to the lane in the bottom of the valley. Turn right, and fork right again past some terraced cottages on your right. A weir and pond below on your left are all that remain of the former silk mill. Follow this path through the Woodland Trust's cool and shady Waulkmill Wood.

3 Leave the wood via a stile and go across the lower part of a sloping field, then in the second field aim for the buildings on the far side. Follow the gated path around to the right, and on through hillside fields.

4 In the second field, fork left for the lower path that, beyond a gate, runs along the bottom edge of a new, mixed plantation, then down a walled track through woodland to reach the main road at Tower Hill.

5 Turn right and walk along the pavement, past the Rising Sun Inn, for 0.5 mile (800m). Turn right into Lidgetts Lane, then as it bends almost immediately left go over a high stile ahead and on to a gated track past a row of hawthorn trees. Swinging left follow this grassy path up to the ridge above – ignore the lower route by the right-hand fence.

6 Follow the obvious hilltop track all the way along the spine of Kerridge Hill, ignoring tracks off left and right.

7 After admiring the views at the monument (White Nancy) at the far end, drop sharply down the pitched path beyond, with Bollington spread out below, then cross a sunken farm lane and continue down across two more steep fields to reach a stile back into Cow Lane/Lord Street.

walk information

➤ **DISTANCE**	3.5 miles (5.7km)
➤ **MINIMUM TIME**	2hrs
➤ **ASCENT/GRADIENT**	1,180ft (360m)
➤ **LEVEL OF DIFFICULTY**	
➤ **PATHS**	Easy field paths and farm tracks, one short, sharp descent
➤ **LANDSCAPE**	Mostly gentle rolling pasture and small pockets of woodland
➤ **SUGGESTED MAPS**	OS Explorer OL24 White Peak
➤ **START/FINISH**	Grid reference: SJ 937775
➤ **DOG FRIENDLINESS**	On lead through farmland, but off lead along lanes
➤ **PARKING**	Kerbside parking on Church Street or Lord Street, Bollington
➤ **PUBLIC TOILETS**	Bollington town centre

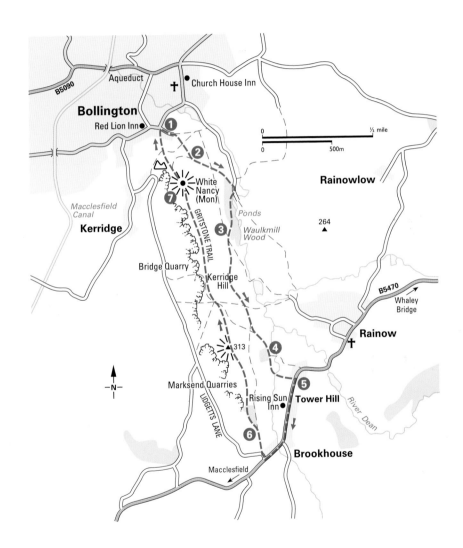

15

A circular walk exploring the old and new Macclesfield Forest, and the mini Matterhorn of Shutlingsloe.

Hunt for Wild Boar in Macclesfield Forest

The Royal Forest of Macclesfield was once the preserve of the nobility, an extensive hunting ground for the royal court where the likes of deer and boar were keenly sought out. It covered a large area, stretching across from the Cheshire Plain to the valleys of the Goyt and Dane; but most of the so-called 'forest' was probably little more than open ground or scrub, with large tracts of high and inhospitable moorland.

ABOVE: Grey clouds gather over fishing at Macclesfield Forest from Croker Hill
RIGHT: Ridgegate Reservoir near Macclesfield Forest

16

Tough Forest Laws

In the 1400s Henry VI appointed John Stanley as Steward of Macclesfield Forest, and it was his son Thomas (later Baron Stanley) who played a crucial role in the Battle of Bosworth in 1485 to ensure the victory of his stepson – the Earl of Richmond, who became Henry VII. The grateful new king made Stanley the Earl of Derby, and the office of Steward of Macclesfield Forest became a hereditary position as a reward.

The Forest Laws that operated in the hunting lands until Elizabethan times were extremely strict. There were severe penalties for anyone caught poaching, as testified by the name of the isolated hilltop pub that the walk visits at Higher Sutton. It's located at a point where a route left the original forest boundary and poachers caught in the act could expect a bleak outcome – the pub is called the Hanging Gate. Other rights in the forest were jealously guarded and fines and punishments were available to reprimand locals who took firewood or let their stock wander. Near the start of the walk is the equally descriptive Crag Inn, tucked away above Clough Brook at Wildboarclough. But whether, according to local tradition, 'the ravine of the wild boar' is indeed the location of the last of its kind killed in England during the 15th century is open to doubt.

Looming above Wildboarclough is the coned peak of Shutlingsloe, which at 1,659ft (506m) offers a full 360-degree panoramic view over Cheshire, Staffordshire and Derbyshire. Especially prominent is Tegg's Nose, a gritstone outcrop to the north that protrudes above the dark green conifers of the present-day Macclesfield Forest. This modern plantation produces timber rather than venison, although native broadleaved trees such as rowan, oak and silver birch have been planted in recent years to break up the regimented rows of spruces and larches and provide encouragement for wildlife. Walkers are welcome to explore the forest's many paths and tracks that climb the often steep hillsides. Look out for the occasional wooden sculpture, and wildlife such as crossbills and woodpeckers, stoats and foxes. The heronry in the larch trees on the eastern shore of Trentabank Reservoir is the largest in the Peak District. In addition, the forest does apparently have red deer, but you'll have to be very quiet and patient to catch a glimpse.

walk information

➤ **DISTANCE**	7 miles (11.3km)
➤ **MINIMUM TIME**	3hrs 30min
➤ **ASCENT/GRADIENT**	2,820ft (860m) ▲▲▲
➤ **LEVEL OF DIFFICULTY**	🚶🚶🚶
➤ **PATHS**	Sloping field paths, lanes and easy forest tracks, steep hillside, lots of stiles
➤ **LANDSCAPE**	Rough pasture, angular hills, plus large tracts of woodland
➤ **SUGGESTED MAPS**	OS Explorer OL24 White Peak
➤ **START/FINISH**	Grid reference: SJ 980681
➤ **DOG FRIENDLINESS**	On lead in fields, off lead on lanes and in woodland, unless notices indicate otherwise
➤ **PARKING**	Lay-by at Brookside, on lane 0.75 mile (1.2km) south of Wildboarclough
➤ **PUBLIC TOILETS**	At Macclesfield Forest Visitor Centre

walk directions

1 Walk along the road for 440yds (402m) to the Crag Inn, then at the foot of its drive go over a stile on the left for a path across a sloping field. This maintains its direction through successive fields (each with a wall gate) until finally you reach the tarmac farm drive at the very top. Turn left and walk along this drive to the lane.

2 Turn right at the far end and walk along the lane as far as Greenway Bridge. Go over a stile on the right and follow the path beside the stream, until it crosses it in order to veer left, up Oakenclough. Keep to the bottom of this little valley, past a ruined stone shelter, and as it rises continue

to its far head, near a small pond. Turn right on to a private drive and then go almost immediately left for a wall-side path uphill.

3 At the top go over a stile and strike out across moorland on a clear grassy track. Maintain your direction until you reach a stile on the far side. Go over this and then descend on a sunken, fenced track to emerge opposite the Hanging Gate pub.

4 Turn right and follow the road for a mile (1.6km), keeping straight on at the junction where the road bends sharply left. Ignore another turning on the left, until finally the lane turns right, into Macclesfield Forest, where there's a wide gate on the right.

5 Don't go through the main gate. Instead go over the stile to the left, signposted 'Shutlingsloe/Trentabank', and follow the footpath which runs parallel with the lane. After dropping down to a newly planted area, cross the footbridge and at the junction of tracks near the wood sculpture carry straight on up a wide, stony route. At the far end turn right, or for the visitor centre and toilets at Trentabank turn left.

6 Walk up the wide forest drive and go left at a fork, then at the far end turn right for a long but quite easy gravel track up through the trees. At the top go through a gate and continue straight on, then turn right to leave the forest for a stone-flagged path across the open moorland up towards the distinctive top of Shutlingsloe.

7 From the summit descend the eroded track down the steep eastern slope of the hill, until you eventually turn right on to an open farm drive. Follow this all the way down to the road and turn right to the car park.

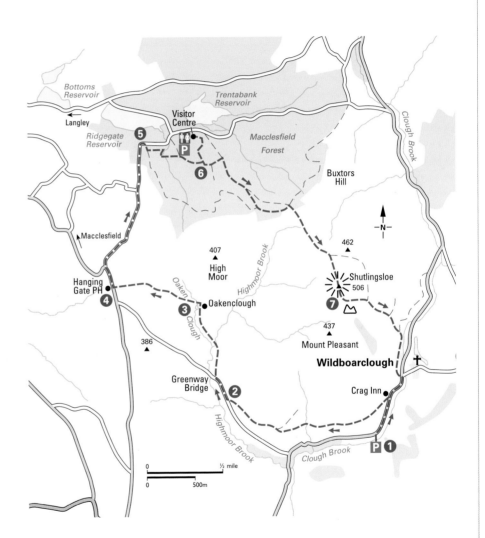

Follow the legend and story of Sir Gawain and find the chapel of the Green Knight.

Lud's Church and the Roaches

The jagged ridge of the Roaches is one of the most popular outdoor locations in the Peak District National Park. The name is a corruption of the French for rocks – roches. It was here on the gritstone crags that the 'working class revolution' in climbing took place in the 1950s. Manchester lads, Joe Brown, a builder, and Don Whillans, a plumber, went on to become legends within the climbing fraternity by developing new rock climbing techniques wearing gym shoes and using Joe's mother's discarded clothes line as a rope.

ABOVE: View towards the Roaches (foreground) with Hen Cloud in the distance
RIGHT: Rock climbers tackle the gritstone escarpment of the Roaches

Sir Gawain and the Green Knight

The greatest legend associated with the Roaches is the Arthurian tale of *Sir Gawain and the Green Knight*. According to the 14th-century poem a knight on horseback, cloaked entirely in green, gatecrashed a feast at Camelot and challenged the Knights of the Round Table. Sir Gawain rose to the challenge and beheaded the Green Knight but the latter retrieved his head and laughingly challenged Sir Gawain to meet with him again, in a year's time, at the Green Chapel. This has been identified as Lud's Church, near the Roaches. In the 1950s Professor Ralph Elliot, now of the University of Adelaide in Australia, identified the Roaches as the general location of the chapel from the text.

> *Great crooked crags, cruelly jagged, the*
> *bristling barbs of rock seemed to brush the sky*

Professor Elliot's theory was supported by a group of linguists, working on the poem at the same time, who placed the work in the same 15-mile (25km) radius. The professor and a group of students from Keele University, where he was then based, tramped all over the countryside looking for a suitable cave to match the poetic description.

> *A hole in each end and on either side,*
> *And overgrown with grass and great patches*
> *All hollow it was within, only an old cavern*
> *Or the crevice of an ancient crag*

Lud's Church fitted the bill. This rocky cleft was created by a mass of sandstone slipping away from the slope of the hill. It was here that Sir Gawain kept his rendezvous with the Green Knight.

RIGHT: View of the Roaches, the landscape of
Sir Gawain's adventures

walk information

➤ **DISTANCE**	6.75 miles (10.9km)
➤ **MINIMUM TIME**	4hrs
➤ **ASCENT/GRADIENT**	1,020ft (311m) ▲▲▲
➤ **LEVEL OF DIFFICULTY**	👥👥
➤ **PATHS**	Rocky moorland paths, forest tracks and road
➤ **LANDSCAPE**	Moor and woodland
➤ **SUGGESTED MAPS**	OS Explorer OL24 White Peak
➤ **START/FINISH**	Grid reference: SK 005621
➤ **DOG FRIENDLINESS**	Keep on lead near livestock
➤ **PARKING**	In lay-by on lane near Windygates Farm
➤ **PUBLIC TOILETS**	None on route

LEFT: The gritstone escarpment landscape of the Roaches is popular with hikers and climbers

walk directions

1 From the lane go through the main gate by the interpretation panel and follow the path half right to the end of the rocks. At a gate in the wall on your right, turn left and straight uphill on a rocky track. Go left through a pair of stone gateposts and continue right on a well-defined track.

2 The path is flanked by rocks on the right and woodland to the left and below. Follow it to the right and uphill through a gap in the rocks. Turn left and then continue uphill. Continue following this ridge path. Pass to the left of Doxey Pool and on towards the trig point.

3 From here descend on a paved path, past the Bearstone Rock to join the road at Roach End. Go through a gap in the wall, over a stile and follow the path uphill keeping the wall on the left. At the signpost fork right on to the concessionary path to Danebridge.

4 Follow this path keeping straight ahead at a crossroads, go through a wall gate and up towards an outcrop. Carry on along the ridge then head down to a signpost by a gate. Turn right and follow the bridleway signed 'Gradbach'. At the next signpost fork right towards Lud's Church.

5 After exploring Lud's Church continue along the path, through woodland, following the signs for Roach End, eventually taking a paved path uphill. Keep the wall on your left-hand side and at the top, cross a stile on to the gated road and follow this back to the lay-by near Windygates Farm.

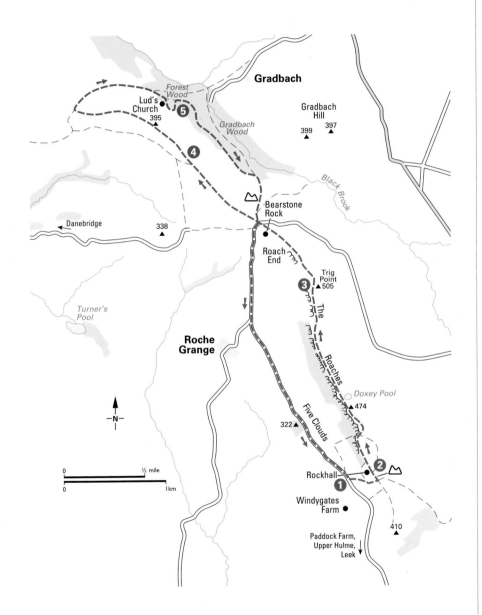

A quiet corner of Derbyshire,

between the Goyt and

Chapel-en-le-Frith.

Combs Reservoir and Across Dickie's Meadow

Combs lies in a quiet corner of north-west Derbyshire, off the road between Chapel-en-le-Frith and Whaley Bridge and beneath the sombre crag-fringed slopes of Combs Moss. This is a beautiful little corner of Derbyshire, tucked away from the crowds of Castleton and Hathersage.

ABOVE: A wooden walkway near Combs Reservoir
LEFT: The view towards Combs Reservoir from
Eccles Pike near Chapel-en-le-Frith

Combs Reservoir

The route starts by the west side of the dam on a narrow path between the lake and Meveril Brook. Red campion, and thickets of dog rose line the path, which rounds the reservoir to its southern tip. You might see a pair of great crested grebes swimming among the rushes. Beyond the reservoir the path tucks under the railway, which brings to mind a mysterious story concerning Ned Dixon, who lived in nearby Tunstead Farm. Ned, or Dickie as he was known, was brutally murdered by his cousin. Locals say his spirit lived on in his skull, which was left outside to guard against intruders. Strange things were said to happen when anybody tried to remove the skull. It is also claimed that the present road from Combs to Chapel was constructed because the railway bridge would not stand over Dane Hey Road. After the first bridge was completed it collapsed, burying the workmen's tools. This was blamed on the skull: Dickie had been against the railway going across Tunstead land.

Combs

A lane with hedges of honeysuckle and hawthorn winds into the village of Combs, where a handful of stone-built cottages are centred on the welcoming Beehive Inn. Combs' most famous son is Herbert Froode. He made his name in automotive engineering as one of the inventors of the brake lining. Starting out in the early 1890s he developed woven cotton brakes for horse-drawn wagons, but his ideas didn't really take off until 1897 when the first motor buses emerged. Froode applied his knowledge of brakes to this much greater challenge and by the end of the century had won a contract to supply brake linings for the new London omnibuses. Ferodo, his company, is an anagram of his surname.

Final Views

Through the village the route takes to the hillsides. Now Combs Reservoir, which is spread beneath your feet, looks every bit a natural lake. Beyond it are the plains of Manchester and the hazy blue West Pennine horizon. In the other direction the gritstone cliffs of Combs Edge, which look rather like those of Kinder Scout.

This very pleasing walk ends as it starts, by the shores of the reservoir. If you look along the line of the dam towards the right of two farms, you'll see where Dickie lived. He's probably watching you, too.

walk directions

1 Follow the path from the dam along the reservoir's western shore, ignoring the first footbridge over Meveril Brook.

2 As the reservoir narrows the path traverses small fields, then comes to another footbridge over the brook. This time cross it and head south across another field. Beyond a foot tunnel under the Buxton line railway, the path reaches a narrow hedge-lined country lane. Turn left along the lane into Combs village.

3 Past the Beehive Inn in the village centre, take the lane straight ahead, then the left fork, signposted to Dove Holes. This climbs out of the village towards Combs Edge.

4 Take the second footpath on the left, which begins at a muddy clearing just beyond Millway Cottage. Go through the stile and climb on a partially slabbed path and then uphill across pasture with the wall on your right. Away to the right is the huge comb of Pygreave Brook. Climb the pathless spur and go through gateways in the next two boundary walls before following a wall on the right. Ignore a gate in this wall – that's a path to Bank Hall Farm – but stay with the narrow path raking across rough grassy hillslopes with the railway line and the reservoir below left.

5 The path comes down to a track that runs alongside the railway line. This joins a lane just short of the Lodge. Turn left to go under the railway and north to Down Lee Farm.

6 Turn left through a kissing gate 200yds (183m) beyond the farmhouse. The signposted path follows an overgrown hedge towards Marsh Hall Farm. The fields can become very boggy on the final approaches. When you reach the farm complex turn right over a stile and follow a vehicle track heading north-west.

7 After 200yds (183m) turn left on a field path that heads west to a stile at the edge of the Chapel-en-le-Frith golf course. Waymarking arrows show the way across the fairway. The stile marking the exit from the golf course is 300yds (274m) short of the clubhouse. You then cross a small field to reach the B5470.

8 Turn left along the road (there's a pavement on the far side), and follow it past the Hanging Gate pub at Cockyard. After passing the entrance to the sailing club, turn left to cross over the dam of Combs Reservoir and return to the car park.

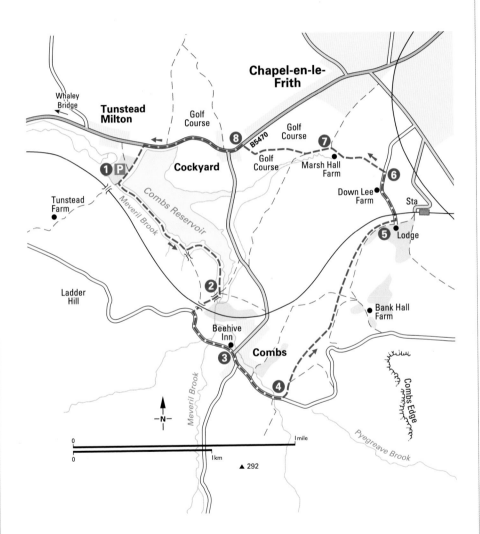

walk information

➤ DISTANCE	3 miles (4.8km)
➤ MINIMUM TIME	2hrs 30min
➤ ASCENT/GRADIENT	164ft (50m) ▲▲▲
➤ LEVEL OF DIFFICULTY	🚶🚶🚶
➤ PATHS	Can be muddy, quite a few stiles
➤ LANDSCAPE	Lakes, meadows, and high moors
➤ SUGGESTED MAPS	OS Explorer OL24 White Peak
➤ START/FINISH	Grid reference: SK 033797
➤ DOG FRIENDLINESS	Farmland – dogs should be kept on leads
➤ PARKING	Combs reservoir car park
➤ PUBLIC TOILETS	None on route

A dramatic route to Kinder Downfall follows the famous trespassers of 1932.

In the Footsteps of the Trespass

f you want to climb one of the quieter ways to Kinder Scout, Hayfield to the west is one of the best places to start. It's also a route with a bit of history to it. From the beginning of the 20th century there had been conflict between ramblers and the owners of Kinder's moorland plateau. By 1932 ramblers from the industrial conurbations of Sheffield and Manchester, disgusted by lack of government action to open up the moors to walkers, decided to hold a mass trespass on Kinder Scout.

ABOVE: A plaque commemorating the mass trespass of Kinder Scout in 1932
RIGHT: View from Kinder Downfall towards the Kinder Reservoir

A Right to Roam

Benny Rothman, a Manchester rambler and a staunch communist, would lead the Kinder Scout trespass on Sunday 24 April. The police expected to intercept Benny at Hayfield railway station, but he outwitted them by arriving on his bicycle, not in the village itself, but at Bowden Bridge Quarry to the east. Here he was greeted by hundreds of cheering fellow ramblers. With the police in hot pursuit the group made their way towards Kinder Scout.

Although they were threatened and barracked by a large gathering of armed gamekeepers the ramblers still managed to get far enough to join their fellow trespassers from Sheffield, who had come up from the Snake Inn. Predictably, fighting broke out and Benny Rothman was one of five arrested. He was given a four-month jail sentence for unlawful assembly and breach of the peace. The ramblers' cause inspired folk singer, Ewan McColl (famous for *Dirty Old Town* and *The First Time Ever I Saw Your Face*) to write The Manchester Rambler, which became something of an anthem for the proliferating walkers' clubs and societies. However it took until 1951, when the recently formed National Park negotiated access agreements with the landowners, for the situation to improve.

Just like the mass trespass this walk starts at Bowden Bridge, where you will see a commemorative plaque on the rock face above the car park. After climbing through the Kinder Valley and above Kinder Reservoir you'll find the same moors of purple heather and the enticing craggy sides of the Scout.

The Downfall

Now you climb to the edge for the most spectacular part of the walk – the part that would have been a trespass all those years ago – and continue along a promenade of dusky gritstone rock. Round the next corner you come to the dark shadow-filled cleft in the rocks of the Kinder Downfall. In the dry summer months the fall is a mere trickle, just enough to wet the rocks, but after the winter rains it can turn into a 100ft (30m) torrent, thrashing against the jumble of boulders below. The prevailing west wind often catches the torrent, funnelling it back up to the top rocks like plumes of white smoke. In contrast, the way down is gentle, leaving the edge at Red Brook and descending the pastures of Tunstead Clough Farm. A quiet leafy lane takes you back into the Kinder Valley.

PAGE 34-35: The windswept upland gritstone plateau of Kinder Scout

walk directions

1 Turn left out of the car park and walk up the lane, which winds beneath the trees and by the banks of the River Kinder. After 550yds (503m), leave the lane at a signposted footpath after crossing a bridge. Follow the path as it traces the east bank of the river before turning left to rejoin the road at a point just short of the treatment plant buildings.

2 Here you fork left through a gate on to a cobbled bridleway, climbing above the buildings. It continues alongside the reservoir's north shore, turning sharp left on White Brow. Beyond a gate, but don't cross over the footbridge, follow the path instead as it climbs alongside William Clough, where it is joined by the Snake Path from the left.

3 The path crosses and recrosses the stream as it works its way up the grass and heather clough. In the upper stages the narrowing clough loses its vegetation and the stream becomes a trickle in the peat. Climb to Ashop Head where you meet the Pennine Way at a crossroads of paths.

4 Turn right to walk along the slabbed Pennine Way path across the moor towards Kinder Scout's north-west edge, then climb those last gritstone slopes on a pitched path to gain the summit plateau. Now it's easy walking along the edge.

5 After turning left into the rocky combe of the River Kinder, the Mermaid's Pool and the Kinder Downfall (waterfalls) come into view. Descend to cross the Kinder's shallow rocky channel about 100yds (91m) back from the edge before turning right and continuing along the edge.

6 Beyond Red Brook, leave the plateau by taking the right fork, which descends south westwards, contouring round grassy slopes beneath the rocky edge.

7 After passing The Three Knolls rocks and swinging right beneath the slopes of Kinderlow End, go through a gate in a fence (grid reference 066867) before taking a right fork to reach another gate in the wall dividing the moor and farmland. Go over a stile next to it and then turn left through a gateway. Descend the trackless pastured spur, passing through several gates and stiles at the field boundaries to pass to the left of Tunstead Clough Farm.

8 Turn right beyond the farmhouse to follow a winding track that descends into the upper Sett Valley. At the crossroads of lanes at the bottom, go straight ahead, and along the road to emerge at Bowden Bridge.

walk information

➤ **DISTANCE**	8 miles (12.9km)
➤ **MINIMUM TIME**	5hrs
➤ **ASCENT/GRADIENT**	1,450ft (440m) ▲▲▲
➤ **LEVEL OF DIFFICULTY**	🚶🚶🚶🚶
➤ **PATHS**	Well-defined tracks and paths, quite a few stiles
➤ **LANDSCAPE**	Heather and peat moorland and farm pastures
➤ **SUGGESTED MAPS**	OS Explorer OL1 Dark Peak
➤ **START/FINISH**	Grid reference: SK 048869
➤ **DOG FRIENDLINESS**	Walk is on farmland and access agreement land, dogs should be kept on leads
➤ **PARKING**	Bowden Bridge pay car park
➤ **PUBLIC TOILETS**	Across bridge from car park

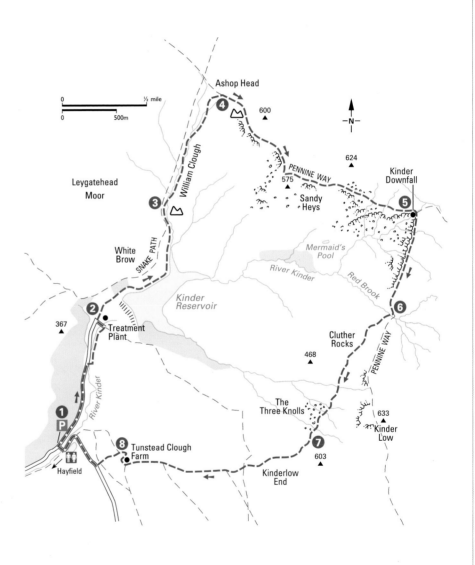

The rural face of the valley between Slaithwaite and Marsden.

Along the Colne Valley

ABOVE: A sunny path beside the Huddersfield Narrow Canal at Slaithwaite
LEFT: A boat on the Marsden Canal next to the Tunnel End Canal and Countryside Museum

Transport across the Pennine watershed has always presented challenges. The Leeds and Liverpool Canal, built during the 1770s, took a convoluted route across the Pennines. Then came the Rochdale Canal; its more direct route came at a high price. Mile for mile, this canal has more locks than any other inland waterway in the country. With the increase in trade between Yorkshire and Lancashire, a third route was soon needed. The Huddersfield Narrow Canal was the answer. Though only 20 miles (32.2km) long, it includes the Standedge Tunnel. Begun in 1798, and dug with pick, shovel and dynamite, the canal was opened to traffic in 1811.

Beads on a String

The Colne Valley, to the west of Huddersfield, is representative of industrial West Yorkshire. Towns with evocative names – Milnsbridge, Linthwaite, Slaithwaite and Marsden – are threaded along the River Colne like beads on a string. In the 18th century this was a landscape of scattered farms and hand-loom weavers, mostly situated on the higher ground. As with Calderdale, a few miles to the north, the deep-cut valley of the Colne was transformed by the Industrial Revolution. Once the textile processes began to be mechanised, mills were built in the valley bottom by the new breed of industrial entrepreneurs. They specialised in the production of fine worsted cloth.

The River Colne provided the power for the first mills, and the canal subsequently improved the transport links. The mills grew larger as water power gave way to steam, towering over the rows of terraced houses built in their shadows. Throughout this walk you can see the mill chimneys and the sawtooth roof-lines of the weaving sheds, though some mills are ruinous and others are now given over to other trades.

Slaithwaite (often pronounced 'Slowitt') is typical of the textile towns in the Colne Valley: unpretentious, a little bit scruffy. It looks to be an unlikely spa town. But that's what it became, albeit briefly, when its mineral springs were compared favourably with those of Harrogate. The town is now undergoing a facelift and its canal is being restored.

RIGHT: The village of Marsden is surrounded on three sides by high moors

walk directions

1 Walk along Britannia Road and at the end go right, up to the A62. Cross over and walk up Varley Road. Beyond the last house go right, through a stile next to a gate. Join a track across a field to a stile on the right-hand end of the wall ahead. Follow a wall to your right, across a stile, to a minor road. Go right and follow the road left to a crossroads. Go straight ahead on a track; after just 20yds (18m) bear left on a track between houses. Squeeze past a gate on to a field path. Follow a wall on your right; towards its end go through a gap and take the steps in the same direction. Follow the obvious route downhill to the road.

2 Go right, along the road, for 20yds (18m) and then turn left on to a track (signed 'Hollins Lane'). Continue as the track becomes rougher; when it peters out, keep left of a cottage and go through a gate. Follow a field-edge path ahead, through a pair of gates either side of a beck. Pass a ruined house to descend on a walled path. When it bears sharp right keep ahead to go through a gate on to a field path. Follow a wall on your right; where it ends keep ahead, slightly uphill across two fields, and meet a walled track. Go left here, towards a farm. Go right, after 50yds (46m), through a stile, on to a path downhill. It soon bears right; take a stile to the left to follow a field-edge path. Cross another field, go through a kissing gate and turn to walk uphill to reach a path that leads up to the B6107.

3 Go right, along the road, for just 75yds (68m), and take a track to your left. Keep left of a house, via a gate. About 150yds (138m) past the house bear right at a fork, taking the less obvious track. You soon follow a wall, beginning a slow descent. Across a beck, the track forks again; keep left, uphill, to skirt the shoulder of much-quarried Hard Hill. The track takes you steeply downhill, then up to a kissing gate, then down again to cross a beck on a stone retaining wall. After another little climb, you have level walking with Butterley Reservoir ahead of you. Bear left, steeply uphill, at a tiny stone building, cross two stiles and meet a tarmac track. Follow it right, downhill, to meet a road.

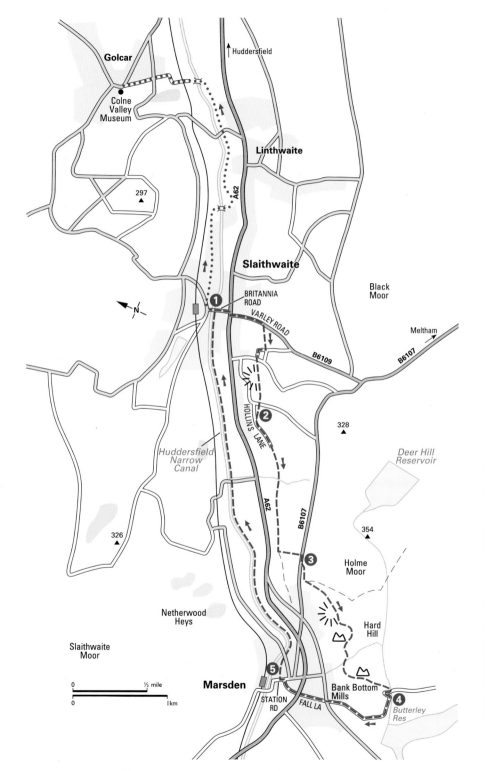

4 Go right, down the road, passing terraced houses dwarfed by Bank Bottom Mills. Keep straight ahead at the roundabout, down Fall Lane, soon bearing left to dip beneath the main road and fork left into Marsden. Take Station Road, at the far end of a green, up to meet the Huddersfield Narrow Canal.

5 Take a path on the right that soon joins the canal tow path. Follow the canal tow path for about 3 miles (4.8km), passing beneath a road, past numerous locks and a couple of road bridges back into Slaithwaite.

Extending the walk

To learn more about the area, you can continue walking alongside the canal into the mill village of Golcar, where you will find the interesting Colne Valley Museum in a weaver's cottage on the hill.

FAR LEFT: A path runs beside the canal on the Huddersfield Narrow Canal at Slaithwaite

walk information	
➤ **DISTANCE**	6 miles (9.7km)
➤ **MINIMUM TIME**	3hrs 30min
➤ **ASCENT/GRADIENT**	550ft (170m) ▲▲▲
➤ **LEVEL OF DIFFICULTY**	👤👤👤
➤ **PATHS**	Field paths, good tracks and canal tow path, many stiless
➤ **LANDSCAPE**	Typical South Pennine country, canalside
➤ **SUGGESTED MAPS**	OS Explorer OL21 South Pennines
➤ **START/FINISH**	Grid reference: SE 079140
➤ **DOG FRIENDLINESS**	Tow path is especially good for dogs
➤ **PARKING**	Plenty of street parking in Slaithwaite
➤ **PUBLIC TOILETS**	Slaithwaite and Marsden

Ramble over hills and dales
in the footsteps of one of
television's favourite doctors.

Peak Practice

ABOVE: *The main street at Longnor*
LEFT: *A walker enjoys the view*
at Hollinsclough

Longnor, a charming Peak village, situated on a high ridge between the Dove and Manifold rivers, developed as a meeting place on the ancient trade routes that once crossed these hills from Sheffield, Chesterfield, Nottingham and the Potteries. More recently it has become famous as the location of the television drama *Peak Practice*, which chronicles the everyday lives of a group of country doctors and their patients. First screened in 1993, the series put Peak District scenery on the television map and has attracted countless visitors. Real life in Longnor, though is somewhat quieter than the TV version, which ceased filming in 2002.

43

Familiar Places

There is plenty that will be familiar to viewers of *Peak Practice*. The fine brick frontage of the fictional Cardale Tearoom is actually a Georgian hotel built to serve the needs of the Crewe and Harpur Estate. It was used as a meeting place for the local farmers when they came to pay their annual rents at the end of March. The Horseshoe has the honour of being the TV doctors' local, the Black Swan. Dating back to 1609 it was an important staging point for the packhorse and carriage trade that crossed these hills. Ye Olde Cheshire Cheese, one of two other pubs in the village, had its origins as a cheese store in 1464. It still has a reputation for fine food but its main attraction is its resident ghost Mrs Robins, a former tenant.

The ancient pubs and cobbled market square are a reminder of Longnor's importance in days gone by as a market town. The turnpike roads with their tolls, and the lack of a railway link, prevented Longnor's development as a major trading centre, but the village retains its Victorian market hall. Now a craft centre and coffee shop, it still has the old market toll charge board, with a list of long-forgotten tariffs, above the front door. However Longnor's old world ambience and location at the heart of ancient paths ensures that it is still busy with walkers, cyclists and tourists.

Local Boy

One of the highlights of a visit to Longnor is the churchyard of St Bartholomew's. Although the church is 18th century, the churchyard has some ancient graves, including that of the remarkable William Billings, who lived to the ripe old age of 112. Born in a cornfield, he was at the capture of Gibraltar in 1704, saw action at the Battle of Ramillies in 1706 and fought against the Stuarts in the Jacobite Risings of 1715 and 1745.

walk directions

1 From the square take the road towards Buxton. Take the first right to turn into Church Street, and then go immediately left, up a lane and right up steps to the footpath. Follow the waymarkers, behind some houses, over a stile and along a wall. Cross another stile, go downhill and turn left on to a farm road.

2 At a fork go left then turn right on to the road. Just before the bend towards the bottom of the hill, take the farm road on the left. At the end, continue through a gate on to the footpath, through a gap stile, downhill, across a bridge and continue straight ahead. Eventually cross a stile and turn left on to the road.

3 Fork left on to a farm road, following the waymarked path. Cross a bridge by a ford and turn left to follow the river bank to the road. Turn right through Hollinsclough, following the road to the right and uphill. Turn right on to a bridleway, through a gate and downhill.

4 After 50yds (46m) fork left by two stones and continue along the flank of the hill. Cross a stile then, at a stone wall, fork left and uphill. At the top turn left at a stone gatepost, through Moorside Farm, through a kissing gate to the road. Turn right then cross a stile to a public footpath on the left.

5 Go downhill to a stream and cross a stile to the left of the ditch. Head uphill, through a stile in the wire fence, through a gap in the wall and round the field to a gap stile. Turn back towards Willshaw Farm, then left on to the well-signposted footpath towards Hill Top Farm.

6 Follow the path over stiles and past the farm to the road. Go left, then take the farm road on the right. Approaching the farm go right, steeply downhill, over a stile and follow the path along the wall. Just before the stream, cross a stile on the left and head uphill to the left of some trees.

7 Continue walking uphill, through a gate in a stone wall to some ruined buildings. Follow the track to the next farm, bear left after the barn, then go left on to a footpath uphill.

8 Go through a stile, follow the wall uphill, over two stiles to the road. Turn left then right towards Longnor. Just before the road bends left, cross a stile on the right, go downhill and over several stiles to a farm road. Turn right and follow this back to the village.

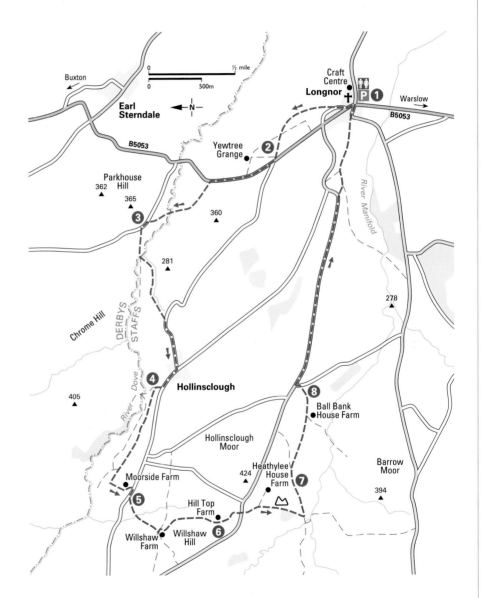

walk information

➤ **DISTANCE**	6 miles (9.7km)
➤ **MINIMUM TIME**	4hrs
➤ **ASCENT/GRADIENT**	459ft (140m)
➤ **LEVEL OF DIFFICULTY**	
➤ **PATHS**	Some on road otherwise good footpaths, can be muddy
➤ **LANDSCAPE**	Valleys, hills and meadows
➤ **SUGGESTED MAPS**	OS Explorer OL24 White Peak
➤ **START/FINISH**	Grid reference: SK 089649
➤ **DOG FRIENDLINESS**	Suitable for dogs but keep on lead near livestock
➤ **PARKING**	Longnor village square
➤ **PUBLIC TOILETS**	Longnor village square

The upper valley of the Dove

has quiet villages

and historic remains.

Pilsbury Castle and the Upper Dove Valley

ABOVE: *A horse grazes peacefully in a field near Hartington*
LEFT: *The 13th century parish church of Saint Giles seen beyond village houses in Hartington*

Hartington, lying in the mid regions of the Dove Valley, is a prosperous village with 18th-century houses and hotels built in local limestone and lined around spacious greens. Its history can be traced back to the Normans, when it was recorded as Hartedun, the centre for the De Ferrier's estate. Hartington Hall, now the youth hostel, was first built in 1350 but was rebuilt in 1611.

As you leave the village the lane climbs past the Church of St Giles, which has a battlemented Perpendicular tower. It continues up the high valley sides of the Dove, then on through emerald high fields and valley.

Pilsbury Castle

Pilsbury Castle hides from the viewer until the very last moment, but then a grassy ramp swoops down to it from the hillsides. Only the earthworks are now visible, but you can imagine its supreme impregnable position on the limestone knoll that juts out into the valley. You can see the motte, a man-made mound built to accommodate the wooden keep, and the bailey, a raised embankment that would have had a wooden stockade round it.

The castle's exact history is disputed. It was probably built around 1100 by the Normans, on the site of an Iron Age fort. It may have been a stronghold used earlier by William I to suppress a local rebellion in his 'Wasting of the North' campaign. Being in the middle of the De Ferrier estate it was probably their administrative centre. In the 1200s this function would have been moved to Hartington.

Views up-valley are fascinating, with the conical limestone peaks of Parkhouse and Chrome Hills in the distance. Now the route descends into Dovedale for the first time, crossing the river into Staffordshire. The lane climbs to a high lane running the length of the dale's east rim. Note the change in the rock – it's now the darker gritstone. The crags of Sheen Hill have been blocking the view east, but once past them you can see for miles, across the Manifold Valley to the Roaches and Hen Cloud. A field path takes the route on its finale, descending along a line of crags with lofty views.

walk directions

1   Turn left out of the car park and follow the road through the centre of the village. Turn left, uphill by the church on Hyde Lane and then take the third path on the left. This descends northwards across fields. Just below a farmhouse, the path swings left to follow a dry-stone wall on the left.

2   The path cuts across the stony drive coming up the hill from Bank Top Farm. Waymarking posts highlight the continuing route along the high valleysides.

3   West of Carder Low (grid ref 126627) the path goes through a gateway by an intersection of walls and becomes indistinct. Here, climb half right to another gateway, then head for a group of trees. Beyond these another footpath signpost shows the way uphill to a step stile in a ridge wall, where you look down into a small valley.

4   Descend into the valley and turn left to reach a high lane by a stone barn. A stile across the road allows you on to the continuing path, rounding the high slopes above Pilsbury. The footpath rakes left down the hillslopes to a farm track and wall alongside the ancient earthworks of Pilsbury Castle. A gate in the stone wall allows further inspection.

5   Turn right and continue down a grassy track, which eventually degenerates into a field path heading up the valley towards Crowdecote.

6   Just past Bridge End Farm turn left to cross the Dove by a little footbridge. Follow the path directly uphill across a field.

7   Beyond the wall stile the path veers right, through scrub, to reach the Longnore road near Edgetop. Turn left along the high lane to Harris Close Farm.

8 A stile on the nearside of an outbuilding at Harris Close starts the path back to Hartington. In all but one field there's a wall on the right for guidance. After going through a wood, the path descends through scrub into the valley. It joins a farm track southwards towards Bridge-end farm.

9 At the signpost 'Hartington' turn left through a gate and across a field. A footbridge, hidden by trees, allows the crossing of the Dove. The intermittent path gradually swings right (south-east) across fields. The path aims for the woods to the left of the dairy and enters them via a gate. At the other side go through a field beside a dairy and turn left along the lane to return to Hartington.

walk information

➤ **DISTANCE**	7.5 miles (12.1km)
➤ **MINIMUM TIME**	4hrs
➤ **ASCENT/GRADIENT**	804ft (245m) ▲▲△
➤ **LEVEL OF DIFFICULTY**	👥👥👥
➤ **PATHS**	Field paths and lanes, some steep climbs, lots of stiles
➤ **LANDSCAPE**	Pastures, limestone valley
➤ **SUGGESTED MAPS**	OS Explorer OL24 White Peak
➤ **START/FINISH**	Grid reference: SK 127603
➤ **DOG FRIENDLINESS**	Keep dogs on lead
➤ **PARKING**	Parson's Field, Hartington, pay car park
➤ **PUBLIC TOILETS**	Near car park

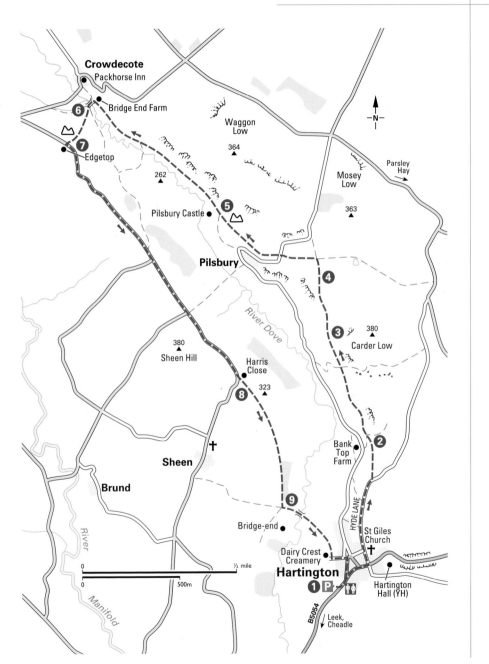

The rural serenity of modern Miller's Dale belies its early role in the Industrial Revolution.

Ghosts of Miller's Dale

I t's all quiet in Miller's Dale these days, but it wasn't always so. Many early industrialists wanted to build their cotton mills in the countryside, far away from the marauding Luddites of the city. The Wye and its tributaries had the power to work these mills. The railway followed, and that brought more industry with it. And so little Miller's Dale and its neighbours joined the Industrial Revolution.

ABOVE: Tideswell's 14th-century parish church, known as the "Cathedral of the Peak"
RIGHT: A view over the rooftops of Tideswell toward the church

Hidden History

The walk starts in Tideswell Dale. Nowadays it's choked with thickets and herbs but they hide a history of quarrying and mining for basalt.

Cruelty at the Mill

Litton Mill will eventually be modernised into holiday cottages, but today it lies damp and derelict in a shadowy part of the dale. The Memoirs of Robert Blincoe, written in 1863, tells of mill owner Ellis Needham's cruelty to child apprentices, who were often shipped in from the poorhouses of London. Many of the children died and were buried in the churchyards of Tideswell and Taddington. It is said that ghosts of some of the apprentices still make appearances in or around the mill. The walk emerges from the shadows of the mill into Water-cum-Jolly Dale. At first the river is lined by mudbanks thick with rushes and common horsetail. It's popular with wildfowl. The river widens out and, at the same time, impressive limestone cliffs squeeze the path. The river's widening is artificial, a result of it being controlled to form a head of water for the downstream mill.

Round the next corner is Cressbrook Mill, built by Sir Richard Arkwright, but taken over by William Newton. Newton also employed child labour but was said to have treated them well. The rooftop bell tower would have peeled to beckon the apprentices, who lived next door, to the works. Like Litton this impressive Georgian mill was allowed to moulder, but is now being restored as flats. The walk leaves the banks of the Wye at Cressbrook to take in pretty Cressbrook Dale. In this nature reserve you'll see lily-of-the-valley, wild garlic and bloody cranesbill; you should also see bee and fragrant orchids. Just as you think you've found your true rural retreat you'll climb to the rim of the dale, look across it and see the grassed-over spoil heaps of lead mines. Finally, the ancient strip fields of Litton form a mosaic of pasture and dry-stone walls on the return route.

PAGE 54-55: Cottages line a road in Tideswell

walk directions

1 Follow the path southwards from beside the car park toilet block into Tideswell Dale, taking the right-hand fork to cross over the little bridge.

2 On entering Miller's Dale, go left along the tarmac lane to Litton Mill. Go through the gateposts on to a concessionary path through a mill yard. Beyond the mill, the path follows the River Wye, as it meanders through the tight, steep-sided dale.

3 The river widens out in Water-cum-Jolly Dale and the path, which is liable to flooding here, traces a wall of limestone cliffs before reaching Cressbrook. Cross the footbridge and then turn left to pass in front of Cressbrook Mill and out on to the road.

4 Turn left along the road and then take the right fork which climbs steadily into Cressbrook Dale. Where the road doubles back uphill, leave it for a track going straight ahead into the woods. The track degenerates into a narrow path that emerges in a clearing high above the stream. Follow it downhill to a footbridge over the stream and then take the right fork path, which climbs high up the valley side to a stile in the top wall.

5 Do not cross the stile, instead take the downhill path to reach the dale bottom, where there's a junction of paths. The one that's wanted here recrosses the stream on stepping stones, and then climbs into Tansley Dale.

6 The path turns right at the top of the dale, follows a tumbledown wall before crossing it on a step stile. Head for a wall corner in the next field, then onwards through a narrow enclosure to reach a walled track just south of Litton village.

7 Turn left along the track, which comes out on to a country lane at the crown of a sharp bend. Keep straight on down the lane but leave it at the next bend for a cross-field path to Bottomhill Road. Across the road, a further field path descends to the lane at Dale House Farm.

walk information

➤ **DISTANCE**	6 miles (9.7km)
➤ **MINIMUM TIME**	3hrs 30min
➤ **ASCENT/GRADIENT**	690ft (210m) ▲▲▲
➤ **LEVEL OF DIFFICULTY**	⅏⅏⅏
➤ **PATHS**	Generally well-defined paths and tracks, path in Water-cum-Jolly Dale liable to flooding, quite a few stiles
➤ **LANDSCAPE**	Limestone dales
➤ **SUGGESTED MAPS**	OS Explorer OL24 White Peak
➤ **START/FINISH**	Grid reference: SK 154743
➤ **DOG FRIENDLINESS**	Dogs can run free in dales with no livestock, but keep under control when crossing farmland
➤ **PARKING**	Tideswell Dale pay car park
➤ **PUBLIC TOILETS**	At car park

Turn left and then right on a lane marked 'unsuitable for motors'. Follow this road into Tideswell.

8 After looking around the village head south down the main street, then right on to Gordon Road, which then heads south.

9 Where this ends, continue down the stony track ahead, which runs parallel with the main road. At the end go through a small gate on the left fork, down to the road into Tideswell Dale. Cross over and turn right for a short path, back to the car park.

Extending the walk

If it's dry you can extend this walk though Monk's Dale. Leave the main route at Point 8 in Tideswell and rejoin it from the Monsal Trail, back at Litton Mill, near Point 2, to retrace your steps to the start of the walk.

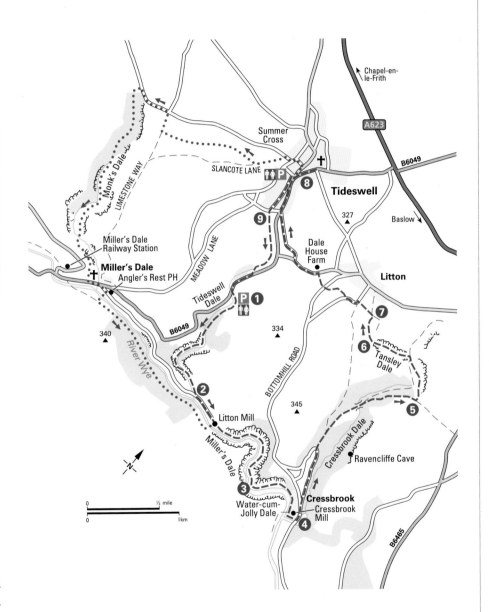

A walk through the alpine-like splendour of the Peak's most famous dale.

Dovedale: Ivory Spires and Wooded Splendour

ABOVE: A tranquil tree-lined lake at Dovedale
LEFT: The view towards Bunster Hill from the isolated limestone Cloud Thorpe Hill

Right from the start there's drama as you follow the River Dove, wriggling through a narrow gorge between Bunster Hill and the towering pyramid of Thorpe Cloud. A limestone path urges you to climb to a bold rocky outcrop high above the river. Lovers' Leap has a fine view across the dale to pinnacles of the Twelve Apostles. It's a view to gladden your hearts – not the sort of place you'd think of throwing yourself from at all. However, in 1761 an Irish dean and his lady companion, who were out horse riding (or were they horsing about?) fell off the rock. The dean died of his injuries but the lady survived to tell the tale.

Spires and Caves

The Dove writhes round another corner. Above your heads, flaky fingers of limestone known as the Tissington Spires rise out from thick woodland cover. Just a few footsteps away on the right there's a splendid natural arch, which is just outside the entrance to Reynard's Cave. This is the result of the cave's roof collapsing.

The dale's limestone walls close in. The path climbs to a place more remote from the rushing river, which often floods around here. As the valley opens out again two gigantic rock stacks face each other across the Dove. Pickering Tor has a small cave at its foot. A little footbridge allows you across to the other side to the foot of Ilam Rock. This 80ft (25m) leaning thumb of limestone has an overhang on the south side that's popular with climbers. It too has a cave at the bottom, which is only 4ft (1.2m) at the entrance but opens out to over 30ft (10m) inside.

You will get a better view of them when you cross the little footbridge to the cave at the foot of the rocks. On this side you're in Staffordshire and the paths are less populated.

Hurt's Wood and Hall Dale

The continuing walk into Hall Dale heralds a less formal landscape. The dale is dry and it climbs up the hillside. Hurts Wood has wych elm, whitebeam, ash and rowan. Some fences have kept grazing animals out, allowing the trees and shrubs to regenerate. Hurts Wood is alive and well. You'll hear and see many birds – warblers, redstarts and black caps; and you'll see wild flowers – dog's mercury, wood anemone and wood forget-me-not.

It seems a shame to leave the dale behind but soon you're walking down a quiet lane with Ilam and the beautiful Manifold Valley on your right and a shapely peak, Bunster Hill, on your left. A path takes you across the shoulder of the hill, across the ridge and furrow of a medieval field system, then back into the valley of the Dove.

walk directions

1 Turn right out of the car park and follow the road along the west bank of the Dove. Cross the footbridge to the opposite bank and turn left along a wide footpath. This twists and turns through the narrow dale, between Bunster Hill and Thorpe Cloud.

2 Follow the path as it climbs some steps up through the woods on to the famous rocky outcrop of Lovers' Leap, then descends past the magnificent Tissington Spires and Reynard's Cave. Here a huge natural arch surrounds the much smaller entrance to the historic cave. As the dale narrows the path climbs above the river.

3 The dale widens again. Leave the main path for a route signposted 'Public Footpath to Stanshope', and cross the footbridge over the Dove. A narrow woodland path turns right beneath the huge spire of Ilam Rock above you. Ignore the path on the left, signposted to Ilam '(steep ascent)'. Beyond a stile the path eases to the left into Hall Dale. Following the valley bottom, as it climbs out of the woods into a rugged limestone-cragged gorge.

4 As the gorge begins to become shallow the path enters pastureland – the attractive village of Stanshope is now on the skyline. At a crossroads of paths turn left through a squeeze stile in the wall and head south with a stone wall on the right. Where the wall turns right, keep walking straight ahead to reach another stile, and then veer half right by a wall in the next field. The path cuts diagonally to the left across the last two fields to reach Ilam-Moor Lane, 250yds (229m) to the south of Damgate Farm.

5 Turn left to walk along the lovely quiet country lane. There are magnificent views from here down to Ilam and the Manifold Valley ahead of you and down to the right.

6 After 800yds (732m) take a footpath on the left, following the drive to Ilamtops Farm for a few paces before turning right over a stile. A field path now heads roughly south-east, traversing low grassy fellsides to the top of Moor Plantation woods.

7 Here the path (fallen away in places) cuts across the steep sides of Bunster Hill, before straddling its south spur and descending to a step-stile in the intake wall. A clear path now descends south-east across sloping pastures to the back of the Izaak Walton Hotel.

8 Turn left (north-east) by the hotel across more fields and back to the car park.

Extending the walk

As so often when walking beside the River Dove, it's difficult to resist the temptation to carry on following its lovely series of dales. You can do this at Point A (see map), continuing up the dale to Viator's Bridge, a packhorse bridge in lovely Mill Dale, before heading back across the fields to rejoin the main route at Point B. The bridge on the route takes its name from a character in Izaak Walton's *Compleat Angler*, who complains to his companion Piscator that the bridge is too small – 'Why a mouse can hardly go over it: Tis not two fingers broad.'

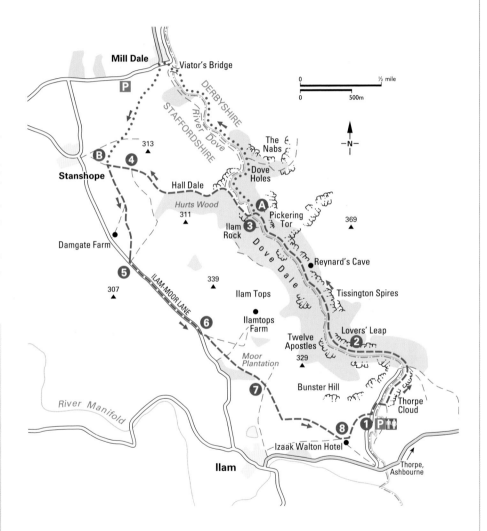

walk information	
► **DISTANCE**	5 miles (8km)
► **MINIMUM TIME**	3hrs 30min
► **ASCENT/GRADIENT**	557ft (170m) ▲▲▲
► **LEVEL OF DIFFICULTY**	🚶🚶🚶
► **PATHS**	Mostly good paths, lanes, a few stiles, one small scramble
► **LANDSCAPE**	Partially wooded dales and high pastures
► **SUGGESTED MAPS**	OS Explorer OL24 White Peak
► **START/FINISH**	Grid reference: SK 146509
► **DOG FRIENDLINESS**	Dogs should be kept under close control
► **PARKING**	Dovedale pay car park, near Thorpe
► **PUBLIC TOILETS**	At car park

Follow in the footsteps
of the immortal Compo,
Foggy and Clegg.

A Taste of the Last of the Summer Wine

Holmfirth and the Holme Valley have been popularised as 'Summer Wine Country'. The whimsical TV series, starring the trio of incorrigible characters Compo, Foggy and Clegg, alongside an extensive cast of friends, has now been running for a quarter of a century. These larger-than-life characters, going back to their second childhoods, have proved to be an irresistible formula in the hands of writer Roy Clarke.

ABOVE: "The Wrinkled Stocking" – a tea room sign based on Nora Batty's character from the TV series Last of the Summer Wine, *set in Holmfirth*
RIGHT: A view along the River Holme in Holmfirth and popular filming location for the TV series

Comedy History

Last of the Summer Wine was first seen in January 1973, as a one-off Comedy Playhouse episode. The response was so good that a six-part series was commissioned. The rest is history, with Summer Wine becoming the UK's longest running comedy programme.

The cast have become familiar faces around Holmfirth. So much so that when Londoner Bill Owen (lovable rogue 'Compo') died in 1999 at the age of 85, he was laid to rest overlooking the little town he had grown to call home. Bill Owen's real-life son Tom joined the cast to play Compo's long lost son, and together with plenty of newcomers, the series seems to have plenty of life in it yet.

Visitors come to Holmfirth in their droves, in search of film locations such as Sid's Café and Nora Batty's house. But Holmfirth takes its TV fame in its stride, for this isn't the first time that the town has starred in front of the cameras. In fact, Holmfirth very nearly became another Hollywood. Bamforths – better known for its naughty seaside postcards – began to make short films here in the early years of the last century. They were exported around the world to popular demand. Local people were drafted in as extras in Bamforths' overwrought dramas. Film production came to an end at the outbreak of the First World War and, sadly, was never resumed.

Holmfirth

Holmfirth town, much more than just a film set, is the real star – along with the fine South Pennine scenery which surrounds it. By the time you have completed half of this walk, you are a mile (1.6km) from the Peak National Park.

The town grew rapidly with the textile trades, creating a tight-knit community in the valley bottom: a maze of ginnels, alleyways and narrow lanes. The River Holme, which runs through its middle, has flooded on many occasions. But the most devastating flood occurred back in 1852 when, after heavy rain, Bilberry Reservoir burst its banks. The resulting torrent of water destroyed the centre of Holmfirth and claimed 81 lives. The tragedy was reported at length on the front page of the London Illustrated News. A public subscription fund was started to help the flood survivors to rebuild the town. These traumatic events are marked by a monument situated near the bus station.

RIGHT: The view over Holmfirth from Heyden Moor

LEFT: View over Holmfirth famous as the location for the long-running BBC series Last of the Summer Wine

walk directions

1 From Crown Bottom car park, walk to the right along Huddersfield Road for just 100yds (91m) before bearing left opposite the fire station, up Wood Lane. The road soon narrows to a steep track. Keep left of a house and through a gate, to continue on a walled path. At the top of the hill, by a bench, follow the track to the right. Follow this track, soon enclosed, as it wheels left, down into a valley. Soon after you approach woodland, you have a choice of tracks: keep left on the walled path, uphill. Join a more substantial farm track and approach a building on the top of the track, take the second stile on the left, across a field path to emerge by the houses of Upperthong. Turn left and follow the road as it bends through the top of the village.

2 Continue along the road, which wheels round to the right. Walk downhill, with great views opening up of the Holme Valley. After 150yds (138m) on the road, take a cinder track on the right. Walk down past Newlands Farm to meet a road. Cross over and take the lane ahead, steeply down into a little valley and up the other side. When this minor road forks at the top, go right, uphill. Immediately after the first house, go left, on a gravel track. Follow this track to Lower Hogley Farm where you keep right, past a knot of houses, to a gate and on to a field path, with a wall to your left. Go through three more fields, aiming for the mast on the horizon, and descend to the road.

3 Go right for just 50yds (46m) to bear left around an old schoolhouse on a grassy path. Follow the walled footpath downhill, through a gate; as the footpath opens out into a grassy area, bear left on a grassy track down into the valley. Follow a high stone wall on your right-hand side,

over a stile, on to an enclosed path. On approaching houses, take a stile and join a metalled track at a fork. Bear right here, then immediately left, on a narrow footpath between houses. Follow a field path through a gate; pass houses and a mill down to meet the main A6024 road.

4 Cross the road then, by a row of diminutive cottages, take Old Road to the left. Keep straight ahead when you reach a junction, down Water Street. Beyond a mill, cross the River Holme on a metal footbridge and follow a riverside path. Soon the footpath veers right through pasture; when the path forks, keep to the right, uphill, to enter woodland. Continue in the same direction, uphill, swinging left to pass below an old quarry in the woods, then forking right (uphill) to emerge at a field. Cross two fields and join a track by a house. Pass some more cottages to meet a road.

5 Go left, along the road. Enjoy fine views down into the Holme Valley, as you make the long descent back to Holmfirth.

walk information

▶ **DISTANCE**	4.5 miles (7.2km)
▶ **MINIMUM TIME**	2hrs 30min
▶ **ASCENT/GRADIENT**	558ft (170m) ▲▲▲
▶ **LEVEL OF DIFFICULTY**	🚶🚶🚶
▶ **PATHS**	Good paths and tracks, plenty of stiles
▶ **LANDSCAPE**	Upland pasture
▶ **SUGGESTED MAPS**	OS Explorer 288 Bradford & Huddersfield
▶ **START/FINISH**	Grid reference: SE 143084
▶ **DOG FRIENDLINESS**	On lead in fields with livestock, off on lanes
▶ **PARKING**	Centre of Holmfirth gets very crowded, so park in Crown Bottom car park (pay-and-display) on Huddersfield Road
▶ **PUBLIC TOILETS**	Holmfirth

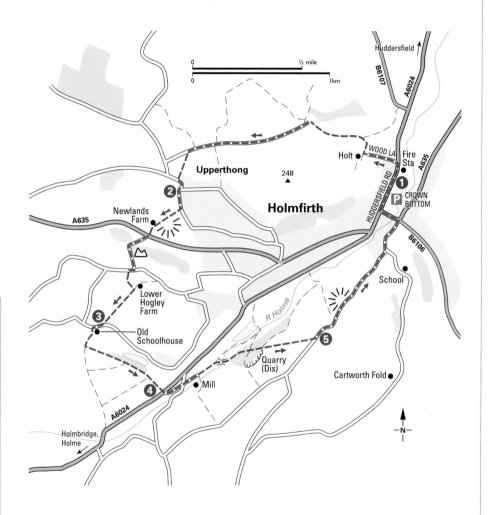

Following the ancient roads over
Win Hill to the Roman fort at Navio,
via the site of an ancient battle.

Marching Roads and Battlefields

ABOVE: *Illuminated Peak Cavern near Castleton*
LEFT: *The beautiful countryside of the Hope Valley*

Leaving Castleton beneath Peveril Castle's Norman keep sets the scene for a walk through history. You're treading the same ground as Roman soldiers and Celtic and Saxon warriors before you. The walk takes you on to the hillside beyond the sycamores of the River Noe. As you amble across green pastures overlooking the Hope Valley, cast your imagination back to the darker days of AD 926. Down there in the valley below you, a furious tribal battle ended in victory for King Athelstan, grandson of Alfred the Great. He would soon become the first Saxon ruler of all England.

Navio – a Roman Fort

In one of those riverside fields the path comes across the earthwork remains of the Roman fort, Navio. Built in the time of Emperor Antoninus Pius, the fort stood at a junction of roads serving garrisons at Buxton, Glossop, and Templeborough. At its peak it would have sheltered over 500 soldiers. It remained occupied until the 4th century, controlling the rich mining area around the Peak. Many Roman relics found near the fort can be viewed at the Buxton Museum.

Win Hill looms large in your thoughts as you cross to the other side of the valley and climb towards it. As you're passing through the hamlet of Aston take a quick look at Aston Hall. Built in 1578, it has an unusual pedimented window with a weather-worn carved figure. The doorway is surrounded by Roman Doric columns and a four-centred arch.

Beyond the hall the climb begins in earnest up a stony track, then through bracken and grass hillside where Win Hill's rocky summit peeps out across the heathered ridge. A concrete trig point caps the rocks. And what a view to reward your efforts! The Ladybower Reservoir's sinuous shorelines creep between dark spruce woods, while the gritstone tors of Kinder Scout, the Derwent Edge, and Bleaklow fill the northern horizon, framed by the pyramidal Lose Hill.

There are several theories on how Win Hill got its name. The most likely one is that it derives from an earlier name, Wythinehull, which meant Willow Hill. The one I prefer though concerns two warlords, Edwin, the first Christian king of Northumbria, and Cuicholm, King of Wessex. Cuicholm murdered Lilla, Edwin's maidservant, and Edwin was looking for revenge. Cuicholm assembled his forces on Lose Hill, while his enemy camped on Win Hill. Edwin was victorious and thus his hill was named Win Hill. Now you follow Edwin down the hill, before continuing across the Hope Valley fields back to Castleton.

RIGHT: Winnats Pass winding through a rocky valley near Castleton
PAGE 70: Part of the village of Castleton from Danby Low Moor

1 Turn left out of the car park along the main street. At the far end of the village turn right on a walled stony lane and continue along a well-defined path accompanying Peakshole Water. Cross the railway with care and continue along the path to its end at Pindale Road.

2 Turn left here, then right at the next junction. After 200yds (183m), go over a stile by a gate on the left and follow the path running roughly parallel to the lane at first, then the River Noe, to reach the site of the Roman fort of Navio. Beyond the earthworks go over a stile in a fence and bear half right across another field to reach the B6049 road at Brough.

3 Turn left through the village and cross the footbridge over the River Noe. Go left over a stile and head north-west to the A6187. Turn left along the road for 200yds (183m) to a small gate just beyond a cottage. Follow the hedge and dyke on the right to pass to the right of some houses.

4 Turn left along the lane heading towards the railway station, then go right along a narrow path, which leads to a footbridge over the line. Cross the bridge and turn right at its far end, then left over a stile to cross yet more fields, this time keeping the fence on your right.

5 When you reach Aston turn left along the road, then almost immediately turn right along a narrow, surfaced lane, signposted 'To Win Hill and Hope Cross'.

6 Beyond Edge Farm an unsurfaced track on the left takes the route along the top edge of some woods to a path junction above Twitchill Farm. Now climb right on a well-used path to Win Hill's summit.

7 From the summit retrace your steps back to the junction above Twitchill Farm. This time descend left past the farm on a tarmac drive, to the railway.

8 Turn left under the railway tunnel for the lane via Kilhill Bridge to Edale Road. Turn right along the road, under the railway bridge, then turn left by a red post box on a field path.

9 By a cottage turn right on a path climbing towards Lose Hill. Take the left fork, which is signposted 'Castleton' to follow a waymarked route westwards to Spring House Farm.

10 In front of the farm, turn right to walk along a track behind Losehill Hall. Where the lane swings left, leave it to follow a cross-field path, which joins a rough lane. After passing the outdoor centre, turn left along Hollowford Road into Castleton.

Shortening the Walk

If you want a shorter walk, without the climb up to Win Hill, you can still get reasonable views if you start the walk in Hope and join the main route at Point 2 Leave it again at Point A, near Twitchill Farm, and follow the raking path up to Wooler Knoll, with fine views over Ladybower Reservoir. Clear tracks lead back into the valley by Fullwood Stile Farm and Edale Road, from where you can pick out field tracks taking you back to Hope.

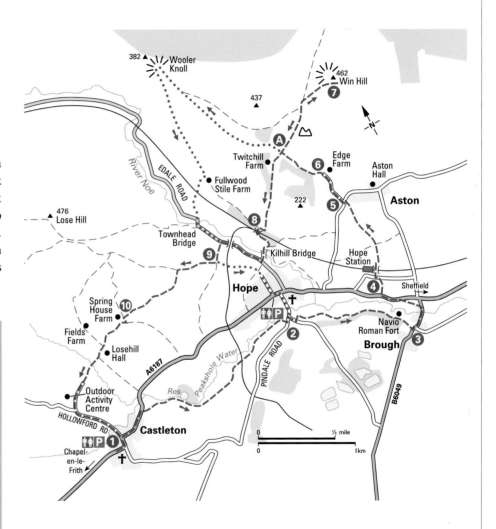

walk information	
➤ **DISTANCE**	8.75 miles (14.1km)
➤ **MINIMUM TIME**	5hrs
➤ **ASCENT/GRADIENT**	1,050ft (320m) ▲▲▲
➤ **LEVEL OF DIFFICULTY**	🚶🚶🚶
➤ **PATHS**	Paths can be slippery after rain, quite a few stiles
➤ **LANDSCAPE**	Riverside pastureland and high peak
➤ **SUGGESTED MAPS**	OS Explorer OL1 Dark Peak
➤ **START/FINISH**	Grid reference: SK 149829
➤ **DOG FRIENDLINESS**	Dogs should be kept on lead, except on lanes
➤ **PARKING**	Main Castleton pay car park
➤ **PUBLIC TOILETS**	At car park

Beneath the beauty of the Ladybower Reservoir lie the remains of the old village of Ashopton.

A High Ridge and Lost Villages at Ladybower

In the north-east corner of Derbyshire, the heather ridges and gritstone tors of Derwent Edge make one last stand before declining to the plains of Yorkshire. It's always been a sparsely populated corner of the country with few references in the history books. Hereabouts, the stories lie beneath the water.

ABOVE: *The viaduct across Ladybower Reservoir*
RIGHT: *The Ladybower Reservoir was constructed between 1935 and 1943 and took more than two years to fill completely*

Farewell to Ashopton

Before the Second World War Ashopton, which lay at the confluence of the rivers Derwent and Ashop, was a huddle of stone-built cottages, a small inn and a blacksmith's shop. A little lane ambled from Ashopton northwards to its neighbouring village, Derwent, which enjoyed an even quieter location in the Upper Derwent valley. But the building of a huge reservoir, the third in the region, shattered the locals' lives. After the completion of its dam in 1943 Ladybower Reservoir gradually filled up, and by 1946 the water level had risen above the rooftops.

Haunting Remains

Before you set off gaze, out at the huge concrete viaduct over the reservoir. Wherever you look there is water. You take a winding track up the next hill, now shaded by a sombre plantation of spruce. The cottages you see here are all that remain of the village of Ashopston. Soon you're through the woods and heading across open moor to the weathered gritstone tors that top the ridge. The rocks of Whinstone Lee Tor are set into a thick carpet of heather. Though the highest hills in the region lie to the north, this is one of the best viewpoints, as the ridge is at its narrowest here. In the west, Kinder Scout's expansive flat top peeps over Crook Hill's rocky crest. In the valley down below, the dark waters of the reservoir still keep their secrets.

After passing the Hurkling Stones, the route descends towards the lakeshore in search of Derwent village. The old gateposts of Derwent Hall still survive by the roadside. A notice board shows the positions of the hall itself, along with the post office, school, church and some of the old cottages. After a dry spell the water level can sometimes fall sufficiently for you to see the crumbling walls and foundations of the village surrounded by the crazed drying mud. One small bridge is almost intact, but the villagers dismantled the main twin-arched packhorse bridge for rebuilding beyond the reach of the rising water at Slippery Stones, higher up the valley.

Leaving the old village behind you return by the shores of the reservoir. Nature has readjusted. The landscape, though more regimented now, is still beautiful; kestrels still scour the hillside for prey, and dippers frequent the streams as they always have done.

walk directions

1 Cross over the road and then take the public bridleway following a private road that zig-zags past a few of Ashopton's remaining cottages.

2 The gated road becomes unsurfaced and where it ends double back left on a forestry track climbing through pines and larches. The track emerges from the forest on to Lead Hill, where Ladybower Reservoir and the rather sombre sprawl of Bleaklow come into view.

3 The path keeps the intake wall to the left as it rakes up the bracken slopes of Lead Hill. Follow the well-worn path as it veers away from the wall up to the ridge. At the junction of paths at the top go second left for the summit of Whistone Lee Tor.

4 The path continues along the peaty ridge past the Hurkling Stones to an unnamed summit. Beyond this it meets a signposted path heading from Ladybower over to Moscar. Descend left until you reach a gate at the edge of the open hillside.

5 Through the gate the path descends westwards and alongside the top wall of a conifer plantation. It fords Grindle Clough's stream beyond another gate and turns past several stone-built barns. The path, now paved, descends further to join the track running along the east shores of Ladybower Reservoir.

6 It's worth a detour here to see the fascinating remains of Derwent village, 400yds (366m) along the track, at the foot of the Mill Brook clough. Retrace your steps along the well-graded track, by the shores of the reservoir. After rounding Grainfoot Clough the track passes beneath woodlands with Whinstone Lee Tor crowning the hilltop.

7 It meets the outward route at a gate above the Ashopton viaduct, opposite the lay-by on the A57 above the reservoir.

Extending the walk

You can extend this walk if you choose, by walking across the moorland edges from Point 4 to Dovestone Tor and Back Tor, then descend to Derwent Reservoir and follow the shore of the reservoir to rejoin the main walk at Point 6.

walk information	
➤ DISTANCE	5.5 miles (8.8km)
➤ MINIMUM TIME	3hrs 30min
➤ ASCENT/GRADIENT	1,200ft (365m) ▲▲▲
➤ LEVEL OF DIFFICULTY	♦♦♦
➤ PATHS	Well-defined moorland paths and a reservoir road
➤ LANDSCAPE	High gritstone moorland
➤ SUGGESTED MAPS	OS OL1 Dark Peak
➤ START/FINISH	Grid reference: SK 195864
➤ DOG FRIENDLINESS	Keep on lead on access agreement land, could run free by reservoir shores
➤ PARKING	Marked lay-by east of Ashopton Viaduct (A57)
➤ PUBLIC TOILETS	Heatherdene car park (A6013)

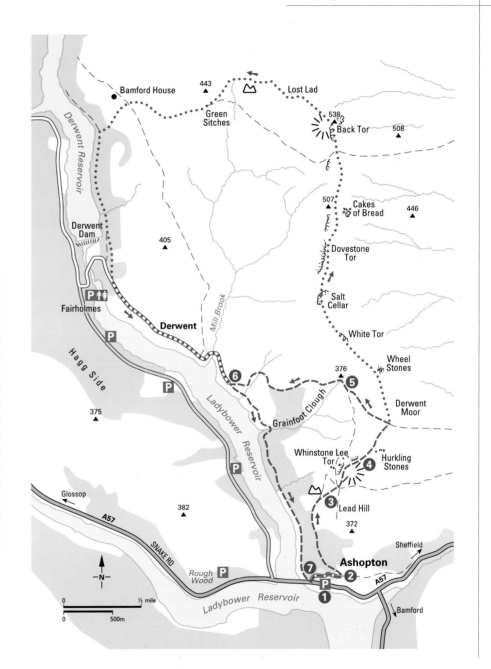

PAGE 76-77: View over Ladybower Reservoir to the hills beyond

*Following the ever-changing River
Wye from Ashford-in-the-Water
through lovely Monsal Dale.*

Through Monsal Dale, the Valley of the Gods

ABOVE: *A medieval village cross stands on the small
green in the limestone-built village of Great Longstone*
LEFT: *Sheep graze beside a cottage in Monsal Dale*

The Wye is a chameleon among rivers. Rising as a peaty stream from Axe Edge, it rushes downhill, only to be confined by the concrete and tarmac of Buxton, a spa town, and the quarries to the east. Beyond Chee Dale it gets renewed vigour and cuts a deep gorge through beds of limestone, finally to calm down again among the gentle fields and hillslopes of Bakewell. The finest stretch of the river valley must be around Monsal Head, and the best approach is that from Ashford-in-the-Water, one of Derbyshire's prettiest villages found just off the busy A6.

Monsal Dale

After passing through Ashford's streets the route climbs to high pastures that give no clue as to the whereabouts of Monsal Dale. But suddenly you reach the last wall and the ground falls away into a deep wooded gorge. John Ruskin was so taken with this beauty that he likened it to the Vale of Tempe: 'you might have seen the Gods there morning and evening – Apollo and the sweet Muses of light – walking in fair procession on the lawns of it and to and fro among the pinnacles of its crags'.

The Midland Railway

It's just a short walk along the rim to reach one of Derbyshire's best-known viewpoints, where the Monsal Viaduct spans the gorge. Built in 1867 as part of the Midland Railway's line to Buxton, the five-arched, stone-built viaduct is nearly 80ft (25m) high. But the building of this railway angered Ruskin. He continued, 'you blasted its rocks away, heaped thousands of tons of shale into its lovely stream. The valley is gone and the Gods with it'.

The line closed in 1968 and the rails were ripped out, leaving only the trackbed and the bridges. Ironically, today's conservationists believe that those are worth saving and have slapped a conservation order on the viaduct. The trackbed is used as a recreational route for walkers and cyclists – the Monsal Trail. The walk continues over the viaduct, giving bird's-eye views of the river and the lawn-like surrounding pastures. It then descends to the river bank, following it westwards beneath the prominent peak of Fin Cop. The valley curves like a sickle, while the path weaves in and out of thickets, and by wetlands where tall bulrushes and irises grow. After crossing the A6 the route takes you into the mouth of Deep Dale then the shade of Great Shacklow Wood. Just past some pools filled with trout there's an entrance to the Magpie Mine Sough. The tunnel was built in 1873 to drain the Magpie Lead Mines at nearby Sheldon. Magpie was worked intermittently for over 300 years before finally closing in the 1960s. It's believed to be haunted by the ghosts of miners from the neighbouring Redsoil Mine who tragically died underground in a dispute with the Magpie men.

Looking back on the beauty of the day's walk it's hard to believe that the gods haven't returned, or at least given the place a second look.

PAGE 80-81: The River Wye flowing fast at the weir in Monsal Dale

LEFT: A five-arched stone viaduct of the former Midland Railway Company spans the River Wye

walk information

➤ **DISTANCE**	5.5 miles (8.8km)
➤ **MINIMUM TIME**	3hrs 30min
➤ **ASCENT/GRADIENT**	656ft (200m) ▲▲▲
➤ **LEVEL OF DIFFICULTY**	🚶🚶🚶
➤ **PATHS**	Well-defined paths and tracks throughout, lots of stiles
➤ **LANDSCAPE**	Limestone dales and high pasture
➤ **SUGGESTED MAPS**	OS Explorer OL24 White Peak
➤ **START/FINISH**	Grid reference: SK 194696
➤ **DOG FRIENDLINESS**	Livestock in Monsal Dale, dogs should be on lead
➤ **PARKING**	Ashford-in-the-Water car park
➤ **PUBLIC TOILETS**	At car park

walk directions

1 From Ashford-in-the-Water car park, walk out to the road and turn right to walk along Vicarage Lane. After 100yds (91m), a footpath on the left doubles back left, then swings sharp right to continue along a ginnel behind a row of houses. Beyond a stile the path enters a field.

2 Head for a stile in the top left corner, then veer slightly right to locate a stile allowing the route to go on to Pennyunk Lane. This walled stony track winds among high pastures. At its end go left uphill along a field edge.

At the top it joins another track, heading north (right) towards the rim of Monsal Dale. The path runs along the top edge of the deep wooded dale to reach the car park at Monsal Head.

3 Take the path marked 'Viaduct and Monsal Trail' here – this way you get to walk across the viaduct. On the other side of the viaduct go through a gate on the left. Ignore the path climbing west up the hillside, but descend south-west on a grassy path raking through scrub woods down into the valley. This shouldn't be confused with the steep eroded path plummeting straight down to the foot of the viaduct.

4 Now you walk down the pleasant valley. The right of way is well away from the river at first but most walkers trace the river bank to emerge at Lees Bottom and a roadside stile.

5 Cross the A6 with great care and go through the White Lodge car park on the path the other side, where the route back to Ashford begins. Beyond the gate carry on along the path, ignoring the turning to Toddington. Go over a wall stile and then up to a rocky path, forking left for the path into Great Shacklow Wood, signposted 'Ashford'.

6 The path now climbs steeply through the trees and stony ground to another gate. Ignore the turning right for Sheldon and continue straight ahead, following a fine ledge path along the steep wooded slopes. Eventually the path comes down to the river, past an old mill, before joining a minor road at the bottom of Kirk Dale.

7 Turn left along the road, down to the A6 and turn right towards Ashford. Leave the road to cross Sheepwash Bridge. Turn right along Church Street, then left along Court Lane to the car park.

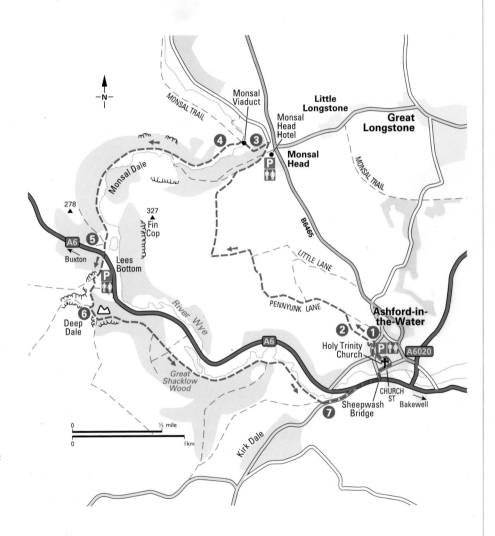

*Follow in the footsteps
of Daniel Defoe to the
lead village of Brassington.*

Skeletons from the Past

*He was as lean as a skeleton, pale as a dead corpse, his hair
and beard a deep black, his flesh lank, and, as we thought,
something of the colour of lead itself.*

So wrote Daniel Defoe on seeing a lead miner, who had been living in a cave at Harborough Rocks. In times past Carsington and Brassington lived and breathed lead. Prior to the construction of Carsington Reservoir, archaeologists discovered a Romano-British settlement here, which could have been the long-lost Ludutarum, the centre of the lead-mining industry in Roman times.

*ABOVE: Carsington Water is a local centre
for outdoor leisure activities including canoeing
and sailing
RIGHT: Picturesque countryside near Brassington*

New Growth

As you walk out of Carsington into the world of the miner, you're using the very tracks he would have used. But the lesions and pockmarks of the endless excavations are being slowly healed by time, and many wild flowers are beginning to proliferate in the meadows and on hillsides.

Brassington

Weird-shaped limestone crags top the hill, then Brassington appears in the next valley with its Norman church tower rising above the grey rooftops of its 17th- and 18th-century houses. Brassington's former post office used to be the tollhouse for the Loughborough turnpike. St James Church is largely Norman, though it was heavily restored in the late 19th century, including the north aisle, which was added in 1880. The impressive south arcade has fine Perpendicular windows. High on the inner walls of the Norman tower is a figure of a man with his hand on his heart. The carving is believed to be Saxon: the man, Brassington's oldest resident.

Climbing out of Brassington the route takes you over Hipley Hill, where there are more remnants of the mines, and more limestone outcrops. On the top you could have caught the train back, but the Cromford High Peak railway closed in 1967, so you are left with a walk along its trackbed. It's a pleasant walk though, through a wooded cutting, with meadow cranesbill and herb Robert thriving among trackside verges and crags.

Harborough Rocks beckon from the left. Archaeologists have uncovered evidence that sabre-toothed tigers, black bears and hyenas once sought the shelter of nearby caves. They also discovered relics and artefacts from Roman and Iron-Age dwellers. For those with extra time, there's an entertaining path winding between the popular climbing crags to the summit, which gives wide views across the White Peak and the lowlands of the East Midlands. Carsington Reservoir is seen to perfection, surrounded by chequered fields, woods and low rounded hills. Leaving the railway behind, there's one last hill, Carsington Pasture, to descend before returning to the lake.

walk directions

1 Take the signposted path northwards towards Carsington. It winds through scrub woods and rounds a finger of the lake before reaching the B5035 road. The path continues on the other side, meeting a lane by Wash Farm and going straight on to enter the village by the Miners Arms.

2 Turn left along the lane to reach the Hopton road. Where the road turns left go straight ahead along a narrow lane passing several cottages. Beyond a gate the lane becomes a fine green track beneath the limestone-studded slopes of Carsington Pasture.

3 Where the track swings left you reach a gate; go through the gate then immediately fork right off the main path on a path climbing the grassy slopes to the west. At the top aim right of a copse and go through a gap in the broken wall before descending into a little valley.

4 Go over two stiles to cross a green lane, then follow a miners' track for 200yds (183m) towards some old mine workings. Here a footpath sign directs you around some limestone outcrops before arcing right towards Brassington. Turn left at the wall stile and follow the waymarked route across the fields into the village.

5 Turn left, then immediately right up Miners Hill. Now go right up Jasper Lane, left up Red Lion Hill, and left again along Hillside Lane. After 200yds (183m) leave the lane for a footpath on the right, which climbs past more limestone outcrops. The faint path gradually veers right, and passes the head of a green lane.

6 Here climb right over the pathless wall stile. Through the next three fields the path climbs parallel to, and to the right of, a line of wooden electricity pylons. In the fourth field bear half right above the rock outcrops and go through the top gate. Now aim for the extensive buildings of Longcliffe Dale Farm. After going over the next stile, turn left up the road, passing the farm. A footpath on the right then cuts a corner to the High Peak Trail, passing an electricity substation and Peak Quarry Farm.

7 Turn right along the trackbed of the High Peak Trail passing the Harborough Rocks.

8 Go right at the footpath signed to Carsington. This descends a small field to cross Manystones Lane. Follow the wall across Carsington Pasture, then descend by woods to a gate by a cottage.

9 Turn left down a little ginnel leading to the road and left again to retrace your earlier route back to Sheepwash car park.

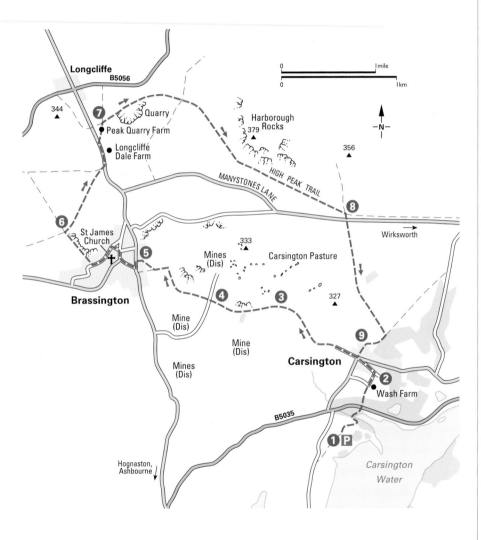

walk information

➤ **DISTANCE**	5.5 miles (8.8km)
➤ **MINIMUM TIME**	3hrs 30min
➤ **ASCENT/GRADIENT**	1,148ft (350m) ▲▲▲
➤ **LEVEL OF DIFFICULTY**	🚶🚶🚶
➤ **PATHS**	Hill paths, some hard to follow, and railway trackbed, numerous stiles
➤ **LANDSCAPE**	Limestone hills
➤ **SUGGESTED MAPS**	OS Explorer OL24 White Peak
➤ **START/FINISH**	Grid reference: SK 249528
➤ **DOG FRIENDLINESS**	Dogs on leads over farmland, can run free on long stretches of enclosed railway trackbed
➤ **PARKING**	Sheepwash pay car park by Carsington Reservoir
➤ **PUBLIC TOILETS**	None on route

Skirting the gritstone cliffs which line Sheffield's moorland edge.

On the Edge at Stanage

From Moscar to Baslow a line of dark cliffs cap the heather moors east of the Derwent Valley. Defoe, ever the scourge of mountain scenery, called it a vast extended moor or waste in which strangers would be obliged to take guides or lose their way. Later Emily Brontë came here to visit her friend Ellen Nussey, the wife of the local vicar. Emily would have found the place much more acceptable, and not unlike her home at Haworth.

ABOVE: *Old millstones, industrial relics, lying in the heather below the cliffs of Stanage Edge north of Hathersage*
RIGHT: *The vicarage at Hathersage is where Charlotte Bronte stayed in 1845 and, inspired by the moorland, set part of Jane Eyre here*

THE OLD
VICARAGE

BED & BREAKFAST

Early Climbers

In the 1890s, the climber, JW Putrell turned to the highest of these cliffs, Stanage Edge, and pioneered several gully routes. Others would follow and today Stanage and its neighbouring 'edges' are one of the most popular climbing venues in Britain. But Stanage is a great place for walkers too, for they can stride out on firm skyline paths with Yorkshire on one side and Derbyshire on the other. High car parks mean that you can walk Stanage without much ascent, but it's more rewarding to work for your fun, so we'll start the route at Hathersage.

The Eyres of Hathersage

Hathersage is a neat village by the banks of the River Derwent. The route starts gently on Baulk Lane and passes the cricket ground on its way through the little valley of Hood Brook. Gradients steepen and the route comes across the 16th-century castellated manor of North Lees Hall, the inspiration for Thornfield Hall, Mr Rochester's home in Jane Eyre. The Eyre family did exist in real life. They were Roman Catholics who lived in the hall until the 17th century, when a narrow-minded Protestant community drove them out. The remains of a chapel, built in 1685, only to be destroyed three years later, can still be seen in the grounds.

Above the hall the route climbs on to the moors and a paved causey track known as Jacob's Ladder takes it to the top of the cliffs. The cliff-edge path to High Neb and Crow Chin is a delight, and the views from it are extensive, taking in a good deal of the Derwent and Hope valleys, Mam Tor and Kinder Scout. It may seem strange to descend to the foot of the cliffs, but the lost height doesn't amount to much and you can now view them from the perspective of the climber.

After rejoining the edge, the path passes above Robin Hood's Cave, where the legendary outlaw perhaps hid from the Sheriff of Nottingham, to reach the high road and climbers' car park. Now there's just Higger Tor to do. The rocky knoll surrounded by an ocean of heather makes a fine finale, one last lofty perch before the descent back to Hathersage.

walk directions

1 At the car park in Hathersage, take the path in the corner past the Methodist church to Main Road. Turn right, cross over, then turn left in Baulk Lane. The lane climbs steadily north, passing the cricket ground. Beyond the buildings it becomes an unsurfaced track.

2 Just short of Cowclose Farm take the signposted left fork, which passes to the right of Brookfield Manor to reach a country lane. Turn right here, then left along a drive to North Lees Hall. After rounding the hall, turn right, climbing some steps that cut the corner to another track. This crosses hillside pastures before continuing through woodland.

3 A stepped path on the left makes a short cut to a roadside toilet block and mountain rescue post. Cross the road for a grassy path heading for the rocks of Stanage Edge. After 200yds (183m) you join the path from the nearby car park. A paved path now climbs through Stanage Plantation before arcing left to the cliff top and turning left.

4 Follow the firm edge-top path north-westwards to see the impressive summit of High Neb and Crow Chin.

5 When you reach Crow Chin, where the edge veers north, descend to a lower path that doubles back beneath the cliffs. This eventually joins a track from the right, which returns the route to the top of the cliffs. Continue walking towards the south-east along the edge to the bouldery east summit (marked on Ordnance Survey maps by a spot height of 457m), whose rocks are capped by a concrete trig point.

6 The track continues to the road at Upper Burbage Bridge. Proceed left along the road for about 150yds (137m), then turn right by the car park, taking the the higher of the two paths which head south to the lofty heights of the summit of Higger Tor.

7 From the rocky top, double back (roughly north of north-west) on a path to the Fiddler's Elbow road. Slightly uphill along the road take the path on the left. This descends Callow Bank to reach a walled track

leading down to the Dale Bottom road. Follow the road for 300yds (274m) to a track on the right that traverses the hillslopes to Toothill Farm. Turn left by the farmhouse on a drive that soon joins a tarred lane taking the route down to Hathersage's impressively spired church and the Roman fort of Camp Green.

8 Turn right down School Lane to reach Main Road, which leads you back into the centre of Hathersage. Go left before the toilets to reach the car park.

walk information

➤ DISTANCE	9 miles (14.5km)
➤ MINIMUM TIME	5hrs
➤ ASCENT/GRADIENT	1,150ft (350m) ▲▲▲
➤ LEVEL OF DIFFICULTY	👤👤👤👤
➤ PATHS	Well-defined paths and tracks, a few stiles
➤ LANDSCAPE	Gritstone and heather moorland
➤ SUGGESTED MAPS	OS Explorer OL1 Dark Peak
➤ START/FINISH	Grid reference: SK 232814
➤ DOG FRIENDLINESS	Dogs are banned from north-western part of Stanage Edge due to nesting birds; elsewhere keep on lead
➤ PARKING	Pay car park, Oddfellows Road, Hathersage
➤ PUBLIC TOILETS	Main road, Hathersage, and on lane above North Lees

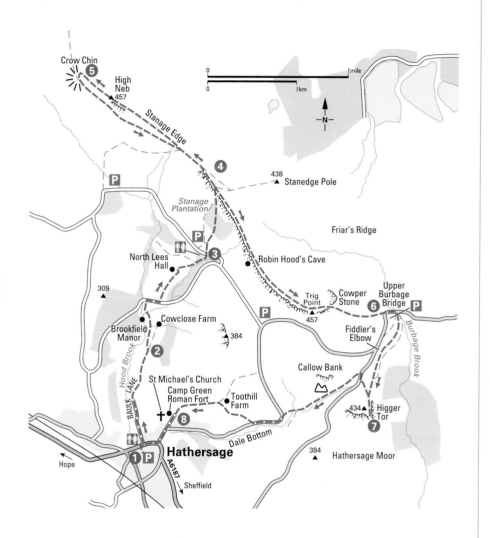

A stroll along the River Derwent past gardens
and through parkland created by 18th-century
landscape guru Lancelot 'Capability' Brown.

Chatsworth Park and Gardens

Sitting on the banks of the River Derwent, surrounded by lush green parkland, moors and a backdrop of wooded hillsides, Chatsworth is one of the most elegant and popular of England's stately homes. First opened to the public in 1844 it continues to attract large numbers of visitors.

ABOVE: The Cascade at Chatsworth House was built over 300 years ago
LEFT: Chatsworth House was home to fourteen generations of the Cavendish family
PAGES 94–95: The Conservatory at Chatsworth

A quiet waterside walk

around the site of a horrific

19th-century industrial tragedy.

Bradfield and the Dale Dike Dam Disaster

Just before midnight on Friday 11 March 1864, when the Dale Dike Dam tragically collapsed, 650 million gallons (2,955 million litres) of water surged along the Loxley Valley towards Sheffield, leaving a trail of death and destruction. When the floods finally subsided 244 people had been killed and hundreds of properties destroyed.

ABOVE: Tree lined hills surround the Dale Dike Reservoir
LEFT: The Damflask reservoir seen from a distance over the rolling hills of Bradfield Dale, near Sheffield

The Bradfield Scheme

During the Industrial Revolution Sheffield expanded rapidly, as country people sought employment in the city's steel and cutlery works. This put considerable pressure on the water supply. The 'Bradfield Scheme' was Sheffield Waterworks Company's ambitious proposal to build massive reservoirs in the hills around the village of Bradfield, about 8 miles (12.9km) from the city. Work commenced on the first of these, the Dale Dike Dam on 1 January 1859. It was a giant by the standards of the time with a capacity of over 700 million gallons (3,182 million litres) of water, but some 200 million gallons (910 million litres) less than the present reservoir.

The Disaster of 1864

Construction of the dam continued until late February 1864, by which time the reservoir was almost full. Friday 11 March was a stormy day and as one of the dam workers crossed the earthen embankment on his way home, he noticed a crack, about a finger's width, running along it. John Gunson the chief engineer turned out with one of the contractors to inspect the dam. They had to make the 8 miles (12.9km) from Sheffield in a horse-drawn gig, in deteriorating weather conditions, so it was 10pm before they got there. After an initial inspection, Gunson concluded that it was probably nothing to worry about. However as a precaution he decided to lower the water level. He re-inspected the crack at 11.30pm, noting that it had not visibly deteriorated. However, then the engineer saw to his horror that water was running over the top of the embankment into the crack. He was making his way to the bottom of the embankment when he felt the ground beneath him begin to shake and saw the top of the dam breached by the straining waters. He just had time to scramble up the side before a large section of the dam collapsed, unleashing a solid wall of water down into the valley below towards Sheffield. The torrent destroyed everything in its path and though the waters

started to subside within half an hour their destructive force swept aside 415 houses, 106 factories or shops, 20 bridges and countless cottage and market gardens for 8 miles (12.9km). Few were spared and some whole families were wiped out, including an 87-year-old woman and a two-day-old baby.

At the inquest the jury concluded that there had been insufficient engineering skill devoted to a work of such size and called for legislation to ensure 'frequent, sufficient and regular' inspections of dams. The Dale Dike Dam was rebuilt in 1875 but it was not brought into full use until 1887, a very dry year.

walk directions

1. Exit the car park and turn right on to the road. At the second junction go right towards Midhopestones. Follow this road uphill passing, on the right, a former inn, Walker House farm and Upper Thornseat. When the road turns right, with Thomson House below, turn left on to an overgrown track.

2. From here go through a gate in front of you and on to Hall Lane, a public bridleway. Follow this along the edge of a wood then through another gate and continue ahead on the farm road. Another gate at the end of this road leads to the entrance to Hallfield.

3. The right of way goes through the grounds of Hallfield but an alternative permissive path leads left through a gate, round the perimeter of the house and through another gate to rejoin the bridleway at the back of the house. Follow the bridleway through a gate and then past Stubbing Farm.

4. The next gate leads to Brogging Farm and the dam at the head of Strines Reservoir. Look out for a sign near the end of the farmhouse and turn left. Go slightly downhill, over a stile, follow the path, then cross a stile and go through a wood.

walk information

➤ DISTANCE	5.5 miles (8.8km)
➤ MINIMUM TIME	3hrs 30min
➤ ASCENT/GRADIENT	394ft (120m)
➤ LEVEL OF DIFFICULTY	
➤ PATHS	Minor roads, bridleways, forest paths
➤ LANDSCAPE	Woodland, reservoir and meadows
➤ SUGGESTED MAPS	OS Explorer OL1 Dark Peak
➤ START/FINISH	Grid reference: SK 262920
➤ DOG FRIENDLINESS	Keep on lead near livestock
➤ PARKING	Car park by Low Bradfield cricket ground
➤ PUBLIC TOILETS	Low Bradfield, near post office

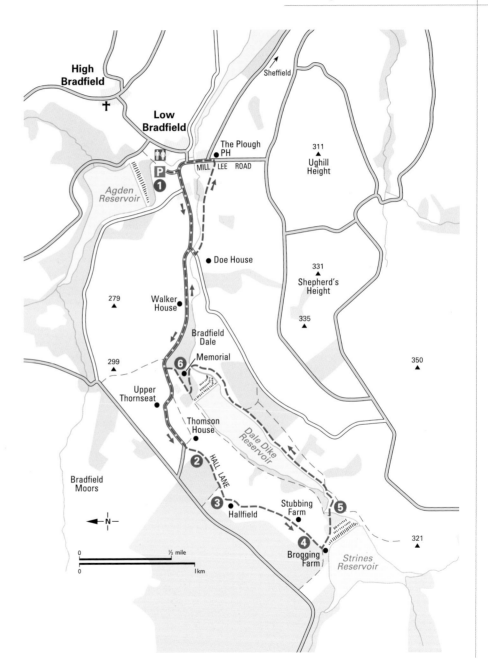

5 Cross the stream by a footbridge, go right at a junction and straight on at the next with the stream on your left. Then follow the path along the bank of Dale Dike Reservoir to the dam head. From here continue through the woods, down several sets of steps and continue on the path looking out for the memorial to those who were killed in 1864.

6 Follow the path until it reaches the road. Cross the stile, turn right on to the road and proceed to the road junction. Turn right, cross the bridge then look for a public footpath sign just before the entrance to Doe House. Cross the stile on the left and follow the path all the way to it's end on Mill Lee Road opposite The Plough. Turn left and follow this road downhill, through the village and back to the car park.

A steady climb raises you above the hurley burley of Matlock Bath to a more familiar Peakland landscape.

Scaling the Heights of Abraham

Between Matlock and Cromford the River Derwent forges its way through a spectacular, thickly wooded limestone gorge. At Matlock Bath it jostles for space with the bustling A6 highway, the railway to Derby and a string of three-storey houses, shops and amusement parlours, built by the Victorians, who flocked here to take in the healing spa waters. On the hillside to the east lies the gaunt castle of Riber, while Alpine-type cable cars glide up the Heights of Abraham, above cliff tops to the west.

ABOVE: *Waterfall near Cromford on the River Derwent in the Peak District, Derbyshire*
RIGHT: *Cable cars sail over the Heights of Abraham; the route is 568m long and climbs 169m*

The Heights in Quebec

The original Heights of Abraham, which the hillside must have resembled, rise above Quebec and the St Lawrence River in Canada. There, in 1759, British troops under General Wolfe fought a victorious battle with the French under General Montcalm. Both generals were killed and the encounter earned Wolfe, and Quebec, an unenviable place in English place-name folklore, to be joined later by Waterloo and later still, Spion Kop.

Matlock Bath

Matlock Bath doesn't have time to catch its breath: it's Derbyshire's mini-Blackpool. Yet there are peaceful corners, and this fine walk seeks them out. It offers fine views across the Matlock Gorge. Spurning the cable car, it climbs through the woods and out on to the hillside above the town. The Victoria Prospect Tower peeps over the trees. Built by unemployed miners a century ago it's now part of the Heights of Abraham complex.

Above the complex, a little path leads you through delectable woodland. In spring it's heavy with the scent of wild garlic and coloured by a carpet of bluebells. Out of the woods, an attractive hedge-lined unsurfaced lane weaves its way through high pastures, giving distant views of the White Peak plateau, Black Rocks and the cliffs of Crich Stand.

Bonsall

At the end of the lane, there's Bonsall, whose Perpendicular church tower and spire has been beckoning you onwards for some time. In the centre of this old lead mining village is a sloping market square with a 17th-century cross. The Kings Head Inn, built in 1677, overlooks the square, and is said to be haunted.

The lane out of Bonsall takes you to the edge of an area of old mine shafts and modern-day quarries. Here you're diverted into the woods above the Via Gellia, a valley named after Philip Gell who built the road from the quarry to the Cromford Canal.

Those who wish can make a short diversion from the woodland path to see the Arkwright Centre and the canal in Cromford. The main route swings north, back into the woods of the Derwent Valley, passing the high hamlet of Upperwood, where fleeting views of Matlock appear through the trees.

walk directions

1 Cross the A6 and then take St John's Road up the wooded slopes opposite. It passes beneath St John's Chapel to reach the gates of Cliffe House. Take the path on the right signposted 'Heights of Abraham'. The path climbs steeply upwards through the woods before veering left across the fields above Masson Farm.

2 Beyond the farmhouse and with Victoria Prospect Tower directly ahead, the waymarked path swings right and climbs up to the top of the field. Beyond this the footpath threads through hawthorn thickets before passing one of the entrances to the Heights of Abraham complex.

3 Ignore an obvious, engineered path and continue uphill along the perimeter of the complex and then turn left, going over a wall stile. After crossing a wide vehicle track the narrow footpath re-enters woodland.

4 At the far side of the woods, turn right on to a farm track close to Ember Farm. Join a pleasant lane that winds down pastured hillslopes into Bonsall village.

5 Turn left by the church along a lane that becomes unsurfaced when you get beyond Town End Farm. The lane finally comes to an abrupt end by the high fences of a quarry. Turn left here and follow a wide track around the perimeter of the quarry.

6 Where the fence ends, continue down the track, bending sharply right then left along a narrow path through woodland high above the Via Gellia, then take the left fork after about 300 yds (274m).

7 Turn left when you reach the next junction, following the footpath waymarked for the Derwent Valley Walk (DVW). This climbs further up the wooded bank, then turns left, tracing a mossy wall on the right. It rakes across the wooded hillside, passes above Cromford Court, then climbs away past some cave entrances to a lane at Upperwood. Ignore the next DVW sign and continue along the lane between cottages and past the West Lodge entrance to the Heights of Abraham showcave.

8 After 100yds (91m) leave the surfaced road for a stepped path through the woods on the left, signed 'Matlock'. Climb some steps to a high wooden footbridge over the Heights of Abraham approach road, and then continue on the woodland path. You'll pass under the Heights of Abraham cable cars before joining a farm track that has come in from the left.

9 This joins St John's Lane and the outward route at Cliffe House. Retrace your steps to the start.

walk information

► **DISTANCE**	8 miles (12.9km)
► **MINIMUM TIME**	4hrs 30min
► **ASCENT/GRADIENT**	1,200ft (365m) ▲▲▲
► **LEVEL OF DIFFICULTY**	🚶🚶🚶
► **PATHS**	Narrow woodland paths, field paths and unsurfaced lanes, lots of stiles
► **LANDSCAPE**	Fields and wooded hillsides
► **SUGGESTED MAPS**	OS Explorer OL24 White Peak
► **START/FINISH**	Grid reference: SK 297595
► **DOG FRIENDLINESS**	Dogs on lead over farmland
► **PARKING**	Pay car park at Artists Corner
► **PUBLIC TOILETS**	At car park

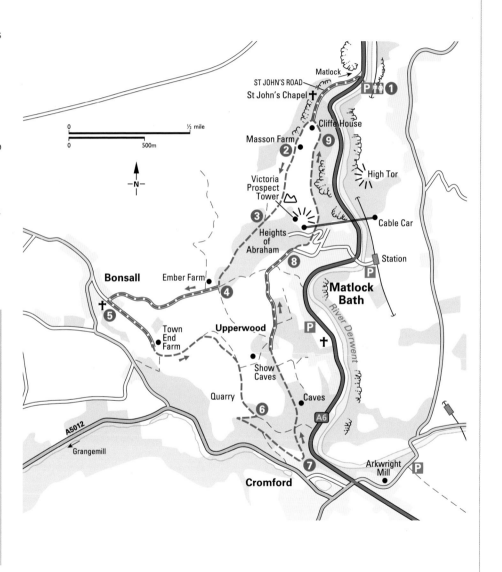

PAGE 106-107: Looking down on the houses of Matlock Bath set in a steep-sided gorge

On Crich Chase through
TV-land to the monument
of Crich Stand.

Climbing up to Crich in Search of Cardale

ABOVE: *A display at Crich Tram*
Museum, which opened in 1959
and now houses over 50 trams
LEFT: *More than a third of the trams at Crich*
Tram Museum are in full working order

The first five minutes of the walk are as uneventful as the rest is fascinating, and include such delights as a modern railway station and a busy road with heavy traffic. But as soon as you've turned the corner and crossed over Chase Bridge you're walking in a different world. An ivy-clad wall effectively blocks sight and sound of the road, the railway and the canal, tangled with irises and pondweed ambles by slowly through the trees. Watch out for the bright yellow-and-black spotted longhorn beetle feeding on the meadowsweet and the holly blue butterflies in springtime.

Familiar to Millions

On this journey you save the greater part of the canal walking to the end, in order to climb through the woodland of Crich Chase, once part of a hunting forest owned by the 13th-century Norman baron, Hubert FitzRalph. After climbing high fields and along a gritstone edge, known as the Tors, you come upon Crich (pronounced so the 'i' rhymes with eye). If you get that déjà-vu feeling it's because Crich was Peak Practice's Cardale until the series moved to Longnor in 2001. Past the market cross and across more fields you come to the National Tramway Museum, which is well worth a visit.

But you can't stay all day: there is a walk to be done! It continues to its high point on Crich Stand, a limestone crag isolated by an area of gritstone. Capping the Stand is a 60ft (19m) beacon tower, rebuilt in 1921 to commemorate the Sherwood Foresters killed in the two World Wars. On a clear day you can pick out Lincoln and its cathedral. Often you'll see kestrels hovering around the cliff edge, searching for their prey.

The path descends through more woodland, beneath the shady gritstone cliffs of the old Dukes Quarry and down to the canal at Whatstandwell. The canal here has been allowed to silt up, and has become a haven for wildlife. It's well known for its many varieties of hoverfly, its azure damselflies and brown chinamark moths.

Wealth of Wildlife

Yellow irises and flowering rush, which has pink flowers, can be seen on the water's edge, while broad-leaved pondweed clogs the middle of the canal. That doesn't seem to impede the moorhens or mallards though. By the time you get back to Ambergate you will have seen a wealth of wildlife, but you can rest assured that much more wildlife will have seen you.

1 Leave the car park at Ambergate Station and walk down the road under the bridge and then turn right along the busy A6. Turn right up Chase Road, which cuts underneath the railway bridge to the Cromford Canal. Follow the tow path northwards to the next bridge.

2 Go over the bridge before following a footpath climbing into the woodland of Crich Chase. In the upper reaches of the wood the waymarked path swings left; follow it to pass through some small clearings. It then follows a wall on the right at the top edge of the wood. Turn right over a stile, then climb across two fields to reach Chadwick Nick Lane.

3 Turn right along the road. After 300yds (274m) a path on the left begins with some steps and a stile, and continues the climb northwards across numerous fields with stiles and gates – and by the rock outcrops of The Tors.

4 The path becomes an enclosed ginnel, which emerges on Sandy Lane. Follow this to the Market Square, where you turn left, then right along Coasthill. Coasthill leads to an unsurfaced lane. Where the lane ends, follow a path in the same direction across fields to join another lane by some houses. Follow this to Carr Lane, then turn right, passing the entrance to the National Tramway Museum.

5 Continue along the road to a sharp right-hand bend, then turn left along the approach road to Crich Stand, topped by the Sherwood Foresters Monument. There's a small fee if you want to go up to the viewing platform on the monument, but otherwise continue along the public right of way on the right. The footpath, signed to Wakebridge and Plaistow, veers half right through shrubs and bramble, before circumnavigating Cliff Quarry.

6 The path then crosses over the museum's tram track near its terminus, before winding down the hillside through attractive scrub woodland. It joins a wide track that descends past Wakebridge and Cliff farms before coming to a road.

7 Turn right along the road for a few paces, then turn left on a footpath. This descends south across fields before swinging right to enter a wood. A well-defined path passes beneath quarried rockfaces, and crosses a minor road before reaching the canal at Whatstandwell.

8 Turn left and follow a most delightful tow path for 2 miles (3.2km) through the shade of tree boughs. At Chase Bridge you meet the outward route and retrace your steps back to the car park.

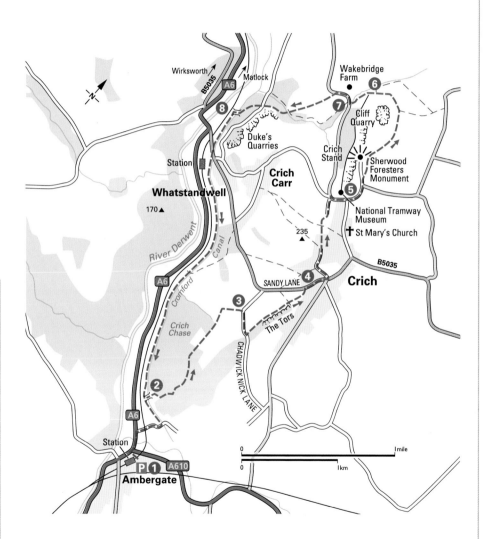

walk information

➤ **DISTANCE**	7.5 miles (12.1km)
➤ **MINIMUM TIME**	5hrs
➤ **ASCENT/GRADIENT**	721ft (220m) ▲▲▲
➤ **LEVEL OF DIFFICULTY**	🚶🚶🚶
➤ **PATHS**	Woodland and field paths and canal tow path, many stiles
➤ **LANDSCAPE**	Woods and pastured hills
➤ **SUGGESTED MAPS**	OS Explorer OL24 White Peak
➤ **START/FINISH**	Grid reference: SK 349517
➤ **DOG FRIENDLINESS**	Keep on lead across farmland, also by canal to protect the wildlife of nature reserve
➤ **PARKING**	Ambergate, car park by station
➤ **PUBLIC TOILETS**	At A6/A610 junction at start and at Crich near Black Swan

Walking in Safety

All these walks are suitable for any reasonably fit person, but less experienced walkers should try the easier walks first. Route finding is usually straightforward, but you will find that an Ordnance Survey map is a useful addition to the route maps and descriptions.

Risks

Although each walk here has been researched with a view to minimising the risks to the walkers who follow its route, no walk in the countryside can be considered to be completely free from risk. Walking in the outdoors will always require a degree of common sense and judgement to ensure that it is as safe as possible.

- Be particularly careful on cliff paths and in upland terrain, where the consequences of a slip can be very serious.
- Remember to check tidal conditions before walking on the seashore.
- Some sections of route are by, or cross, busy roads. Take care and remember traffic is a danger even on minor country lanes.
- Be careful around farmyard machinery and livestock, especially if you have children with you.
- Be aware of the consequences of changes in the weather and check the forecast before you set out. Carry spare clothing and a torch if you are walking in the winter months. Remember the weather can change very quickly at any time of the year, and in moorland and heathland areas, mist and fog can make route finding much harder. Don't set out in these conditions unless you are confident of your navigation skills in poor visibility. In summer remember to take account of the heat and sun; wear a hat and carry spare water.
- On walks away from centres of population you should carry a whistle and survival bag. If you do have an accident requiring the emergency services, make a note of your position as accurately as possible and dial 999.

Acknowledgements

The Automobile Association would like to thank the following photographers, companies and picture libraries for their assistance in the preparation of this book.

Abbreviations for the picture credits are as follows: (t) top; (b) bottom; (l) left; (r) right; (AA) AA World Travel Library.

Front Cover AA/T Mackie; Back Cover AA/A J Hopkins; Back Flap AA/T Mackie;

2/3 AA/T Mackie; 5 AA/T Mackie; 6 AA/T Mackie; 7bl AA/A J Hopkins; 7bcl AA/A Tryner; 7bcr AA/T Mackie; 7br AA/A J Hopkins; 11 AA/T Mackie; 12/13 © Andrew Paterson/Alamy; 13 AA/N Coates; 16 AA/N Coates; 16/17 AA/M Birkitt; 20/21 AA/A J Hopkins; 21 AA/T Mackie; 22/23 AA/T Mackie; 24 AA/T Mackie; 26/27 © Robert Morris/Alamy; 27 AA/R Ireland; 30 AA/M Birkitt; 30/31 AA/T Mackie; 34/35 AA/T Mackie; 36/37 AA/M Trelawny; 37 AA/J Morrison; 38/39 © Paul Harvard Evans/Alamy; 40 AA/J Morrison; 42/43 AA/J Beazley; 43 AA/A J Hopkins; 46/47 AA/T Mackie; 47 AA/T Mackie; 50 AA/T Mackie; 50/51 AA/T Mackie; 54/55 AA/T Mackie; 56/57 AA/T Mackie; 57 AA/A J Hopkins; 60 AA/T Mackie; 60/61 A J Hopkins; 62/63 AA/T Mackie; 64 AA/T Mackie; 66/67 AA/T Mackie; 67 AA/M Birkitt; 68/69 AA/A J Hopkins; 70 AA/M Kipling; 72 AA/T Mackie; 72/73 AA/P Brown; 76/77 AA/T Mackie; 78/79 AA/T Mackie; 79 AA/M Birkitt; 80/81 AA/T Mackie; 82 AA/M Birkitt; 84 AA/T Mackie; 84/85 AA/T Mackie; 88/89 AA/N Coates; 89 AA/A J Hopkins; 92/93 AA/A J Hopkins; 93 AA/A Midgley; 94/95 AA/A Midgley; 98/99 AA/J Morrison; 99 AA/N Coates; 102 AA/T Mackie; 102/103 AA/T Mackie; 107 AA/T Mackie; 108/109 AA/T Mackie; 109 AA/T Mackie;

Every effort has been made to trace the copyright holders, and we apologise in advance for any accidental errors. We would be happy to apply the corrections in the following edition of this publication.